Consort Suites and Dance Music by Town Musicians in German-Speaking Europe, 1648–1700

This companion volume to *The Courtly Consort Suite in German-Speaking Europe* surveys an area of music neglected by modern scholars: the consort suites and dance music by musicians working in the seventeenth-century German towns. Conditions of work in the German towns are examined in detail, as are the problems posed by the many untrained travelling players who were often little more than beggars. The central part of the book explores the organisation, content and assembly of town suites into carefully ordered printed collections, which refutes the concept of the so-called 'classical' suite. The differences between court and town suites are dealt with alongside the often-ignored variation suite from the later decades of the seventeenth century and the separate suite-writing traditions of Leipzig and Hamburg. While the seventeenth-century keyboard suite has received a good deal of attention from modern scholars, its often symbiotic relationship with the consort suite has been ignored. This book aims to redress the balance and to deal with one very important but often ignored aspect of seventeenth-century notation: the use of blackened notes, which are rarely notated in a meaningful way in modern editions, with important implications for performance.

Michael Robertson completed his PhD in 2004. In addition to working as a teacher, harpsichordist and organist, he writes about seventeenth-century music and has a fruitful music-editing partnership with a leading German publisher of early music. He is a visiting research fellow at the University of Leeds.

Consort Suites and Dance Music by Town Musicians in German-Speaking Europe, 1648–1700

Michael Robertson

LONDON AND NEW YORK

First published 2016
by Routledge
2 Park Square, Milton Park, Abingdon, Oxon OX14 4RN

and by Routledge
711 Third Avenue, New York, NY 10017

Routledge is an imprint of the Taylor & Francis Group, an informa business

© 2016 Michael Robertson

The right of Michael Robertson to be identified as author of this work has been asserted by him in accordance with sections 77 and 78 of the Copyright, Designs and Patents Act 1988.

All rights reserved. No part of this book may be reprinted or reproduced or utilised in any form or by any electronic, mechanical, or other means, now known or hereafter invented, including photocopying and recording, or in any information storage or retrieval system, without permission in writing from the publishers.

Trademark notice: Product or corporate names may be trademarks or registered trademarks, and are used only for identification and explanation without intent to infringe.

British Library Cataloguing in Publication Data
A catalogue record for this book is available from the British Library

Library of Congress Cataloging in Publication Data
Robertson, Michael, 1949– author.
Consort suites and dance music by town musicians in German-speaking Europe, 1648–1700 / by Michael Robertson.
  pages cm
Includes bibliographical references and index.
ISBN 9781409470199 (hardcover: alk. paper)—ISBN 9781315573519 (ebook)
1. Suite (Music)—17th century. 2. Suite (Music)—18th century. 3. Dance music—Europe, German-speaking—17th century—History and criticism. 4. Dance music—Europe, German-speaking—18th century—History and criticism. I. Title.
ML3420.2.R62 2016
784.18'83094309032—dc23   2015033075

ISBN: 9781409470199 (hbk)
ISBN: 9781315573519 (ebk)

Bach musicological font developed by © Yo Tomita

Typeset in Times New Roman
by codeMantra

Printed in the United Kingdom
by Henry Ling Limited

In memory of John Railton, MBE (1929–2013)

Contents

List of figures viii
List of tables x
List of music examples xiii
List of abbreviations xix
Acknowledgements xxi
Preface xxiii

1 Towns and town musicians: Governance, status and performance   1

2 Dances, collections and national styles   19

3 The aftermath of war: 1648–59   43

4 Concepts of careful organisation: 1660–75   65

5 A time of decline: 1676–1700   90

6 Leipzig   108

7 Hamburg   149

8 Keyboard suites by town composers   172

9 Note blackening and mensural notation   195

Appendix 1 211
Appendix 2 215
Bibliography 219
Index 231

List of figures

1.1 J. Pezel, *Musicalische Gemüths-Ergetzung / Bestehend [in] Intraden, Allemanden, Balletten, Gavotten, Alle breven, Courenten, Sarabanden und Chiqven* (Leipzig, 1672), Preface, shelfmark II.6.10a: Leipzig, Städtische Bibliotheken-Musikbibliothek. Reproduced by kind permission.   5

2.1 A. Hammerschmidt, *Erster Fleiß: Allerhand newer Paduanen, Galliarden, Balleten, Mascharaden, Francoischen [sic] Arien, Courenten und Sarabanden* (Freiberg, 1636, repr. 1650), Cantus II, X. Courente à5, shelfmark c.53: London, The British Library Board. Reproduced by kind permission.   23

3.1 Knoep, *Erster Theil Newer Paduanen*, 'XVIII. Ballet', 'XXIX. Courant', 'XXX. Ballet', 'XXXI. Courant'. 'Cantus I' part-book, shelfmark Utl.instr.mus.i tr. 13: Uppsala, universitetsbibliotek. Reproduced by kind permission.   57

3.2 H. Hake, *Ander Theil Newer Pavanen, Sonaten, Arien, Balletten, Brandlen, Covranten, und Sarabanden, Mit 2.3.4.5. und 8. Instrumenten mit dem Basso Continuo* (Stade, 1654), 'Register', shelfmark K.8.d.18 (second page of 'Register'): London: The British Library Board. Reproduced by kind permission.   58

6.1 J.C. Horn, *Parergon musicum Oder Musicalisches Neben-Werck / Bestehend in allerhand ammuthigen / Sonatinen, Alleman- / den, Couranten, Ballet- / ten, Sarabanden und Chiqven, Mit Fünff Stimmen / ... Fünfftem Theil* (Leipzig, 1676), 'Violino 1' part-book, '4. Ballo', shelfmark H 930 [1]: Kraków, Biblioteka Jagiellońska. Reproduced by kind permission.   132

8.1	J. Krieger, *Sechs Musicalische Partien ... auf einem Spinet oder Clavichordio zu spielen* (Nuremberg, 1697), Partia I, 'Allemande', shelfmark 2 Mus. pr. 1293: Munich, Bayerische Staatsbibliothek. Reproduced by kind permission.	183
8.2	Niedt, *Handleitung zur Variation*, 'X. Capitel', shelfmark a.31: London, The British Library Board. Reproduced by kind permission.	184
8.3	J.J. Froberger, *Diverse Ingegnosissime, Rarissime & non maj piu viste Curiose Partite ... Dal Eccellentissimo e Famosissimo Organista* ([Mainz], 1693), 'Capriccio 13', shelfmark c.51: London, The British Library Board. Reproduced by kind permission.	185
9.1	M. Praetorius, *Syntagmatis Musici, Michaelis Praetorii C., tomus tertius* (Wolfenbüttel, 1619), p. 53, shelfmark M.K.8.f.1: London, The British Library Board. Reproduced by kind permission.	196
9.2	N. Genbenbach, *Musica nova, Newe Singekunst* (Leipzig, 1626), p. 54, shelfmark 498.1 Quod. (7): Wolfenbüttel, Herzog August Bibliothek. Reproduced by kind permission.	198

List of tables

2.1	Strain analysis of movements entitled 'Ballet' in N.B.N. (ed.), *Exercitium musicum* (Frankfurt am Main, 1660)	33
2.2	Contents of J. Schop, *Erster Theil Newer Paduanen, Galliarden, Allmanden, Balletten, Couranten, unnd [sic] Canzonen* (Hamburg, 1633; repr. 1640)	34
3.1	Ballet construction in A. Hammerschmidt, *Erster Fleiß Allerhand newer Paduanen, Galliarden, Balleten, Francoischen [sic] Arien, Courenten und Sarabanden, Mit 5. Stimmen auff Violen zu spielen/sampt dem General Baß* (Freiberg, 1636, repr. 1639 and 1650)	44
3.2	Ballett construction in Neuebauer, 'Newe Pavanen'	52
3.3	Contents of L. Knoep, *Erster Theil Newer Paduanen, Galliarden, Balletten, Mascaraden, Arien, Allemanden, Couranten und Sarabanden, Mit 3. Stimmen auff Violen zu Spielen/sampt dem General Bass* (Bremen, 1652)	56
3.4	Contents of M. Kelz, *Primitiæ musicales, seu concentus novi harmonici. Italis dicti: le Sonate, Intrade, Mascarade, Balletti, Alemande, Gagliardi, Arie, Volte, Serenade, è Sarabande* (Augsburg, 1658)	61
4.1	English music in N.B.N. (ed.), *Exercitium musicum, Bestehend in auszerlesenen Sonaten, Galliarden, Allemanden, Balletten, Intraden, Arien, Chiquen, Couranten, Sarabanden, und Branlen* (Frankfurt am Main, 1660)	67
4.2	Movements in the second section of Beck (ed.), *Continuatio exercitii musici*	74
4.3	English sources in J.H. Beck (ed.), *Continuatio exercitii musici secunda, Bestehend in außerlesenen Paduanen, Intraden, Allemanden, Balletten, Gavotten, Giqven, Couranten und Sarabanden* (Frankfurt am Main, 1670)	76

4.4	Movements in Section 2 of L. Knoep, *Ander Theil Newer Paduanen, Galliarden, Arien, Allemanden, Balletten, Couranten, und Sarabanden, Mit 2. und 3. Stimmen nebenst dem Basso Continuo* (Bremen, 1660)	80
4.5	Contents of G.W. Druckenmüller, *Musicalisches Tafel-Confect; Bestehend in VII. Partyen / Balleten, Allemanden, Couranten, Sarabanden &c.* (Schwäbisch Hall, 1668)	83
4.6	Contents of H. Kradenthaller, *Deliciarum musicalium Erster Theil à4. Viol. Von Sonatinen, Arien, Sarabanden und Giquen* (Nuremberg, 1675)	86
5.1	Contents of J.F. Meister, *Il giardino del piacere overo raccolta de diversi fiori musicali, come Sonate, Fughe, Imitationi, Ciaccone, Passagaglie, Allemande, Correnti, &c.* (Hamburg, 1695)	100
5.2	Key relationships in Meister, *Il giardino del piacere*, 'La Musica Ottava'	101
6.1	Ballo details in Rosenmüller, *Studenten-Music*	112
6.2	Contents, J. Rosenmüller, *Sonate da camera cioe Sinfonie, Alemande, Correnti, Balletti, Sarabande, Da Svonare Con Cingue Stromenti Da Arco, et altri* (Venice, 1667)	113
6.3	Rosenmüller, *Sonate da camera*, details of 'Sinfonia' movements	116
6.4	Pezel, *Musicalische Gemüths-Ergetzung*, contents	121
6.5	Contents of J. Pezel, *Delitiæ musicales, oder Lust-Music, Bestehend in Sonaten, Allemanden, Balleten, Gavotten, Couranten, Sarabanden, und Chiquen* (Frankfurt am Main, 1678)	122
6.6	Contents of Horn, *Parergon musicum ... Fünfftem Theil*	133
6.7	Movement sequences in J. Pezel, *Fünff-stimmigte blasende Music, Bestehend Intraden, Allemanden, Balleten, Couranten, Sarabanden und Chiquen* (Frankfurt am Main, 1685)	140
6.8	Contents of J.C. Horn, *Parergon musicum Oder Musicalisches Neben-Werck / Bestehend in allerhand lustigen Intraden, Gagliarden, Couranten, Balletten, Sarabanden, Chiqven &c. ... Sechsten Theil* (Leipzig, 1676)	144
7.1	Contents of D. Becker, *Musicalische / Frühlings-Früchte / Bestehend In drei-vier-und fünff-stimmiger Instrumental-Harmonia, Nebenst dem Basso Continuo* (Hamburg, 1668)	153

xii   *List of tables*

7.2	Details of sections one and two of manuscript *S-Uu* Ihre 281–3	159
8.1	Manuscript *D-Lr* Mus. ant. pract. KN 147, suites by Matthias Weckmann	179
8.2	Movements from select suites in J.S. Cousser, *La cicala della cetra D'Eunomio* (Stuttgart, 1700) and J.C.F. Fischer, *Les Pièces de Clavessin* (Schlackenwerth, 1696), J. Kuhnau, *Neüer Clavier Übung Andrer Theil* ([Leipzig], 1692)	180
A.1	Contents of A. Hammerschmidt, *Erster Fleiß Allerhand newer Paduanen, Galliarden, Balleten, Francoischen [sic] Arien, Courenten und Sarabanden, Mit 5. Stimmen auff Violen zu spielen / sampt dem General Baß* (Freiberg, 1636, repr. 1639 and 1650)	211
A.2	Contents of G. Zuber, 'Erster Theil newer / Paduanen, Arien, Balletten, / Couranten, Sarabanden und / einer Sonat: / Mit 5 Stimmen nebenst dem / Baßo Continuo componirt / von / Georg Zubern: / beställter Violista und Musicus in / Lübeck' (manuscript *D-UDa* 38a/9)	212
A.3	Contents of A. Hammerschmidt, *Dritter Theil, Neuer Paduanen, Galliarden, Canzonen, Sonaten, Balleten, Intraden, Couranten und Sarabanden, Mit 3. 4 und 5 Stimmen* (Leipzig, 1650)	212

List of music examples

2.1 A. Hammerschmidt, *Ander Theil newer Paduanen, Canzonen, Galliarden, Balleten, Mascharaden, Francoischen [sic] Arien, Courenten und Sarabanden* (Freiberg, 1639, repr. 1658), 'XIV. Sarabande 2. à5'. 22

2.2 Openings of: M. Cazzati, *Correnti, e Balletti Per Sonora nella Spinetta Leuto, ò Tiorba ... Opera XXX*, (Bologna, 1662), 'Corrente nona'; *D-Kl* 2° Ms. mus. 61d², '3. Courant. Mr. Werdier'. 23

2.3 J.-B. Lully, *Ballet du temple de la paix. Dansé devant Sa Majesté à Fontainebleau* (Paris, 1685), 'Gigue'. 25

2.4 J. Pachelbel, *Musicalische Ergötzung, bestehend in Sechs Verstimten Partien â 2. Violin nebst den Basso Continuo* (Nuremberg, n.d.), 'Partie.VI', 'Gigè'. 26

2.5 G.B. Bassani, *Balletti, Correnti, Gighe, e Sarabande à Violino, e Violone, overo Spinetta, con il Secondo Violino à beneplacito ... Opera prima* (Bologna, 1677, repr. 1684), 'Giga Prima'. 27

2.6 J. Rosenmüller, *Studenten-Music / Darinnen zu befinden Allerhand Sachen Mit drey und fünff Violen / oder auch andern Instrumenten zu spielen* (Leipzig, 1654), '7. Paduan à 3'. 28

2.7 J. Pezel, *Fünff-stimmigte blasende Music, Bestehend In Intraden, Allemanden, Balleten, Courenten, Sarabanden und Chiquen* (Frankfurt-am-Main, 1685), '49. Galliarda à5'. 29

2.8 Manuscript *F-Pn* Rés F 496, 'Recüeil de Plusieurs Anciens Ballets Dancez Sous les Regnes de Henry 3. Henry 4. Et Louis 13. Depuis l'An 1575 Jusqu'à 1641', 'Allemande En G. re, sol, Becar'. 30

2.9 N. Hasse, *Delitiæ musicæ, Das ist Schöne / lustige und anmuthige Allemanden, Couranten und Sarabanden* (Rostock, 1656), '40. Allemand'. 31

xiv *List of music examples*

2.10	First strain of J.C. Horn, *Parergon musicum Oder Musicalisches Neben-Werck / Bestehend in allerhand ammuthigen Sonatinen, Alleman-den, Couranten, Ballet-ten, Sarabanden und Chiqven ... Fünfftem Theil* (Leipzig, 1676), '4. Ballo'.	33
2.11	G.W. Druckenmüller, *Musicalisches Tafel-Confect; Bestehend in VII. Partyen / Balleten, Allemanden, Couranten, Sarabanden &c.* (Schwäbisch Hall, 1668), [Partie] 3, openings of '1. Allem', '2. Courant'.	36
2.12	Manuscript *D-Kl 2°* Ms. mus. 61a [I], 'Branles à4 de M. Brülar. 1664 ex. G.♮ dur'.	39
3.1	First treble part of G. Zuber, 'Erster Theil newer Paduanen, Arien, Balletten, Couranten, Sarabanden und einer Sonat. Mit 5. Stimmen nebenst dem Basso Continuo' (*D-UDa* 38a/9 and 38b/8), '10. Paduan'.	48
3.2	J. Neuebauer, 'Newe Pavanen, Galliarden, Balletten, Couranten, Allmanden, Und Sarabanden, Mitt 4. Und 5. Stimmen Nebenst einem Basso Continuo' (*D-Kl* 4° Ms. mus. 27 (1–5)), '9. Pavan', '10. Galliard', '11. Ballett', '12. Couranta'.	51
3.3	Hake, *Ander Theil Newer Pavanen*, openings of the component dances of 'XXXV. Brandle a 4'.	59
3.4	N. Hasse, *Delitiæ musicæ, Das ist Schöne/lustige und anmuthige Allemanden, Couranten und Sarabanden* (Rostock, 1656), '61. Allemand' and '62. Courant'.	61
3.5	Kelz, *Primitiæ musicales*, '15. Couranta'.	62
4.1	Comparison between J. Playford, *Court-Ayres or Pavins, Almains, Corant's and Sarabands* (London, 1655), and *Exercitium musicum*, 'XXVI. Allemande'.	68
4.2	J.A. Leborgne, 'CXII. La Bouree dartus' in N.B.N. (ed.), *Exercitium musicum*, and 'Petite Bouree' (manuscript *US-NH* Ma.21 H59).	69
4.3	J.H. Beck (ed.), *Continuatio exercitii musici, Bestehend in außerlesenen Allemanden, Balletten, Gavotten, Giquen, Couranten und Sarabanden* (Frankfurt am Main, 1666), 'XXXII. Sarabande'.	72
4.4	Knoep, *Ander Theil Newer Paduanen*, openings of 'XIX. Aria' and 'XX. Aria'.	81
4.5	Knoep, *Ander Theil Newer Paduanen*, openings of 'I. Paduana' and 'II. Galliard'.	82
4.6	Openings of Druckenmüller, *Musicalisches Tafel-Confect*, 'Partie IV'.	84

List of music examples xv

4.7 Kradenthaller, *Deliciarum musicalium Erster Theil*,
'24. Aria', '32. Aria'. 87
4.8 Kradenthaller, *Deliciarum musicalium Erster Theil*,
'5. Gique'. 87
4.9 Kradenthaller, *Deliciarum musicalium Erster Theil*,
'1. Sonatina'. 88
5.1 Linking material in J. Scheiffelhut, *Musicalischer Gemüths Ergötzungen Erstes Werck* (Augsburg, 1684),
'3. Courant', '4. Ballett' and '5. Saraband'. 93
5.2 J. Scheiffelhut, *Lieblicher Frülings-Anfang / oder Musicalischer Seyten-Klang* (Augsburg, 1685), first strain of '10. Courant'. 95
5.3 Scheiffelhut, *Lieblicher Frühlings-Anfang*, '15. Præludium'. 96
5.4 Movement linking in D. Speer, *Musicalisch-Türckischer Eulen-Spiegel* (n.p., 1688). 98
5.5 Meister, *Il giardino del piacere*, 'La Musica Quinta', 'Arioso'. 101
5.6 J. Pachelbel, *Musicalische Ergötzung / bestehend in Sechs Verstimten Partien â 2. Violin nebst den Basso Continuo* (n.p., n.d.), 'Partie I', first strains of 'Ballet' and 'Variatio'. 103
5.7 D. Buxtehude (*BuxWV* 273), 'Sonata a 2 ex B. Con le Suite Violino è Violadagamba di Sig: Dieter: Buxtehude' (manuscript *S-Uu* Instr.mus.i hskr.13:25), first strain of 'Allamanda' and 'Courand'. 105
6.1 Rosenmüller, *Studenten-Music / Darinnen zu befinden Allerhand Sachen Mit drey und fünff Violen* (Leipzig, 1654), openings of '10. Courant' and '11. Courant'. 111
6.2 Rosenmüller, *Sonate da camera*, 'Sinfonia Terza', 'Ballo'. 115
6.3 Rosenmüller, *Sonate da camera*, 'Sinfonia Seconda', 'Correnta'. 116
6.4 Comparisons between Rosenmüller, *Studenten-Music*, '38. Ballo' and W. Fabricius, *Deliciæ Harmonicæ, oder Musicalische Gemüths-Ergätzung* (Leipzig, 1657), '38. Ballo'. 118
6.5 J. Pezel, *Musica vespertina Lipsica oder Leipzigische Abend-Music* (Leipzig, 1669), '16. Prælude'. 119
6.6 Comparisons between J. Pezel, *Musicalische Gemüths-Ergetzung Bestehend Intraden, Allemanden, Balletten, Gavotten, Alle breven, Couranten, Sarabanden und Chiqven* (Leipzig, 1672), '9. Sarabande', and Rosenmüller, *Sonate da camera*, 'Sinfonia Prima', 'Sarabanda'. 121
6.7 Movement openings in J.C. Horn, *Parergon musicum, Oder Musicalisches Neben-Werck / Bestehend in allerhand*

xvi *List of music examples*

	anmuthigen *Allemanden, Couranten, Ballo und Sarabanden ... Ersten Theil* (Erfurt, 1663, repr. Leipzig, 1670), '13. Allemande', '14. Courante', '15. Ballo', '16. Sarabande'.	125
6.8	Comparisons between Horn, *Parergon musicum ... Ersten Theil*, '22. Courante' and J.C. Horn, *Parergon musicum, Oder Musicalisches Neben-Werck / Bestehend in fünff angenehmen Grossen – Balletten ... Andern Theil* (Erfurt, 1663, repr. Leipzig, 1670), '19. Courante; L'Adolescence & les quatre saisons de l'Année'.	129
6.9	Movement linking in J.C. Horn, *Parergon musicum, Oder Musicalisches Neben-Werck / Bestehend in allerhand anmuthigen Intraden, Allemanden, Couranten, Ballo, Sarabanden, Chiquen, &c. Mit Fünff Stimmen ... Dritten Theil* (Leipzig, 1672), '19. Intrada', '20. Allemande', '21. Courante'.	131
6.10	Movement linking in Horn, *Parergon musicum ... Fünfftem Theil*, fourth suite.	134
6.11	Comparison between J. Pezel, *Bicinia Variorum Instrumentorum ut à2. Violinis, Cornet, Flautinis, Clarinis, Clarino et Fagotto* (Leipzig, 1675), '28. Treza', and J.H. Schmelzer, 'Zu den geburts Tag Ihro Maÿ: der Khönigin in Spanien' (*A-Wn* Mus. Hs. 16583[II]), 'Trezza 97ᵃ'.	137
6.12	Pezel, *Bicinia*, 'Appendix', '14. Courente'.	138
6.13	Pezel, *Fünff-stimmigte blasende Music*, '17. Allemande' and '18. Courente'.	141
6.14	Pezel, *Fünff-stimmigte blasende Music*, '26. Galliard'.	142
6.15	Horn, *Parergon musicum ... Sechsten Theil*, '28. Intrada à 12'.	145
7.1	J.J. Froberger, openings of 'Allemande', 'Gigue', 'Courante' in 'Libro Quarto: Toccate, Ricercari, Capricci, Allemande, Gigue, Courante, Sarabande' (*A-Wn* Mus. Hs. 18707), fols 100v–102v.	151
7.2	Becker, *Musicalische Frühlings-Früchte*, openings of '10. Sonata à4', '11. Allmand à4', '12. Courant à4', '13. Sarband à4', '14. Giquæ à4'.	154
7.3	D. Becker, *Erster Theil zwey-stimmiger Sonaten und Suiten Nebest einem gedoppelten Basso Continuo* (Hamburg, 1674), 'II. Allmandt'.	157
7.4	Manuscript *S-Uu* Ihre 281–3, Section 1, openings of '16. Allem:' and '17. Cour'.	160
7.5	D. Becker, 'Sonata â 4, 2 Violini & due Viola da gambæ, Nummer 2' (*D-Hs* M B/2463), Sonata, closing section.	163

List of music examples xvii

7.6	D. Becker, 'Sonata â 4, 2 Violini & due Viola d[a gambæ], Nummer 4' (*D-Hs* M B/2463), 'Allemande'.	164
7.7	A. Reincken, *Hortus musicus recentibus aliquot Flosculis Sonaten, Allemanden, Couranten, Sarbanden et Giquen Cum 2 Violin. Viola, et Basso continuo* (n.p., n.d.), 'Sonata 1ma', 'Allmand 2da'.	166
7.8	Linking material in anonymous manuscript *S-Uu* Instr.mus. i hs.11:10, 'Sonata', 'Allemand', 'Courant', 'Ballett' and 'Sarabanda'.	167
7.9	Manuscript *S-Uu* IMhs 009:001; linking between 'Courante', 'Ballo' and 'Sarabande'.	168
8.1	D. Buxtehude (*BuxWV* 242), 'Gigue' (manuscript *DK-Kk* 6806.1399).	173
8.2	Comparison between J.A. Reincken, *Hortus musicus recentibus aliquot Flosculis Sonaten, Allemanden, Couranten, Sarbanden et Giquen* (n.p., n.d.), 'Allemande 27^{tima}' and 'Suite ex C♮, Allemand' (manuscript *D-B* Mus. Ms. 40644).	174
8.3	D. Buxtehude, 'Suite in E minor' (*BuxWV* 237), linking between movements.	176
8.4	Manuscript *D-Lr* Mus. ant. pract. 1198, 'Allemanda' and 'Current'.	178
8.5	M. Weckmann, manuscript *D-Lr* Mus. ant. pract. KN 147, 'Gigue'.	179
8.6	F.E. Niedt, *Handleitung zur Variation* (Hamburg, 1706), 'X. Capitel'.	182
8.7	B. Schultheiss, *Muth- und Geist-ermuntrender Clavier-Lust / Erster Theil* (Nuremberg, 1679), '12. Allemande'.	186
8.8	B. Schultheiss, *Muth- und Geist-ermuntrender Clavier-Lust / Anderer Theil* (Nuremberg, 1679), '24. Gigue'.	187
8.9	J. Kuhnau, *Neüer Clavier Übung Erster Theil* (Leipzig, 1689), '25. Courante'.	189
8.10	J. Kuhnau, *Neüer Clavier Übung Erster Theil*, '10. Gigue', opening of each strain.	189
9.1	W. Brade, *Newe außerlesene Paduanen / Galliarden / Cantzonen / Allmand und Couranten* (Hamburg, 1609), 'Coranta à5'.	200
9.2	G. Knüpfer, 'Sonata a 7. 2.Violin, 3.Viol, 1.Fag., 1.Violon con Continuo' (manuscript *GB-Ob* MS Mus.Sch.c.93), 'Sonata'.	201
9.3	J.C. Horn, *Parergon musicum Oder Musicalisches Neben-Werck ... Fünfftem Theil* (Leipzig, 1676), '15. Courante'.	202

xviii *List of music examples*

9.4	J.R. Ahle, *Dreyfaches Zehn allerhand newer Sinfonien, Paduanen, Balletten, Alemanden, Mascharaden, Arien, Intraden, Couranten und Sarabanden* (Erfurt, 1650), 'Bassus', 'XVI. Ballet à3'.	203
9.5	J.J. Froberger, 'Libro di capricci, e ricercati … Libro Terzo' (manuscript *A-Wn* Mus. Hs. 16560), 'Ricercar 8', excerpt.	203
9.6	J. Rosenmüller, *Studenten-Music / Darinnen zu befinden Allerhand Sachen Mit drey und fünff Violen* (Leipzig, 1654), '52. Courant', start of second strain.	204
9.7	J. Rosenmüller, *Sonate da camera cioe Sinfonie, Alemande, Correnti, Balletti, Sarabande* (Venice, 1667), 'Sinfonia Sesta', 'Sarabanda'.	205
A.1	Incipits of 'Gregorig Zubern ander Theil', *GB-Lbl* Add. MS 31438.	216
A.2	Incipits of 'a 3 Diderich Becker' in manuscript *D-Dl* Mus. 1/B/101.	218

List of abbreviations

The following abbreviations are used throughout this book:

BuxWV	*Buxtehude-Werke-Verzeichnis* (Wiesbaden: Breitkopf und Härtel, 1974; 2nd edition, 1985)
CCS	M. Robertson, *The courtly consort suite in German-speaking Europe, 1650–1706* (Farnham: Ashgate, 2009)
DDT	*Denkmäler deutscher Tonkunst*, 65 vols (Wiesbaden: Breitkopf und Härtel, 1892–1931, repr. Graz, 1957–61)
FbWV	J. Froberger (ed. S. Rampe) *Neue Ausgabe sämtliche Werke* 6 vols (Kassel: Bärenreiter, 1993–)
GH	*German History*
Göhler	A. Göhler (comp.), *Verzeichnis der in den Frankfurter und Leipziger Messkatalogen der Jahre 1564 bis 1759 angezeigten Musikalien* (Leipzig: Kahnt, 1902)
LWV	H. Schneider, *Chronologisch-thematisches Verzeichnis sämtlicher Werke von Jean-Baptiste Lully* (Tutzing: Schneider, 1981)

Library Sigla used in this book

A-Wn	Vienna, Österreichische Nationalbibliothek
D-B	Berlin, Staatsbibliothek zu Berlin Preussischer Kulturbesitz
D-Dl	Dresden, Sächsische Landesbibliothek
D-EFu	Erfurt, Universitätsbibliothek
D-Hs	Hamburg, Staats- und Universitätsbibliothek Carl von Ossietzky
D-Kl	Kassel, Landesbibliothek und Murhardsche Bibliothek der Stadt Kassel
D-Lr	Lüneburg, Ratsbücherei
D-OB	Ottobeuren, Benediktiner-Abtei, Bibliothek

D-UDa Udestedt, Evangelisch-lutherisches Pfarramt, Archiv
DK-Kk Copenhagen, Det Kongelige Bibliotek
F-Pn Paris, Bibliothèque nationale de France
GB-DRc Durham, Cathedral Library
GB-Lbl London, British Library
GB-Lgc London, Gresham College
GB-Ob Oxford, Bodleian Library
PL-Kj Cracow, Biblioteka Jagiellońsk
S-Uu Uppsala, universitetsbibliothek, Carolina Rediviva
S-VX Växjö, Stadsbibliothek
US-NH New Haven, Yale University, music library
US-NHub New Haven, Yale University, Beinecke rare book and manuscript library

Acknowledgements

Given the partial roots of this book in a 2004 PhD dissertation, I should start by acknowledging my supervisors at that time, John Butt and Peter Holman. Both of them, particularly Peter, have continued to help and encourage me over the years and I am deeply grateful for their unfailingly good guidance. I am also grateful to the following who have helped in so many ways, either with my original dissertation or with the more recent work on this book: Andrew Ashbee, Ulli Burchette, Tassilo Erhardt, Victoria Holmes, Tanya Kevorkian, Simon McVeigh, David Marsh, Christoph Meinel, Samantha Owens, Stephen Rose, Shirley Thompson, Bryan White, Andrew Wooley.

My visits and enquiries to various institutions have been met with unfailing help and courtesy, but I would particularly like to thank the staff at the following: the British Library; Cambridge University Library; Bodleian Library, Oxford; the Cathedral Library, Durham; the Brotherton Library, Leeds; Universität der Künste Berlin; Bibliothèque nationale de France; Universitätsbibliothek, Freiburg in Breisgau; Staats- und Universitätsbibliothek Carl Von Ossietzky, Hamburg; Universitätsbibliothek Kassel – Landesbibliothek und Murhardsche Bibliothek der Stadt Kassel; Stadtbibliothek – Musikbibliothek, Leipzig; Gesamtkirchengemeinde Library, Regensburg; Kirchenbibliothek, Katharinenkirche, Salzwedel; Universitetsbibliotheket, Uppsala; Landsbiblioteket i Växjö; Biblioteka Jagiellońska, Warsaw; Hochschule für Musik Franz Liszt, Weimar; Deutsches Musikgeschichtliches Archiv, Kassel.

My deepest thanks go to my wife, Barbara. Without her help and constant support, this book could never have been contemplated, let alone finished. The term 'inspirational teacher' is frequently over-used, but John Railton MBE was indeed such a person. He helped me to recognise the importance of music in my life and continued to inspire me through my formative years at school. This book is dedicated to his memory.

Preface

One of the focal points of my PhD dissertation, 'The consort suite in the German-speaking lands, 1660–1705' (University of Leeds, 2004) was the division of the genre into two distinct traditions: suites written by court-based musicians and suites written by town-based musicians. I dealt with the former in *The Courtly Consort Suite in the German-Speaking Lands 1650–1706* (Farnham: Ashgate, 2009, hereafter *CCS*); this companion volume, greatly expanded from the original dissertation, examines the dance music of the towns.

In defining the German lands, it is likely that most of the composers considered in the following chapters would have thought of themselves as being German, even if they were nominal citizens of the Holy Roman Empire. But Germany was not a single entity: rather, it was a number of largely autonomous individual states and principalities of varying sizes. The area that these states covered had shrunk as a result of the Thirty Years War: Sweden enjoyed considerable territorial gains along the Baltic and North Sea coasts, and France reached the Rhine for the first time. The German states were theoretically part of the Holy Roman Empire and its legislative framework but, especially after the ending of the Thirty Years War in 1648, they became increasingly independent. In fact, the Empire after 1648 was 'a political power only in a passive sense'.[1] For the purposes of this study, we can describe the German lands in a geographical sense as stretching from the Baltic and North Sea coasts in the north to the Bavarian lands of the ruling Wittelsbach family in the south, and from the borders of the Spanish Netherlands in the west to the Archduchy of Austria and the Kingdom of Bohemia in the east. France made further inroads into German territory when it formally annexed the ten imperial cities of Alsace, including Strasbourg, in 1681.

I have used the term 'consort' to denote ensembles of two or more instruments in addition to the continuo. For larger-scale pieces, I have avoided the use of the term 'orchestral'; as Peter Holman has pointed out, it is inappropriate for ensembles of this period.[2] Works for single instrument and continuo have been excluded. I have also excluded viol consorts of the type by Johann Michael Nicolai 'a3 viol da gamba' (manuscript *GB-DRc* MS Mus.D 10). Along with those in the lute repertoire, these suites for viols alone are a different genre from the consort suites considered here, and would benefit from fresh study elsewhere. The keyboard suite is considered, but only in the context of its relationship with the consort suite.

Throughout this book, the term 'suite' will be used carefully, especially in the earlier chapters dealing with the decades immediately following the Thirty Years War. In the seventeenth century, the term was used in the same way that we use 'entourage' now. So royalty or diplomats would have their accompanying 'suites' and the term even found similar employment on the dramatic stage; to give just one example, the printed libretto to Jean-Baptiste Lully's *Le triomphe de l'amour* (*LWV* 59) has an entrée for 'Indiens de la suite de Bacus'.[3]

Away from royalty and the stage, the term could also be used simply to indicate the continuation of a piece of music over a page turn.[4] Court musicians sometimes used 'de suite', 'en suite' or just 'suite' to indicate like movements that followed each other without a break, and 'suite' was sometimes used in conjunction with the Bransle sequence.[5] But it was not until the end of the century that the term started to be used with any frequency and, even then, it was mostly in the printed editions issued by publishers in Amsterdam. For most German town composers (or their publishers) it was enough to simply list dance types on the title pages of their collections. Dieterich Becker's *Erster Theil zwey-stimmiger Sonaten und Suiten* is a rarity in this sense, even if the composer (or his publisher) may have been using 'suite' in terms of what follows rather than specifically referring to a sequence of dances.

While there are exceptions, which are documented in this book, it was usual for suites or sequences of associated dances to be written with their component movements using the same key. Therefore, it is on this premise that the terms 'pairing', 'sequence' and 'suite' are used in the following chapters.

As we will discover in later chapters, the 1650s and 60s saw important changes in conceptual attitudes towards town suites and suite collections and, in order to understand these changes, this survey starts in 1648, the end of the Thirty Years War. It finishes at the end of the seventeenth century when the era of the consort suite written by town musicians was over, even if parts of the tradition lingered on in the keyboard-suite writing of the early years of the eighteenth century.

An important objective in writing this book has been to argue against a perception of suite and dance-music composition that has remained largely unchallenged throughout the twentieth century since its inception up to the present day. In his 2001 *New Grove* article, which remains unchanged in the present online version, David Fuller divided his material under the headings of the 'classical suite' before and after the addition of the Gigue.[6] In doing so, Fuller was following a twentieth-century view of the suite that all but ignored the differences between court and town repertoires and subjected the suite as whole to the concept of the so-called 'classical order'. The latter arose in the early part of the century with the work of Tobias Norlind and Karl Nef, who saw the suite as a poor relation to the sonata.[7] There is historical precedent for this especially, if surprisingly, in court circles, where dance was an important part of royal entertainment. Philipp Heinrich Erlebach's manuscript inventory of music and instruments at the court of Rudolstadt lists sonatas by instrumental groupings, whereas most of the suites in the inventory are referred to simply as '47 Partien'.[8] An inventory of music at the court of Leopold I in Vienna lists different categories of sonatas, but suites are barely mentioned.[9] There were some exceptions: under the heading 'Balletti', the 1695 inventory of the music assembled for Bishop Karl Liechtenstein-Castelcorno at Kroměříž contains a separate and detailed list of the suites in the collection.[10]

Norlind and Nef attempted to redress the perceived difference between dance and sonata by imposing a sequence of 'Haupttänze' (principal dances).[11] The *Haupttänze* were the Allemande, Courante, Sarabande and, later, Gigue. Every example of the genre could then be judged by its relationship to these movements and movement order. A similar, but less dogmatic, approach was adopted by Paul Whitehead in his 1996 PhD dissertation.[12] He identified the Allemande, Courante, Sarabande and Gigue sequence as a 'pan-German phenomenon', but qualified this by suggesting that 'Particular dance groupings need to be viewed within the context of a diffuse and pluralistic repertoire that expressed itself in kaleidoscopic terms.'[13] However, this did not stop him from identifying one particular sequence of movements that did not conform to a particular pattern as being 'idiosyncratic'.[14]

While not abandoning it, Whitehead was not the only late-twentieth-century writer to doubt the classical concept. In 1992, Alexander Silbiger suggested that 'a new paradigm' had emerged in musical form 'after ca. 1650' and included the suite as part of 'a set of genres based on discrete extended movements, each with a constancy of tempo, texture, and mood'.[15] Similarly, David J. Buch defined French suites as 'A flexible hierarchy of types of movements, marked by a sense of proportion (and perhaps decorum) achieved by a somewhat loose ordering of dances of a specific meter, character and tempo.'[16] But, as we will see in the following chapters, the concept of the 'classical order' still carries considerable weight among present-day scholars.[17]

In *CCS*, I argued that 'the idea of a well-defined and specific order of movements spread across the repertoire does not apply to suites by court musicians' and that 'the fluid, lively and rich tradition of the courtly suite is at odds with the concepts of a 'classical' ordering.[18] Another example of this tradition lies in the many instances documented in this book and *CCS* of performers from both court and town being required to make a choice of performing material; the suggestion that such choice 'would be an impertinent combination, dependent on the performer's fancy, and not a unity created by the will of the composer' cannot be sustained.[19]

However, town-music consort suites of the seventeenth-century German lands often contain sequences that appear to support, albeit partially, the idea of an established order of movements. For example, many dance-music sequences start with an Allemande–Courante pairing. But as the following chapters will demonstrate, it was the metrical relationship between duple- and triple-time dances of all kinds that held the greatest importance. And in the following decades, it was the ordering of complete suites within a collection that became the overriding factor. If there is a hierarchy in consort suites by German town musicians, it is one imposed by careful organisation of the suites themselves and not movement types within them.

Perhaps the only dance-music tradition that comes near to an established order of movement types is the keyboard suite. But even here, twentieth-century

xxvi *Preface*

writing has confused the issue, Willi Apel considering consort suites by Schein and Peuerl in the same breath as keyboard suites by Froberger.[20] If a convention of Allemande, Courante and Sarabande does seem to have dominated the keyboard-suite repertoire in the middle of the seventeenth century, the increasing use of engraving techniques also saw the adoption of the organisational concepts once inhabited by the consort collections of the 1670s and 1680s (see Chapter 8). Again, it is an issue of careful organisation and not of movement types.

Printed editions seem often to have been the result of direct collaboration between composer and publisher. At times, the composer himself was responsible for the publishing. That did not prevent error, sometimes substantial. Until the arrival of music-engraving in the German lands at the very end of the seventeenth century, few if any composers seem to have had control over the highly specialised work of the typesetters, and it is here that mistakes were most likely to happen. However, printed editions remain our most important sources of suites and suite collections by town musicians. In the course of the following chapters, I will be comparing prints with often-inferior manuscript copies, and it is clear that many copyists could be ignorant of various aspects of music notation or apparently wilful in their selections of movements and dance types. But as we shall see in later chapters, copyists often appear to have had direct links with town *Collegia* ensembles, and it may be that their selections were dictated by the needs and technical limitations of these amateur musicians.

Seventeenth-century German music is beset with problems of movement nomenclature and inconsistency of spelling. Spelling of movement titles can differ within the same manuscript part and, just as frequently, within a set of printed part-books. To give one example; sources often fail to distinguish between 'Courante' and 'Corrente'. In order to avoid confusion and a proliferation of italics, I have used 'Courante' as a generic term throughout except where it has been necessary to identify specific examples in the Italian manner. Likewise, Allemande, Sarabande and Gigue have all been used in a similar generic manner.

Almost without exception, the title pages of German suite collections contain large amounts of material. The titles themselves are often substantial, involving lists of included movements. In the captions, I have tried to include as much of this material as possible within the space of a few lines. But to avoid unnecessary duplication of words, particularly within the main text, titles there have been subsequently truncated. I have modernised the seventeenth-century convention of using a 'v' as a 'u'.

A number of books cited in the chapter end notes and bibliography are from specialist publishers. In all citations of work from the twentieth or twenty-first centuries, I have therefore included the name of the publisher as well as the place of publication. Where German translations are newly provided, the original text has been included; where they have been taken from existing publications, the original text has been omitted. 'Modern' in terms of publication has been taken to mean twentieth and twenty-first centuries.

There is considerable scholarly disagreement over the use and influence of modes in the seventeenth century.[21] Solely for identification, I have employed the

Preface xxvii

terms of modern tonality in all discussions of key and relationships between keys. Where it has been necessary in the text to differentiate between notes of different pitches, I have used the system where c' is the middle of the modern piano keyboard and c" the octave above; c is the octave below and C the octave below that. The terms *à3*, *à4* and *à5* have been used to denote three-, four- and five-part ensembles.

The music examples are not intended to be paradigms of modern critical editing. Apart from specific examples where the poor quality of the source is central to the discussion, obvious printing and scribal errors have been corrected without comment. Reconstructed material has been presented on small staves or with cue-sized notes. For clarity, I have used modern bar lines throughout, even when they do not appear in the sources, and note beams or groupings have been applied accordingly. In both printed and manuscript sources, the use of ties, particularly at the end of dance-movement strains, is often inconsistent. Where editorial ties have been added, they are identified by a vertical line through the tie. Accidentals follow modern usage and are extended throughout the bar unless cancelled. Articulation and dynamic markings are shown as they appear in the sources, but bass-line figures have been placed under, and not over, the notes to which they refer. I have used the standard treble and bass clefs along with the alto and tenor C clefs as they are given in the sources. I have only made a change where the French-violin clef or other C clefs have been used, and these changes have been marked by incipits at the start of the examples under consideration.

In my original dissertation, I lamented the inaccuracies of the *RISM A/II* database. Since 2004, the situation has greatly improved, but the relatively small number of manuscript sources dealt with in this book has made the use of the database unnecessary except in a small number of cases. On the other hand, specific exemplars of a collection have warranted the use of the *RISM A/I* catalogues on CD-ROM and the numbers from these catalogues have been used in the bibliography or where specifically required in the text. Unfortunately, I have to make the same plea for these catalogues to be revised as I did for *RISM A/II*. As we shall see, some of the information they contain is still inaccurate or has been superseded.

Collections are considered in chronological order along with manuscript derivatives. Manuscripts with no connection to printed editions are dealt with separately at the end of the relevant chapter. Rhythmic and metrical characteristics of various dances are often given as being in duple or triple time. Duple is to be understood as anything essentially in rhythmic groups of two or four and triple as anything in three.

Notes

1 R. Vierhaus, trans. J. Knudsen, *Germany in the age of absolutism* (Cambridge: Cambridge University Press, 1988 repr. 1991), p. 10.
2 P. Holman, 'From violin band to orchestra' in J. Wainwright and P. Holman (eds), *From Renaissance to Baroque: change in instruments and instrumental music in the seventeenth-century* (Aldershot: Ashgate, 2005), pp. 241–57 at p. 241.
3 [P. Quinault], *Le triomphe de l'amour: ballet dansé devant sa Majesté à S. Germain en Laie* ([Paris], c. 1680), p. 10. Online facsimile at http://digital.library.unt.edu/ark:/67531/metadc1689 (accessed 10 April 2013).

xxviii *Preface*

4   For example, see the 1687 keyboard manuscript copied by 'Mademoiselle La pierre' (*F-Pn* Rés. Vmd. ms. 18) (facsimile: Geneva: Minkoff, 1983).
5   *CCS*, p. 46.
6   D. Fuller, 'Suite' in D.L. Root (ed.), Grove music online (www.oxfordmusiconline.com) (accessed 31 December 2014).
7   T. Norlind, 'Zur Geschichte der suite' in *Sammelbände der Internationalen Musikgesellschaft*, vol. 7 (Leipzig, 1905–1906), pp. 172–203; K. Nef, *Geschichte der Sinfonie und Suiten* (Leipzig, 1921).
8   *Inventarium*, ThStA Rudolstadt, Geheimes Archiv B VII 4c Nr.2. The page is reproduced in M. Robertson, 'The consort suite in the German-speaking lands, 1660–1705', PhD dissertation (University of Leeds, 2004).
9   'Distinta Specificatione. Dell Archivio Musicale per il Servizio della Cappella, e Camera Cesaiea Prima' (manuscript *A-Wn* S.m. 2451).
10 The inventory is reproduced in J. Sehnal and J. Pešková, *Caroli de Liechtenstein Castelcorno episcopi Olumucensis operum artis musicae collectio Cremsirii reservata*, Artis Musicæ Antiquioris Catalogorum Vol. V/1 (Prague: Editio Supraphon, 1998), pp. 41–76.
11 Norlind, 'Zur Geschichte der suite', p. 187; Nef, *Geschichte*, p. 74.
12 P. Whitehead, 'Austro-German printed sources of instrumental music, 1630 to 1700', PhD dissertation (University of Pennsylvania, 1996).
13 Ibid., p. 174.
14 Ibid., p. 170.
15 See A. Silbiger, 'Music and the crisis of seventeenth-century Europe' in V. Coelho (ed.), *Music and science in the age of Galileo* (Dordrecht: Kluwer, 1992), pp. 35–44 at p. 40.
16 D.J. Buch, 'The influence of the *ballet de cour* in the genesis of the French baroque suite' in *Acta Musicologica* 57/1 (1985), pp. 94–109 at pp. 96–7.
17 For example, see P. Wollny (ed.), *Johann Jacob Froberger, Toccaten, Suiten, Lamenti; die Handschrift SA 4450 der Sing-Akademie zu Berlin* (Kassel: Bärenreiter, 2004), Preface, p. xxii, and M. Seares, *Johann Mattheson's Pièces de clavecin and Das neu-eröffnete Orchestre* (Farnham: Ashgate, 2014), p. 70.
18 *CCS*, p. 64.
19 W. Apel (trans. H. Tischler), *The history of keyboard music to 1700* (Bloomington: Indiana University Press, 1972), p. 555.
20 Ibid., p. 555.
21 While not dealing specifically with Germany, the best discussion of modes and modal theory is to be found in: R. Herissone, *Music theory in seventeenth-century England* (Oxford: Oxford University Press, 2000). For a discussion of twentieth-century writings on modes, see M.G. Vaillancourt, 'Instrumental ensemble music at the court of Leopold I (1658–1705)', PhD dissertation (University of Illinois at Urbana-Champaign, 1991), pp. 103–161.

1 Towns and town musicians
Governance, status and performance

'In this year 1618 the most horrific comet appeared ..., it remained for thirty days in the sky, just as war in Germany too lasted thirty years, and thus each day means a year, as the experience of it has unfortunately and sufficiently proven.'[1] This extract from the journal of Joachim Rese, a German small-town official, is not alone in viewing the comet as a portent of the Thirty Years War,[2] and a time of 'misery, fear, distress, and heartrending suffering among all the people'.[3]

Albeit in terms of classical antiquity, Hieronymus Kromayer, professor of rhetoric in mid-seventeenth-century Leipzig, saw the war as a 'happy catastrophe',[4] though the extent of this catastrophe and its aftermath has been a source of 'long and often heated debate among historians'.[5] But there is little doubt that many parts of the German lands suffered very badly in the conflict. In the end, it seems that Germany 'lost some 40 per cent of its rural and 33 per cent of its urban population', substantial figures by any consideration.[6] To add to this disaster, the plague returned to western and southern areas in the 1630s and by 1650, as a result of war and pestilence, the population of Germany had fallen, for the first time, below that of France.[7]

But there was also regeneration in the second half of the century: Schwäbisch Hall, for instance, which had suffered particularly badly at the hands of Bavarian, French and Swedish occupying forces, had all but returned to its pre-war levels of prosperity by the 1680s.[8] And urban renewal was certainly not limited to this area of the German lands. While the accounts of foreign travellers cannot always be considered reliable, there is a persuasive similarity to their observations that contradicts the worst portraits of widespread urban poverty.[9]

According to Claude Jordan de Colombier's 1698 *Voyages historiques de l'Europe*,

> Cette Ville est trés-recommandable par sa grandeur, qui a trois grandes lieuës de France de circuit; elle est ceinte de trois murailles de pierre de taille, flanquées de 183. Tours, & d'un Fossé large & profond: Sa Bibliotheque est remplie d'un grand nombre de Livres & Manuscrits trés-rares; son Arsenal est garni de tout ce qui peut servir à sa défense. Il y a de trés-belles Eglises.

2   *Towns and town musicians*

> (This town [Nuremberg] is to be highly recommended for its grandeur, and has a circumference of three French leagues. It is enclosed by three cut-stone walls, flanked by 183 towers and a large and deep moat. Its library is filled with a great number of very rare books and manuscripts, and its arsenal is provided with everything necessary for defence. There are some very fine churches.)[10]

Colombier's observations are confirmed by De Blainville, a widely travelled Spanish diplomat. Writing in 1705, the latter judged Nuremberg to be 'twice as large as Francfort, and the Commerce carried on renders it very rich and populous ... The streets of this Town are large, open, well paved'.[11] A similar portrait of flourishing town life is presented nearly fifty years earlier in Priorato's *The History of the Sacred and Royal Majesty of Christina Alessandra Queen of Swedland*. The entry for 20 October 1655 reads:

> Auspurge is one of the fairest, most noble and famous Cities of Germany, seated in a very pleasant plain, abundantly watered with streams which make the ground most fertile. The structures are great and magnificent, the streets large and long, and the traffique very great. 'Tis replenisht with Merchants, and opulent Citizens, the Town-house is one of the most beautifullest Fabriques of *Germany*, and the rest are noble and majestick.[12]

In contrast to this relative prosperity, there was a sharp and apparently widespread decline in urban population. Lady Mary Wortley Montagu found some streets in the Nuremberg of 1716 to be 'wretchedly thin of inhabitants' even if she saw other towns in the same light as De Blainville: 'well built and full of people'.[13] Given that Lady Mary was writing in the immediate aftermath of the War of the Spanish Succession, another conflict that took its toll of the German lands, her comments do seem to be accurate. In 1622, Nuremberg had 40,000 inhabitants but, by 1800, only 27,000.[14] And other travellers agreed with her. William Carr was an English diplomat and traveller; his 'Remarks', an account of his travels across much of Europe, were published in 1688.[15] Like De Blainville in Nuremberg, he found the streets of Cologne to be 'very large' but was struck by the comparatively sparse population; 'The streets are so thin of people, that one may pass some of them and not meet ten men or women, unless it be Church men or Religious sisters'.[16] Carr also found Cologne to be 'much decayed within these hundred years ... the houses dayly fall to ruine'. But he saw the reasons for this as being religious rather than economic and put it down to the influence of the Jesuits who 'had so great influence upon the Magistrates, that they banish all Protestants'.[17] This seems a rather confused or simply biased view, especially as the 1648 Peace of Westphalia 'dictated that in biconfessional cities ... all properties and buildings – such as churches, cloisters, hospitals and schools – would be restored to both Catholics and Protestants based upon whichever confession had owned them in 1624'.[18] But it does seem that the terms of the Peace were not always observed, and there appears to have been a degree of re-Catholicisation across some areas of the German lands that supports De Blainville's observation.[19]

The general picture, then, is one of uncertain economic recovery, and, if not as disastrous a picture as modern historians have suggested, not all towns and cities seem to have been 'great and magnificent'. The situation was not helped by a lack of political stability. Even after the 1648 Peace of Westphalia, which marked the official end of the war, 'the half century which began in the later 1660s saw inter-state struggles which changed the political face of Europe more, and more lastingly, than any since the reign of the Emperor Charles V five generations earlier'.[20] But one factor, more than any other, lay at the heart of the indifferent economy: the often-exorbitant levels of taxation in the towns.

During the Thirty Years War, the structure of taxation had changed from direct to indirect; more importantly, the levels of taxation were 'totally unprecedented'.[21] And the accumulated debt at the end of the war prevented a return to the lower levels enjoyed prior to 1618. This was apparent to De Blainville when he also spent time in Cologne; he commented on the 'exorbitant Contributions' that the Elector levied 'every Day from this City'.[22] Even so, the situation was not uniformly bad. De Blainville praised the Elector at 'Coblentz' (Koblenz), who 'contents himself with a very moderate Revenue, rather than overwhelm them with Taxes',[23] and Carr commented on 'Francfort' (Frankfurt am Main), where 'the government is easy to the people, they not being taxed as other cities are'.[24] Of course, geographically well-placed towns and cities were able to benefit from foreign trading. Carr also noted that 'the citie [Frankfurt] is populous and frequented by all sorts of Merchants, from most parts of Europe, & part of Asia also, becaus of the two great faires that are yearly kept there'.[25] The 'great faires' were trade fairs and, as Carr observed, it was foreign trade that enabled stronger economic recovery in places such as Frankfurt, Leipzig and Hamburg.

The governance of the towns presented an equally diverse state of affairs. Fifty-one *Reichsstädte* (imperial towns or cities) were recognised in the 1648 Peace. They were 'territorially independent estates ... directly subject to the Empire and not to other territorial states' and, as such, paid direct taxes to the Empire in return for its protection.[26] But protection did not guarantee prosperity; in fact, rather the opposite. The promotion by the territorial states of rural industry, privileged monopolies and toll barriers all 'undoubtedly drew some commerce and industry away from the imperial cities'.[27] In any case, not all towns were able to afford such 'protection' and there was an extraordinarily wide range of sovereignty and jurisdiction.[28] In addition to the *Riechsstädte*, there were the *Landstädte*, towns and cities that fell under the jurisdiction of individual territorial princes. Some towns were entirely autonomous, independent of princely or imperial authority, but this did not stop some princes and dukes from attempting to change the situation. Braunschweig, for example, only managed to retain its independence from the ducal court of Braunschweig-Lüneburg-Wolfenbüttel by military action. But the independence was temporary; the town was eventually subsumed into royal 'protection' in 1671.[29]

For those towns that did manage to avoid direct royal interference, the governing officials were members of the so-called 'Inner Councils'. Membership of

4   *Towns and town musicians*

these was made up of one or more *Bürgermeister*, and members 'usually held office for life or for a very long time'.[30] And if a burgher moved away from the town of his appointment, citizenship in his new home had to be purchased 'for cash or by marriage, or a mixture of both'.[31]

The Inner Council could be comparatively large; De Blainville noted that 'Cologne is governed by its Chapter and by its Magistrates, consisting of two Burgo-masters and 49 Councellors'.[32] This resulted in a good deal of independence in the day-to-day affairs of the towns though, even here, royal influence could still be felt. De Blainville observed that the Elector of Cologne 'nominates a Magistrate who is Judge in Criminal Causes'[33] and the royal courts were still called on to appoint mediators in disputes between the citizenry and municipal governing bodies.[34]

An important function of the Inner Council lay in the appointing of civic posts, and this included the town musicians. So it is hardly surprising that the latter sought the approval and patronage of their civic masters. And such patronage was forthcoming from the *Honoratioren* or 'honourable families' that formed the highest social levels of town society.[35] The conspicuous wealth of the richest members of this social group was exhibited not only in impressive houses with elaborate gardens, but in a willingness to provide 'substantial philanthropic endowments' that enriched the musical life of the largest towns.[36] But even in the less exalted levels of town society, the prosperous merchants, artisans and tradesmen of centres such as Leipzig were still a source of patronage.

Figure 1.1 shows the list of dedicatee civic dignitaries from the group of 'Weitberühmten Kauff- und Handels-Leuten' (well-known buyers and traders) given at the start of Johann Pezel's *Musicalische Gemüths-Ergetzung* (Leipzig, 1672).

Dedications and dedicatee lists such as this indicate the importance of such patronage in town music-making, and it appears that presentation copies for some or all of the patrons could form a substantial part of any print run.[37] It is difficult to be precise about the nature of this patronage but, as Arne Spohr has pointed out, the dedication of Johann Schop's 1633 *Erster Theil newer Paduanen* to members of the Hamburg city council may well be an acknowledgement of a substantial increase in his salary.[38] And, in an era of self-publication, when, as Rosenmüller complained, publishers expected their authors to pay for both ink and paper, it is possible that many similar dedications reflected contributions towards printing costs.[39] The preface of Schein's 1624 *Diletti pastorali* seems to imply that patrons could also guard against 'unbecoming calumnies'.[40] Perhaps the latter included the 'slanderers' that Schein complained about two years later in his *Opella nova II*.[41]

While individual patronal motivation may often have been little more than an attempt to procure status as leaders of municipal society, many towns and cities 'relied on the arts to strengthen some of the civic values and ideologies they wished to promote'.[42] The support from the *Bürgerschaft* gave town musicians secure employment, especially compared with their colleagues at court, who could be dismissed at any time. According to Johann Beer's *Musikalische Discurse durch die Principia der Philosophie deducirt* (Nuremberg, 1719), 'there are numerous courts which, at the least sign of stress, will lay off or reduce their staff to

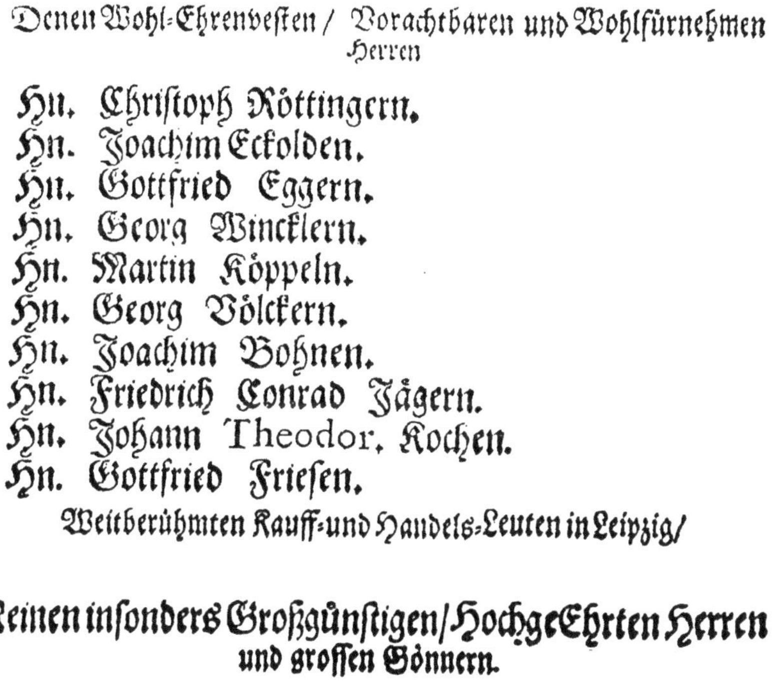
Denen Wohl-Ehrenvesten / Vorachtbaren und Wohlfürnehmen Herren

Hn. Christoph Röttingern.
Hn. Joachim Eckolden.
Hn. Gottfried Eggern.
Hn. Georg Wincklern.
Hn. Martin Köppeln.
Hn. Georg Völckern.
Hn. Joachim Bohnen.
Hn. Friedrich Conrad Jägern.
Hn. Johann Theodor. Kochen.
Hn. Gottfried Friesen.

Weitberühmten Kauff- und Handels-Leuten in Leipzig/

Meinen insonders Großgünstigen/Hochgeehrten Herren und grossen Gönnern.

Figure 1.1 J. Pezel, *Musicalische Gemüths-Ergetzung / Bestehend [in] Intraden, Allemanden, Balletten, Gavotten, Alle breven, Courenten, Sarabanden und Chiqven* (Leipzig, 1672), Preface, shelfmark II.6.10a: Leipzig, Städtische Bibliotheken-Musikbibliothek. Reproduced by kind permission.

such an extent that the entire court must dissolve as a result'.[43] Working in towns often seems to have been the only means of fresh employment, and Beer, a court employee, ruefully notes, 'consequently, there are many court musicians who long to be town musicians if the compensations were as great. For what is more splendid than stability?'[44] Even when court musicians were promised a proper income, its payment was often irregular. At Dresden, Schutz complained that, over a period of four years, some members of the *Hofkapelle* had received only three out of the expected sixteen quarterly payments.[45] Despite all this, there is a suggestion in Beer's novel, *Teutsche Winter-Nächte* (Nuremberg, 1682), that members of the *Hofkapelle* are superior musicians and, by implication, have higher social status. The town musicians quarrel about titles and have to be reminded that 'many a cantor also composes better than many a *Kapellmeister*'.[46]

Elsewhere in his satirical novels, and for reasons that seem to border on sensationalism, Beer is scathing about musicians in general, incompetent cantors and elderly organists being singled out for particular ridicule.[47] But these comments on the lack of competence of town musicians need to be treated with caution; at its best, the town tradition could produce virtuosi of the highest quality. Thomas Baltzar was a pupil of Johann Schop and of the Lübeck town musician Georg Zuber. In 1655,

6   *Towns and town musicians*

he moved to England after spending time at Queen Christina's court in Sweden.[48] The Oxford antiquarian Anthony Wood 'saw him run his Fingers to the end of the Finger-Board of the Violin, and run them back insensibly, and all in alacrity and in very good tune'.[49] Wood concluded that 'Mr. Davis Mell was accounted hitherto the best Violin in England ... but after Baltzar came into England, and shew'd his most wonderful parts on that Instrument, Mell was not so admired.'[50]

Beer's implied difference of status between court and town employment is also suspect. While some musicians may have felt a loss of status in moving from court to town, in reality, the difference between the two states of employment was often nebulous; with the possible exception of trumpeters, musicians were able to move freely between *Hofkapelle* and *Stadt*.[51] Matthias Weckmann, one of Hamburg's most celebrated town musicians, started his career as a court organist in Dresden. He then moved to Sweden, where he became *Kapellmeister* to Crown Prince Christian, before returning to Dresden and then Hamburg, taking up the town post of organist at the latter's *Jacobikirche*.[52] The same applied to musicians of lesser calibre. In Lübeck, Peter Grecke had trained with Franz Tunder, spent three years as a member of the Güstrow *Hofkapelle*, and was then appointed town musician on his return to Lübeck in 1669. He became a burgher in 1675.

There was always the chance of additional temporary work for town musicians – they were frequently brought into court *Hofkapellen* as extras when the occasion demanded. In Lübeck, town musicians were 'regularly engaged' by the surrounding courts,[53] and in neighbouring Hamburg Johann Schop, director of the city's *Ratsmusik*, continued to play for special occasions at the court of his former employer, Christian IV of Denmark.[54]

Town musicians were subject to strict regulation, with hiring and training being similar to that of the guilds of tradesmen. Guild training dictated that journeymen in all trades had to satisfy the so-called *Wanderschaft* requirement before becoming masters, and this entailed an apprentice travelling between towns seeking employment in order to 'refine his occupational skills, learn new techniques, and broaden his knowledge of the world'.[55] The *Wanderschaft* also had the effect of limiting the number of journeymen seeking to become masters.

For musicians, the equivalent was an association formed in 1653 by the town musicians of Saxony that 'aimed to unite musicians from across central German lands in a code of shared values'.[56] Possibly influenced by the imperial privileges issued for court trumpeters, 'The Imperial confirmation of the articles of the Union of Instrumental Musicians in the districts of Upper and Lower Saxony and other interested places' was submitted to Emperor Ferdinand III as a code of practice, and then printed.[57] Article VIII of the code forbids the use of 'dishonourable instruments, such as bagpipes, sheep-horns, hurdy-gurdies, and triangles, which beggars often use for collecting alms at house doors'. Article X expected musicians to 'shun and avoid' contact with 'jugglers, hangmen, bailiffs, gaolers, conjurors, rogues, or any other such low company'.[58] Articles XII and XIII also stated, as a safeguard of playing standards, that 'no apprentice [musician] shall be free under five years' followed by a further period of three years as 'assistants to other famous masters'. In addition to the strictures of the code, there were locally imposed further layers of regulation. In Munich, the period of training apparently lasted for eighteen years, which, for the established musicians themselves provided the additional benefit of controlling the number of players and maintaining fee levels.[59] In Erfurt, there were lists of instruments that could properly be used and those associated with begging; there was also a stipulation of 'honourable birth' for the employed musicians.[60]

The importance of honourable birth reflected the demands of society as a whole and the presence of powerful social hierarchies. Schwäbisch Hall had strict, regulated codes not just for events such as baptisms, weddings, funerals and banquets, but for the quality of the dress worn by its inhabitants at these gatherings.[61] Social hierarchy was therefore maintained by visible distinctions of rank, and Schwäbisch Hall was certainly not alone in enforcing such regulations.

Given this social background, it is not surprising that there were well-established hierarchies of musical status, especially in the larger towns and cities. The *Stadtpfeifer* were at the top of this hierarchy and the most highly trained. Beneath them were groups of lesser-qualified musicians, albeit still highly regulated, and with clearly defined lower-grade duties. Such groups were given a variety of titles, *Kunstgeiger*, *Rollbrüder*, *Zunftmusicker*, *Chorbrüder* or *Köstenbrüder* to name but a few.[62] In Graz in 1701, the nine *Geigerkompagnien* (each consisting of four men) were permitted to play violins, bass viols and dulcimers at the weddings of lower social classes.[63] And this clearly demonstrates an important difference in musical status. Instruments such as dulcimers were encouraged for these lesser ensembles – they were not to be played in public by the *Stadtpfeifer*. However, movement between ensembles was possible, and suitably trained members of the *Kunstgeiger* could be elevated to the *Stadtpfeifer*. In Leipzig, Johann Pezel started his career as a *Kunstgeiger* and then qualified as both a violinist and trumpeter. Accordingly, he became a member of the *Stadtpfeifer*.[64]

There was also a third group of players, the tower musicians (*Türmer*), whose 'duties were a blend of guarding and music-making that varied depending on the size of a town'.[65] *Stadtpfeifer* sometimes had to take part in these duties alongside tower musicians and it seems that, in many cases, the latter were just as highly trained. As with members of the *Kunstgeiger*, it seems to have been possible to move between *Türmer* and *Stadtpfeifer* ensembles although, in most cases, it is unlikely that further training was required.

The numbers of musicians involved in town-music performances could vary considerably; the *Abendmusiken* at Lübeck drew on the services of 'almost forty people', many brought in for the occasion.[66] But, as with the courts, the number of musicians in regular employment varied greatly. Not surprisingly, the size and wealth of individual towns and cities governed the size of the municipal ensembles, and the numbers of regularly employed players were small. Away from the *Abendmusiken*, Buxtehude's Lübeck normally relied on 'an excellent band of [seven] municipal musicians who greatly enhanced the musical environment of the city'. In addition to these seven, there were two trumpeters, a piper and a drummer.[67] In wartime Hamburg during the 1630s, there were only eight town musicians, albeit with the possibility of augmentation by the *Rollbrüder* who could add their services when the occasion demanded.[68] There were five town musicians in Erfurt, mostly members of the Bach family and, in Gotha, there were only two, albeit augmented when the occasion demanded. These numbers often remained small at the request of the musicians themselves, who wished to retain their levels of fee income.

The bulk of these fees came from weddings. Once again, there was a strict framework of regulation and hierarchy, with the more qualified musicians playing at the larger, more profitable matrimonial ceremonies. The duties could be split between the various ensembles. Payment of fees was made as a single sum to be distributed among those who took part, so it was in the interests of the musicians to keep their numbers to a minimum. For example, in Augsburg, there were two ensembles for providing music at weddings, one for Protestants and one for Catholics.[69] Clearly this involved a relatively large number of players, and the town council was petitioned by the musicians in 1686 to reduce their number from twenty-four to twenty. It was the same among the *Rollbrüder* in Braunschweig; in 1668, they applied to the council to reduce their membership from nine to six.[70]

Given the importance of this fee income, often worth more than salaries, any competition was a source of anxiety. The main cause for concern was the presence of ill-qualified and ill-educated wandering musicians. If the latter were sometimes itinerant journeymen travelling from place to place in order to gain experience, there were also many who were little more than beggars and demanded rather less than the regulation fees.[71] So it is not surprising that playing standards were jealously guarded and, as we have seen, closely regulated.

The requirement to be proficient on more than one instrument was common to many, if not all, town musicians. In Daniel Speer's novel *Simplicianischer lustig-politischer Haspel-Hannß* (n.p., 1684), the fictional musician, 'Bobbin Jack', becomes a town musician and is expected to play the 'trumpet, recorder, viol and trombone'.[72] Elsewhere in the novel, he serves an apprenticeship as a bass viol player, and also plays the zither. This formidable versatility – even if we do not know the standard of the playing – was exceeded by Hans Iwe, a municipal musician in Hamburg. In his 1672 application for the post, he wrote that 'I do not hesitate to play violin, viola da gamba, violone, all manner of woodwinds, cornetto, dulcian, trombone, bass trombone and flutes in a suitable manner'.[73] Iwe later became an assistant to Buxtehude, so we must assume at least a reasonable proficiency in some, if not all, of these instruments; his versatility is even more noteworthy given the 'remarkably high' quality of Hamburg's *Ratsmusik* with its 'extremely demanding' selection processes.[74] The same versatility explains the appearance of a single movement for '2.Violino: 2.Cornetto è Basso' in Becker's *Musicalische Frülings-Früchte* when the remainder of the collection is devoted to string music. Manuscript *D-UDa* 38a/9 contains the first treble line music for Andreas Hammerschmidt's *Dritter Theil newer Paduanen* (Leipzig, 1650), and there are frequent references to wind instruments. But in '13. Sonata à5' from this collection, the player is expected to play both 'Cornetto' and 'Trombona' during the same piece, sufficient bars' rest allowing the change from one to the other.[75] Likewise, the part-books of Johann Caspar Horn's *Geistliche Harmonien über die gewöhnlichen Evangelia ... Der Sommer-Theil* (Dresden, 1680) make it clear that the same players are required to alternate between violin and *Cornetto* while the viola players are also expected to play the trombone.

Away from the expertise of ensembles and players in the leading towns, however, it seems that such wide-ranging proficiency was rare. Even if town musicians had the ability to play many different instruments, it is unlikely that they managed all of them with equal skill. This is clear from the interchangeable instrumentation that is specified in a number of dance-music collections and perhaps expected without comment elsewhere. The third volume of Kindermann's 1643 *Deliciæ studiosorum* gives *Cornetti* and recorders as an alternative to violins, and a trombone or *Fagott* instead of a string bass. The large-scale suites in the sixth volume of Horn's *Parergon musicum* also allow for a wide range of alternative instrumentation, not only between wind and string instruments but also in terms of what may be omitted without serious harm to the musical textures.[76]

Likewise, Johann Rosenmüller's *Sonate da camera* (Venice, 1667) offers the performer the alternative of instruments 'Da Arco, et altri' (strings and others). The identity of the 'altri' instruments is not specified, but Rosenmüller was a trombone player and it is likely that he had a consort of *Cornetti* and trombones in mind. And while the collection was published in Venice, Rosenmüller would have learned the need to provide for different types of ensemble well before he left his native Germany (see Chapter 6). Even in Hamburg, the title page of Johann Theile's now-lost 1683 publication, *Sonaten, Prael, Allem, Cour, Arien & Chiquen*, apparently gave a number of alternatives for all the parts except the first violin:

> For 3 parts: 2 Violinen and 1 Fagotto or Viola da Gamba: alternatively, 1 Violino and 2 Viola da Gamba, or 1 Trambona or 1 Fagotto, [all] in addition to the B[asso] c[ontinuo].[77]

While such alternatives were surely not required in Hamburg, Theile clearly desired the widest possible dissemination of his music: he did not want its use limited by problems of instrumentation.

The widest possible dissemination of a composer's music was another way of dealing with the perceived threat of beggar musicians. It was here that printed editions played a major part. Stephen Rose has pointed out that 'Protestants believed that composers had received their talent from God and should not keep it to themselves', but it was the appearance of work in print that, more than anything else, raised the status of its author and made the expense of a printed edition worthwhile.[78] As Rose has also pointed out, 'typically the publisher oversaw and financed the venture, supplied the printer with paper, and took responsibility for marketing'.[79] The printer set the type and produced a specified number of copies. At times, the jobs of printer and publisher were carried out by the same person or publishing house, but it was more usual for the two roles to be separate.

The prolific Andreas Hammerschmidt only started to issue his music in print after taking up a municipal post and, apparently on the strength of his printed collections of consort music, the Leipzig town musician Johann Pezel was offered a senior position at Bautzen without audition.[80] Printing also offered the opportunity for wide dissemination of a composer's work, especially at trade fairs. The Rudolstadt court inventory of music, drawn up at the end of the century, lists the 1656 *Deliciæ Harmonicæ* by the Leipzig town musician Werner Fabricius among its contents. It is highly likely that the collection was purchased at a book fair.

The preface of a printed edition could be a place where a composer might show his erudition and learning. We cannot be sure if Matthias Kelz was employed by either court or town, but the preface to his *Primitiæ musicales* (Augsburg, 1658) is typical of many. His wide reading is showcased by references to the biblical Moses, the classical Roman writers Pliny the elder and Lucretius, the Greek tragic poet Aeschylus, and the Christian writing of both St Ambrose and the abbot Rupert of Deutz. The origins of music itself are traced from the triumph of water over fire, leading in turn to the creation of the reed bed of the river and the *fistularum* (reed) of the musical instrument. The status of Kelz as an educated musician is established; it is a very long way from that of the itinerant beggar.

If the printed edition was an essential weapon in the battle for status, it is not surprising that manuscript copies of these printed collections seem to have been a source of genuine irritation. In the preface to his *Studenten-Music* (Leipzig, 1654), Johann Rosenmüller complains that his pieces were subject to frequent faulty and unauthorised copying:

> [U]nd ich auch mehrmals nicht ohne ziemlichen Verdruß sehen und erfahren müssen / daß sie mir teils heimlich und wider meinen Willen und Wissen abgeschrieben / und hin und her getragen / auch durch so vielfältiges Abschreiben (wie es zu gehen pfleget) je länger je mehr verfälschet worden.

> ([A]nd I have had to observe and experience, not without some dismay, that they copied me sometimes secretly and against my wish and knowledge, and carried [the music] back and forth; as usually happens, the more often it was copied, the more it was distorted.)

The unauthorised copying that he is referring to here is manuscript; pirate editions of German consort-suite collections were not unknown, but they were rare.[81] Even allowing for the expense of printing and the frequent errors in typesetting, it is clear that town composers still considered the printed publication to be the most desirable way of disseminating their music.

If foreign musicians, usually French or Italian, did not offer the same threat as beggar musicians, they were still regarded with suspicion by some town musicians. The preface to Johann Kuhnau's *Frische Clavier-Früchte* keyboard collection (Leipzig, 1696) warns against the dangers of preferring music solely on the grounds that it was foreign. And it is no coincidence that, in the same composer's satirical novel, *Der musicalische Quack-Salber* (Dresden, 1700), the imposter musician at the heart of the story pretends to come from an Italian background, while the *Collegium musicum* he attempts to mislead is lampooned as a 'silly company who think a composer or *musicus* who hasn't seen Italy is a foolish dunderhead'.[82] While the attempts of the imposter to portray himself as a skilled musician are more satirical than real, there can be little doubt that the *Collegium* itself is portrayed with some accuracy. According to Kuhnau,

> As is usual in cities, the musicians hold their *Collegium Musicum* once or twice a week, which is indeed a praiseworthy undertaking, partly because they thereby continue to improve themselves in their splendid profession and partly because from their pleasant harmony they also should learn an even, harmonious agreement among their personalities.[83]

Such bodies met throughout the German lands and practised their art for most, if not all, of the seventeenth century. Kuhnau is sparing on information regarding his ensemble's vocal or instrumental accomplishments. We are not told if it is made up of professional musicians, amateurs or a mixture of both. But they are referred to, probably sarcastically, as 'die Hoff-Capelle' and it seems that self-aggrandising court musicians are also intended as objects of the satire.[84] The story's imposter is invited to sit at the harpsichord to play a continuo part, and there is also mention of an organ pumper, which implies a chamber organ, presumably for the same purpose. There are also tenor and bass singers along with the instrumentalists. None of the members are *virtuosi*, but at least some of them do have a reasonable musical knowledge. For example, there is awareness of the limitations of the natural trumpet. The imposter's claim to have imitated the alto voice on the trumpet is met with incredulity as the instrument 'scarcely reaches into the range of this voice and which is not suited for the present melody by letting itself be extended in the manner of the trombone'.[85] Tellingly, there is no mention of public performance; the *Collegium* plays together for its own edification and, each week, two members are expected to provide new music (*Musicalischen Stücken*).[86]

A similar ensemble is described in the first volume of Friederich Erhardt Niedt's *Musicalische Handleitung* (Hamburg, 1700).[87] The fictitious *Collegium* here seems to comprise a wider mixture of experience and expertise than Kuhnau's; the ensemble leader is a 'Director *Chori Musici*' and presumably a professional musician, but clearly others are not of this standard and a number of 'piglets (if not big fat sows)' creep into the performance.[88] It is telling that part distribution was varied during the course of the *Collegium*'s meeting, 'in such a way that the one who had played the violin before now had to take the *Violabranio* [*di braccio*] and so on'.[89] Once again, we see the tradition of playing different instruments, albeit in a limited way.

The preface to Hieronymus Kradenthaller's *Deliciarum musicalium Erster Theil* (Nuremberg, 1675) clearly implies this type of domestic music-making:

> … denen diese meine *Deliciæ Musicales* lang nicht gleichen warden / und ist nicht dahin gemeinet denen Virtuosen etwas vor zuschreiben / sondern welchen es beliebig zur Delectation zu gebrauchen.
>
> (… these *Deliciæ Musicales* of mine are not the same in length and do not have those qualities that are usually attributed to virtuosi; instead they should be used at will for delectation.)

The 'Hoff-Capelle' meets at a various private houses, and, along with Niedt and Kradenthaller, Kuhnau seems to be suggesting the existence of less skilled quasi-domestic ensembles existing in parallel with the long-established well-regarded *Collegia* in towns such as Leipzig and Hamburg. As we shall see in Chapter 6, membership of the Leipzig student *Collegium* was highly desirable and it is difficult to reconcile the apparent expertise of such ensembles with the object of Kuhnau's or Niedt's satire. So it is important to make a distinction between these two types of *Collegia* and, throughout this book, I will be drawing attention to music that may have been intended solely for domestic ensembles.

If we assume that the main market for printed suite collections was the *Collegia* in either of its manifestations, there were other occasions when dance music could have been played, either by the hated itinerant players, or at a professional level by the registered town musicians, and it is important to consider the circumstances for these performances. For the larger towns and cities, there were visits by foreign dignitaries. The *Diarii Europæi* records the arrival and short stay in Hamburg of Queen Christina of Sweden, during which she was entertained with charming music ('und mit einer lieblichen Music belustigen liesse').[90] Given Christina's reported love of dancing, we may suppose that dance was also included in the entertainment. In Lübeck, Sunday evening concerts of *Abendmusiken* took place in St Mary's Church; from 1668 until his death in 1707, their organisation was entrusted to Buxtehude. As we have seen, large numbers of players took part and, by the end of the century, they were celebrated in *Die Beglückte und Geschmückte Stadt Lübeck* as:

> The great Abend-Music, consisting of pleasant vocal and instrumental music, presented yearly on five Sundays between St. Martin's and Christmas, following the Sunday vesper sermon ... This happens nowhere else.[91]

It is understandable for a guidebook to stress the unique quality of the *Abendmusiken*, but concerts were given elsewhere, even if not on the scale of those in Lübeck. The preface to Becker's *Erster Theil zwey-stimmiger Sonaten und Suiten* (Hamburg, 1674) states that secular instrumental pieces had been performed in church in Hamburg, a possible reference to the public concerts in the cathedral refectory organised by Matthias Weckmann. On a more mundane level, and not for church performance, Rosenmüller's *Studenten-Music* was written, according to the preface, at the request of the Leipzig students when they wished to entertain the town's gentry in the evening ('wenn sie etwan vornehme Herren und Standspersonen mit einer Nacht-Music beehren wolle'). Likewise, the title page of Johann Pezel's 1669 *Musica Vespertina Lipsica* tells us that dance music in Leipzig was played for the evening entertainment of the town's citizens.

There were also occasions when functional dance was required. For civic or family purposes, the title page of Gottfried Taubert's *Rechtschaffener Tanzmeister* dance treatise (Leipzig, 1717) lists the following occasions where it might be encountered: 'Assemblées, Balls, Hochzeit-Täntze' (wedding dances). Taubert also deals with the question of dancing away from the ballroom and dramatic stage, where the association of dance with lewd and licentious behaviour was clearly an issue. A large part of the opening of his treatise is concerned with the morality of dancing and the question of sinful indulgence by 'those of our rural folk, young farmers and shepherds who are unimpressed by art and elegance in dancing ... joining hands in a jolly round dance; or also [those of city folk] who [dance] in the open streets in front of beer halls and taverns at the annual fairs and other festive events'.[92] The music of the 'jolly round dances' was clearly a matter for lesser players.

For the professional *Stadtpfeifer*, weddings were of the greatest importance; as we have seen, they were an essential part of their fee income. Weddings in seventeenth-century German often lasted for two days, with music and dancing playing a large part in the festivities.[93] There were opportunities for music during the various feasts where it is possible that suites were played, and there was certainly a good deal of Taubert's 'Hochzeit-Täntze'. At least part of the music was for the dancing, for which the wedding hosts should 'hire a skilled dancing master and principal dancers [to] prepare them prior to the wedding'.[94] And in an interesting parallel with town musicians, 'the dancers themselves should be honourable and well brought up people'.[95] Taubert places this type of dancing at the same level as 'dancing at assemblies, balls, and other festive occasions' and clearly sees it as being more formal, perhaps even an emulation of court entertainment.[96] It is highly likely that the *Stadtpfeifer* would have provided the accompaniment at such occasions.

What was played at this type of wedding? The French-inspired Bransle sequence of four or six dances that features in many town-suite collections did not emanate from the dramatic stage; it was traditionally danced in the ballroom. It is barely mentioned by Taubert, but given that it had fallen completely out of fashion by the start of the eighteenth century, this is hardly surprising. For the higher levels of Leipzig society at this time, it is unlikely that the Bransle sequence would have been included among their preferred dances. But in the previous century, and the heyday of the town-music suite, the Bransle and its associated dances were an essential part of any ball. Its use as functional dance music in the German towns is confirmed in the preface to Georg Druckenmüller's *Musicalisches Tafel-Confect* (Schwäbisch Hall, 1668) where it is suggested that the suite of Bransles in the collection has a dual purpose. When used as instrumental music, it can be played by viola da gambas. When used as practical dance music, it can be played an octave higher by the violins ('Wo keine Violen di gam. vorhanden / oder nicht beliebig / oder zu Tanz / kan man die II. Partie eine Octav höher / mit Violinen versuchen').[97] The Bransle's frequent musical partner in the seventeenth-century ballroom was the Courante; at court, and perhaps in the towns, the latter was often used to start the proceedings. Unlike the Bransle sequence, it was still fashionable in 1717 and Taubert devotes considerable space to it. Along with the later Menuet and Bourée, it is a 'Fundamental-Täntze' used on every occasion ('so zu allen Zeiten, und an allen Orten üblich seyn').[98]

If Druckenmüller is suggesting a dual-purpose role for at least some of the dance-music repertoire, was this widespread, or limited to a few examples of dance types? The more formal type of dancing itself was certainly not confined to weddings and civic assemblies. Taubert was certainly aware of music 'indoors on plank floors or a stage',[99] and Horn wrote the music for the *Grossen-Balletten* performed by the Leipzig student group known as the 'Pindus Gesellschaft', later including it in his *Parergon musicum* collection (see Chapter 6). The music, and presumably the dancing, largely follows the format of the French *Ballet de cour* with its *Entrées* for various groups of characters.

However, it is telling that Horn's *Grossen-Balletten* do not include the Allemande, a cornerstone of the town repertoire and, except as a character dance, Taubert avoids all mention of it. In the light of this, the omission of the Allemande from Horn's Ballets becomes highly significant. And while French traditions are not necessarily relevant to German town traditions, it is noteworthy that Sebastien Brossard's 1701 *Dictionaire de Musique* classes movements such as Passepieds, Courantes and Menuets as 'Danse' while the Allemande is a 'Symphonie grave'.[100] The music itself appears to be suggesting the same and, as we shall see during the course of examples later in this book, an important part of the Allemande's music language was the interplay between the various instrumental voices. This places it at odds with functional dance music that was often disseminated as a single treble line, and it is reasonable to assume that town-music Allemandes were not danced.

As part of a concept to which I will often return, Allemandes in the town-music repertoire were frequently linked to other dances in a pair or a suite. So should the repertoire as a whole be regarded in the same light and mostly be considered as instrumental? The theorist and town musician Friederich Erhardt Niedt appears to think that it should; indeed, he makes a clear distinction between dance music that is functional and that which is 'only played and not danced, as with Minuets and other types that were never intended for the dance'.[101] However, Niedt may not, like Druckenmüller, be the most reliable guide; the Menuet, in both its French and Italian versions, was an essential part of the functional-dance repertoire of the early eighteenth century. But the main distinction in Niedt's writing between the functional and the abstract is clear enough. It is also difficult to see how dances such as the Ballo, which existed in a variety of forms (see Chapter 2) could ever have been associated with an established choreography.

In conclusion, we can be certain that specific dances, particularly those of the Bransle sequence, often started life as functional dance music for weddings and other festivities but later became music to be played instrumentally once placed into a suite or sequence of dances in a printed collection. This could apply equally well to music for the dramatic stage. Horn's *Grossen-Balletten* surely underwent a change of purpose when they were printed as part of a six-volume series of suites clearly intended for instrumental performance – otherwise it is hard to see why they should have been included if they were not to be played away from the dramatic stage. And with the proviso that the music needed to be idiomatically written, no doubt the transformation could take place in reverse – Bransles starting life in otherwise-instrumental suite collections taking on a new identity as functional dance music. But such crossing of boundaries was limited; for the remainder of the suite repertoire, we cannot escape the conclusion that town-music suites were only intended for instrumental performance. We may question the identity of Niedt's movements 'never intended for the dance', but it seems that the bulk of the dances in town-music collections were unlikely to be used as functional dance music.

Notes

1 Translation in H. Medick, 'The Thirty Years' War as experience and memory: contemporary perceptions of a macro-historical event' in L. Tatlock (ed.), *Enduring loss in early modern Germany: cross disciplinary perspectives* (Leiden: Brill, 2010), pp. 25–49 at p. 33.
2 Ibid., p. 34.
3 Translated from the 1640 journal of Caspar Preis, an 'Upper Hessian Catholic peasant'. Quoted in ibid., p. 41.
4 Ibid., pp. 26–7.
5 J. Gagliardo, *Germany under the old regime, 1600–1790* (London: Longman, 1991), p. 90.
6 E. Sagarra, *A social history of Germany, 1648–1914*, 2nd edition (New Brunswick: Transaction, 2003), p. 5.
7 R. Vierhaus (trans. J.B. Knudsen), *Germany in the age of absolutism* (Cambridge: Cambridge University Press, 1988, repr. 1991), p. 3.
8 T. McIntosh, *Urban decline in early modern Germany: Schwäbisch Hall and its region, 1650–1750* (Chapel Hill: University of North Carolina Press, 1997), pp. 43, 45.
9 As Percy Adams has pointed out, 'the impulse was great to change, or at least exaggerate, the facts as the traveler attempted to recall them'. P.G. Adams, *Travelers and travel liars, 1660–1800* (New York: Dover, 1962; repr. 1980), p. 132.
10 [C. Jordan de Colombier], *Voyages historiques de l'EuropetTome VI ... Par Mr. De B.F. Nouvelle edition*, 2nd edition (Amsterdam, 1718), pp. 200–1.
11 De Blainville (trans. G. Turnbull and W. Guthrie), *Travels through Holland, Germany, Switzerland and Other Parts of Europe ... by the late Monsieur de Blainville*, 3 vols (London, 1757), Vol. 1, p. 218, entry for 26 June 1705.
12 Count G. Priorato (trans. J. Burbery), *The History of the Sacred and Royal Majesty of Christina Alessandra Queen of Swedland With the Reasons of her late Conversion to the Roman Catholique Religion* (London, 1658), Vol. 2, pp. 116–17.
13 Lady M. Wortley Montagu, *Letters of the Right Honourable Lady M--y W---y M----e*, 4 vols (London, 1763–7), Vol. 1, entry for 22 August 1716.
14 McIntosh, *Urban decline*, p. 2.
15 W. Carr, *Remarks of severall Parts of Germanie, Denmark, Sweedland, Hamburg, Lubeck, and Hansiactique Townes* (Amsterdam, 1688).
16 Ibid., p. 121.
17 Ibid., p. 120.
18 D.J. Corpis, 'Losing one's place' in L. Tatlock (ed.), *Enduring loss in early modern Germany: cross disciplinary perspectives* (Leiden: Brill, 2010), pp. 327–367 at p. 339.
19 Arno Herzig has suggested that approximately a quarter of the population of Germany ('ungefähr ein Viertel der Bevölkerung Deutschlands') migrated as a result of *Rekatholisierung* between the sixteenth and eighteenth centuries. It is unclear how much of this was a direct result of the Thirty Years War. A. Herzig, *Der Zwang zum wahren Glauben: Rekatholisierung vom 16. bis zum 18. Jahrhundert* (Göttingen: Vandenhoeck & Ruprecht, 2000), p. 10.
20 M. Anderson, *War and society in Europe of the old regime 1618–1789* (London: Fontana, 1988, repr. Guernsey, 1998), p. 77.

21 R.G. Asch, 'Estates and Princes after 1648: the consequences of the Thirty Years War' *GH*, 6/2 (1988), pp. 113–32 at p. 129. See also pp. 128–9 as a whole.
22 De Blainville, *Travels*, Vol. 1, p. 93, entry for 21 March 1705.
23 Ibid., entry for 13 April 1705.
24 Carr, *Remarks*, p. 129.
25 Ibid., pp. 129–30.
26 M. Walker, *German home towns: community, state, and general estate 1648–1871*, 2nd edition (Ithaca: Cornell University Press, 1998), p. 19. See also Vierhaus (trans. Knudsen), *Germany in the age of absolutism*, pp. 105–106.
27 McIntosh, *Urban decline*, p. 3.
28 Walker, *German home towns*, p. 18.
29 G. Jaacks, 'Ducal courts and Hanseatic cities: political and historical perspectives' in K. Snyder (ed.) *The organ as a mirror of its time* (Oxford: Oxford University Press, 2002), pp. 31–59 at p. 32.
30 Walker, *German home towns*, p. 46.
31 Sagarra, *Social history*, p. 68.
32 De Blainville, *Travels*, Vol. 1, p. 93, entry for 21 March 1705.
33 Ibid., entry for 21 March 1705.
34 Walker, *German home towns*, pp. 67–8.
35 Gagliardo, *Germany under the old regime*, p. 163.
36 Ibid., p. 163.
37 See S. Rose, 'Music, print and presentation in Saxony during the seventeenth century' *GH*, 23/1 (2005), pp. 1–19 at p. 8.
38 J. Schop (ed. A. Spohr), *Erster Theil newer Paduanen* (Middletown, WI: A-R Editions, 2003), Preface, p. x.
39 For an overview of self-publication, see: S. Rose, 'The composer as self-publisher in seventeenth-century Germany' in E. Kjellberg (ed.), *The dissemination of music in seventeenth-century Europe: celebrating the Düben collection* (Bern: Peter Lang, 2010), pp. 239–60. For the comment regarding ink and paper, see p. 248.
40 S. Rose, 'Publication and the anxiety of judgement in German music life of the seventeenth century' *Music & Letters*, 85/1 (2004), pp. 22–40 at p. 25.
41 Ibid., p. 25.
42 T. Munck, 'Keeping up appearances: patronage of the arts, city prestige, and princely power in Northern Germany and Denmark, 1600–1670' *GH*, 6/3 (1988), pp. 213–232 at p. 214.
43 J. Beer, *Musikalische Discurse durch die Principia der Philosophie deducirt* (Nuremberg, 1719), p. 17, translated in H.W. Schwab, 'The social status of the town musician' in W. Salmen (ed.; trans. H. Kaufman and B. Reisner), *The social status of the professional musician from the middle ages to the 19th century* (New York: Pendragon, 1983), pp. 33–59 at p. 37.
44 Ibid., p. 37.
45 Munck, 'Keeping up appearances', p. 213. As Munck quite correctly notes later in the article, not every member of the *Hofkapelle* may have been treated in the same way; Schutz himself owned houses in Dresden, Halle and Weissenfels. Ibid., p. 215. See also *CCS*, p. 18.
46 J. Beer (trans. J. Russell), *German winter nights* (Rochester, NY: Camden House, 1998), p. 79.
47 See S. Rose, *The musician in literature in the age of Bach* (Cambridge: Cambridge University Press, 2011), pp. 120–21. See also S. Zohn, 'Die vornehmste Hof-Tugend: German musicians' reflections on eighteenth-century court life' in S. Owens, B. Reul and J. Stockigt (eds), *Music at German courts, 1715–1760: changing artistic priorities* (Woodbridge: Boydell & Brewer, 2011), pp. 413–25 at pp. 419–21.
48 P. Holman, 'Thomas Baltzar (?1631–1663), the "Incomparable Lubicer on the Violin" *Chelys*, 13 (1984), pp. 3–38, particularly pp. 3–5.

49 A. Wood, 'The life of Mr Anthony a Wood ... written by himself, and now first printed from a Copy, transcrib'd by the Publisher' in T. Caius, *Vinidiciæ antiquitatis academiæ Oxoniensis*, 2 vols (Oxford, 1730), pp. 438–603 at p. 513. Wood's opinion was confirmed by John Evelyn, who heard Baltzar play in 1656. Evelyn wrote 'I stand to this houre amaz'd that God should give so greate perfection to so young a person.' E.S. de Beer, *The diary of John Evelyn*, 6 vols (Oxford: Clarendon Press, 2000), Vol. 3, p. 167.
50 Wood, 'Life', p. 514.
51 For details of the rivalry between court and town trumpeters, see: T.A. Collins, 'Of the differences between trumpeters and city tower musicians: the relationship of *Stadtpfeifer* and *Kammeradschaft* trumpeters' *Galpin Society Journal* 53 (2000), pp. 51–9.
52 The biographical information on Weckmann has been taken from the Preface to M. Weckmann (ed. S. Rampe), *Sämtliche Freie Orgel- und Clavierwerke* (Kassel: Bärenreiter, 1991), pp. xxi–xxii.
53 Jaacks, 'Ducal courts', p. 45.
54 Schop (ed. Spohr), *Erster Theil newer Paduanen*, Preface, p. ix.
55 McIntosh, *Urban decline*, p. 161.
56 Rose, *Musician in literature*, p. 79.
57 It is noteworthy that these imperial privileges forbade any association with town trumpeters. See Collins, 'Differences', pp. 51–2.
58 The complete code is translated into English in P. Spitta (trans. C. Bell and J.A. Fuller Maitland), *Johann Sebastien Bach: his work and influence on the music of Germany, 1685–1750*, 3 vols (London: Novello, 1899), Vol. 1, pp. 145–51. Articles VIII and X are given on p. 146, XII and XIII on p. 147.
59 Ibid., p. 358. See also: Rose, *Musician in literature*, p. 81.
60 T. Kevorkian, 'Town musicians in German baroque society and culture' *GH*, 30/3 (2012), pp. 350–71 at p. 357.
61 T. McIntosh, *Urban decline*, p. 110.
62 See W. Greve, *Braunschweiger Stadtmusikanten: Geschichte eines Berufstandes 1227–1828* (Braunschweig: Stadtarchiv und Stadtbibliothek, 1991), p. 71.
63 Ibid., p. 71.
64 E. Wienandt, *Johann Pezel (1639–1694): a thematic catalogue of his instrumental works* (New York: Pendragon, 1983), Preface, p. xii.
65 Kevorkian, 'Town musicians', p. 355.
66 K.J. Snyder, *Dieterich Buxtehude: organist in Lübeck*, 2nd edition (Rochester, NY: University of Rochester Press, 2007), p. 61.
67 Ibid., p. 50.
68 See Schop (ed. Spohr), *Erster Theil newer Paduanen*, Preface, pp. xii–xiii. See also J. Spitzer and N. Zaslaw, *The birth of the orchestra: history of an institution, 1650–1815* (Oxford: Oxford University Press, 2004), p. 239.
69 Here and for the remainder of the paragraph, the information is taken from Kevorkian, 'Town musicians', pp. 353–6.
70 Greve, *Braunschweiger Stadtmusikanten*, p. 71.
71 For a portrayal of a beggar musician, see Rose, *Musician in literature*, pp. 67–74.
72 H. Howey, 'The lives of Hoftrompeter and Stadtpfeiffer as portrayed in three novels of Daniel Speer' *Historical Brass Society Journal*, 3 (1991), pp. 65–78 at p. 72.
73 Snyder, *Dieterich Buxtehude*, p. 51.
74 Jaacks, 'Ducal courts', p. 45.
75 The collection and its manuscript copies are considered in detail in Chapter 3.
76 The complete Preface and its translation are given in Chapter 6.
77 Göhler, 2/1539.
78 Rose, 'Publication', p. 22.
79 Rose, 'Composer as self-publisher', p. 241. The remainder of the paragraph is also taken from the same source.
80 H. Biehle, *Musikgeschichte von Bautzen* (Leipzig: Kistner und Siegel, 1924), p. 35.

81 One of the few examples of piracy may be Becker's 1668 *Musicalische Frühlings-Früchte*, which was issued in Antwerp in 1673 as *Musicalische Lendt-Vruchten bestaend in dry, vier, vyf, Instrumentale-Hermoniale stemmen*. It is likely that the composer did not sanction this edition (see Chapter 7).
82 J. Kuhnau (trans. J.R. Russell), *The musical charlatan* (Columbia, SC: Camden House, 1997), p. 4.
83 Ibid.
84 J. Kuhnau, *Der musicalische Quack-Salber* (Dresden, 1700), p. 12.
85 Kuhnau (trans. Russell), *Musical charlatan*, p. 26.
86 Ibid., p. 4.
87 Translated as P.L. Poulin and I.C. Taylor, *The musical guide* (Oxford: Clarendon Press, 1989).
88 Ibid., p. 9.
89 Ibid., p. 10.
90 M. Merian (comp.), *Diarii Europœi* (Frankfurt am Main, 1667), Vol. 14, p. 413.
91 Quoted in Snyder, *Dieterich Buxtehude*, p. 54.
92 T. Russell (trans.), *The compleat dancing master: a translation of Gottfried Taubert's Rechtschaffener Tantzmeister*, 2 vols (New York: Peter Lang, 2012), pp. 143–4. The original German text is given in G. Taubert, *Rechtschaffener Tantzmeister oder gründlicher Erklärung der Frantzösischen Tantz-Kunst* (Leipzig, 1717). Facsimile edition, ed. K. Petermann (Munich: Heimeran Verlag, 1976), p. 141.
93 Kevorkian, 'Town musicians', p. 363.
94 Russell, *Compleat dancing master*, p. 923.
95 Ibid., p. 930.
96 Ibid., p. 922.
97 As I have already pointed out in *CCS*, p. 48, Druckenmüller appears to have been uncertain of the Bransle idiom and we must exercise some caution over his comments. However, it is reasonable to assume that, in a general sense, he was correct in identifying the dual role of the Bransle sequence in the towns.
98 Taubert, *Rechtschaffener Tantzmeister*, p. 378.
99 Taubert, *Rechtschaffener Tantzmeister*, p. 140. Translation from Russell, *Compleat dancing master*, p. 143.
100 S. de Brossard, *Dictionaire de Musique, contenant une explication des termes Grecs, Latins, Italiens, & François les plus usitez dans la Musique* (Paris, 1703); facsimile edition (Hilversum: Fritz Knuf, 1965). For the Allemande, see p. 9; for the other dances see the *Table Françoise*.
101 Niedt (ed. and trans. Poulin and Taylor), *Musical guide*, pp. 138–9.

2 Dances, collections and national styles

In the previous chapter, I argued that the distinction between royal and municipal states of employment was often nebulous. But, for the dance music emanating from the courts and towns, the opposite is true. Each possessed distinct and separate concepts of organisation and style. Dances emanating from court musicians were often directly linked with entertainment on the dramatic stage, resulting in frequent changes of order and movement type reflecting different performing conditions. The manuscripts of dance music written for performance at the court of Hessen-Kassel frequently reflect this, and as I have already pointed out elsewhere, changes to order and content appear to have been made even while copying was in progress.[1] In such circumstances, there was little point in committing dance music to print and much of the dance music of the courts was disseminated in a lively, often-fluid manuscript tradition.

The dance music of town musicians in the second half of the seventeenth century had little in common with this tradition. While many dance-music collections before the end of the Thirty Years War seem to have relied on performers making their own choice of movement type when putting together sequences of dance music, those from the 1650s onwards increasingly removed this choice. They replaced it with carefully ordered content in which movement relationships to each other were of primary importance. Printed editions were the principal medium for the dissemination of these collections and, even in manuscript copies where the choice of movement type could be highly selective, the order of dances was rarely changed. As we shall see, it was only the music for outdoor performances in towers and balconies that continued to reflect *ad hoc*, and perhaps last-minute, choice.

Particularly in the second half of the century, these published collections of dance music and suites developed an increasingly formulaic identity of their own. And on the occasions when court musicians such as August Kühnel and Esaias Reusner did decide to go against the courtly trend and issue printed collections of suites, they chose to follow closely the format used by their colleagues in the towns. Indeed, it is remarkable that Kühnel's *Sonate ô Partite*, published in 1698, still largely follows the traditions of the town-music suite, even though the genre had largely ceased to exist by this time.[2]

Careful organisation, something that I will return to frequently during the course of this book, was not the only concept that separated court and town dance-music traditions. There was also the important question of perceived national style. For much of the seventeenth century, particularly the second half, the language of the German courts was French. The language of their music was also French, especially when the music of Lully and his imitators became so fashionable. And we may be certain that any *Kapellmeister* who wished to remain in princely employment was, at the very least, able to produce music that contained easily discernible elements of the *frantzösischen Manier*.[3]

In the towns, composers had no such imperatives although, in contrast to a *Kapellmeister*, any director of town music might risk censure if his music was considered to be too courtly. Most municipal dance music was written in what its composers considered to be the Italian style – the *italiänischen Manier*, even if a worthwhile definition of this and the opposing French style seems to have eluded many of them. At the start of the eighteenth century, the Hamburg-based Johann Mattheson showed some determination in trying to define the differences, and devoted an entire chapter of his treatise *Das neu-eröffnet Orchestre* (Hamburg, 1713) in consideration of the matter.[4] But despite his warning that 'Whoever wishes to reach a general, completely unprejudiced and sound judgement concerning contemporary Italian, French, English and German music must not confuse the composition and execution of such national music',[5] Mattheson is disappointingly silent on dance-music characteristics and can offer little more than subjective judgements on performance: 'The Italians surprise, the French like to charm, the Germans study and the English reward.'[6]

For the Bremen town musician Lüder Knoep, it was the rather more practical matter of instrumentation that marked out the *frantzösischen Manier*. The preface of his *Ander Theil Newer Paduanen, Galliarden, Arien, Allemanden, Balletten, Couranten, und Sarabanden* (Bremen, 1660) describes the final part of the collection as 'nach der Frantzösischen Manier mit einem Bass und Discant gesetzet' (set in the French manner with a bass and treble).

Knoep's emphasis on treble and bass lines is linked with the instrumentation of violin, two or three violas and bass. This combination had been a feature of violin-band playing throughout the sixteenth century. But, as the seventeenth century progressed, it became specifically associated with France.[7] In performance of French music, and that of its German imitators, both treble and bass lines were frequently doubled while the inner viola parts – three, sometimes two – were played by single players.[8] Knoep himself recommends the use of a number of violins in unison ('mit unterschiedlichen Geigen in unison') for the 'Discant' part in the French section of his *Ander Theil*. We must also take into account that dance music in the German courts was often disseminated as nothing more than a bass and treble or single treble line; it was up to individual musicians to add the inner parts and sometimes the bass according to their own tastes and circumstances.[9] With this in mind, Knoep's view of the French manner – as we shall see, he was by no means the only one to hold this view – is hardly surprising.

On the other hand, five-part writing with two violins, two violas and bass was a feature of Italian instrumentation from the early seventeenth century.[10] This combination, though sometimes with a single viola, was regularly used by the majority of German town composers; in contrast to the often-simple inner parts of the French manner, second violins frequently take a major part in the *Invention*,[11] the violas less so. But it is important to remember that players of town-music suites were often given the option of playing the music as trios with just two violins and bass.

It is curious that these issues of instrumentation are barely mentioned in prefaces or treatises. Instead, it is aspects of performance that define the French style for many German musicians, and not just those in the towns. The title pages of dance-music collections often refer to the contents as 'lustig' (lively), and this came to be synonymous with the *frantzösischen Manier*. 'Nach der lustigen Frantzösischen Manier zu spielen' (to be played in the lively French manner) is the instruction on the title page of the second volume of Johann Caspar Horn's *Parergon musicum* (Erfurt, 1663). 'Lustig' does not seem to have been solely a question of tempo; a light manner of playing was also expected, particularly in the execution of bow strokes and a uniformity of bowing.[12]

If the *frantzösischen Manier* was associated with *lustig* performance, then it follows that the opposing Italian style was rather more serious. And this seems to have been not just a characteristic of performance, but of the music itself. Georg Muffat speaks of 'Certain melancholy, exquisite affects of the Italian manner' in the foreword of his 1701 *Auserlesene Instrumental-musik*, and the dissonance used in some of the slow movements of this collection show precisely what he meant.[13] Not surprisingly, the *italiänischen Manier* was often linked to vocal music and the expressing of strong emotions. Beyond this, it is difficult to find meaningful seventeenth-century definitions of the Italian style and Horn is one of many who seems to have experienced difficulty in this respect. The title page of the first volume of *Parergon musicum* (Erfurt, 1663) can manage no more than proclaiming its contents as 'nach der ietzigen italiänischen manier zu spielen' (to be played in the current Italian manner). As we shall see in Chapter 6, Horn does give indications of how certain dances should be played, but he is disappointingly vague when it comes to linking them with specific national style.

A clearer picture emerges in the often-substantial musical differences between certain French and Italian dances. These differences were most pronounced in Sarabandes, Courantes and Gigues. The Sarabande, often employed as the closing movement to a suite until the late 1660s, existed in three guises during the seventeenth century: sung Spanish, fast French, and the last to emerge, the slow French.[14] The fast French was later imported into Italy, and Richard Hudson has suggested that this version of the dance is recognisable by its 'distinctive rhythmic figure' of ♩♩♩|♩. ♪♩ in triple time.[15] But if German Sarabandes clearly have their roots in the fast-French/Italian version, Hudson's 'distinctive' figure is not used with any consistency. Instead, off-beat accents are frequently applied in the form of note blackening, often disrupting any rhythmic pattern and bringing the dance

22 *Dances, collections and national styles*

Example 2.1 A. Hammerschmidt, *Ander Theil newer Paduanen, Canzonen, Galliarden, Balleten, Mascharaden, Francoischen [sic] Arien, Courenten und Sarabanden* (Freiberg, 1639, repr. 1658), 'XIV. Sarabande 2. à5'.

Note: the extra line above the Cantus I part clarifies the rhythmic changes brought about by the note blackening. All blackened semibreves would almost certainly have been accented by the performers. The blackened minim in the penultimate bar of the bass parts is unaccented.

nearer to the slow-French model.[16] Example 2.1 shows just such a Sarabande in Andreas Hammerschmidt's widely disseminated *Ander Theil newer Paduanen, Canzonen, Galliarden, Balleten, Mascharaden, Francoischen [sic] Arien, Couranten und Sarabanden* (Freiberg, 1639, repr. 1658). In this highly imaginative treatment of the dance, Hammerschmidt gives the inner parts simple and uneventful rhythms, but contrasts this simplicity with a series of off-beat accents marked by note blackening in the treble and then the bass.

Not everyone showed such imagination in Sarabande writing; it is telling that the only structural or stylistic comment on this dance in Friederich Erhardt Niedt's *Handleitung zur Variation* (Hamburg, 1706) is that it 'must have eight measures in each reprise'.[17] Compared with Hammerschmidt's example above, those written in the later part of the century cannot always escape the charge of being routine and formulaic.

The Courante is arguably the most importance dance type in the entire genre and was certainly its most popular. Example 2.2 shows an Italian *Corrento* from Mauritio Cazzati's *Correnti, e Balletti ... Opera XXX* (Bologna, 1662) along with a French Courante from the second suite in *D-Kl* 2° Ms. mus. 61d^2 – one of the Kassel manuscripts of dance music.[18] The Italian example is rhythmically uncomplicated apart from the cross-rhythm at the end-of-phrase cadence. The French example shows a near-continuous rhythmic ambiguity.

As with the Sarabande, hybrid forms of the Courante were popular with some German town composers.[19] Hammerschmidt, Rosenmüller, Pezel and Horn all used the relative simplicity of the Italian style, but with note blackening again giving off-beat accents in the middle of phrases. Figure 2.1 shows the Cantus II part of 'X.

Dances, collections and national styles 23

Example 2.2 Openings of: M. Cazzati, *Correnti, e Balletti Per Sonora nella Spinetta Leuto, ò Tiorba ... Opera XXX*, (Bologna, 1662), 'Corrente nona'; D-Kl 2° Ms. mus. 61d², '3. Courant. Mr. Werdier'.

Figure 2.1 A. Hammerschmidt, *Erster Fleiß: Allerhand newer Paduanen, Galliarden, Balleten, Mascharaden, Francoischen [sic] Arien, Courenten und Sarabanden* (Freiberg, 1636, repr. 1650), Cantus II, X. Courente à5, shelfmark c.53: London, The British Library Board. Reproduced by kind permission.

Courente à5' from Hammerschmidt's *Erster Fleiß: Allerhand newer Paduanen, Galliarden, Balleten, Mascharaden, Francoischen [sic] Arien, Courenten und Sarabanden* (Freiberg, 1636, repr. 1650). It shows the off-beat blackened accentuation at the start of the second strain.

Often allied to the Sarabande and the Courante was the *Double*. (This should not be confused with the Bransle Double, where elaboration was a matter of dance steps and not music.) Brossard, Walther and Niedt all link the *Double* with diminution and, by implication, technical display. The diminution was in the form of elaboration of a melody but mostly with retention of the original harmonies. At its simplest, it was nothing more than an arpeggiated version of the main dance mainly belonging to the solo instrument repertoires, especially the keyboard and lute. Given the simplicity of construction, it is not surprising that some examples are of dubious quality and surely added by other composers or performers.

Apart from occasional use in trio suites, *Doubles* rarely appear in larger instrumental combinations, although it is possible that they were improvised. The court composer Adam Drese lists them in the title page of his *Erster Theil Etlicher Allemanden, Couranten, Sarabanden, Balletten, Intraden und andern Arien mit theils darbei befindlichen Doublen, oder Variationen* (Jena, 1672). Unfortunately the treble part, the most likely source of *Double* variations, does not survive, but Drese describes how a *Double* may be played in a consort: a single violin elaborates the treble line of a dance while the original lines are quietly played by the remainder of the ensemble.[20] We should not forget that the concept of elaborating a treble part over repetitions of harmony or bass line was an essential part of the Chaconne. So it was therefore familiar territory to many German musicians, especially those who had served at courts as well as in the towns. If *Doubles* did not appear as written-out movements in the town-suite repertoire, they may have been improvised, especially in larger ensembles with high-quality players. In which case, the method of performance described by Drese may well have applied here as well.

Despite its French name, the *Double* was not a specific product of national style; it was merely an elaboration of its parent dance. But the Gigue or *Giga* did follow the Courante and Sarabande in having separate and distinct national characteristics. And, once more, German town composers produced their own distinctive version.

According to Niedt and Walther, the Gigue had English antecedents but, for most town musicians, it was again the Italian and French styles that appear to have held most meaning. The Italian *Giga* is characterised by simple textures and a strong, forward-driving rhythmic impetus and, while both French and Italians used imitation in their Gigues, the French versions were more complicated affairs with frequent irregular phrase lengths. Example 2.3 shows the start of a Gigue from Lully's *Ballet du temple de la paix*, *LWV* 69/13 (Paris, 1685) with its characteristic dotted rhythms.[21] We should also notice that the imitation is only between treble and bass: another example of the emphasis on these parts in French music.[22]

Dances, collections and national styles 25

Example 2.3 J.-B. Lully, *Ballet du temple de la paix. Dansé devant Sa Majesté à Fontainebleau* (Paris, 1685), 'Gigue'.

As Bruce Gustafson has pointed out, counterpoint was also at the heart of the German version, albeit in a more sophisticated form; in addition to imitative openings at the start, the opening of the second strain was often an inversion, if sometimes approximate, of the parallel passage in the first strain.[23] But the movement still retains the propulsion of the Italian *Giga*, and this no doubt assisted in the gradual adoption of the Gigue as a suite finale. In such cases, the counterpoint could bring about a pleasing symmetry with that of an opening sonata.

An association between the Gigue and the Allemande, especially in the lute repertoire of the early seventeenth century, may explain the existence of a common-time variant of the former found in Italy, France and Germany.[24] Example 2.4 gives the opening of the final 'Gigè' in Johann Pachelbel's *Musicalische Ergötzung* (Nuremberg, n.d.).[25]

26 *Dances, collections and national styles*

Example 2.4 J. Pachelbel, *Musicalische Ergötzung, bestehend in Sechs Verstimten Partien â 2. Violin nebst den Basso Continuo* (Nuremberg, n.d.), 'Partie.VI', 'Gigè'.

Note: the two violin parts are in *scordatura* tuning. For clarity, these have been notated at their sounding pitch. The original key signatures, scordatura tunings and starting notes are all given in the incipit.

It raises the question of how such music was performed. It has been suggested that the common-time rhythms were sometimes performed as the more usual triple-time groups, and some sources in the keyboard repertoire do suggest that this was sometimes the case.[26] But it is hard to see how examples such as Pachelbel's piece could be played in this way without significant loss of detail. Furthermore, the remaining Gigues in *Musicalische Ergötzung*, all using significantly different material to the common-time example, are notated without exception in 12/8.

Further light can be shed on the performance of common-time Gigues by a version of the dance found in Giovanni Battista Bassani's 1677 *Balletti, Correnti, Ghighe, e Sarabande* (Example 2.5), even if it does not come from a German source. In 'Giga Prima' from this collection, there is a clear separation between the triplet quavers, all carefully marked, and the duple-time quavers and semiquavers. If Bassani had wished the whole Gigue to be performed as if it were in 12/8, he would surely have notated it in a different way. None of the other Gigues in the collection have this dual notation; the common-time 'Giga duodec[ima]' is written almost entirely in equal quavers – needing substantial adjustment for triple-time performance – and, apart from the semiquaver-driven 12/16 of 'Giga Terza', the remaining examples are all in the usual 12/8.

Taken as a whole, the Sarabandes, Courantes and Gigues of the town suite all show us that, while their composers mostly wrote in a style that is nearer to the Italian than anything else, they certainly did not slavishly

Example 2.5 G.B. Bassani, *Balletti, Correnti, Gighe, e Sarabande à Violino, e Violone, overo Spinetta, con il Secondo Violino à beneplacito ... Opera prima* (Bologna, 1677, repr. 1684), 'Giga Prima'.

imitate the *italiänischen Manier*. And as we shall see later in this chapter, the one set of French-origin dances regularly used by town composers, the Bransle sequence, was subject to substantial modification. Other dances used by town musicians – and their repertoire was modest in comparison with court composers – were not subject to national variation in anything like the same way. And it is to these that I now turn.

The imposing character of the Paduan (apparently derived from the Padua region of Italy) made it a popular choice for blocks of like dances that often started collections.[27] It was also popular as a way of starting individual sequences of dances and we can see it as a precursor of the Preludes and Sonatas that fulfilled the same function in the suites of the 1670s and 80s. Richness of texture and frequent use of imitation are characteristic of the Paduan, and composers seem to have regarded it as an opportunity to demonstrate their learned credentials. Walther, writing in 1732, describes the Paduan as a 'gravitätischer Tantz' with three strains ('aus 3. Repetitionen') of eight, twelve or sixteen bars, and this accords with seventeenth-century usage.[28] But there is one important facet in seventeenth-century German usage that he does not mention: the intensification of rhythm that often took place during the course of the dance. As we can see in Example 2.6, taken from Rosenmüller's *Studenten-Music* of 1654, the opening *gravitas* is achieved through the use of a rich chordal texture, sometimes with the addition of dissonant harmonies. These are followed by quaver divisions, usually with imitation between the instrumental parts. In the third strain, there is often further rhythmic diminution with the quavers giving way to semiquavers. If these semiquaver and quaver divisions allow some opportunity for technical display, they are still within the confines of the dance's structure.

28   *Dances, collections and national styles*

Example 2.6 J. Rosenmüller, *Studenten-Music / Darinnen zu befinden Allerhand Sachen Mit drey und fünff Violen / oder auch andern Instrumenten zu spielen* (Leipzig, 1654), '7. Paduan à 3'.

The later part of the century saw a substantial decline in the Paduan's popularity. This is clearly shown in manuscript copies of the 1660s made from printed editions of earlier decades: the *Paduanen* are routinely omitted. And it is telling that Niedt omits all mention of it. Curiously, Walther's definition of the Paduan ends with a warning that each strain must not have fewer than eight bars 'because of the four steps' ('weniger aber nicht haben muß, wegen der 4 Tritte oder *Passuum*, so darinn observirt werden müssen').[29] This seems to imply functional dance music, but it is more likely that, in dealing with a near-obsolete dance, Walther had little personal experience of it and was forced to rely on definitions from earlier times.

Dances, collections and national styles 29

In the sixteenth and early seventeenth centuries, German composers followed their English counterparts in the frequent addition of a Galliard to form a pair with the Paduan. Originally a triple-time 'lively hopping and kicking dance', the Galliard also suffered something of a decline in later seventeenth-century Germany.[30] Despite this, examples can still be found in the suites of the 1670s and 80s. It features prominently, for example, in the latter part of the sixth volume of Horn's *Parergon musicum* (Leipzig, 1676), even if the material in this part of the collection does seem to come from an earlier time. There also appears to have been a slow version; as we can see in Example 2.7, '49. Galliarda' from Johann Pezel's

Example 2.7 J. Pezel, *Fünff-stimmigte blasende Music, Bestehend In Intraden, Allemanden, Balleten, Courenten, Sarabanden und Chiquen* (Frankfurt-am-Main, 1685), '49. Galliarda à5'.

30 *Dances, collections and national styles*

Fünff-stimmigte blasende Music (Frankfurt am Main, 1685) is marked 'adagio' and is rather more serious in character.

Perhaps not aware of the slow version, Niedt calls it 'a cheerful, happy dance' but then describes it as 'set in even [i.e. duple] time'.[31] This definition reflects the great transformation of the Galliard not in the towns, but in court circles during the last decades of the seventeenth century when it changed from a triple- to duple-time dance. 'Dixiême Air, Galliarde' from the fifth suite of *Composition de musique* (Stuttgart, 1682) by the court composer Jean Sigismond Cousser has an opening duple-time rhythm of ♪|♩. ♪♩. ♪|♩. ♪♩. ♪|♩♩; it mirrors Niedt's comments precisely.[32]

Another dance that significantly changed its character was the Allemande, although this happened at the start of the seventeenth century rather than the end. As its name suggests, this duple-time dance of serious character probably originated in Germany. The so-called 'Philidor manuscripts' of ballet music at the French court contain a number of examples dating from between 1575 and 1602 that were, without doubt, performed on stage. Example 2.8 shows the first of the series, all being in a similar style and with simple rhythmic characteristics.[33]

Albeit in modified form, this simple style of Allemande remained in the repertoire of dances used in Viennese court ballets, although it is unlikely to have ever been associated with a specific choreography.[34] Elsewhere, the Allemande underwent a complete transformation and, as I argued in the previous chapter, became an entirely instrumental movement in the process, divorced from functional dance. Example 2.9 shows the extent of this transformation in '40. Allemand' from Nicolaus Hasse's *Delitiæ musicæ* (Rostock, 1656).

Example 2.8   Manuscript *F-Pn* Rés F 496, 'Recüeil de Plusieurs Anciens Ballets Dancez Sous les Regnes de Henry 3. Henry 4. Et Louis 13. Depuis l'An 1575 Jusqu'à 1641', 'Allemande En G. re, sol, Becar'.

Dances, collections and national styles 31

Example 2.9 N. Hasse, *Delitiæ musicæ, Das ist Schöne / lustige und anmuthige Allemunden, Couranten und Sarabanden* (Rostock, 1656), '40. Allemand'.

Note: The 'Alto' and 'Violon' parts are editorial reconstructions.

With its serious and complex character – Martin Heinrich Fuhrmanns' 1706 *Musicalische-Trichter* singing treatise refers to the dance as a 'proposition' – it is not surprising that the Allemande became a commonly used opening to a suite or sequence of dance movements in both keyboard and consort repertoires.[35] It is even possible that specific motifs and musical figures were associated at times with the dance, particularly in the keyboard version (see Chapter 8). However, it could never fully replace the same function of the longer and more imposing Paduan; so it is not surprising that, as we shall see, composers wishing for a larger-scale start to their suites should later turn to the Sonata rather than the Allemande to fulfil this need.

It was not always the case that dances changed character during the course of the seventeenth century; the Mascharada was used by, among others, Hammerschmidt and Zuber until the 1650s. Thereafter, it disappeared from the town-music repertoire. Praetorius equates it with a 'mummery' in which 'several persons disguise themselves with masks and costumes and appear at musical banquets and weddings ... they have their particular melodies and step patterns'.[36] While the melodies do not appear to have survived into the town repertoire, Hammerschmidt's examples all start with variants of ♩. ♪ ♫ | ♩, suggesting Praetorius' particular step patterns. The dance was multi-sectioned and often long; perhaps this was the reason for its disappearance in the second half of the century.

If some dances disappeared or changed character, the Menuet was a relative newcomer to both court and town repertoires in the seventeenth century. Fuhrmann includes it in one of his group of 'Frantzöis. Blümchen' (little French flowers). By the time of Taubert's 1717 *Rechtschaffener Tanzmeister*, it was clearly a highly fashionable dance and the treatise lists it as one of three 'Haupt-und Fundamental-Täntzen' along with the Courante and Bourée.[37] Niedt considers it to be 'the smallest and shortest dance' with two strains that each have 'at least eight measures and cannot have more than sixteen'.[38]

Finally, we come to a group of dances that have both specific and generic uses. Walther simply calls the Ballo 'ein Tanzt' but this is not as simple as it first appears.[39] As well as being individual movements, Ballett, Balletti and Ballo were all used at various times, and in various places, as generic terms for complete sequences of dances. For example, the French-manner final section of Lüder Knoep's *Ander Theil Newer Paduanen* idiosyncratically uses the Italian 'Ballo' heading to identify each sequence of movements (see Chapter 4).[40]

To add to this, when the terms are used for individual movements, they often cover the widest range. During the first half of the century, along with the near-identical 'Aria', they are often non-specific and often-substantial dances, sometimes alternating between duple and triple time. Along with the Mascharada, these multi-section movements were the nearest that town composers came to court character dances derived from dramatic stage music, even if they were not danced. However, duple- and triple-time alternations within a single movement were declining in popularity by the end of the 1650s, and the Ballett itself settled into a lively, straightforward duple-time dance of two short strains. But even then, there seems to have been little in the way of standardisation. We can see a typical example of the variety involved in Table 2.1 that gives a strain analysis of movements entitled 'Ballet' in the wide-ranging dance collection *Exercitium musicum* (Frankfurt am Main, 1660).[41]

In its Ballo form, the dance took on an even more lively character, frequently using dotted rhythms throughout. Example 2.10 shows the opening of '4. Ballo' from the fifth volume of Horn's *Parergon musicum* (Leipzig, 1676).[42]

All these changes suggest that many composers of dance music did not recognise, or feel bound by, conventions of genre or title. They also add weight to the argument that I put forward in the introduction to this book; concepts of a 'classical' order are too simplistic. And if we now turn from individual dances to the

Table 2.1 Strain analysis of movements entitled 'Ballet' in N.B.N. (ed.), *Exercitium musicum* (Frankfurt am Main, 1660)

Movement title	Time signature	Upbeat to each strain	Number of bars in first strain	Number of bars in second strain
XVII. Ballett	¢	♪	6	6
XXIX. Ballett	¢	♩♪	6	6
XXXIIX. Ballett	¢	♪	4	4
LI. Ballett	¢	None	8	8
LII. Ballett	¢	None	5	5
LV. Ballett	¢	None	5	5
LVI. Ballett	¢	None	5	5
LVII. Ballett	¢	None	5	5

Example 2.10 First strain of J.C. Horn, *Parergon musicum Oder Musicalisches Neben-Werck / Bestehend in allerhand ammuthigen Sonatinen, Alleman-den, Couranten, Ballet-ten, Sarabanden und Chiqven ... Fünffiem Theil* (Leipzig, 1676), '4. Ballo'.

printed collections of dance music, we will see that it is the relationship of movements to each other rather than the choice of movement type that was uppermost in the minds of seventeenth-century town composers.

At the start of the century and throughout the Thirty Years War, it was common for collections to comprise a number of movement pairs in the same key, the first of each pair in duple time and the second in triple. Table 2.2 summarises the contents of a typical example: Johann Schop's *Erster Theil newer Paduanen* (Hamburg, 1633; repr. 1640).[43]

From 1621 until 1665 Schop was director of Hamburg's town music, which continued to thrive in spite of the Thirty Years War, and there can be little doubt that the collection contains music played by the town musicians.[44] It shows a

34 *Dances, collections and national styles*

Table 2.2 Contents of J. Schop, *Erster Theil Newer Paduanen, Galliarden, Allmanden, Balletten, Couranten, unnd [sic] Canzonen* (Hamburg, 1633; repr. 1640)

Movement numbers	Movement type	Comment
1–5	Paduana à3	All in G minor or G major
6–7	Paduana – Galliard à3 pair	
8	Canzon à3	Substantial multi-section movement to end the *à3* group
9–11	Paduana à4	Both in F major
11–13	Paduana à4 – Allmand à4 – Paduana à4	11, 12 in G major; 13 in G minor
14–15	Paduana – Galliard à4 pair	G minor. Linked melodically at the start
16–17	Paduana à4	
18	Allmand à4 / Galliard à4	The lack of a movement number for the Galliard may be a printer's error or it may denote a pairing (see also 35)
19	Canzon à4	Substantial multi-section movement to end the *à4* group
20–30	Paduana à5	20 in G major, 21–4 in G minor
31–2	Paduana – Galliard à5 pair	
33–4	Paduana à5	
35	Allmand à5 / Galliard à5	No separate number for Galliard (see also 18)
36–37	Intrada à5	
38–39	Allmand à5 – Courandt à5	?intended as a pair
40–45	Intrada à5 – Allmand à5 [×4] – Courandt à5	All in G minor. Final Allmand and Courandt ?intended as a pair
46–55	Ballett à5 – Allmand à5 – Courandt à 5 – Ballett à4 – Allmand à5 [×5] – Courandt à5	The reason for the 'Ballett à4' being in this part of the collection is unclear. Printer's error is likely
56–60	Paduana à6	

good deal of English influence, including direct quotations from the music of John Dowland, and there is some movement towards careful ordering of content.[45] This is built around the increase in instrumentation from three to six parts along with a good deal of grouping by dance type. Only one pair of dances ('14. Paduana à4' and '15. Galliard à4') is linked through the use of shared material and it seems that Schop preferred to leave the responsibility of choosing sequences of dances largely to the performer.

Similar organisational priorities can be seen in Hans Hake's *Ander Theil Newer Pavanen, Sonaten, Arien, Balletten, Brandlen, Couranten, und Sarabanden* (n.p., 1654).[46] Here, movements are ordered by ensemble size, starting with two violins *senza basso*, and finishing with choirs of violins and trombones

('1. Cohr, Violinen, und 1. Cohr, Trombonen'). As we shall see in the following chapter, the collection does contain key-related sequences of different movements but they appear to be subservient to the overall plan of organisation by sonority. It is surely no coincidence that the edition carries a carefully produced and unusual index setting out the different ensemble sizes.

In a similar way, the title page of Hasse's *Delitiæ musicæ* highlights the fact that the contents are largely ordered by ensemble size and type, 'mit 2. 3. und 4. Stimmen Auff 2. oder 4. Violinen, 1. Violon / Clavicymbel oder Teorbe' and, twenty years later, Volume 6 of Johann Caspar Horn's *Parergon musicum* (Leipzig, 1676) reverts to this type of organisation with a gradual increase in instrumentation from *à5* at the start of the collection to *à12* at the end. Once again, Horn's title page makes it quite clear that this is an important feature, 'mit zwey Chören / auff Violen / Cornetten / Schalmeyen / Flöten / u. nach Belieben in 5.7.10.11. und 12. Stimmen'.

In the second half of the seventeenth century, organisation by sonority tended to give way to the arrangement of whole sequences of dances by key and content; in other words, the grouping together of suites with the same or similar movement type. Such arrangement was not new. The ten suites of Paul Peuerl's *Neue Padouan, Intrada, Däntz und Galliarda* (Nuremberg, 1611) all employ the same dance types – *Padouan / Intrada / Dantz / Galliarda* – and the twenty suites of Johann Hermann Schein's *Banchetto musicale* (Leipzig, 1617) all have the identical sequence of *Padouana à5 / Gagliarda à5 / Courente à5 / Allemande à4 / Tripla à4*. The deliberate ordering of the latter collection is highlighted in the prefatory 'Ad Musicum candidum' where Schein (or his publisher) tells us that the contents 'correspond to one another in tone and invention'.[47] The tone and invention in this case presumably refer to the use of a common key for every movement of a suite. Collections from the second half of the century take this one stage further; suites and sequences were often arranged in ascending order of key. For instance, Horn's suites in Volume 1 of *Parergon musicum* are arranged in this way and, to give another example, the suites in the *Hortus musicus* collection by the Hamburg town composer Johann Adam Reincken are set in ascending order of key from A to E with the last one returning to A.

It is possible that Schein's 'tone and invention' may also refer to the techniques of the so-called 'variation suite', also used in Peuerl's collection.[48] These techniques declined in popularity during the time of the Thirty Years War but, in conjunction with the greater interest in ordering, they underwent a reawakening in the 1650s that grew into a full-scale revival during the following three decades. The revival took place in the towns, not in the courts, and the reason for this is clear: the *ad hoc* organisation of suites by court musicians meant that order and contents were often subject to change, which made little point in using devices relying on a relationship between a pair of movements that might later become separated. By their very nature, variation techniques brought stability to movement sequences and it is telling that linked pairs of movements seem rarely to have been broken up by manuscript copyists.

36 *Dances, collections and national styles*

At its simplest, movements in a variation suite were linked by shared fragments of common melodic or harmonic material, sometimes both. This was particularly applied at the start of movements or strains. Example 2.11 shows movement linking taken from the third suite of Georg Wolffgang Druckenmüller's *Musicalisches Tafel-Confect* (Schwäbisch Hall, 1668); the two violin lines and bass are linked at the opening of each dance.

On rare occasions, a common bass line was used to link movements. Niedt recommends it as a basis for keyboard improvisation in his 1706 *Handleitung zur Variation* (see Chapter 8), and it is found in the works of Daniel Speer.[49] But this was the exception rather than the rule. As an extension of the technique, duple-time dances could be re-cast by using the same material set in triple time. Again, this was common in the early 1600s and underwent a revival in the second half of the century. Triple-time re-casting had its roots in the proportional notation

Example 2.11 G.W. Druckenmüller, *Musicalisches Tafel-Confect; Bestehend in VII. Partyen / Balleten, Allemanden, Couranten, Sarabanden &c.* (Schwäbisch Hall, 1668), [Partie] 3, openings of '1. Allem', '2. Courant'.

of the sixteenth century and, as we shall see in later chapters, Allemande and Courante pairings became the preferred option for this type of treatment.[50] Subsequent chapters in this book will show that many town musicians of the later seventeenth century, particularly in Hamburg and Leipzig, were capable of producing fine examples of variation technique in their consort-suite writing. And we should not forget that Kuhnau, Handel and Mattheson continued to employ the technique in keyboard-suite collections published well into the eighteenth century.[51]

We have seen that Schein's and Peuerl's collections used the same sequence of movements throughout and this is a further feature of ordering that again became popular in the second half of the century. For example, the 1660 first volume of Horn's extended *Parergon musicum* collection (see Chapter 6) has the same sequence of Allemande, Courante, Ballo and Sarabande throughout. At the heart of such dance-music sequences and suites was the relationship between duple and triple time. As we shall see in the next chapter, collections issued during the Thirty Years War and its aftermath were often dominated by groups of duple-/triple-time pairings. By the 1660s, these pairings were being combined to form larger groupings, and in the light of this, we can see Horn's Allemande, Courante, Ballo and Sarabande as a combined pairing of duple–triple–duple–triple. Like Horn, the great majority of suite composers opened their sequences with the Allemande and Courante pairing, often linked together by variation techniques. However, the second pairing of many dance suites could be more fluid and the duple–triple relationship not always maintained.

The duple-/triple-time pairing was also at the heart of the Bransle sequence, an 'alternative' suite used many town composers during the second half of the seventeenth century. 'Alternative' suites, deliberately differing in style and content to the rest of the collection, provided an effective contrast, especially in collections employing identical or near-identical movement sequences. As we have seen, Bransles were the functional dance music of the ballroom and a widely disseminated French export. In England, the sequence was not used instrumentally, being 'the only contemporary dance that was more or less confined to the dance floor'.[52] The inclusion of the sequence in German town-music collections may seem strange, but it provided composers with the ideal vehicle for contrast within a carefully organised framework. It may well have had the additional purpose of demonstrating the ability of the town musician to write functional or quasi-functional dance music in the French style. The Bransle sequence remained in both court and town repertoires for much of the seventeenth century, although Niedt at the start of the eighteenth seems to be unaware of its true nature and discusses it as a single dance.[53]

In its native French form, the sixteenth-century version of the sequence included more than twenty varieties and it was up to individual musicians to make their choice of movements.[54] By the 1630s, it had settled into a regular sequence of six differently characterised movements:

Bransle Simple – Bransle Gay – Amener – Bransle Double – Montirande – Gavotte

Example 2.12 shows the treble-line openings of the 'Branles à4 de M. Brülar. 1664'. Bruslard was a member of Louis XIV's musical establishment in Paris,[55] and the source, *D-Kl* 2° Ms. mus. 61a [I], is one of the manuscripts of French dance music preserved in the Landesbibliothek und Murhardsche Bibliothek der Stadt Kassel.[56]

Given its importance in seventeenth-century dance music, it is perhaps no coincidence that the opening part of the sequence is, once more, a duple-/triple-time pairing. The Bransle Simple comprises three- or six-bar phrases with a quaver upbeat while the following Bransle Gay uses a recurring ♩♩.♪ rhythm throughout. The Amener is also in a triple metre but with six-bar phrases split either into three plus three bars, or four plus two. In the opening bar, the rhythm is prefaced by a quaver–crotchet upbeat. The Bransle Double is again in triple time, but with simple four-bar phrasing, while the concluding Montirande and Gavotte are both duple-time movements.

While the Gavotte entered the town-music repertoire as part of the Bransle sequence, it had become detached from the sequence by the end of the seventeenth century and emerged as a dance in its own right. Once detached, it was often grouped among 'Galanterien', and Fuhrmann also includes it as one of his group of 'Frantzöis. Blümchen'.[57] Unlike the well-known eighteenth-century version that starts halfway through the bar, most seventeenth-century examples start on the first beat, and this can be seen in Bruslard's Gavotte in Example 2.12.

In the German lands, there was one consistent change to the Bransle sequence: the six movements were frequently shortened to four by omitting the Bransle Double and Montirande. This did not just apply to new compositions; native French six-movement Bransle sequences were truncated in the same way by their German copyists. Indeed, the shortened version was so widespread that it is possible that many German town musicians were not even aware of the original six movements. When added to printed suite collections with movement numbering, it is telling that the sequence was, almost without exception, grouped together under a single number and regarded as a single entity. It is reasonable to assume that this tradition originated with composers and not their publishers. And, as we shall see in later chapters, not every town composer produced completely idiomatic versions of the sequence. It is possible they were unaware of the individual characteristics of each part of the sequence, or they simply were not bothered to follow them.

Finally, it has been suggested that 'the music [in printed sources] might be arranged in an actual performing order... or it might reflect some altogether more abstract criterion'.[58] But given the degree of careful organisation in many of the collections issued between 1660 and 1690, it is hard to see why the same movement order in a sequence of dances should not have been intended for both publication and performance. For the carefully ordered collections surveyed during the course of the following chapters, it is assumed that the published order of movements within a suite represent the composer's intentions for performance.

Example 2.12 Manuscript *D-Kl* 2° Ms. mus. 61a [I], 'Branles à4 de M. Brûlar. 1664 ex. G.♮ dur'.

40 *Dances, collections and national styles*

Notes

1. *CCS*, p. 77; see also Chapter 4 of *CCS* in its entirety.
2. Charles Brewer, *The instrumental music of Schmelzer, Biber, Muffat and their contemporaries* (Farnham: Ashgate, 2011), p. 302, links Kühnel's collection with Biber's 1680 *Mensa Sonora*. He claims that Biber's 'heterogenous mixture of abstract and dance movements' is 'the earliest such collection presently known'. But Becker's *Erster Theil zwey-stimmiger Sonaten und Suiten* was published in Hamburg in 1674. Four years earlier, Reusner's *Musicalische Gesellschaffts ergetzung* (Brieg, 1670) also presents a similar mixture of abstract and dance movements; see *CCS*, pp. 105–106. The juxtaposition of abstract and dance music is discussed further in Chapter 3.
3. The *frantzösischen Manier* at the courts is discussed in detail in *CCS*.
4. J. Mattheson, *Das neu-eröffnet Orchestre, oder Universelle und gründliche Anleitung* (Hamburg, 1713). Translated as M. Seares, *Johann Mattheson's Pièces de clavecin and Das neu-eröffnet Orchestre* (Farnham: Ashgate, 2014), Appendix.
5. Ibid., Appendix, §1.
6. Ibid., Appendix, §12.
7. See P. Holman, 'From violin band to orchestra' in J. Wainwright and P. Holman (eds), *From Renaissance to Baroque: change in instruments and instrumental music in the seventeenth century* (Aldershot: Ashgate, 2005), pp. 241–57 at pp. 243–4.
8. See *CCS*, pp. 20–21.
9. For a further discussion of this single-line transmission, see *CCS*, pp. 39–42.
10. Holman, 'From violin band', p. 244.
11. Throughout this book, I have used the term 'Invention' – commonly used by seventeenth-century writers – to describe the general act of composition. For example, see Mattheson (trans. Seares), *Das neu-eröffnet Orchestre*, Appendix, §4.
12. *CCS*, pp. 25–6.
13. D.K. Wilson (ed. and trans.), *Georg Muffat on performance practice* (Bloomington and Indianapolis: Indiana University Press, 2001), p. 71.
14. R. Hudson, *The Folia, the Saraband, the Passacaglia, and the Chaconne: the historical evolution of four forms that originated in music for the five-course Spanish guitar*, 4 vols (Neuhausen and Stuttgart: Hänssler Verlag, 1982), Vol. 2, xvi–xx.
15. Ibid., xvi.
16. Note blackenings and their performance are discussed in detail in the final chapter.
17. F.E. Niedt, *Handleitung zur Variation* (Hamburg, 1706). Available online at http://petrucci.mus.auth.gr/imglnks/usimg/0/05/IMSLP296207-PMLP480263-Niedt_Handleitung_zur_Variation__1706__bsb10527644.pdf (accessed 28 October 2015). Translated by P.L. Poulin and I.C. Taylor as *The musical guide* (Oxford: Clarendon Press, 1989), p. 171.
18. For further discussion of the Kassel manuscripts, see *CCS*, pp. 66–83.
19. Writing in the early eighteenth century, Mattheson may well have been thinking of these hybrid dances when he observed that 'the Germans take pains to combine the Italian and French styles'. Mattheson (trans. Seares), *Pièces de clavecin*, Appendix, §9.
20. *CCS*, p. 27.
21. Available online: http://digital.library.unt.edu/ark:/67531/metadc69 (accessed 13 September 2013).
22. We should be wary of the belief that Lully employed others to write the inner parts of his music. See: J. Spitzer and N. Zaslaw, *The birth of the orchestra: history of an institution, 1650–1815* (Oxford: Oxford University Press, 2004), p. 92.
23. B. Gustafson (ed.), *Lüneburg, Ratsbücherei, Mus. ant. pract. 1198*, 17th Century Keyboard Music 22 (New York and London: Garland, 1987), Introduction, p. vii.
24. See: B. Scheibert, *Jean-Henry D'Anglebert and the seventeenth-century clavecin school* (Bloomington: Indiana University Press, 1986), p. 155.

25 A further example by Pachelbel can be found in his manuscript 'Partie a 4; 1 Violin, 2 Viole e Cembalo' (*D-B* Mus. Ms. 16481/2); modern edition, ed. R. Gwilt (Hungerford: RG editions, 1998). The opening of this gigue is also given in *CCS*, p. 39.
26 M.E. Little, 'Gigue (i)' in D.L. Root (ed.) *Grove music online* (www.oxfordmusiconline.com), accessed 19 March 2012.
27 The Paduan in the early part of the seventeenth century is discussed in M. Kokole, *Isaac Posch 'diditus Eois Hesperiisque plagis – Praised in the Lands of Dawn and Sunset'* (Frankfurt am Main: Peter Lang, 2009), pp. 143–6.
28 J.G. Walther, *Musicalisches Lexicon oder Musicalische Bibliothec* (Leipzig, 1732); modern edition, ed. F. Ramm (Kassel: Bärenreiter, 2001), p. 415.
29 Ibid., p. 415.
30 P. Holman, *Dowland: Lachrimae (1604)* (Cambridge: Cambridge University Press, 1999), p. 27.
31 Niedt (trans. Poulin and Taylor), *Musical guide*, p. 137.
32 For further examples of the duple-time Galliard, see M.E. Little and C.G. Marsh, *La danse noble: an inventory of dances and sources* (New York: Broude Bros., 1992), pp. 40, 72 and 81.
33 The Allemande is dated 1575 in the manuscript's index and at the head of the movement.
34 *CCS*, pp. 206–7.
35 M.H. Fuhrmann, *Musicalischer-Trichter: Dadurch Ein geschickter Informator seinen Informandis die Edle Singe-Kunst* (Brandenburg, 1706), p. 87. The idea of the Allemande as a 'proposition' was copied by Walther in his definition of the dance: *Musicalishes Lexicon* (ed. Ramm), p. 31.
36 M. Praetorius *Syntagmatis Musici, Michaelis Praetorii C[apellmeister], tomus tertius* (Wolfenbüttel, 1619); edited and translated by J. Kite-Powell as *Syntagma musicum III* (Oxford: Oxford University Press, 2004), p. 43.
37 G. Taubert, *Rechtschaffener Tanzmeister oder gründlicher Erklärung der Frantzösischen Tantz-Kunst* (Leipzig, 1717), p. 378.
38 Niedt (trans. Poulin and Taylor), *Musical guide*, pp. 139–40.
39 Walther, *Musicalishes Lexicon* (ed. F. Ramm), p. 64.
40 In Vienna and the surrounding area, 'Balletto' was the standard terminology for a suite. Many instances of this may be found in the Liechenstein collection in Kroměříž; see: J. Sehnal and J. Pešková, *Caroli de Liechtenstein Castelcorno episcopi Olumucensis operum artis musicae collectio Cremsirii reservata*, Artis Musicæ Antiquioris Catalogorum Vol. V/1 (Prague: Editio Supraphon, 1998). Richard Hudson sees the *Balli* in this part of Knoep's collection as 'even simpler pieces' but makes no mention of the composer's stated stylistic distinctions: R. Hudson, *The Allemande, the Balletto, and the Tanz*, 2 vols (Cambridge: Cambridge University Press, 1986), Vol. 1, p. 183.
41 The three-volume series of *Exercitium musicum* is discussed in Chapter 4.
42 RISM A/1 falls to list the complete exemplar of this work in *PL Kj* H 930 [1]. See A. Patalas, *Catalogue of early music prints from the collections of the former Preußische Staatsbibliothek in Berlin, kept at the Jagiellonian library in Cracow* (Cracow: Musica Iagellonica, 1999), p. 183.
43 Modern edition, J. Schop (ed. A. Spohr), *Erster Theil newer Paduanen* (Wisconsin, WI: A-R Editions, 2003).
44 Ibid., Preface, pp. ix–x.
45 Ibid., Preface, p. xi.
46 The index to this collection is given in the following chapter.
47 'das sie beydes in Tono und invention einander sein respondiren'. The prefaces and introductions to Schein's collection are given in facsimile in the modern edition, ed. D. Krickeberg (Kassel: Bärenreiter, 1967).
48 Metoda Kokole has argued that this is not the case as variation techniques are only used in three suites of the collection. See Kokole, *Isaac Posch*, p. 123.

42 *Dances, collections and national styles*

49 The work of Speer and Niedt is further discussed in Chapters 4 and 8.
50 Proportional notation is discussed under performance practice in the final chapter.
51 Twentieth-century scholars have all but ignored the important revival of variation techniques in the second half of the seventeenth century. For example, see P. Nettl, *Die Wiener Tanzkomposition in der zweiten Hälfte des siebzehnten Jahrhunderts*, Studien zur Musikwissenchaft 8 (Vienna: Universal Edition, 1921), p. 61. The first edition of *The New Grove Dictionary of Music and Musicians* does allow that 'suites of thematically related dances continued to be written throughout the 17th century and into the 18th', but only mentions Reincken's *Hortus musicus*: D. Fuller, 'Suite' in S. Sadie (ed.), *The New Grove Dictionary of Music and Musicians*, Vol. 18 (London: Grove, 1980), p. 339. Robert S. Hill has correctly argued against 'the present music-historical perspective [that] predominantly gives the Variation suite a special place at the beginning of the 17th Century', but then, like *The New Grove*, mainly limits his comments on the later works to *Hortus musicus*; see R.S. Hill, 'Stilanalyse und Überlieferungsproblematik' in A. Edler and F. Krummacher (eds) *Dietrich Buxtehude und die europäische Musik seiner Zeit: Bericht über das Lübecker Symposion 1987* (Kassel: Bärenreiter, 1990), pp. 204–214 at p. 205.
52 P. Holman, *Four and twenty fiddlers: the violin at the English court* (Oxford: Clarendon Press, 1993, repr. 1995), p. 312.
53 Niedt (trans. Poulin and Taylor), *Musical guide*, p. 135.
54 *CCS*, pp. 50–51.
55 Ibid., p. 67.
56 For a full discussion of these frequently misunderstood manuscripts, see *CCS*, pp. 67–82.
57 Fuhrmann, *Musicalischer-Trichter*, p. 87.
58 P. Whitehead, 'Austro-German printed sources of instrumental music, 1630 to 1700', PhD dissertation (University of Pennsylvania, 1996), p. 126.

3 The aftermath of war: 1648–59

The period immediately following the end of the Thirty Years War saw a renewal of interest in printed editions of dance music, either as new collections or reprints of earlier volumes. Reprinted volumes indicate clear commercial demand and, as we shall see, their contents exerted a continuing influence on the dance music of other musicians. And while this chapter deals principally with suites and dance music issued between 1648 and 1659, it is important for the reprints of earlier collections to be included in this part of the survey. Accordingly, the chapter starts with the dance collection by Andreas Hammerschmidt originally issued during the years of war but reprinted in 1639 and 1650.

Hammerschmidt was appointed organist of Freiberg's leading church in 1635, and the dedication to the town's mayor and councillors in the original print of *Erster Fleiß Allerhand newer Paduanen, Galliarden, Balleten, Mascharaden, Francoischen [sic] Arien, Courenten und Sarabanden* (Freiberg, 1636) is surely in recognition of this. *Erster Fleiß* was the composer's first publication, and Table A.1 (see Appendix 1) lists the contents. The reprints were presumably timed to coincide with Hammerschmidt's issue of a second and third collection of dance music. While a small number of minor errors crept into the later prints, the only significant difference between the various editions lies on the title page; in 1636 and 1639, Hammerschmidt is described as 'Organisten in S. Peter zu Freybergt', in the 1650 reprint, he is 'dieser Zeit Organisten zur Zittaw in OberLausitz'.

The instrumentation of the collection is the standard one adopted by most town composers in the period covered by this book – two violins, two violas and bass. The part-books are given the titles 'Cantus I', 'Cantus II', 'Altus', 'Tenor', 'Bassus' and 'General-bass'. Both the bass parts are figured, although this may be more a question of the printer not wishing to set up a new unfigured part for the string bass than a desire to provide two parts for chordal instruments. Hammerschmidt's use of Altus and Tenor for the viola parts implies different instruments, and this is supported by Daniel Speer in his *Grund-richtiger / Kurtz / leicht und nöthiger Unterricht der musicalischen Kunst* (Ulm, 1687). Speer confirms the two types of viola, alto and tenor, and identifies them as separate instruments, albeit with the same c–g–d′–a′ tunings of the standard viola.[1]

At the start, middle and end of *Erster Fleiß*, we find dances grouped together by type: first, four *Paduanen* and two *Courenten*: at the halfway point, seven

Courenten: and, finally, four *Balleten*. There also substantial numbers of duple-/triple-time dance pairings, and it is significant that Hammerschmidt, or perhaps his publisher, took the trouble to highlight these pairings in the movement titles (for example, 'XI. Mascharada 1. à5', 'XII. Sarabande 2. à5'). The collection is unusual in being so explicit in this respect; normally it was left to the performers to discover such things for themselves.

The dances themselves exhibit considerable variety. The opening group of *Paduanen* is clearly intended to be a demonstration of the composer's credentials as a learned musician. Counterpoint is used at the start of each one, and every instrument is involved in the imitation of the opening material. In contrast to collections that allow the omission of the viola parts, it would be impossible for the inner parts in these *Paduanen* to be removed without seriously damaging the *Invention*. It is also difficult to think of anything further away from the treble and bass emphasis of courtly dance music.

Multi-sectioned movements are a feature of *Erster Fleiß*, mostly under the titles of 'Ballet à5' or 'Aria à5'. Table 3.1 shows the structural contents of these Ballets.

In the previous chapter, Table 2.1 demonstrated the variety of construction in the Ballets of the 1660 *Exercitium musicum* collection. The earlier Ballets in *Erster Fleiß* show the same characteristics. The introduction of triple time is not uniform and there is considerable variety in the length of each strain. 'VII. Ballet à5', for example, is fifty-nine bars long with three duple-time (¢) strains followed by two of 3/2, while 'XVI. Ballet 1. à5' has only two strains, each in duple time, and each of nineteen bars. There is also little uniformity of rhythm at the start of strains; some start on upbeats, some, albeit the majority, on downbeats. It is clear that Hammerschmidt saw them as generalised dance movements, lacking specific characteristics.

Table 3.1 Ballet construction in A. Hammerschmidt, *Erster Fleiß Allerhand newer Paduanen, Galliarden, Balleten, Francoischen [sic] Arien, Courenten und Sarabanden, Mit 5. Stimmen auff Violen zu spielen/sampt dem General Baß* (Freiberg, 1636, repr. 1639 and 1650)

Title	Strain 1	Strain 2	Strain 3	Strain 4	Strain 5
VII. Ballet à5	¢; 13 bars	¢; 10 bars	¢; 11 bars	3/2; 12 bars	3/2; 13 bars
VIII. Ballet à5	¢; 8 bars	¢; 10 bars	3/2; 17 bars	N/A	N/A
XVI. Ballet 1. à5	¢; 7 bars	¢; 12 bars	N/A	N/A	N/A
XVIII. Ballet à5	¢; 8 bars	¢; 8 bars	3/2; 11 bars	N/A	N/A
XXVI. Ballet 1. à5	¢; 12 bars	¢; 12 bars	N/A	N/A	N/A
XXX. Ballet 1. à5	¢; 7 bars	¢; 8 bars	N/A	N/A	N/A
XXXII. Ballet 1. à5	¢; 6 bars	¢; 8 bars	N/A	N/A	N/A
XXXIII. Ballet 2. à5	¢; 4 bars	¢; 4 bars	N/A	N/A	N/A
XXXVI. Ballet à5	¢; 7 bars	¢; 8 bars	3/2; 13 bars	N/A	N/A
XXXVII. Ballet à5	¢; 6 bars	¢; 5 bars	3/2; 16 bars	N/A	N/A
XXXVIII. Ballet à5	¢; 8 bars	¢; 6 bars	3/2; 15 bars	N/A	N/A
XXXIX. Ballet à5	¢; 8 bars	¢; 8 bars	3/2; 20 bars	N/A	N/A

The four Arias in *Erster Fleiß* show a similarly mixed construction; 'XXVIII. Aria 1. à5' has three duple-time strains, 'XV. Aria à5' has a third strain in 3/2 and the remaining two each have two duple-time strains. If it is difficult to distinguish these movements from the Ballets of the collection, it is also difficult to understand why Hammerschmidt (or his printer) used different titles for similar movement types.

In the previous chapter, I argued that 'compound movements were the nearest that town composers came to court character dances derived from dramatic stage music, even if they were not danced'. Hammerschmidt's Arias and Ballets frequently use 'langsam', 'starck', 'stille' and 'geschwind' to modify their performance. In 'XVIII. Ballet à5', for example, the end of each duple-time strain is marked 'langsam', clearly indicating a broadening of tempo. Such markings suggest a flexibility of style, if not radical changes of tempo, that would make dancing difficult. It is further confirmation that town musicians saw their collections primarily as instrumental entertainment probably intended as material for musicians in the various *Collegia*. Even when used for civic occasions such as wedding ceremonies, they were not, with the likely exception of the Bransles, providing functional dance music.

Unlike the *Paduanen*, the triple-time music in *Erster Fleiß* tends to be harmonically simpler with less interest in the middle parts; most of the Galliards in the collection could easily be disseminated in the court tradition with only treble and bass parts and not lose anything substantial in quality. But even in these lighter-textured triple-time dances, Hammerschmidt is clearly intent on showing that he can produce different versions of the same movement type. So 'XIX. Courente à5' has simple inner parts and starts each of its strains on an upbeat, but the following *Courente* starts on the downbeat and is characterised by groups of quavers for each instrument. Not all pairings are between duple- and triple-time movements. 'XXXII. Ballet 1. à5' is paired with 'XXXIII. Ballet 2. à5', but the second has quite a different character with dotted rhythms anticipating the variety of Ballo that was to become so popular in later decades of the century. This second dance is also marked to be played quicker on each repetition ('geschwinde und alle mal geschwinder').

As I have already said, the 1639 reprint of *Erster Fleiß* was presumably timed to coincide with the issue of Hammerschmidt's second volume of dance music, *Ander Theil newer Paduanen, Canzonen, Galliarden, Francoischen Arien, Courenten und Sarabanden* (Freiberg, 1639). This second volume, apparently never reprinted, follows a similar pattern to its predecessor. Again there is an opening group of *Paduanen*, but three of them are paired with *Galliarden* and use linked material. Curiously, and perhaps as a result of a printer's error, the three related *Galliarden* are placed at the end of the main part of the collection, albeit with titles that clarify the identity of each linked Paduan.

As with *Erster Fleiß*, the collection is built around the pairings of duple- and triple-time music, sometimes during the course of a single movement and sometimes spread across pairs of dances. Hammerschmidt also repeats his use of instructions to modify the speed or character of sections within individual dances. Once again, the quality of the dances is high; we can see this in 'XIV. Sarabande 2. à5' with its characteristic note blackening, given above in Chapter 2 (Example 2.1).

Ander Theil has one significant departure in content from *Erster Fleiß*: the instrumentation of the main part of the collection is the same *à5* combination Hammerschmidt used in *Erster Fleiß*, but a separate group of *à3* dances for two violins and bass ends the collection after the additional *Galliarden*. The reduction from five-part to three-part instrumentation clearly sets them apart as an appendix, even if it is not marked as such. The first of these dances is 'LI. Ballet à3', with a set of seventeen variations.[2] It is likely that Hammerschmidt was only thinking in terms of a greatly extended set of *Double* variations and many are little more than different sets of divisions over the same bass line, barely departing from the basic melodic and harmonic material.

If linking material across volumes is very rare, 'LI. Ballet' and its variations are followed by three *à3 Canzonen*, two of which are harmonically and melodically linked to movements in the previous *Erster Fleiß*.[3] In all three, the frequent use of imitation as an important part of the *Invention* shows Hammerschmidt demonstrating himself to be capable of esoteric composition and a high standard of musicianship.

A number of similarities exist between the two Hammerschmidt collections discussed so far and Georg Zuber's *Erster Theil newer Paduanen, [Gaillarden,] Arien, Balletten, Couranten, Sarabanden und einer Sonat. Mit 5. Stimmen nebenst dem Basso Continuo* published in 1649 in Lübeck. Little is known of Georg (or Gregor) Zuber. He had some training as a court musician as he was a member of the Gottorf *Hofkapelle* during most of the 1630s,[4] but he is not listed in Mattheson's *Grundlage einer Ehren-Pforte* (Hamburg, 1740). Some of the manuscript sources of *Erster Theil* describe him as 'beställter Violista und Musicus in Lübeck' (official violinist and musician in Lübeck), and it could well be that this was the phrase used on the title page of the 1649 printed edition. Walther's *Musicalisches Lexicon* describes him as a 'Hochwiesen Raths der Stadt Lübeck bestallt gewesener Violinist und Musicus' (well-known former official town violinist and musician in Lübeck).[5] 'Gewesener' (former) implies that Zuber left Lübeck, and it seems that he spent some time in Sweden in the company of his pupil, the violinist and composer David Petersen.[6]

Unfortunately, it seems that the printed edition is now lost, but it is possible to discern a good deal of its content from surviving manuscript sources. The first violin part is preserved in *D-UDa* 38a/9 and the bass in *D-UDa* 38b/8. Both are in the same hand, but the latter is missing its final page.[7] The 'Tenor' (second viola) part, also in the same hand as 38a/9 and 38b/8, may well have been part of the same manuscript set, and is preserved as manuscript *D-EFu* 13M. 8° 1222. The likely parts for second violin and first viola have not survived. These manuscripts all point to performance by the Udestedt *Adjuvantenchor* 'amateur musicians from the village who performed music at Sunday church services'.[8] Given the repertoire of Zuber's collection, they must have played at social gatherings as well. Despite their amateur status, the players of the *Adjuvantenchor* must have been proficient musicians, especially the first violinist.

Zuber avoids the *scordatura* tuning and double stopping of the solo and trio repertoires; but with the exception of the second viola part, and presumably the first, he still expects a standard of playing that is higher than that of many consort-suite publications.

Another copy of the first violin part, albeit heavily truncated and not associated with the Udestedt ensemble, forms part of *GB-Lbl* Add. MS 31438, where a note in the margin describes it as 'Gregorius Zubern 1.d° 1649. a. 5 ... u[nd] Franckfurt am Maÿn 1660'. This may imply a re-issue, perhaps to accompany Zuber's 1659 second volume and, as we have seen, this was common practice. But it is also possible that the anonymous scribe thought the 1659 new second volume to be a re-issue of the first, and created additional confusion by getting the date wrong.

At first sight, manuscripts 38a/9, 38b/8 and 13M. 8° 1222 all appear to be full copies of the original. But Albert Göhler's compilation of seventeenth-century book-fair catalogues and Walther both list 'Galliarden' as part of the original title, and no Galliards are present in any of the manuscripts.[9] While it is possible that both Göhler and Walther were mistaken, a similar reduction in content is confirmed by Hammerschmidt's *Dritter Theil newer Paduanen* (see below) that was copied into the same manuscripts and probably by the same copyist. And in manuscript 31438, not only are Zuber's *Galliarden* omitted, but the *Paduanen* as well.

If it is difficult to be certain over the copying dates of 38a/9, 38b/8 and 13M. 8° 1222, it is possible to be more precise over 31438 as the '1660' in the title of the Zuber's collection gives us the earliest possible date of this part of the manuscript. The date also explains the omission of the *Galliarden* and *Paduanen*: both were starting to lose their places in dance-music collections in the 1660s, and it is likely that the copyists were influenced by this trend. Fortunately, all sources are in agreement about the order of the remaining movements. Table A.2 in Appendix 1 details the contents of both 38a/9 and 31438.

Even allowing for truncated transmission of 38a/9, 38b/8 and 13M. 8° 1222, it is clear that Zuber's collection marks an important point in the development of the printed suite. There is careful organisation of the content into six sequences of four or five movements. Each sequence starts with a Paduan and all but one end with a Sarabande.

The *Paduanen* all follow the general three-strain pattern described in the previous chapter; they are sophisticated movements and represent some of the most interesting music in the collection. Example 3.1 shows the violin part of the second and third strains of '10. Paduan' with its solistic divisions and intensification of rhythm following the simplicity of the first strain. It is clear from this that Zuber was thinking in terms of single players to a part. And while he was certainly not the first composer to end a Paduan with a rising chromatic treble line, the closing bars are undeniably effective.

If the other dances may sometimes lack the same degree of sophistication, they are rarely routine. Variation techniques do not play a major part, but their imaginative use is apparent in the '10. Paduan' – '13. Sarabande' sequence where a three-note head-motif linking the first three dances is inverted at the start of the fourth. It is difficult to know where the *Galliarden* fitted into the contents of the

48 *The aftermath of war: 1648–59*

Example 3.1 First treble part of G. Zuber, 'Erster Theil newer Paduanen, Arien, Balletten, Couranten, Sarabanden und einer Sonat. Mit 5. Stimmen nebenst dem Basso Continuo' (*D-UDa* 38a/9 and 38b/8), '10. Paduan'.

printed edition, but it is possible that they were grouped together at the start of the collection or, perhaps more likely, formed a duple-/triple-time pair with the Paduan at the start of each sequence.

Sarabandes and Courantes are all in the Italian manner. None of the Udestedt manuscripts contain blackened notation in these movements denoting off-beat accentuation, but there is blackening in Hammerschmidt's *Dritter Theil newer Paduanen* that was also copied into the manuscripts by the same hand that dealt with Zuber's collection (see below). So it is reasonable to assume that there was no blackening in the original print. Arias feature prominently in the collection; they are all multi-sectioned movements starting in duple time and finishing in triple and exhibiting a variety of tempo markings in the manner of Hammerschmidt's *Erster Fleiß*. As with the latter, the implied flexibility of performing style seems to have little in common with functional dance music.

The title 'Balletto' is used specifically for the simple twin-strain dance that appears in all but two of the Paduan-led sequences. But it is also used generically for '29. Balletto' and '31. Balletto', two large-scale sequences of movements at the end of the collection. There is a clear suggestion of functional dance music in both of these latter sequences, setting them apart from the rest of the collection. As we have seen, it was common for town composers to provide an 'alternative' suite in their carefully ordered collections and Zuber's *Balletti* are a very early example of this 'alternative', perhaps even the first. It is possible that Zuber conceived the idea for ending the collection in this way from the Appendix in Hammerschmidt's *Ander Theil*.

'29. Balletto' and '31. Balletto' have nine and thirteen dances respectively, separated by a Sonatina for recorder consort ('Flautini').[10] While most of the movements in each sequence are untitled, both contain a 'Bataglia' and a closing 'Sarabanda'; there is also a striking similarity of content and style to the French-manner 'Ballet à4. Zu Stockholm getantzt' probably danced at the court of Queen Christina's Swedish court during the late 1640s or early 1650s and now preserved as one of the Kassel manuscripts of dance music (*D-Kl 2° Ms. mus. 61k⁴*). Markings at the start of Zuber's movements ('u[nd]') seem to suggest that each sequence was intended to played without a break. For both sequences, the first violin part uses a French violin clef rather than the mixture of treble G and soprano C clefs of the earlier part of the collection. But the true French nature of the writing here can be found in the idiomatic French Courante that forms part of the first *Balletto*. Zuber was clearly at ease with the *frantzösischen Manier*.

If the tenor viola part seems little more than functional chord filling in some of the dances, it does appear to play a more important part in the *Invention* elsewhere, especially the *Paduanen*. It is possible that, like Rosenmüller's 1667 *Sonate da camera* (see Chapter 6), the two viola parts may have been intended as optional for some, but not all, of the dances. With so much missing, it is difficult to make comments on the precise nature of the 'Tenor' part in both *Balletti*. In '29. Balletto', the clef is changed from the tenor C used up to this point to alto C. The tessitura still suggests the viola even if the range of the part never descends below the lowest string of the violin. In the second '31. Balletto' sequence, the clef is changed again, this time to a second-line C clef, but it is still the viola that seems to be the intended instrument. As the music for this part is different from that of the first violin at this point, we can be certain that Zuber is not employing the two-part treble and bass texture used in the final section of Knoep's *Ander Theil Newer Paduanen* (see Chapter 2). Neither of the two *Balletti* seems to be linked to the recorder-consort Sonatina that separates them.

'30. Sonatina' may not be the only example of parts of the collection being used by wind instruments. The bass part of '21. Balletto' is transposed down a tone in the fragmentary manuscript *D-UDa* 38b/1. Presumably this was to make it playable by a trombone as part of a brass ensemble.

Taken as a whole, the importance of Zuber's *Erster Theil* cannot be overstated. While it was certainly not the first seventeenth-century publication of dance music to be carefully and clearly organised, it was one of the earliest, if not the first, to return to such concepts after the Thirty Years War. Even with the omission of movements in the manuscript sources, it is still clear that it is the careful arrangement of content and not the choice of a specific dance type that was of primary importance to Zuber. As we shall see in the following chapter, the 'alternative' *Balletto* sequences at the end of the collection may well have influenced both composers and publishers in the following decades. The collection also gives us a snapshot of dance-movement sequences before the Allemande of the keyboard suite became so dominant. It can only be hoped that the missing parts of this collection will one day come to light.

Similar trends of careful organisation to Zuber's *Erster Theil* are to be found in a collection by the Kassel musician Johann Neubauer, in manuscript *D-Kl* 4° Ms. mus. 27 (1–5), dated 'den 9. augusti, 1.6.49'.[11] The standard of the copying is precise and careful; the ornate title page suggests that it was intended as a scribal publication and the collection as a whole was clearly meant to impress. Nothing is known about Neubauer; the manuscript carries a courtly dedication to 'Willhelm, Landgraffen zu Hessen', but that does not preclude him from being a town musician; the perfunctory description 'Musi: Instrumentalÿ' without any reference to royal employment status does suggest *Stadt* rather than *Hofkapelle*. It is possible that Neubauer was presenting this suite collection as part of an application for a post at the Kassel court. If this is the case, it is unlikely that he was successful as there are no records of him in the court archives. On the other hand, the dedication could have been an attempt to enlist royal support for an application to join one of the town-music ensembles.

The collection's title, 'Newe Pavanen, Galliarden, Balletten, Couranten, Allmanden, Und Sarabanden, Mitt 4. Und 5. Stimmen Nebenst einem Basso Continuo' emulates a collection in the town-music manner, as does the content with its movement linking, numbered movements that mostly fall into readily discernible suite patterns, and arrangement in ascending order of key from E minor to D major. There are five part-books, 'Canto primo', 'Canto Sec[und]°', a figured organ part and two that are unlabelled. The latter are clearly alto and tenor viola parts; one is in the tenor clef, the other is in the alto clef. The present binding of the 'Canto primo' book is faulty; the page containing movements 14–17 is bound in after '33. Pavan'.

The collection is divided up into three sequences of Pavan / Galliard / Ballett / Couranta in *à4* instrumentation – surprisingly omitting the alto viola and not the tenor – and five with the same movement type in *à5*. After the second *à5* sequence, Neubauer inserts an Allemande and Sarabande paring but he is careful to maintain the rising-key ordering; the Allemande–Sarabande pair is in A major following the A minor of the previous Pavan-led sequence. In a similar fashion, a pair of Allemandes and Sarabandes is also placed after the fourth and fifth suites.

This is clearly a much higher level of organisation than Hammerschmidt's collections and even Zuber's. And we have to look back to Schein's 1617 *Banchetto musicale* to find anything that would provide a suitable model. Schein's collection comprises twenty suites, all with the same movement sequence of Padouana, Gagliarda, Courente, and Allemande with re-cast Tripla. There are a number of striking parallels between Neubauer and Schein's work; both mix *à4* and *à5* ensembles even if Schein uses both ensemble sizes within the same suite while Neubauer keeps them separate. There is similarity between the choice of dance type, although Neubauer does not attempt to match Schein's 'Tripla' re-castings of previous Allemandes. And, with the exception of the Allemande–Sarabande pairs, Neubauer further emulates Schein in keeping to the same sequence of movements throughout. The two collections share similar arrangement of content in ascending

The aftermath of war: 1648–59 51

order of key and, above all, demonstrate nothing less than delight in using variation techniques at nearly every opportunity. Example 3.2 shows the openings of the third of Neubauer's Paduan-led sequences. Here, '10. Galliard' is a triple-time re-casting of the previous Pavan, and the movement linking extends at a melodic level throughout the entire sequence.

Example 3.2 J. Neuebauer, 'Newe Pavanen, Galliarden, Balletten, Couranten, Allmanden, Und Sarabanden, Mitt 4. Und 5. Stimmen Nebenst einem Basso Continuo' (*D-Kl* 4° Ms. mus. 27 (1–5)), '9. Pavan', '10. Galliard', '11. Ballett', '12. Couranta'.

If this is reminiscent of the way in which variation techniques were used by Schein, not everything in the collection derives from *Banchetto musicale*. In the manner of Hammerschmidt, the duple-/triple-time relationship is at the heart of each sequence, and Neubauer's *Ballett* movements are also tri-partite multi-sectioned movements. Again following Hammerschmidt, the sections of the latter are varied in a most imaginative way; their contents are detailed in Table 3.2.

The quality and diversity of these movements are typical of the collection as a whole. Example 3.2 above shows how the opening figuration of '9. Pavan' is transformed into a triple-time Galliard of the most extraordinary vitality that not even Schein could equal. If such movements exerted little influence on the development of the suite, we must remember that Neubauer's collection was apparently never printed and remained in manuscript. It is unlikely to have been known outside Kassel itself.

A year later, and perhaps to coincide with a reprinting of *Erster Fleiß*, a third volume of Hammerschmidt's dance music was issued – his *Dritter Theil neuer Paduanen, Galliarden, Canzonen, Sonaten, Balletten, Intraden, Couranten und Sarabanden* (Leipzig, 1650). Given the failure of the reprints of his earlier dance-music collections to rectify obvious errors, it may be significant that Hammerschmidt chose a new publisher, Samuel Scheibe in Leipzig. However, if this is the case, it is strange that the printer remained the same Georg Beuther in Freiberg who had acted as publisher of *Erster Fleiß* and *Ander Theil*.

As with Zuber's *Erster Theil*, manuscripts 38a/9, 38b/8 and 13M. 8° 1222 provide most of the source material and Hammerschmidt's *Dritter Theil* must also have been in the repertoire of the Udestedt *Adjuvantenchor*. Unlike Zuber's collection, the 'Bassus Continuus' part-book of the printed edition has survived for comparison, albeit incomplete.[12] The first forty-two movements are complete in the part-book, but all else is lost apart from a fragmentary page giving the start of 'LI. Ballett'. In the same way as Zuber's material in the three Udestedt manuscripts, the copyist was selective in his choice of movements and it is

Table 3.2 Ballett construction in Neuebauer, 'Newe Pavanen'

Title	Section 1	Section 2	Section 3	Comments
3. Ballett	C Allegro	[C] Adagio	3 Presto	Ending of Section 1 is re-cast into triple time for the ending of Section 3.
7. Ballett	C Allegro	3 Presto	C Adagio	
11. Ballett	C Allegro	[C]	3 Presto	Section 2 has no tempo marking.
15. Ballett	C Adagio	3 Allegro	C Adagio	
19. Ballet	C Presto	[C] Adagio	3 Presto	Ending of Section 1 is re-cast into triple time for the ending of Section 3.
25. Ballet	C Allegro	3 Presto	C Adagio	
29. Ballet	C Allegro	[C] Adagio	3 Presto	
35. Ballet	C Allegro	[C] Adagio	3 Presto	While not formally linked, both Sections 2 and 3 start with a rising chromatic figure in the treble line.

The aftermath of war: 1648–59 53

the *Galliarden* that are again omitted. The remainder appears to be complete. In a seemingly coincidental further parallel with Zuber's *Erster Theil*, 'XXV. Ballet à5' and 'XXVI. Sarabanda à5' were copied into manuscript *GB-Lbl* Add. MS 31438 where both dances are part of a twelve-movement section marked 'Andr. Hamershmidt'. I have not been able to find concordances for the remaining ten movements and, given the problems of attribution with this manuscript that I have discussed above, we cannot be certain of their origin or authorship.

The Udestedt manuscript sources of *Dritter Theil* tell us that the instrumentation is for three, four and five parts, although the dance music without exception is marked 'à5'. This is confirmed on the title page of the 'Bassus Continuus' part-book. It is reasonable to assume that a string ensemble was expected for the dances, but it seems that a consort of *Cornetti* and trombones are required for the *Intraden* that close the collection as well as other abstract movements not connected with dance. As we have already seen in the previous chapter, the player of the 38a/9 treble part-book is expected to alternate between the 'Trombona' and *Cornetto* during the course of a single movement. We have no way of telling if these instructions were added for the particular circumstances of the Udestedt performances or whether they belonged to Hammerschmidt's original print.

The contents of the bass part-book of *Dritter Theil* are shown in Table A.3 in Appendix 1, along with the manuscript concordances. The missing movement titles have been reconstructed from the latter. The collection starts and ends with sequences of movements organised by type; there is a greater emphasis on abstract, non-dance music than in either of Hammerschmidt's previous volumes. Once again, there is a group of *Canzonen*, this time in both *à3* and *à4* instrumentation, which are given a prominent place near the start of the collection and not relegated to the end as they were in *Ander Theil*. They are followed by three *à5* Sonatas and, unusually, an *à5* Quodlibet so that, in this section of abstract pieces, Hammerschmidt (or his publisher) has arranged the content in order of increasing sonority.

As in Hammerschmidt's earlier collections, the dance music is arranged almost entirely in duple-/triple-time pairings; only the single 'I. Paduan à5' at the start of the collection stands alone as a type of prelude. The content of these pairings is more rigid than in *Erster Fleiß* or *Ander Theil*; the first dance of the pair is always a multi-sectioned Ballet that rarely departs from a format of two duple-time sections followed by a third in triple time. The third and fourth pairs of *à5 Paduanen* and *Galliarden* (VI-IX) have linked bass lines at the start, and it is likely that there would have been further linking of opening material from first violin part. Movement linking is rarely used elsewhere.

Given the anticipation of the careful organisation of suite collections in the 1660s that we see in many of the collections discussed in this chapter, Hammerschmidt's reliance on the formats of his collections originating in the 1630s makes his *Dritter Theil* appear old-fashioned. It is not surprising that, unlike the first volume of his dance music, the third was never reprinted.

As with Hammerschmidt's *Dritter Theil* and Zuber's *Erster Theil*, Johann Rudolf Ahle's *Dreyfaches Zehn allerhand newer Sinfonien, Paduanen, Balleten, Alemanden, Mascheraden, Arien, Intraden, Courenten und Sarabanden; Mit 3.*

4. und 5. Stimmen survives incomplete; the first viola part-book is lost, leaving Cantus I and II, Tenor (second viola) and figured Bassus parts. The collection was printed in Erfurt in the same year as Hammerschmidt's *Dritter Theil*. Ahle was a town musician in Mühlhausen, where he was organist at the church of St Blasius, and he was a civic official for the last period of his life.

Writing in 1932, Friederich Noack suggested that *Dreyfaches Zehn* was a very early example of placing an abstract movement at the start of a sequence of dance movements.[13] Perhaps he was misled by the title; grouped together by type along with five *Paduanen* at the start of the collection, three à5 *Sinfonien* are used to preface the collection as a whole, and not individual dances or sequences. While it is possible that the performers may have used them in conjunction with the latter, it would be a mistake to view them as a precursor of the sonata and suite combination.

After this opening group, Ahle (or his printer) has a central section devoted to a series of à3 and à5 dances, mostly in duple-/triple-time pairings. The collection ends with a sequence of two Intradas and a Sarabande before the Appendix – a single 'Canzon à5 ad imit. Germanicæ cantilenæ'. Along with the Intradas, there are options here for wind instruments. Next to Zuber's multi-movement *Balletti*, this single-movement Appendix is hardly an outstanding feature of the collection, but it does again show the start of a trend that resulted in the 'alternative' suite of later decades. Göhler lists another collection of dance music, apparently arranged in increasing order of sonority, but this has been seemingly lost.[14]

The 1650s were a time of relative popularity for the trio format even if, as Rosenmüller suggests in his 1667 *Sonata da camera*, trios could also be created by the simple expedient of omitting the viola parts of à4 and à5 music in order to give a texture of two violins and bass. The development of the trio suite largely mirrors that of the suite in general and there is the same move towards careful organisation of content. We can see this in Lüder Knoep's *Erster Theil Newer Paduanen, Galliarden, Balletten, Mascaraden, Arien, Allemanden, Couranten und Sarabanden* (Bremen, 1652). Knoep came from a family background of town musicians and became organist of St Stephani in Bremen from 1641 until his death in 1665.[15]

The collection demonstrates a desire to place at least some of the contents into clearly discernible groupings even if the concepts of organisation are not as tight as Neubauer's or Zuber's.[16] Set for two violins, bass and *General-Bass*, the edition's preface is dated '1. Junii Anno 1651', but some time elapsed before going to press – the title page has 'Ao.1652'.[17] There are thirty-five movements, a relatively small number for a printed collection, but the first thirty-one are grouped together into nine sequences or pairings and, apart from the last two pairs of dances, in ascending order of key. Table 3.3 on page 56 details the collection. Unfortunately, the 'Cantus II' part has not survived.

The contents of each sequence are clearly defined by key groupings and, in most cases, the use of a Paduan or 'Area' as a starting movement. The relationship between duple and triple time again plays an important part. The six movements of the first and second sequences are all made up of three sets of duple–triple pairs. The arrangement is varied only slightly for the third sequence. In three cases, 'XXI. Area', 'XXVII. Area' and the probably mis-named 'XXIII. Almand', the relationship is within the movements themselves; all three start in duple time and finish in triple. The triple-time section of last of these is marked 'alleg: 3. mahl'; if the three-fold repeat is carried out to the full, this part of the dance becomes a substantial piece in its own right.

Movement linking also plays an important part; Knoep uses it between the opening Paduana–Galliard pairings of the first two sequences and then, in a way that anticipates the Hamburg suites of Becker and Reincken by more than a decade, it is extended across the entire sequence of 'XVIII. Ballet' to 'XXXI. Courant'. The 'Cantus I' part for the latter is shown in Figure 3.1. 'Courant, XXIX', 'Ballet XXX' and 'Courant XXXI' all open with the note sequence a'–d"–a', while 'Ballet XXVIII' uses the inverted d"–a'–d", albeit with a filling of the gaps between the notes.

The 'Cantus I' part was partially copied into manuscript *GB-Lbl* Add. MS 31438 under the title 'Lüder Knoep. a3. 1652'. While the copying of individual movements has been accurate, considerable licence has been taken over what has been included. As with the copy of Zuber's *Erster Theil newer Paduanen* found in the same manuscript, the collection has been modernised by omitting all the *Paduanen* and *Galliarden*. In addition, the copyist has restricted himself to the Ballets, Sarabandes and Courantes from the beginning and end of the collection; nothing is taken from the middle. Knoep's rising order of key is still apparent, but the balance and structure of his carefully ordered sequences have largely been lost.

As we have seen in the previous chapter, one of the clearest examples of ordering by sonority is Hans Hake's *Ander Theil Newer Pavanen, Sonaten, Arien, Balletten, Brandlen, Covranten, und Sarabanden, Mit 2.3.4.5. und 8. Instrumenten mit dem Basso Continuo* (Stade, 1654). At the time of the collection's publication, the title page tells us that Hake was a 'bestalten [appointed] Violisten und Musico der Stadt Stade'. But dedications to Swedish courtiers suggest either close personal contact or the use of this publication supporting an application for a position at court. If the latter is correct, Hake was apparently unsuccessful as, ten years later, it appears he was still in municipal employement, working in Hamburg with Becker.[18]

The organisation of *Ander Theil Newer Pavanen* is by increasing range of sonority – the instrumentation ranges from two violins without bass to a two-choir ensemble of strings and trombones, and it is telling that this is highlighted in the *Register* (index) given at the start of each part-book. The second page is reproduced in Figure 3.2.

The opening section of the collection comprises two Sonatas, the first followed by a single Courante, the second by a pair. And while the Courantes are in the Italian style and presumably intended only as instrumental music, the placing of two together in this section follows court practice where 'de suite' pairs of like dances were played consecutively without a break in order to provide enough music for functional dance.[19] Each Courante is in the same key as its preceding Sonata and appears to be paired with it although there is no linking to make the composer's intention completely clear. While this is clearly not an example of a Sonata preceding a suite, it seems to be another early example of the juxtaposition

Table 3.3 Contents of L. Knoep, *Erster Theil Newer Paduanen, Galliarden, Balletten, Mascaraden, Arien, Allemanden, Couranten und Sarabanden, Mit 3. Stimmen auff Violen zu Spielen/sampt dem General Bass* (Bremen, 1652)

Movement title	Key	Time signature	Comments
I. Paduana		¢	Linked to I. Paduana
II. Galliard a3		3	Single section, two strains
III. Ballo		¢	
IV. Saraband		3	Single section, two strains
V. Ballo	C major	¢	
VI. Courant		3	
VII. Paduana		¢	
[VIII.] Galliard a3		3	Linked to VII. Paduana
IX. Ballo		¢	Linked to VIII. Galliard
X. Courant	D minor	3	Linked to IX. Ballo
XI. Ballet		¢	Linked to X. Courant. Single section, two strains
XII. Saraband		3	No links
XIII. Paduana		¢	
XIV. Ballo	F major	¢	
XV. Courant		3	No linking between any movement in this sequence
XVI. Almand		¢	
XVII. Saraband		3	
XVIII. Paduana		¢	
XIX. Area	G minor	¢	Three sections, last in triple time
XX. Courant		3	Linked to XIX. Area
XXI. Area		¢	Linked to XVIII. Paduana. Three sections, last in triple time
XXII. Paduana		¢	
XXIII. ?Almand	A minor	¢;3	Three sections, last in triple time, '3. mahl'. 'Almand' is probably a misnaming of 'Area'
XXIV. Saraband		3	
XXV. Paduana		¢	
XXVI. Area	C minor	¢;3	Three sections, last in triple time
XXVII. Area		¢;3	Four sections, last two in triple time, last '3. mahl'
XXVIII. Ballet	D major	¢;3;¢	Three sections, duple–triple–duple. Linked to XXVII. Area
XXIX. Courant		3	Linked to XXVIII. Ballet
XXX. Ballet		¢	Single section, two strains. Linked to XXIX. Courant
XXXI. Courant		3	Linked to XXX. Ballet
XXXII. Ballet		¢	Single section, two strains

Movement title	Key	Time signature	Comments
XXXIII. Courant	G major	3	
XXXIV. Mascharada		¢;3;¢	Three sections, duple–triple–duple
XXXV. Saraband	C major	3	

Note: the strong similarity between 'XXIII. Almand' and the 'Areas' in the collection make it highly likely that the dance has been mislabelled.

Figure 3.1 Knoep, *Erster Theil Newer Paduanen,* 'XVIII. Ballet', 'XXIX. Courant', 'XXX. Ballet', 'XXXI. Courant'. 'Cantus I' part-book, shelfmark Utl.instr. mus.i tr. 13: Uppsala, universitetsbibliotek. Reproduced by kind permission.

of abstract and dance music. The closing part of the collection is devoted to two single Pavans written for *Cornetti* and trombones followed by a third for a polychoral ensemble of violin and trombone choirs. The part-books are unclear about the precise allocation of the instruments in the middle parts.

Music for two violins and bass, first in normal tuning and then in *scordatura*, makes up the central part. But ordering by sonority is not the only way in which the material is arranged. In the section written for 'zwo Violinen & Bass' (in normal tuning), there are five sequences, each one starting with a Paduan/Ballet combination, or just a Ballet, and ending with a Courante and Sarabande. The *Paduanen* are the expected substantial three-strain movements, and the first three Ballets are hardly less imposing. They are multi-sectioned and alternate between duple and triple time. The section using *scordatura*-tuned violins (25–32) contains two sequences of Pavan / Ballet / Courant / Saraband. Both Ballets are simple twin-strained affairs lacking the complexity of those in the previous section.

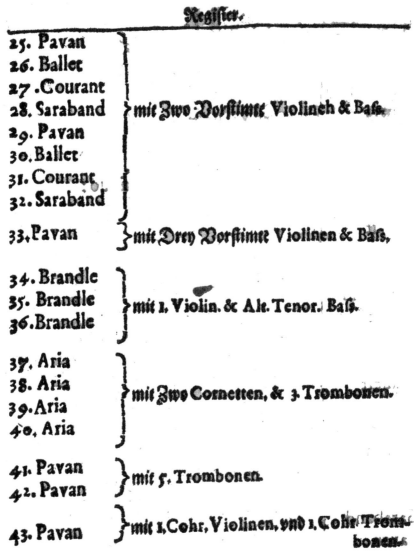

Figure 3.2 H. Hake, *Ander Theil Newer Pavanen, Sonaten, Arien, Balletten, Brandlen, Covranten, und Sarabanden, Mit 2.3.4.5. und 8. Instrumenten mit dem Basso Continuo* (Stade, 1654), 'Register', shelfmark K.8.d.18 (second page of 'Register'): London: The British Library Board. Reproduced by kind permission.

Despite their numbering as single items in the index, all three Bransles are complete sequences. The first two (34 and 35) use the full six-movement version including the Bransle Double and Montirande. The last of the three (36) uses the truncated four-movement version, so popular in the German lands. The use of both long and short versions of the sequence suggests a familiarity with the court repertoire where, as we have seen, Bransles were a mainstay of the ballroom. The openings of the movements in the second of the sequences (35) are shown in Example 3.3.

Comparison with the Bransle sequence by Bruslard given in the previous chapter as Example 2.12 shows the musical language to be completely idiomatic. Hake also takes care to use the equally idiomatic instrumentation of single violin, two violas and bass and goes to the trouble of writing the treble part in the French violin clef, its only appearance in the entire collection. All this seems to suggest a clear knowledge of the French-orientated music of the Swedish court and supports the assumption of contact with the Swedish courtiers of the dedication.

Nicolaus Hasse was organist of the *Marienkirche*, Rostock, from 1642 until 1671; his *Delitiæ musicæ* was published in Rostock in 1656. We cannot know if he knew of Hake's *Ander Theil*, but the two editions are similar in their organisation by sonority. The title page lists dances for '2. 3. und 4. Stimmen / Auff 2. oder 4. Violinen, 1. Violon' and, unusually, 'Clavicymbel oder Teorbe'. At the end of the collection, there is an 'Auffzug. 2 Clarin[i], 2 Heerpauken'. Unfortunately, not all the parts have survived; there is a figured 'Bassus Generalis' but not string bass and, more seriously, the wide gap in tessitura between 'Cantus II' and 'Tenor' shows that an 'Alto' part has been lost.[20]

The centre of the collection is made up of ten suites that are marked 'à4' in the *Bassus Generalis* part-book and these correspond to the '4. Violinen [two violins and

Example 3.3 Hake, *Ander Theil Newer Pavanen*, openings of the component dances of 'XXXV. Brandle a 4'.

two violas], 1. Violon' of the title page. In other words, the 'à4' marking implies four instruments plus continuo. The opening group of movements, eleven suites marked 'à2' in the *Bassus Generalis*, are therefore for one violin, one viola and continuo. A final *à2* group, placed after the *à4* suites comprises thirteen duple-time, treble and bass *Taniec* 'nach Pohlischer Arth gesetzet' (set in the Polish manner) along with a triple-time 'Proportion' re-casting for each one. The final *Auffzug* is also re-cast in triple time. The ordering of the collection by sonority is therefore clear; suites for two instruments and bass followed by the set for '4. Violinen' and bass, followed in turn by pairs of movements and their re-castings for just treble and bass.

This is not the only element of careful organisation. The suites in both three- and four-part instrumentation all have the same sequence of three movements, 'Allemand', 'Courant' and 'Serraband'. The Courantes and Sarabandes are all in the Italian style and follow broadly similar patterns. Movement linking is used throughout the collection in a variety of ways. In addition to the usual Allemande–Courante linking, the opening suite has links carried across all three movements while, in the third of the four-part suites, it is the Allemande and Sarabande that share material. Perhaps the most interesting example of variation technique is in the last suite, where it is not the melodic writing that principally links the Allemande and Courante, but the fanfare-like dialogue between the first and second violin. Example 3.4 shows the opening of both movements.

There are no examples of tertiary re-castings in the suites themselves. It is likely that Hasse wished to make a clear distinction between these and the following *Taniec* and 'Proportion' pairs. The re-casting of the latter is not the usual relationship of half a bar of duple time equalling a complete bar of triple time. Instead, the bar of triple time equals the complete bar of duple time. The last *Taniec* and 'Proportion' pair is not marked for any specific instrument, but the treble writing is obviously for a trumpet, matching the closing *Auffzug*.

This third section of the collection represents another early example of an Appendix containing 'alternative' music, this time Polish dances, and further reinforces the trends that we have seen in the dance-music collections of the 1650s. If we add the attractive quality of the suites in this collection, particularly those with the larger ensemble, it is hoped that, perhaps in the company of a more thoughtful modern edition, the music will gain greater recognition.

Matthias Kelz's self-published *Primitiæ musicales seu concentus novi harmonici* was published in Augsburg in 1658. Kelz was educated in Augsburg and spent his working life there. So it is curious that the title page has the place of his birth, 'Schongauiensis, &c' (Schongau in Bavaria) under his name on the title page. The title page also gives a clue to the character of the collection with instrumentation and a list of movement types conspicuously marked 'Italis dicti:' and therefore given in Italian. It is a trio collection, for two violins, 'Basso Viola' and 'organo, overo Basso Continuo'. Table 3.4 lists the contents of the collection.

Example 3.5 shows the first strain of '15. Couranta' and the 'Tardissimo' indication over the note blackening at the end of the strain. The blackened notes mark three accented semibreves played across the beat. Apart from the unusual tie between the last two, Kelz's use of them at the cadence of a strain is

The aftermath of war: 1648–59 61

Example 3.4 N. Hasse, *Delitiæ musicæ, Das ist Schöne/lustige und anmuthige Allemanden, Couranten und Sarabanden* (Rostock, 1656), '61. Allemand' and '62. Courant'.

Table 3.4 Contents of M. Kelz, *Primitiæ musicales, seu concentus novi harmonici. Italis dicti: le Sonate, Intrade, Mascarade, Balletti, Alemande, Gagliardi, Arie, Volte, Serenade, è Sarabande* (Augsburg, 1658)

Movement title	Key	Time	Movement title	Key	Time
1. Sonata	C major	¢ – 3/2	15. Couranta	B minor	3/2
2. Intrada	C major	¢	16. Serenada	B minor	3/2
3. Mascarada	C major	¢	17. Couranta	B minor	3/2
4. Mascarada	C major	¢	18. Sarabanda	B minor	3/4
5. Couranta	C major	3/2	19. Sonata	D major	¢
6. Aria	C major	C	20. Ballet	D major	¢
7. Sonata	D major	¢ – 3/2	21. Alemande	D major	¢
8. Mascarada	D major	¢	22. Gagliarda	D major	¢
9. Ballet	D major	C	23. Volta	D major	3/2
10. Aria	D major	3/2	24. Serenada	D major	3/2
11. Gagliarda	D major	3/2	25. Sarabanda	D major	3/2
12. Sarabanda	D major	3/2	26. Sonata	A major	¢ – 3/2
13. Ballet	B minor	¢	27. Couranta	A minor	3/2
14. Volta	B minor	3/2			

62 *The aftermath of war: 1648–59*

Example 3.5 Kelz, *Primitiæ musicales*, '15. Couranta'.

in keeping with the usage of this musical device in the town repertory, and the 'Tardissimo' drawing-out of the rhythm is in keeping with end-of-strain broadening in Hammerschmidt's collections. Once again, we have a movement in a collection that clearly displays the considerable distance between the town-music repertoire and functional dance music. Elsewhere, the collection is unusually detailed in its performing indications; many movements have indications such as the 'Dolcemente' at the start of '17. Couranta' and 'Moderatè' at the head of '18. Sarabanda'.

If Kelz had particular players in mind when assembling this collection, their technical standards must have been high. Both violins are given passages extending to both ends of their compasses and the frequently high tessitura for the first violin suggests a player specialising in the high register of the instrument. In keeping with the title page, all the *Correnti* and Sarabandes are firmly in the Italian style. Kelz does not even use the hybrid versions of the dances that were popular with other town musicians.

At first sight, it would seem that the Sonatas at the start of the C major and first D major sequences are early examples of an abstract movement being used to preface dance sequences. But we should be wary of considering Kelz's Sonatas to be examples of Sonatas preceding suites. *Primitiæ musicales* is no more than a collection of pieces arranged by key. There is none of the duple-/triple-time relationship that characterises Hammerschmidt's collections, and the use of variation technique is completely absent. In addition, the final '27. Couranta' is clearly separated from its preceding '26. Sonata' as it is written for 'Variatio Chordarum' – *scordatura*-tuned violins. As the Sonata keeps to standard tuning, it is difficult to see how the two pieces can be thought of as a single unit. In common with Ahle's *Sinfonien* and Hake's *Sonaten* considered above, the presence of the Sonatas is clearly part of the same trend in the 1650s juxtaposing abstract and dance music; but it is nothing more than that.

The final collection to be considered in this chapter clearly demonstrates the problems often posed by manuscript copies claiming to be taken from printed collections. Georg Zuber apparently issued a second volume of *newer Paduanen* in 1659, ten years after the appearance of his first collection. Göhler lists it in abbreviated form as 'Ander Theil, neuer Pad. Gall. Alam. Ball. Cour. u. Sarab. m. 2. & 4. St. nebenst d. B. c.' published by Wust in Frankfurt am Main.[21] Walther also lists a second volume, presumably the same, comprising fifty-four pieces and written for two and four voices along with continuo.[22] Unfortunately, the only surviving possible source is a 'Cantus I' part in manuscript Add. MS. 31438, where it is described as 'Gregorig Zubern ander Theil'. The contents are detailed along with music incipits in Example A.1 in Appendix 2, although the unreliability of this source is clearly demonstrated by its inclusion without attribution of 'XXII. Mascharada I à5' and 'XXVI. Courente à5' from Hammerschmidt's 1639 *Ander Theil*.

However, even with such problems of authorship taken into account, it is still possible to see the remnants of a similar plan of organisation to Zuber's 1649 collection, with sequences of movements grouped together by key and some use of linking. It is likely that the opening sequence of Allemande, Courante, Sarabande, Ballet and second Sarabande was repeated elsewhere in the collection. But even here, problems are still apparent; the title of 'Allemand' for the opening movement that ends in triple time is highly questionable, especially in the light of Zuber's avoidance of the dance type in the 1649 collection. It is possible that this is a mislabelling emanating from the original printed edition and, as we have seen, it would not be the only instance of this type of error. The unreliability and scarcity of sources for Zuber's *Ander Theil* are frustrating, and it must be hoped that more material may be discovered at some time in the future.

The rise of, and increasing interest in, the concept of careful organisation of content that has been described above came to dominate suite collections from the 1660s until the end of the town-suite era. And while we cannot have any idea of day-to-day conversations between composer, publisher and printer where they existed as separate entities, the question of who was responsible for this trend is of great importance. Was it principally the influence of the composer, the publisher or both? The next chapter deals with the period 1660–75, a time that saw the issue of a number of compilations of dance music as well as the standard single-composer collections, and it is these compilations that enable an attempt at separating out the roles of publisher and town composer.

Notes

1 D. Speer, *Grund-richtiger/Kurtz/leicht und nöthiger Unterricht der musicalischen Kunst* (Ulm, 1687), pp. 84–5. The description of the viola types is repeated in the second, expanded and revised, edition published ten years later. The viola or 'viola basso' that often appears as the bass instrument in some ensembles was considered by Walther to be a 'kleine Baß-Geigen' and the equivalent of the cello. See: J. Walther, *Musicalisches Lexicon Oder Musicalische Bibliothec* (Leipzig, 1732); modern edition, ed. F. Ramm (Kassel: Bärenreiter, 2001), p. 573. Speer also describes a 'Bass-Violon' of six strings with GG–C–F–A–d–g tuning: *Grund-richtiger* (1687), pp. 87 and 89.
2 Hammerschmidt, or his printer, marks the first variation 'Variatio 2'. The 1957 modern edition of *Ander Theil* moves this entire movement to the end of the collection without any explanation. See A. Hammerschmidt (ed. H. Mönkemeyer), *"Ander Theil": instrumentalwerke zu 5 und 3 stimmen*, Das Erbe deutsche Musik 49 (Kassel: Nagels, 1957).
3 Speer's linking across collections is dealt with in Chapter 5.
4 G. Karstädt, 'Zuber, Gregor' in L. Finscher (ed.), *Die Musik in Geschichte und Gegenwart*, 29 vols (Kassel: Bärenreiter, 2005), Personenteil 17, pp. 1563–4.
5 Walther (ed. Ramm), *Musicalisches Lexicon*, p. 593.
6 R.A. Rasch, 'David Petersen [Pietersen]' in D.L. Root (ed.) *Grove music online* (www.oxfordmusiconline.com) (accessed 26 November 2014).
7 Both manuscripts are catalogued in S. Voss, *Die Musikaliensammlung im Pfarrarchiv Udestedt* (Schneverdingen: Karl Dieter Wagner, 2006).
8 J. Schop (ed. A. Spohr), *Erster Theil newer Paduanen* (Middleton, WI: A-R Editions, 2003), Preface, p. xii.
9 Göhler 2/1726. Walther (ed. Ramm), *Musicalisches Lexicon*, p. 593.
10 These movements are not given in Voss, *Musikaliensammlung*.
11 The manuscript is digitally reproduced online at http://orka.bibliothek.uni-kassel.de/viewer/image/1414585425981/1 (accessed 12 November 2014).
12 RISM lists further exemplars of the printed edition under H 1962 and HH 1962. Despite diligent searches, the staff at the Gesamtkirchengemeinde library in Regensburg and the Katherinenkirche library in Salzwedel have been unable to find them. It seems that the supposed exemplars have been confused with copies of Hammerschmidt's *Erster Fleiß* and *Ander Theil*. I am most grateful to the staff of the libraries concerned and also to Christoph Meinel for making further enquiries on my behalf.
13 F. Noack, *Sinfonie und Suite von Gabrieli bis Schumann* (Leipzig: Breitkopf und Härtel, 1932), p. 38.
14 Göhler, 2/20: 'Neuer Sonaten, Pad., Intr., Arien, Ball., Alem., Cour. U. Sarab. m. 2. 3. 4. 5. St.'
15 F. Piersig and D. Schröder 'Knop [Knoep, Knopff], Lüder' in D.L. Root (ed.) *Grove music online* (www.oxfordmusiconline.com) (accessed 26 November 2014). I have retained the spelling 'Knoep' in favour of 'Knöp' or 'Knop' as it the version used on the title pages of his printed editions.
16 P. Whitehead, 'Austro-German printed sources of instrumental music, 1630 to 1700', PhD dissertation (University of Pennsylvania, 1996), p. 566, dismisses the collection as 'arranged by key into groupings of from two to six dances'.
17 Both RISM A/1 and *Grove music online*, give the incorrect date of 1651.
18 U. Grapenthin, 'Becker [Bekker, Bäkker], Dietrich [Diederich, Diedrich, Dierich] in D.L. Root (ed.), *Grove music online* (www.oxfordmusiconline.com) (accessed 20 November 2014).
19 *CCS*, p. 46.
20 In the modern edition (ed. A. Bares (Albese con Cassano: Musedita, 2010)), the editor has not realised that the 'Alto' part is missing. There are also numerous other errors. See also Example 2.9 in the previous chapter, where the missing parts have been reconstructed.
21 Göhler, 2/1727.
22 Walther (ed. Ramm), *Musicalisches Lexicon*, p. 593.

4 Concepts of careful organisation: 1660–75

Especially when we take into consideration the music by Leipzig and Hamburg composers (dealt with separately in Chapters 6 and 7), the period from 1660 to 1675 can be seen as a golden age for consort-suite composition in the seventeenth-century German lands. While the 1650s saw the rise of collections in which careful ordering of content played some part, the 1660s and early 70s were a time when careful organisation became fundamental to the construction of dance-music publications. By dealing with the single-composer collections from 1660–75 outside Leipzig and Hamburg, and contrasting them with three publisher-led compendium editions from the same time, I will shed light on the questions of influence posed at the end of the previous chapter. The three compendium editions are the collections of dance music issued in 1660, 1666 and 1670 by the publisher Balthasar Christoph Wust.

Wust was born into a family of well-established Frankfurt am Main booksellers, and became a leading figure in this important trading centre with its long associations with the printing industry. Principally a Bible publisher, he also appears to have had a particular interest in music. Wust was the dedicatee of Johann Caspar Horn's sixth volume of *Parergon musicium* and was described by the latter as a 'Berühmten Buchhändlern in Franckfurt am Mayn' (well-known book seller in Frankfurt am Main) and 'einem hornischen guten Freunde / und grossen Liebhaber der Music' (a good friend of Horn's and great lover of music). While Wust played no apparent part in the production of this volume of *Parergon musicum* – Georg Heinrich Fromman was the publisher – it is possible that he contributed something towards the printing costs of this or other volumes in the series.

The first of Wust's own compendium editions, *Exercitium musicum Bestehend in auszerlesenen Sonaten, Galliarden, Allemanden, Balletten, Intraden, Arien, Chiquen, Couranten, Sarabanden, und Branlen* (Frankfurt am Main, 1660; hereafter *EM 1*), is scored for two treble parts and bass. While the two trebles are labelled 'Cantus I' and 'Cantus II', the inclusion of music using *scordatura* violin tuning makes it clear that violins were intended for at least part of the collection, if not all. Given the inclusion in many printed suite editions of two bass parts, one figured and one unfigured, *EM 1*'s single bass part suggests that either a further part has been lost or that the single 'Bassus continuus' part, with its occasional figuring, was an economy measure to keep printing costs as low as possible.

'Zusammen getragen' (collected and arranged in order) was how Wust described the contents. *EM 1* is not the work of a single composer, but a collection of 113 pieces spanning both court and town repertoires; after the 12 multi-section Sonatas and one Sonatina at the start, the remainder is exclusively dance music. However, Wust was not the first person to produce a compendium edition of this type; Michael Praetorius had issued his *Terpsichore* collection in 1612, but only two years before the publication of *EM 1*, Johann Ernst Rieck had issued *Neue Allemanden, Giques, Balletten, Couranten, Sarabanden, und Gavotten* (Strasbourg, 1658).

Rieck was a town musician, but he had connections at the court of the Margrave of Brandenburg and it is hardly surprising that some of the material in his collection comes from the courtly repertoire.[1] While *Neue Allemanden* has pieces for *à4* ensembles, the major part of the collection is made up of trios, some of keyboard or lute origin, with Rieck providing a middle line to existing treble and bass parts where required.

The material in *EM 1* also appears to be assembled from a variety of sources and it is not fanciful to suggest that Rieck clearly influenced Wust's decision to issue a wide-ranging volume of trios. If sources are mostly identified in *Neue Allemanden*, there is noticeable reticence on the part of Wust to name his composers. The preface of *EM 1* baldly states that the music is 'von den fürnembsten Componisten dieser Zeit' (by the foremost composers of our time) but only two are named: Guillaume Dumanoir and Jean Artus Leborgne, the latter commonly identified, as he is here, simply as 'Artus' ('CXII. La Bouree dartus').[2] Both were dancing masters in Louis XIV's 'petite Escurie' and Parisian violinists; it seems that their dance music was widely disseminated in the German lands. Dance movements by the two of them are included in the Kassel manuscripts of *D-Kl* 2° Ms Mus.61, and the manuscript collection *S-Uu* IMhs 409.

Wust's 'XL. Sarabande' in *EM 1* also exists in manuscript *S-VX* Mus. Ms. 4b where it is part of 'Ouverture d'Experience', a suite in the French manner. As the name of the composer is not given in either source, it is difficult to say if it is genuinely French or the work of a German composer imitating the French style. Only the treble line has been written into the manuscript, but space has been left for a second treble part and bass to be inserted later, a further example of the single-line transmission of so much dance music.

There is English music as well as French in Wust's collection, again without attribution. Gordon Dodd's *Thematic index of music for viols* for the Viola da Gamba Society of Great Britain has identified pieces by Charles Coleman and William Lawes, and these are shown in Table 4.1 along with concordances from John Playford's *Court-Ayres or Pavins, Almains, Corant's and Sarabands* (London, 1655).[3] The numbers next to the composers' names are those given in Dodd's index.

Table 4.1 English music in N.B.N. (ed.), *Exercitium musicum, Bestehend in auszerlesenen Sonaten, Galliarden, Allemanden, Balletten, Intraden, Arien, Chiquen, Couranten, Sarabanden, und Branlen* (Frankfurt am Main, 1660)

Exercitium musicum	Composer	Court-Ayres
XXVI. Allemande	Charles Coleman (396)	145 Ayre
XXIIX. Sarab:	Charles Coleman (398)	147 Saraband
XXXI. Allemande	William Lawes (232)	136 Ayre
XXXII. Cour. Sara.	? John Jenkins	N/A
XXXIII. Allem.	William Lawes (221)	134 Almaine
XLIV. Cour.	Charles Coleman (106)	N/A
LX. Paduana	Charles Coleman (213)	189 Pavin
LXI. Allem.	Charles Coleman (216)	190 Almaine
LXII. Cour.	Charles Coleman (221)	N/A
LXIV. Allem.	Charles Coleman (220)	N/A
LXIIX. Aria	Charles Coleman (292)	2 Ayre

Note: 'XXXII. Cour. Sara.' is concordant with Jenkins 54/10 in Dodd (rev. Ashbee), *Thematic index* where the latter is described as 'spurious or doubtful'. The *EM 1* concordance is incorrectly described as '2 pieces'.

The four pieces in the table not included in *Court-Ayres* maybe explained by the re-issue of Playford's volume in Amsterdam in 1657 under the title *Engels Speel-thresoor* ('English Treasury of Instrumental Music').[4] As this publication does not survive, it is difficult to know if Wust used Playford or the Amsterdam copy as his source. But *Court-Ayres* comprises 245 pieces while *Engels Speel-thresoor* apparently had 12 more in its corresponding section, presumably of English origin.[5] So it is possible that the latter was Wust's source and the four dances in *EM 1* not found in *Court-Ayres* were among those included as extras in the Amsterdam version.

Playford only gave the treble and bass parts of the dances in *Court-Ayres* and it is likely that there was no attempt to add anything further in *Engels Speel-thresoor*.[6] So it was necessary for *EM 1*'s editor to add a second violin part in the manner of both Praetorius and Rieck, who had carried out similar tasks for their compendium editions. Wust's editor, only identified as 'N.B.N.', was presumably responsible for these additional parts, often of dubious quality. The lack of competence is clearly shown in Example 4.1. The new 'Cantus II' part of 'XXVI. Allemande' does not provide the expected second-treble to Playford's original ('145 Ayre' by Charles Coleman in *Court-Ayres*); instead, it imposes what can only be seen as a new first treble part over the top of the existing one. Apart from the curious bare fifths of the opening, this was mostly achieved by the addition of sixths and thirds to the original treble line. The harmonic consequences of this formulaic construction are often, as in the third and seventh bars, unconvincing.

Playford's pieces were probably not the only ones that needed the addition of at least one extra part. As with the extract from 'Ouverture d'Experience' discussed

68 *Concepts of careful organisation: 1660–75*

Example 4.1 Comparison between J. Playford, *Court-Ayres or Pavins, Almains, Corant's and Sarabands* (London, 1655), and *Exercitium musicum*, 'XXVI. Allemande'.

above, it is likely that most, if not all, of the French dance music at the end of the collection was received as a single treble line. As we have seen, Wust's 'CXII. La Bouree dartus' is a version of a widely disseminated Bourée by Leborgne. The same dance also appears in a hitherto-unrecorded concordance with the so-called Hintze manuscript of keyboard pieces (*US-NH* Ma.21 H59) copied by the Hamburg town musician Matthias Weckmann.[7] The first strains of each version are compared in Example 4.2. Unfortunately, Leborgne's original appears to have been lost, so it is difficult to know the extent of Weckmann's elaboration or any simplification in Wust's version.

Concepts of careful organisation: 1660–75 69

Example 4.2 J.A. Leborgne, 'CXII. La Bouree dartus' in N.B.N. (ed.), *Exercitium musicum*, and 'Petite Bouree' (manuscript *US-NH* Ma.21 H59).

Despite this, the difference in competence between the two is clear; in the sections that I have marked with an 'x', the harmonic progression in *EM 1* is weak and ineffectual. With only a small change, the version copied and probably harmonised by Weckmann becomes very much stronger. And while there are similarities between the two bass lines, they seem to be no more than coincidental. If, as seems highly likely, Wust (or his editor) was working from nothing but a treble line, it shows the lack of imagination, if not incompetence, in parts of *EM 1*.

There are times, however, when standards are higher, especially in the six anonymous pieces using two *scordatura* violins. 'XIIX. Courante' in this group displays the frequent and imaginative use of note blackening used to disrupt the rhythm of an Italian *Corrente*; it is typical of the work of a skilled German town musician of the 1650s.[8] The second treble part is also a model of its kind. Given such disparity throughout the collection, it seems that some sources were received as complete trios and were printed unchanged. If others needed rather more work, it is difficult to believe that the additional second-treble and bass parts are from the hand of an experienced musician. The suggestion that 'N.B.N.' was Johann Hector Beck, the editor of the two later *Exercitium* editions, is highly unlikely; the latter show his standard of work to have been very much higher and he surely would not have been responsible for the incompetence shown in the examples above.[9] It is more likely that 'N.B.N.' was the publisher Wust himself, or one of his employees.[10]

70 *Concepts of careful organisation: 1660–75*

If the musical standards of parts of *EM 1* are often dubious, the organisation of the collection is more interesting; it mirrors trends of the middle and late 1650s and, as we shall see, may well have exerted a major influence on town-suite collections of the next decade. Wust's preface is unhelpful; he merely tells us that

> Diese Sonaten, Galliarden, Balletté, &c. ... zusammen getragen / und in eine solche Ordnung gerichtet / daß zweiffels ohne / einem jeden Music verständigen dieses alles / zumahlen die verstimte Stücke auff der Violino nicht unangenehm seyn.
>
> (These Sonatas, Galliards, Ballets etc. are collected and arranged in such an order that, without doubt, each musical [composition] is fully understood and, in particular, that the scordatura pieces on the violin are not made unpleasant.)

Care is certainly taken with the *scordatura* pieces; they are headed '6 movements for two re-tuned violins' ('6. Drück/mit 2. verstimbten Violinen') at the opening, and 'End of the re-tuned ballets' ('Ende der verstimbten Balletten') at the close.

The 'understanding' of the title page also appears to be based on the use of an Allemande, Intrada or Paduan to start nearly every fresh sequence of pieces. Apart from the sonatas at the start of the collection and the Bransles at the end, the sequences are also arranged in ascending order of key. However, there is little consistency over the choice of dance types. For example, the single sequence in C minor has the following that seems to be nothing more than a succession of duple- and triple-time pairings:

> XXXI. Allemande – XXXII. Cour[ante] Sara[bande] – XXXIII. Allem. – XXXIV. Courante – XXXV. Allem: – XXXVI. Sarab.

On the other hand, the second of the D minor sequences has a sequence that appears to have been intended as a suite:

> XLVII. Allem: – XLIIX.Courante – XLIX. Sarabande – L. Chique

The five Bransle suites placed at the end of *EM 1* provide a clear distinction between functional dance music and the town-music repertoire in other parts of the collection.[11] Wust draws attention to the French origins of the music by including, for the first time, the composer's name for three of them – Dumanoir. Two of the five Bransles use all six movements of the sequence but three, including two by Dumanoir, use the shortened four-movement version favoured in the German lands. They are unlikely to have originated from France in this form (see Chapter 2). 'CVI. La du Chesse', the widely circulated 'La Duchesse' Courante, is placed between the fourth and fifth Bransles; it appears to be unrelated to either. In grouping these Bransles together at the end, Wust was not doing anything new. He was merely following collections such as Zuber's 1649 *Erster Theil newer*

Paduanen where, as we have seen, two sequences of functional dance music provided a conclusion. Indeed, it is likely that Wust knew of this collection, for he had published Zuber's second volume only a year before *EM 1*.[12] By following Zuber's example and helping to bring the concept of an 'alternative' suite (see Chapter 2) of functional dance music to a wider audience, *EM 1* may have exerted an organisational influence well beyond its artistic worth. And while little care seems to have taken about the music itself, the ordering of the collection shows that, as a publisher, Wust was receptive to concepts of careful organisation. It may be that publishers elsewhere also saw the advantages of these concepts and were happy to promote them.

EM 1 is the probable source for a sequence of movements copied into manuscript *GB-Lbl* Add. MS 31438. As we have seen in previous chapters, it contains music from various printed editions. Out of twenty-four movements in the manuscript that make up a sequence headed in a later hand 'Matthew Locke', the first fifteen are taken from Wust's collection. With some omissions, they largely correspond with movements 'XXXI. Allemande' to 'LIII. Sarab[ande]' of *EM 1*. The omissions were presumably down to whims of the copyist. I have not been able to find a source for the remaining nine movements of the manuscript sequence, but it is possible that some of them came from *Engels Speel-thresoor*.[13]

The second volume of Wust's *Exercitium* series, *Continuatio exercitii musici Bestehend in außerlesenen Allemanden, Balletten, Gavotten, Giquen, Couranten und Sarabanden* was published in 1666 (hereafter *EM 2*). Unlike the *à3* instrumentation of the first volume, it uses the four-part combination of two violins, viola and bass. Despite the seeming success of *EM 1*, this may well reflect the apparent decline in the popularity of the trio suite during the 1660s. This time, the editor of *EM 2* is identified: Johann Hector Beck, a one-time town musician in Frankfurt am Main, where Wust had his publishing house.[14] The collection is divided into two and the title page makes a clear separation between the source for the first fifty pieces and the rest:

> außerlesenen Allemanden, Balletten, Gavotten, Giquen, Couranten und Sarabanden, Welche theils von den besten Violisten dieser Zeit mit Discant und Baß gesetzt / den Liebhabern aber der edlen Music zu gefallen zwey Stimmen und General Baß neben den ersten funffzig Stücken darzu componirt / und also alle mit zweyen Discänten / einer Braccio und zweyen Bässen.
>
> (exquisite Allemandes, Ballets, Gavottes, Gigues, Courantes and Sarabandes, set for the treble and bass by the leading violinists of our time, but in order to find favour with lovers of fine music, there have been additionally composed two voices and a *Generalbass* to match the first fifty pieces, so that all of them are [now] for two treble parts, one viola and two basses.)

For these first fifty pieces, the initials 'J.H.B.' appear at the head of every page of the part-books and it is reasonable to assume that most, if not all, are by Beck himself. On the evidence presented here, Beck is at least competent and often more than that. Example 4.3 shows 'XXXII. Sarabande'. While its rhythm and structure are perhaps over-dependent on the common rhythmic formula used by town musicians, the inner parts show an imaginative use of dissonance and further highlight the differences in quality between *EM 2* and parts of *EM 1*. The example also shows Beck's interest in dynamic contrast; while the *piano* passages in 'XXXII. Sarabande' are not strict echoes, they look back to the type of echo movement that Hammerschmidt was writing in his suite collections of the previous decade.

Example 4.3 J.H. Beck (ed.), *Continuatio exercitii musici, Bestehend in außerlesenen Allemanden, Balletten, Gavotten, Giquen, Couranten und Sarabanden* (Frankfurt am Main, 1666), 'XXXII. Sarabande'.

Beck (or Wust) also took care to organise the contents of these fifty pieces; every sequence contains a core Allemande, Ballet, Courante, Sarabande and Gigue, with extra movements added at the end. The group of extra movements always ends with a second Sarabande. The beginning and end of each sequence are therefore completely clear to the performer. The opening sequence of movements is typical:

I. Allemande – II. Ballet – III. Courante – IV. Sarabande – V. Giqve – VI. Gavotte – VII. Gavotte – VIII. Sarabande

Curiously, there is no attempt to arrange the sequences in ascending order of key. For the second part of *EM 2*, Playford's editions were again a source of material. The London publisher was clearly aware of foreign piracy and drew attention to it in the preface of his *Courtly Masquing Ayres* (London, 1662). The latter was a re-issue of 'only about a 100 of the most Choice' pieces from *Court-Ayres* along with another '200 [pieces] joyned with them [that] were never till now Printed'; the reasons for producing such a volume lay in the unexpected success of the earlier collection that 'found so good acceptance both in this kingdome and beyond Seas, that there it was Reprinted to my great damage'.

Playford may well have had the Amsterdam edition of *Court-Ayres* in mind when he wrote this, but it did not stop further piracy; *Courtly Masquing Ayres* appeared in Amsterdam in 1664 as a second volume of *Engels Speelthresoor*.[15] And it did not stop Wust, or Beck, from plundering on a far greater scale than *EM 1*. Of the 104 movements in *EM 2*, 45 are taken from Playford or the Amsterdam re-issues. Not surprisingly, Wust is silent over the origins of these pieces; his preface merely refers to 'den fürnehmsten Componisten dieser Zeit' (the foremost composers of this time) and the title page to 'den besten Violisten dieser Zeit' (the best violinists of this time). Table 4.2 details the movements in this part of the collection along with their known sources. In the case of 'XCVII. Ballet' (Coleman 268), which appears in both Playford collections, I have given the details of each. None of the concordances given below have hitherto been recognised.

Beck's task of providing additional instrumental parts for this half of the collection was less than the title page suggests. Both *Court-Ayres* and *Courtly Masquing Ayres* (and presumably the now-lost Amsterdam editions) contain bass lines, and Beck uses them every time albeit with occasional minor modifications. The second bass part is merely a figured version of the first.

The choice of organisation of the Playford pieces was presumably made with the intention of producing a parallel with the sequences by Beck in the first half of the collection. This was not difficult; a good deal of *Court-Ayres* and *Courtly Masquing Ayres* was already arranged in quasi-suite sequences. With one exception, which may be the result of a printer's error in its title (LVI. Ballet), all the movements in this part of *EM 2* are similarly arranged, starting with an Allemande and finishing with either a Sarabande or Gigue (see Table 4.2). In addition, it seems that Beck sometimes selected pieces with a similar melodic outline in order to give an impression of movement linking. For example, 'LX. Allemande' and 'LXII. Sarabande' appear to be linked together and therefore the work of the same composer; but the Allemande is by Davis Mell and the Sarabande by Benjamin Rogers.

While a careful selection process is often evident, there remain other times when Beck's choice of movement from his Playford sources is curious.[16] The *Courtly Masquing Ayres* sequence of '276 Ayre' / '277 Corant' / '278 Saraband' – all by Locke – is broken up after '277 Corant' by the insertion of a different Sarabande

Table 4.2 Movements in the second section of Beck (ed.), *Continuatio exercitii musici*

Continuatio exercitii musici	Composer	Key	Source
LI. Allemande	Davis Mell (2/26)	A minor	*CMA* 207 Ayre
LII. Courante	Davis Mell (2/27)	A minor	*CMA* 208 Coranto
LIII. Courante	Davis Mell (2/28)	A minor	*CMA* 209 Coranto
LIV. Sarabande	Davis Mell (2/29)	A minor	*CMA* 210 Saraband
LV. Giqve	Davis Mell (2/30)	A minor	*CMA* 211 Country dance
LVI. Ballet	?	A minor	?
LVII. Ballet	?	A minor	?
LVIII. Sarabande	?	A minor	?
LIX. Gavotte	Matthew Locke (19/67)	A minor	*CMA* 273 A dance
LX. Allemande	Davis Mell (4/42)	B flat major	*CMA* 216 Ayre
LXI. Courante	?	B flat major	?
LXII. Sarabande	Benjamin Rogers (4/60)	B flat major	*CMA* 154 Saraband
LXIII. Allemande	Davis Mell (4/46)	B flat major	*CMA* 225 Ayre
LXIV. Ballet	Thomas Prat (1/1)	B flat major	*CMA* 186 Ayre 'or Amsterdam'
LXV. Courante	Thomas Prat (1/2)	B flat major	*CMA* 187 Coranto
LXVI. Sarabande	Davis Mell (4/44)	Bflat major	*CMA* 223 Saraband
LXVII. Gavotte	Benjamin Rogers (4/58)	B flat major	*CMA* 152 A Morisco
LXVIII. Ballet	Matthew Locke (19/63)	B flat major	*CMA* 269 Ayre
LXIX. Giqve	?	B flat major	?
LXX. Courante	William Gregory (3/50)	B flat major	*CMA* 264 Corant
LXXI. Sarabande	Matthew Locke (19/64)	B flat major	*CMA* 270 Saraband
LXXII. Allemande	John Jenkins (55/31)	B minor	*CA* 29 Almaine
LXXIII. Ballet	Christopher Simpson (4/20)	B minor	*CA* 38 Ayre
LXXIV. Courante	William Lawes (12/163)	B minor	*CMA* 6 Corant
LXXV. Sarabande	?	B minor	?
LXXVI. Allemande	Thomas Gibbes (1/11)	E minor	*CMA* 292 Ayre
LXXVII. Ballet	Thomas Gibbes (1/12)	E minor	*CMA* 293 Ayre

LXXVIII. Courante	Thomas Gibbes (1/13)	E minor	CMA 294 Corant
LXXIX. Sarabande	Thomas Gibbes (1/14)	E minor	CMA 295 Saraband
LXXX. Gavotte	Thomas Gibbes (1/15)	E minor	CMA 296 Morisco
LXXXI. Giqve	Thomas Gibbes (1/16)	E minor	CMA 297 A Jigg
LXXXII. Allemande	John Banister	E minor	CMA 247 Ayre
LXXXIII. Courante	John Banister	E minor	CMA 248 Corant
LXXXIV. Sarabande	John Banister	E minor	CMA 249 Saraband
LXXXV. Giqve	John Banister	E minor	CMA 250 Jigg
LXXXVI. Allemande	Matthew Locke (19/74)	A major	CMA 280 Ayre
LXXXVII. Ballet	Matthew Locke (19/70)	A major	CMA 276 Ayre
LXXXVIII. Courante	Matthew Locke (19/71)	A major	CMA 277 Corant
LXXXIX. Sarabande	Davis Mell (2/34)	A major	CMA 215 Saraband
XC. Giqve	Matthew Locke (19/73)	A major	CMA 279 The Simerons Dance
XCI. Sarabande	Matthew Locke (19/72)	A major	CMA 278 Saraband
XCII. Allemande	Benjamin Rogers (4/50)	G major	CMA 144 Ayre
XCIII. Ballet	William Lawes (12/170)	G major	CMA 25 Ayre
XCIV. Courante	William Lawes (12/171)	G major	CMA 26 Corant
XCV. Sarabande	?	G major	?
XCVI. Allemande	?	G major	?
XCVII. Ballet	Charles Coleman (8/268)	G major	CA 60 Ayre; CMA 58 Ayre
XCVIII. Courante	Davis Mell (2/21)	G major	CMA 203 Coranto
XCIX. Sarabande	Benjamin Rogers (4/53)	G major	CMA 147 Saraband
C. Allemande	Benjamin Rogers (4/54)	G major	CMA 148 Ayre
CI. Ballet	Davis Mell (2/18)	G major	CMA 202 Ayre
CII. Courante	Davis Mell (2/22)	G major	CMA 204 Coranto
CIII. Allemande	Benjamin Rogers (4/55)	G major	CMA 149 Saraband
CIV. Sarabande	?	G major	?

Notes: *CA* = *Court-Ayres*, *CMA* = *Courtly Masquing Ayres*. LXXII–LXIV are transposed from Playford's G minor. The index numbers next to the composers' names are those in Dodd (rev. Ashbee), *Thematic index of music for viols*. The pieces by John Banister are not given in the thematic index. Three pieces used in *EM 2*, 'LXXIV. Courante', 'XCIII. Ballet' and 'XCIV. Courante', are also found in Playford's *A Musicall Banquet* (London, 1651).

76 *Concepts of careful organisation: 1660–75*

by Davis Mell and the so-called 'Simerons Dance' also by Locke (see Table 4.2). Why did Beck change the logical original sequence? We can only assume that he wanted to enlarge it but still, for reasons that are not clear, retain Locke's '278 Saraband' as the final movement.

EM 2 must have sold well, for Wust re-issued it in 1670 bound together with *Continuatio exercitii musici secunda, bestehend in außerlesenen Paduanen, Intraden, Allemanden, Balletten, Gavotten, Giqven, Couranten und Sarabanden* (Frankfurt am Main, 1670; hereafter *EM 3*). No separate preface was given in the single surviving copy of the new collection and we have to rely on the minimal title page to tell us that the treble and bass pieces are said to be 'mit zweyen Stimmen und General-Bass vermehrt / und also alle mit zweyen Discanten einer Braccio und zweyen Bässen' (enlarged with two [additional] instruments and *General-Baß*, and thus all with two treble, one viola and two bass parts).

The contents of *EM 3* are rather more disparate than Wust's previous collection and there is no suggestion of two separate sections. But of the 102 movements in *EM 3*, 47 are still taken from Playford (or the Amsterdam re-issues). As the supply of music from *Courtly Masquing Ayres* had been partially depleted by its use in *EM 2*, it is no surprise that Beck (or Wust) returned to the earlier *Court-Ayres* for material in *EM 3*. Table 4.3 lists the concordances between Wust's and Playford's volumes, all of them hitherto unknown. Where the material used by Beck appears in both *Court-Ayres* and *Courtly Masquing Ayres*, I have again provided details from each edition.

For the pieces in *EM 3* not taken from Playford, 'LXXXV. Courante. à4' concords with *D-UDa* 38a/9 and 38b/8, manuscript sources of Georg Zuber's otherwise-lost collection of *Paduanen, Galliarden, Arien, Balletten, Cour. Sarab. und einer Sonate* published in Lübeck in 1649, and again in 1660 (see Chapter 3). That only a single movement was taken from a complete printed collection suggests that Beck used a wide variety of sources for those pieces not taken from Playford. The initials 'J.H.B.' do not appear at any point, so it is reasonable to assume that Beck did not include any of his own music.

Table 4.3 English sources in J.H. Beck (ed.), *Continuatio exercitii musici secunda, Bestehend in außerlesenen Paduanen, Intraden, Allemanden, Balletten, Gavotten, Giqven, Couranten und Sarabanden* (Frankfurt am Main, 1670)

Continuatio exercitii musici secunda	*Composer*	Court-Ayres	Courtly Masquing Ayres
I. Paduana à4	Benjamin Rogers (18)	219 Pavan	164 Pavan
II. Allemande à4	Benjamin Rogers (65)		168 Ayre
III. Courante à4	Silas Taylor (5)	217 Coranto	
IV. Ballet à4	Silas Taylor (4)	216 Ayre	
V. Sarabande à4	William Lawes (383)	215 Saraband	
XIV. Ballet à4	Davis Mell (31)		212 Ayre

(*Continued*)

Concepts of careful organisation: 1660–75 77

Continuatio exercitii musici secunda	Composer	Court-Ayres	Courtly Masquing Ayres
XV. Courante à4	Davis Mell (32)		213 Corant
XVI. Courante à4	Davis Mell (33)		214 Corant
XXXIX. Allemande à 4	William Lawes (391)	162 Ayre	41 Ayre
XL. Courante à4	Davis Mell (37)		
XLII. Sarabande à4	Davis Mell (52)		231 Saraband
XLIV. Courante à4	John Carwarden (11)	177 Coranto	
XLV. Ballet à4	Davis Mell (49)		228 Ayre
XLVI. Sarabande à4	William Gregory (51)		265 Saraband
XLVIII. Allemande à4	Benjamin Rogers (43)		137 Ayre
XLIX. Courante à4	William Lawes (180)	100 Coranto	
L. Ballet à4	Benjamin Rogers (42)		136[a] Almaine 'Pleasant Spring'
LXIV. Allemande à4	Benjamin Rogers (30)	238 Ayre	178 Ayre
LXV. Courante à4	Charles Coleman (176)	236 Coranto	
LXVII. Allemande à4	Charles Coleman (172)	232 Ayre	
LXVIII. Courante à4	Benjamin Rogers (32)	240 Coranto	180 Coranto
LXIX. Sarabande à4	Charles Coleman (177)	237 Saraband	
LXX. Allemande à4	Charles Coleman (175)	235 Almaine	
LXXII. Sarabande à4	Charles Coleman (174)	234 Saraband	88 Saraband
LXXIII. Allemande à4	Benjamin Rogers (31)	239 Ayre	179 Ayre
LXXV. Sarabande à4	Benjamin Rogers (37)	245 Saraband	185 Saraband
LXXVI. Allemande à4	Benjamin Rogers (62)		156 Symphony
LXXVII. Courante à4	Benjamin Rogers (13)	204 Coranto	159 Coranto
LXXVIII. Sarabande à4	Benjamin Rogers (14)	205 Saraband	160 Saraband
LXXX. Ballet à4	John Banister		247 Ayre
LXXXI. Courante à4	Davis Mell (67)		234 Corant
LXXXII. Sarabande à4	John Banister		253 Saraband
LXXXIII. Allemande à4	Benjamin Rogers (12)	203 Ayre	158 Ayre
LXXXIV. Ballet à4	Benjamin Rogers (15)	206 Ayre	161 Ayre
LXXXV. Courante à4	Benjamin Rogers (16)	207 Coranto	162 Coranto
LXXXVI. Sarabande à4	Benjamin Rogers (17)	208 Saraband	163 Saraband
XCI. Sarabande à4	William Lawes (312)	68 Saraband	20 Saraband
XCIII. Courante à4	Ben Sandley (3)	84 Coranto	
XCIV. Sarabande à4	Ben Sandley (4)	85 Sarabanda	
XCV. Allemande à4	Charles Coleman (49)	128 Almaine	
XCVI. Courante à4	William Lawes (230)	132 Coranto	
XCVII. Allemande à4	William Lawes (231)	135 Almaine	
XCVIII. Sarabande à4	William Lawes (224)	133 Saraband	
XCIX. Allemande à4	John Jenkins (43)		99 Almaine
C. Ballet à4	Benjamin Rogers (5)	108 Ayre	131 Ayre
CI. Courante à4	William Lawes (267)		34 Corant
CII. Sarabande à4	William Lawes (268)		35 Saraband

Notes: The index numbers next to the composers' names are those in Dodd and Ashbee, *Thematic index of music for viols*. The pieces by John Banister are not listed in the index.

In common with *EM 2*, there are some changes to the Playford originals that are not always for the better. A change of bass line in Wust's 'XCI. Sarabande à4' from the version given in Playford weakens the harmonic progression and some changes from the latter's treble lines seem to be a result of copying error rather than a deliberate attempt at improvement. It is impossible to tell if these came from Beck or from *Engels Speel-thresoor*.

In its organisational concepts, *EM 3* reflects the trends in single-author printed collections of the late 1660s; the music is mostly arranged in ascending order of key and many of the sequences contain a similar selection of dance types. The start of each sequence is mostly indicated by the use of an Allemande. Beck (or Wust) uses an 'alternative' suite in the form of a nine-movement Intrada-led sequence in D major (LII. Intrada – LX. Sarab.) placed at the mid-point rather than the end of the collection. Here, we find the suggestion of functional dance music and even dramatic-stage origins; it is telling that none of these nine movements are taken from Playford. Functional dance music origins for this sequence are also suggested by the French instrumentation: one violin, two violas and bass in contrast to the two violins, single viola and bass used almost without exception for the rest of the collection. However, the Courantes are very much in the German hybrid style popular in the middle decades of the century, and it is unlikely that they were written in France. It is more likely that the entire sequence was extracted from music for a German court entertainment in the French manner.

It is possible that a second Intrada-led group of movements near the end of the collection (LXXXVII. Intrada – XCI. Sarabande à4) exercises a similar alternative function. But they have few of the characteristics of the first Intrada sequence; the instrumentation is for two violins, viola and bass, while the Sarabande, taken from Playford, is by Lawes. Wust issued no more of these compendium editions after *EM 3* and this is probably a reflection of the decrease in popularity of the town-music suite collection that, as we shall see in the next chapter, occurred during the 1680s. Taken together, the three *Exercitium* volumes offer a fascinating glimpse into the workshop of a publisher and the manner of editing large-scale collections of dance music. If Wust indulged in large-scale piracy, we should not see this as a reason for disapproval; concepts of the rights of authorship were in their infancy in seventeenth-century Germany.

I argued earlier that *EM 1* may well have reinforced some of the trends of the 1660s and the later volumes may also have exerted some sort of influence, even if no more than commercial. It is possible that the now-lost *Exercitium musicum* by Johann Guth, published in Frankfurt am Main in 1672, was influenced by Wust. It apparently lists 'auserl[esene] Sonaten, Allem, Ball, Capriccen, Giquen, Cour. & Sarab'. on its title page, all set in the 'neuester ital. Manier' (latest Italian style) and scored for '2. Violin, 1. Braccio, Violon & B.c.'[17]

A direct single-composer comparison with *EM 1* is provided by Lüder Knoep's *Ander Theil Newer Paduanen, Galliarden, Arien, Allemanden, Balletten, Couranten, und Sarabanden, Mit 2. und 3. Stimmen nebenst dem Basso Continuo* (Bremen, 1660).[18] Like his earlier *Erster Theil* (see Chapter 3), it is a trio collection for two violins (*Cantus* I and II), *Bassus* and *Bassus Continuus*. Both bass parts are figured but, as I suggested in the previous chapter, this may be for reasons of economy rather than the desire to produce two part-books for chordal continuo instruments.

Unlike his previous collection, Knoep's *Ander Theil* is clearly divided into three sections and the contrast between the third section – six *à2* suites considered by the composer to be in the French manner – and the rest of the work is highlighted by changing the movement numbering from Roman to Arabic. The first section comprises eight examples of the increasingly old-fashioned Paduan, either on their own or with a linked Galliard. The second and much larger section is detailed in Table 4.4 and features a wider selection of Allemandes, Balletts, Courantes and multi-sectioned Arias along with the occasional Sarabande. Even if Knoep did not see them in this light, it is difficult not to think of these sections in terms of the new Allemande supplanting the older Paduan.

At the heart of the section two movements is the duple-/triple-time relationship, not only between the duple-time Allemandes and Balletts and the triple-time Courantes, but also in the Arias. The latter all follow a similar format familiar from Hammerschmidt's collections: two strains of duple time followed by a single strain of triple time. Curiously, the triple-time strains are marked '3. mahl' (three times) in the two bass parts, but not always in the first and second violin parts. This is likely to be a printing error, but it may suggest that Knoep expected the ensemble to be directed by the continuo players. Perhaps wary of an over-formulaic approach, Knoep does introduce some variety to the duple-time sections of these Arias; Example 4.4 shows the difference between the crotchet-led opening of 'XIX. Aria' and the restless and repetitive opening of 'XX. Aria' that is near to the style of constantly dotted Ballo starting to find its way into the repertoire.

Throughout Knoep's collection, considerable use is made of movement linking, some of it using the variation technique of re-casting a duple-time movement into triple time. The usage is looser than the norm of the late 1650s and early 1660s, where half a bar of duple time was extended to become a whole bar of triple time. As Example 4.5 demonstrates, he mostly proceeds on a note-for-note basis and adjusts the rhythms to match the character of the dances.

In his choice of movements for re-casting, Knoep does not always follow the usual duple–triple relationship. As Table 4.4 shows, 'X. Courante' has harmonic and melodic links not with the expected preceding 'IX. Allemand', but with the later 'XII. Courante'. In using common material for two separated triple-time movements, we must assume that Knoep wished to demonstrate his ability to create two different Courantes from a common opening.

In the end, however, it is the final part of *Ander Theil* that provides the greatest interest. Here, there are six clearly defined sequences of movements. In a section that openly claims to be French in manner, it is curious that an Italian collective title of 'Ballo' is given to each of them. Perhaps the printer did not understand its significance and used it to avoid confusion with two movements in the second section entitled 'Ballett'.

80 *Concepts of careful organisation: 1660–75*

Table 4.4 Movements in Section 2 of L. Knoep, *Ander Theil Newer Paduanen, Galliarden, Arien, Allemanden, Balletten, Couranten, und Sarabanden, Mit 2. und 3. Stimmen nebenst dem Basso Continuo* (Bremen, 1660)

Movement titles	Key	Comment
IX. Allemand	B flat major	
X. Courante	B flat major	Linked to 'XII. Courante'.
XI. Allemand	B flat major	
XII. Courante	B flat major	
XIII. Allemand	B flat major	Linked to 'XIV. Courant. Saraband'.
XIV. Courant. Saraband	B flat major	
XV. Allemand	B flat major	
XVI. Saraband	B flat major	
XVII. Allemand	G minor	
XVIII. Courante	G minor	
XIX. Aria	G minor	Multi-sectioned duple- then triple-time movement. Triple-time section marked '3. mahl' (3 times).
XX. Aria	G minor	Multi-sectioned duple- then triple-time movement. Triple-time section marked '3. mahl'.
XXI. Allemand	F major	Linked to 'XXII. Saraband'.
XXII. Saraband	F major	
XXIII. Allemand	F major	
XXIV. Courante	F major	
XXV. Ballett	C major	
XXVI. Courante	C major	
XXVII. Ballett	C major	
XXVIII. Courante	C major	
XXIX. Ballett	D major	
XXX. Courante	D major	
XXXI. Ballett	D major	
XXXII. Courante	D major	
XXXIII. Aria	B flat major	Multi-sectioned duple- then triple-time movement. Finishes in G minor. Triple-time section marked '3. mahl' (3 times).
XXXIV. Aria	B flat major	Multi-sectioned duple- then triple-time movement. Triple-time section marked '3. mahl' (3 times).
XXXV. Ballett	B flat major	
XXXVI. Saraband	B flat major	

Despite the dubious linguistics, it does seem that Knoep intended his *Balli* to reflect the type of dance sequence usually associated with the French staged ballet. Every one of the six sequences concludes with a Sarabande and four contain a Bataglia. 'Ballo Secundo' and 'Ballo Tertio' do not include Courantes, but all six sequences conclude with a Sarabande. The similarities between this part

Concepts of careful organisation: 1660–75   81

Example 4.4 Knoep, *Ander Theil Newer Paduanen*, openings of 'XIX. Aria' and 'XX. Aria'.

of Knoep's collection and parts of *Erster Theil Etlicher Allemanden, Couranten, Sarabanden, Balletten, Intraden und andern Arien* (Jena, 1672), by the Weimar and Jena court musician Adam Drese, are striking.[19] There is good reason to think that these parts of Drese's collection are extracts from genuine dramatic works; perhaps Knoep's *Balli* fulfill the same purpose.

82 Concepts of careful organisation: 1660–75

Example 4.5 Knoep, *Ander Theil Newer Paduanen*, openings of 'I. Paduana' and 'II. Galliard'.

The desire for careful ordering of the contents of Knoep's *Ander Theil* is stronger than in the contemporary *EM 1*, and while it is impossible to know with complete certainly if the impetus for this desire came from composer or publisher, we must suspect the composer. However, the next collection in our survey was published by the composer himself, so the issue of responsibility does not arise.

Georg Wolffgang Druckenmüller's *Musicalisches Tafel-Confect; Bestehend in VII. Partyen / Balleten, Allemanden, Couranten, Sarabanden &c.* was issued in 1668, midway between *EM 2* and *3*. Little is known of Druckenmüller's life and career; it seems that he was a town organist in Schwäbisch Hall, but not a court musician. *Musicalisches Tafel-Confect* is a highly original example of a town musician attempting to produce suites in distinctly different styles of composition and instrumentation.

There are seven sequences identified by the composer as *Partyen*. The movement numbering in each *Partie* always starts from '1', so the layout of the collection (detailed in Table 4.5) is presented with great clarity. The opening *Partie* is followed by three Bransle suites alternating with three Allemande-led suites.

The collection is again unusual in requiring a variety of different instrumentations ranging from viol consort to five-part violin band; 'Partie II', one of the French-inspired Bransle sequences, is scored for a three-part viola da gamba consort with the third part doubled by a figured continuo part. As we have seen in Chapter 2, the preface states that the two upper viola da gamba parts may be played an octave higher on violins when there are not enough instruments, or for dancing. And while the role of the Bransle as music for the ballroom was seemingly widely understood, this is one of the few specific indications of practical dance music in a suite collection by a town composer.

However, none of the three Bransle sequences follows the established order of movements. In the first two, the Bransle Double is omitted from the standard six-movement sequence; in the third, the Bransle Double is included, but the Gavotte omitted. As we can see in Table 4.5, the instrumentation also goes

Table 4.5 Contents of G.W. Druckenmüller, *Musicalisches Tafel-Confect; Bestehend in VII. Partyen / Balleten, Allemanden, Couranten, Sarabanden &c.* (Schwäbisch Hall, 1668)

Movement titles	Key	Instrumentation
1. Ballet / 2. [untitled] / 3. [untitled] / 4. [untitled] / 5. Lam. / 6. Viv. / 7. Masc. / 8. Aria / 9. Cour. / 10. Sarab.	D major	Violin 1 – Violin 2 – Viola 1 – Viola 2 – Violon – Continuus
1. Brandle / 2. Gay / 3. Amener / 4. Montir. / 5. Gavot	G major	Viol. di gam.[I] – Viol. di gam.[II] – Viol. di gam.[III] – Continuus
1. Allem. / 2. Courant / 3. Ballo / 4. Sarab. / 5. Chique	D major	Violin 1 – Violin 2 – Viola 1 – Viola 2 – Violon – Continuus
1. Brandle / 2. Gay / 3. Amener / 4. Montir. / 5. Gavot	G major	Violin 1 – Violin 2 – Violon – Continuus
1. Allem. / 2. Courant / 3. Sarab. / 4. Chique	G minor	Violin 1 – Viola 1 – Viola 2 – Violon – Continuus
1. Brandle / 2. Gay / 3. Amener / 4. Montir. / 5. Double	D major	Violin 1 – Violin 2 – Viola 1 – Viola 2 – Violon – Continuus
1. Allem. / 2. Courant / 3. Sarab. / 4. Chique	A minor	Violin 1 – Viola 1 – Viola 2 – Violon – Continuus

against the usual practice. The French-style combination of one violin, two violas and bass is reserved not for the Bransles, but for the fifth and seventh suites that reflect the German and Italian manner. The more Italian combination of two violins, two violas and bass is given instead to the last of the Bransle suites.[20] Example 4.6 gives the treble-part openings of the movements of 'Partie IV', which is scored for the *à3* combination of two violins and bass.

While the rhythms of '1. Brandle' are arguably too busy for a Bransle Simple, the movement is set in the traditional three-bar phrase lengths, while rhythms and phrase lengths in the remaining parts of the sequence all follow idiomatic French models.[21] So it is clear that Druckenmüller had a good understanding of at least part of the Bransle idiom, even if he chose to ignore or misunderstood other aspects of it. But the Bransles may not be the only example of functional dance music. The opening sequence, starting with a Ballet and three untitled movements was perhaps intended as an imitation of dance music for the dramatic stage. It is similar in content to the first Intrada-led sequence in *EM 3*.

In contrast to the Ballet and Bransles are three Allemande-led suites that are clearly meant to be seen as instrumental music not intended for dancing. So it seems that Druckenmüller's purpose for this collection was to provide clearly defined examples of different types of dance sequence: quasi-functional dance music from both the dramatic stage and ballroom along with instrumental suites reflecting the standard town-music repertoire. In addition, the standard of the music with its inner-part writing for the two violas provides an example of the town-music repertoire at its best.

Example 4.6 Openings of Druckenmüller, *Musicalisches Tafel-Confect*, 'Partie IV'.

Concepts of careful organisation: 1660–75   85

If *Musicalisches Tafel-Confect* is one of the most clearly defined and carefully ordered collections of the seventeenth century in the German lands, did it come about as a result of the composer acting as self-publisher, or can we see parallels in other collections where publisher and composer are separate?

Certainly, there is a parallel in Hieronymus Kradenthaller's *Deliciarum musicalium Erster Theil à4. Viol. Von Sonatinen, Arien, Sarabanden und Giquen* (Nuremberg, 1675). Kradenthaller ('Gradenthaller' in his subsequent publications) was a town organist in Regensburg and it appears that he was held in high regard as a 'wohlberühmter und kunstreicher Organist' (a well-known and very artistic organist).[22] *Deliciarum musicalium Erster Theil* was not his first collection of suites; two volumes of *Musicalische Recreation* for solo violin and continuo had been issued in Regensburg in 1672. If the title page of *Erster Theil* suggests the music-making of the domestic *Collegia* as the focus for Kradenthaller's work – 'allen Music-Freunden zur Delectation' (for the delectation of all music lovers) – *Musicalische Recreation* confirms it.

Erster Theil was not published by the composer; this and the printing were carried out by Wolf Eberhard Felsecker who, like Wust, seems to have had considerable experience in producing editions of consort music.[23] There are part-books for two violins, *Violetta*, *Violon* and *Cembalo*. Curiously, the 'Violino II' part is written in the soprano clef throughout, normally an indication of the French *haute-contre* viola. Perhaps reflecting its intended domestic use, the organisation of the collection is a model of clarity. There are nine suites of five movements and, apart from the last, each one starts with a Sonatina, and ends with a Gigue. Perhaps surprisingly, there are no linked movements. The contents of the collection (detailed in Table 4.6) are organised not by using the same sequence of dance types for each suite, but by a clearly defined metric relationship between movements. Apart from the 'alternative' Bransle sequence at the end, the centre of each suite is the triple-time Sarabande preceded by a duple-time Sonatina and an opening dance. After each Sarabande comes another duple-time dance and a closing 6/4 Gigue.

While it is clear that Kradenthaller was using 'Balleto', 'Ballo' and 'Aria' in generic terms to indicate a duple time dance, the Arias themselves fall into two types. Example 4.7 gives examples of both: '24. Aria' shows the restless dotted rhythms strongly associated with the Ballo in most of the town repertoire, while '32. Aria' is a rhythmically simpler and straightforward duple-time dance of two strains. Neither bears any relationship to the multi-sectioned version of Hammerschmidt or his contemporaries.

The opening and closing movements of each sequence also retain the air of deliberate simplicity; all but one of the Gigues rely on simple propulsion for their main character and only one is polyphonic. The Sonatinas are similarly unpretentious. Example 4.8 shows the first strain of '5. Gique' and Example 4.9 shows the opening of '1. Sonatina'.

If the music of the above examples is well written and effective, but rarely demanding on a technical level, the issue of a second volume a year later suggests

Table 4.6 Contents of H. Kradenthaller, *Deliciarum musicalium Erster Theil à4. Viol. Von Sonatinen, Arien, Sarabanden und Giquen* (Nuremberg, 1675)

Movement title	Keys and time signatures	Movement title	Keys and time signature
1. Sonatina	D minor ¢	24. Aria	A minor ¢
2. Aria	D minor, ¢	25. Gique	A minor 6/4
3. Sarabande	D minor, 3	26. Sonatina	E minor ¢
4. Aria	D minor ¢	27. Allemande	E minor ¢
5. Gique	D minor, 6/4	28. Sarabande	E minor 3
6. Sonatina	F major ¢	29. Aria	E minor ¢
7. Aria	F major ¢	30. Gigue	E minor 6/4
8. Sarabande	F major 3	31. Sonatina	D major ¢
9. Aria	F major ¢	32. Aria	D major ¢
10. Gique	F major 6/4	33. Sarabande	D major 3
11. Sonatina	G minor ¢	34. Aria	D major ¢
12. Balleto	G minor ¢	35. Gique	D major 6/4
13. Sarabande	G minor 3	36. Sonatina	G major ¢
14. Aria	G minor ¢	37. Ballo	G major ¢
15. Gique	G minor 6/4	38. Sarabande	G major 3
16. Sonatina	C major ¢	39. Aria	G major ¢
17. Aria	C major ¢	40. Gique	G major 6/4
18. Sarabande	C major 3	41. Bransle	B flat major ¢
19. Aria	C major ¢	42. Gay	B flat major 3
20. Gique	C major 6/4	43. Amener	B flat major 3
21. Sonatina	A minor ¢	44. Gavotte	B flat major ¢
22. Aria	A minor ¢	45. Courante	B flat major 3
23. Sarabande	A minor 3	46. Sarabande	B flat major 3

that the formula had appeal for its intended market and sold well. (The second volume will be dealt with in the following chapter.)

At the end of the previous chapter, I posed the question of responsibility for the increasingly popular trend that brought concepts of careful organisation to printed suite collections by German town composers. As we have seen, the weakest organisationally is Wust's publisher-led *EM 1*, even if it does contain an early example of the 'alternative' suite concept. It is telling that, when Beck assumed the editorship of *EM 2*, much greater care was taken to organise the contents in a way that gave increased clarity for the performer. But it was in single-author collections that the greatest advances were made, and while we can never be certain of day-to-day relationships between publishers, printers and musicians, it is hard to see how these changes could have been anything other than at the behest of the composer.

Concepts of careful organisation: 1660–75   87

Example 4.7 Kradenthaller, *Deliciarum musicalium Erster Theil*, '24. Aria', '32. Aria'.

Example 4.8 Kradenthaller, *Deliciarum musicalium Erster Theil*, '5. Gique'.

Example 4.9 Kradenthaller, *Deliciarum musicalium Erster Theil*, '1. Sonatina'.

Notes

1 See: *CCS*, pp. 93 and 96.
2 The identification of 'Artus' as Leborgne was first put forward in *CCS*, pp. 74–5.
3 G. Dodd (rev. A. Ashbee), *Thematic index of music for viols* (Viola da Gamba Society of Great Britain, online edition, www.vdgs.org.uk) (accessed 12 November 2013).
4 See R.A. Rasch, 'Seventeenth-century Dutch editions of English instrumental music' *Music & Letters*, 53/3 (1972), pp. 270–73. I am grateful to Peter Holman for drawing my attention to this and other Dutch sources of Playford's editions.
5 The Amsterdam publication concluded with '40 ingenious Pavanes, Airs, Courantes, Sarabandes, composed by Matthew Locke' (translation from ibid., p. 272).

6   Ibid.
7   For a description of the manuscript and its contents, see M. Weckmann (ed. S. Rampe), *Sämtliche Freie Orgel- und Clavierwerke* (Kassel: Bärenreiter, 1991), Preface, pp. xxvii–xxix.
8   The implications for performance of note blackening in Courantes will be discussed in Chapter 9.
9   E. Kjellberg and P. Whitehead, 'Beck, Johann Hector' in D.L. Root (ed.), *Grove music online* (www.oxfordmusiconline.com) (accessed 23 October 2013).
10 It is possible that 'N.B.N.' is not a set of initials but the Latin phrase '*Non bene notus*' (not well known) and this would further point to Wust or a member of his staff as the editor.
11 See also *CCS*, pp. 97–8.
12 According to Göhler, 2/1727, Wust was the publisher of the second volume of Zuber's *newer Paduanen* only a year before *Exercitium musicum*.
13 The incorrect ascription to Locke may possibly be explained by the addition of forty pieces by him in *English Speel-thresoor*. See Rasch, 'Seventeenth-century Dutch editions'.
14 It appears that, during the 1660s, Beck had been expelled from the town, which may explain why his connection with Frankfurt am Main is not mentioned on the title page of *EM 2*. See Kjellberg and Whitehead, 'Beck, Johann Hector'.
15 Rasch, 'Seventeenth-century Dutch editions', p. 272. The collection has not apparently survived.
16 Given the lack of evidence, we can only assume that the Amsterdam versions followed Playford's orginal movement order.
17 Göhler 2/649.
18 A facsimile of this collection is available online at http://gallica.bnf.fr/ark:/12148/btv1b90099414.r=Knoep%2C+Lüder.langEN (accessed 1 November 2015).
19 For a description of the dramatic excerpts in Drese's collection, see *CCS*, pp. 46–7.
20 No music or indication of doubling is given in the 'Violin II' part-book for the fifth and seventh suites.
21 The treble lines of a French-origin Bransle sequence are given in Chapter 2, p. 39.
22 H. Kradenthaller (ed. K. Ruhland), *Vier kurze Suiten* (Magdeburg: Edition Walhall, 2006), Preface.
23 *Erster Theil* has the publisher's name as 'Felßecker', while *Anderer Theil* (see following chapter) has 'Felsecker'.

5 A time of decline: 1676–1700

If Chapter 4 dealt with a golden period for consort-suite composition in the German lands, this chapter deals with the tradition's gradual decline outside of Leipzig and Hamburg, and eventual extinction during the last two decades of the seventeenth century. As we shall see, this decline is in terms of output and not necessarily in quality of music as, again with the exception of Leipzig and Hamburg, very little of the suite repertoire seems to have been published in the 1670s. In court circles, composers such as Johann Wilhelm Furchheim issued collections of suites in the first half of the decade, but few printed editions of consort suites seem to have emanated from the *Hofkapellen* in the second half. It is possible that the picture is obscured by an accident of preservation, but given the absence of references to suite publications in trade catalogues from this time, this seems unlikely. Certainly, the decline of music printing during the last two decades of the century must have played a part.[1] But the trade and commerce on which the towns and therefore musical patronage depended continued to flourish in all but a few places. And while it is true that there was political uncertainty during the 1670s with wars against Sweden in the north and France in the south, these were relatively minor affairs compared with the Thirty Years War, and settled by the Peace of Nijmegen in 1678. So even if the decline in publishing was a contributory factor, we must look to culture rather than commerce for reasons explaining the demise of the town tradition.

Publishers, composers and their patrons may simply have lost interest in the relatively narrow confines of town-suite publications, but it is far more likely that the genre was overtaken by a cultural phenomenon, the revolution in suite composition brought about by the music of Jean-Baptiste Lully. It is telling that, while Jacob Scheiffelhut, a town musician in Augsburg, published two sets of consort suites in the 1680s that were firmly in the town-music tradition, his third set of suites, *Musicalisches Klee-Blatt*, published in 1707, was described by the composer as being 'Auf jetziger Zeit wol-bekannte Frantozösische Art' (in the well-known French manner of the present time). And they were written in the Lullian manner. As we shall see in Chapter 8, the town-music tradition only continued to flourish in the keyboard repertoire where it was rescued by the advent of music-engraving techniques in the German lands. But given the expense of the new technique, it is hardly surprising that most composers seem to have preferred the cheaper option of printing two-stave keyboard music rather than costly sets of part-books.

Against this gloomy background, a second volume of Kradenthaller's *Deliciarum musicalium* was issued in 1676 (*Deliciarum musicalium Anderer Theil / Etlicher Sonatinen, Arien, Sarabanden und Giquen, &c.*), published and printed by Felsecker. In the same manner as many other second-volume collections, *Anderer Theil* appears to have been bound together with a re-issue of *Erster Theil*.[2] The Preface confirms that, as with the first volume, the collection was intended for 'contentment and recreation', and this may provide the reason for its publication. There was surely still a need for technically undemanding but attractive consort publications.

Anderer Theil comprises twelve suites; as in *Erster Theil*, the start of each one is marked by a Sonatina. But there, the similarities end. The careful metric relationships of the earlier collection are all but abandoned and the movement choice is broader; Trezzas and even old-fashioned Gagliardes are added to the movement types. A Bransle sequence is again used as an 'alternative' suite, but not placed at the usual end of the collection. Instead the collection is ended, after the twelfth suite in E flat major, by four movements, '71. Courante', '72. Aria', '73. Trezza' and '74. Aria', all in the key of B flat major. It is difficult to discern a purpose for these movements; perhaps they were added for the performer to use in any way he desired.

An important feature of this second volume is the apparent influence of Johann Heinrich Schmelzer and the Viennese court tradition even though there is no evidence that Kradenthaller ever visited Vienna. Suites in this tradition – usually known in the seventeenth century as *Balletti* – were often brought to a close by a *Retirada*, a deeply serious and sometimes-chromatic movement that could also employ sharp dissonance.[3] Kradenthaller does not use *Retirada* as a title, but two of the suites in *Anderer Theil* have Gigues (29 and 34) finishing with sections marked 'Adagio' apparently serving the same purpose. And while he was not the only composer outside Vienna to do so (see Chapter 6), Kradenthaller also uses the Viennese Trezza in the second and eleventh suites as well as the four-movement group of dances at the end of the collection.

However, it is the use different keys within the same suite that is most telling in terms of Viennese influence. While the normal prerequisite of suite construction is that all movements should be in the same key, in Vienna, this stricture was often ignored. Many of Schmelzer's *Balletti* were sequences of dances extracted from music for the dramatic stage, and consequently employ one or more changes of key. However, the changes of key are not seemingly random; in many cases, they are part of a clearly discernable circular structure.[4] For example, Schmelzer's 'Gran Ballo della Deita', part of the music for an opera given for Leopold's birthday in 1667 ('Arien der dreÿ Balletti in der Opera zu dem geburts dag [sic] Ihro Meÿl: des kaisers Leopoldi. den 9. Junÿ 1667', manuscript *A-Wn* Mus. Hs. 16583) contains the following sequence of movements and keys:

> Allemande (G minor) / Saltarella (B flat major) / Guige (G minor) / Sarabande (D minor) / Aria per la Retirada (G minor)

The second suite of Kradenthaller's *Anderer Theil* contains this sequence:

> 6. Sonatina (F major) / 7. Ballo (F major) / 8. Aria (F minor) / 9. Gagliarda (F minor) / 10. Aria (A flat major) / 11. Trezza (F major) / 12. Aria (F major)

While the use of tonic major and minor combinations is found in other areas of the German suite repertoire, the move to A flat major is noticeably similar to Schmelzer's practice. Individually, the similarities between *Anderer Theil* and the Viennese imperial tradition might seem little more than coincidence but, taken as a whole, the case for Schmelzer's influence on Kradenthaller is striking. On a musical level, there is nothing in the second volume of *Deliciarum musicalium* that can match the work of Schmelzer. But Kradenthaller's pieces are well crafted and frequently rise above the commonplace.

Jacob Scheiffelhut's *Musicalischer Gemüths Ergötzungen Erstes Werck* was published by Jacob Koppmayer in 1684. Scheiffelhut was an important figure in the musical life of Augsburg during the latter part of the seventeenth century and into the early years of the eighteenth. He received his musical education there and, from 1673, was a musician at St Anna's choir school.[5] He remained in the town until his death in 1709. The suggestion that his suites 'reflect the pronounced French influence' in Augsburg is presumably based on the contents of *Musicalisches Klee-Blatt* but, as we shall now see, this is certainly not true of Scheiffelhut's two collections issued in the seventeenth century.[6]

If the 'Erstes Werck' of the 1684 collection suggests a second volume under the same title, nothing appears to have been issued apart from *Lieblicher Frülings-Anfang oder Musicalischer Seyten-Klang* that appeared in the following year. Perhaps 'Erstes Werck' was intended to remind the purchaser that this was the composer's first volume, the equivalent of an 'Opus 1'. Unfortunately, the collection has not survived complete; in 1931, all the part-books except the 'Basso Viola' were extant, but the first violin part was subsequently lost, presumably in the Second World War.[7] No modern edition had been made before this loss. According to the title page, the collection is scored for the trio combination of 'zwey *Violinen, Basso Viola* und *Basso Continuo*'. The 'Basso Continuo' part-book is unusual in containing pencilled corrections. There are eight suites, all with the same sequence of movements:

> Sonata / Allemand / Courant / Ballett / Saraband / Gique

The keys of the collection are mostly arranged in ascending fourths or fifths as follows:

> A major – E minor – B flat major – F major – D major – G major – C minor – G minor

The Sonatas are all substantial multi-sectioned movements. The dances follow the town-music tradition with hybrid Courantes and propulsive, often imitative Gigues.

A time of decline: 1676–1700 93

Despite the loss of so much, we can see that considerable use is made of linked material; Scheiffelhut varies the technique in a number of ways and with considerable invention. In the first suite, '1. Sonata' has shares elemants of its bass-line material with the following Courant, Ballett and Saraband. The 'Violino Secundo' part remains separate for these movements, and the bass figuring suggests that the first violin does the same. Example 5.1 gives the openings of these movements and reconstructs the 'Violino Primo' part on this basis. It is likely that the 'Basso Viola' part was the same as the continuo part at these places.

In the seventh suite, there is a network of linking that includes the Sonata and all the dances except the final Gigue. The interval of C to A♭ provides the framework for much of this, especially in the bass lines with shared material in '37. Sonata', '39. Courant' and '40. Ballett'. At the same time, the 'Violino Secundo' part links the Sonata and '41. Saraband'. Presumably, the first violin part did the same. A further layer is provided by common material in the second (and presumably first) violin parts at the start of '38. Allemand', '39. Courant'

Example 5.1 Linking material in J. Scheiffelhut, *Musicalischer Gemüths Ergötzungen Erstes Werck* (Augsburg, 1684), '3. Courant', '4. Ballett' and '5. Saraband'.

94 A time of decline: 1676–1700

and '40. Ballett'. So there is separate linking going on between the Sonata and its following dances, not only in the treble but also, independently, in the bass.

The final suite uses chromaticism to link the bass line. The Sonata, Allemande and Sarabande are linked in this way, while the treble lines appear to remain separate throughout the suite. Unlike the rest of the collection, the Gique is also a part of the movement linking; the chromatic bass line is the subject for its imitative entries.

Despite the loss of the important first-violin part-book, we can be certain that Scheiffelhut was writing in a manner firmly wedded to the German town-music tradition. The material is carefully organised and the dances are mostly in the Italian style apart from the Gigues in the German hybrid manner. It is difficult to see evidence of any 'pronounced French influence' (see above) and it is reasonable to suggest that *Musicalischer Gemüths Ergötzungen Erstes Werck* may be one of the finest trio collections to be published by a German composer during the second half of the seventeenth century. It is nothing less than a tragedy that the first violin part has been lost in comparatively recent times and we must hope for its recovery.

Scheiffelhut's second collection, the 1685 *Lieblicher Frühlings-Anfang, oder Musicalischer Seyten-Klang*, was also published by Koppmayer in Augsburg. This time, the collection is in *à4* instrumentation of 'zwey Violinen, Viola di Braccio, Basso Viola & Continuo'.[8] The musical quality is as fine as the 1684 publication and, this time, the collection survives complete. In a similar manner to suite collections elsewhere, particularly Leipzig (see Chapter 6), Scheiffelhut separates the opening abstract movements from their following dances by allowing the viola part to be omitted. According to the preface: 'die Viola di Braccio kan wol im Rohtfall in den Allemanden, Couranten, Ballo, Sarabanden und Arien außgelassen werden' (if necessary, the viola di braccio may be omitted from the Allemands, Courants, Sarabandes and Arias). We must assume that performances of the dances alone were acceptable, even if not desirable. Gigues are an exception to this list, presumably because their contrapuntal textures require the presence of a middle part.

There are eight suites in the collection, all of which use the following movement sequence:

Præludium / Allemand / Courant / Ballo / Saraband / Aria / Gique

Scheiffelhut is clearly concerned to provide the widest range of material within his framework of dances; this is particularly the case with the closing Gigues in each suite; all have widely differing characters.

The *Balli* lack the propulsive dotted rhythms often found in the town-music repertoire and appear, at first sight, to require a slower tempo than the norm. Presumably this is why Scheiffelhut's preface points out that they should, along with the Courantes and Gigues, still be played quickly. Despite this instruction, and 3/4 signatures that might indicate the Italian style, the Courantes themselves are more clearly French in character than those of the earlier collection.

A time of decline: 1676–1700 95

The typical rhythmic ambiguity of '10. Courant' is clearly shown in Example 5.2, which reproduces the original barring, though the latter is not without error.[9]

If the Gigues are often contrapuntal, the Preludes of the collection, all multi-sectioned, show that Scheiffelhut was capable of a high standard of fugal writing. The first half of '50. Præludium', the final Prelude of the collection, contains counterpoint that is easily the equal of the Sonatas in Reincken's *Hortus musicus* from three years later (see Chapter 7). The use of chromatic bass lines and rich, often dissonant, harmony also appears in many of these Preludes; Example 5.3 shows the *Adagio* section that links the opening *Lente* to the following *Vivace* in '15. Præludium'.[10]

Movement linking does not have the same prominence as in the earlier collection; three suites are entirely free of variation techniques and none of the suites have the layers of linking that Scheiffelhut used in 1684. Finally, the notation of the dance music has a more modern appearance than other collections

Example 5.2 J. Scheiffelhut, *Lieblicher Frülings-Anfang / oder Musicalischer Seyten-Klang* (Augsburg, 1685), first strain of '10. Courant'.

Notes: the 'Violino Secundo' part contains an additional bar line at the halfway point of bar 3, presumably in error. The bar line at the end start of the final bar in the 'Viola da Braccio' part has been moved to the halfway point of the previous bar, again presumably in error.

96 *A time of decline: 1676–1700*

Example 5.3 Scheiffelhut, *Lieblicher Frühlings-Anfang*, '15. Præludium'.

from around this time. Note blackening is completely avoided, and cross-bar rhythms are notated by tied notes. In a clear move away from the mensural concepts of previous generations, the preface links the requested quick tempi of the duple-time Balli specifically to their ¢ signature, and the mensural '3', often found in seventeenth-century Courantes, has been replaced by '3/4' throughout. The casual use of bar lines is typical of many printed publications in the seventeenth century, but *Lieblicher Frühlings-Anfang* suggests that Scheiffelhut (or his printer) was clearly keen to avoid anything that, notationwise, looked old-fashioned.

Printed dance music was not limited to collections of suites; Daniel Speer's three 'Quodlibets', collections of popular songs and instrumental music published between 1685 and 1688, all contain examples of the genre. A town musician, albeit one who never remained in any place for more than a short time, Speer is mostly remembered as a writer of satirical novels. But he was also a theorist and his treatise *Grund-richtiger ... Unterricht der musicalischen Kunst* was published in Ulm in 1687 with a revised version following ten years later. Speer's habit of writing under various pseudonyms has resulted in questions of authorship, but both novels and music are now generally accepted as his work.[11]

The index to Speer's first 'Quodlibet', *Recens Fabricatus Labor, Oder Neugebachene Taffel-Schnitz* (n.p., 1685), lists twenty-five sets of pieces, the twenty-fourth of these being 'Eine Sonata und Party. â 5. Viol.' The movements of the 'Party' (*Partie*) are 'Sonatina', 'Ballet', 'Courant', 'Gavott', 'Sarabant' and 'Gigque'. The '5. Viol.' are two violins, two violas and bass. The purpose of the Sonata in the same key as the suite is unclear. Speer may have intended it as a prelude to the 'Party', but the additional presence of a Sonatina makes this unlikely even if examples of suites with two opening abstract movements are not unknown elsewhere. We can be more certain about the relationship between the dance movements. The Ballet, Sarabande and Gigue are linked by a three-note sequence (A–E–F♯) that Speer, perhaps wishing to emphasise his credentials as a theorist, uses in inversion to link the remaining Courante and Gavotte.

In Speer's second Quodlibet, *Musicalischer Leuthe Spiegel / Das ist: Ein Extract auß dem Welt-berühmten Ertz-Schelmen Judas Tractat* (n.p., 1687), there is no confusion about the place of the sonatas; their presence in the suite sequence is confirmed by the 'Party' title at the head of the music in each case. The Quodlibet contains two suites that are listed in the index as:

Eine Party auß dem E. dur. à 5. Instr. 2. V[iolini], 2. Violæ.
Item, noch eine auß dem E. à 5. 1. Violino, 3. Violæ.

Given the instrumentation of the second of these, we must assume that the '2. Violen / so ad placitum [i.e. *ad libitum*]' instruction of the Quodlibet's title page does not apply here. Both suites have the same movement sequence of Sonata / Ballet / Courant / Gavott / Sarab. / Gique, and it seems that Speer intended them to be seen as a pairing of opposites. The first is in E major, the second in E minor; the Italian instrumentation of the first suite with two violins, two violas and bass is presumably meant to contrast with the French single violin, three violas and bass of the second.

In the light of this, it is surprising that the dances themselves show little in the way of contrasting characteristics although, as we have seen, Horn was similarly disinterested in his *Parergon musicum*. The Courante of the second suite is certainly not in the French manner, but firmly in the Italian, while the example in the first suite approaches the German hybrid manner. Likewise, both Sarabandes are Italian. If Speer was aware of the differing characteristics of French- and Italian-style dances, he chose to ignore them. In both suites, he uses the same tonic–leading note–tonic bass-line motif for linking movements. In the first, it links the Ballet, Courant and Sarabande; in the second, it links all the movements including the Sonata. There is no linking of the treble lines at any point in either suite.

Speer clearly saw this pluralistic use of the same bass-line motif as central to his method of suite composition. The two suites in the third Quodlibet, *Musicalisch-Türckischer Eulen-Spiegel* (n.p., 1688), are written for two violins, two 'ad placitum' violas and bass. While he uses the more common melodic linking in the treble lines of parts of the the first suite, there is once again the tonic–leading note–tonic bass line and, as before, it links every movement. The linking in the first suite is shown in Example 5.4.

98 *A time of decline: 1676–1700*

Example 5.4 Movement linking in D. Speer, *Musicalisch-Türckischer Eulen-Spiegel* (n.p., 1688).

Other composers used bass-line linking as part of a vocabulary of variation techniques and, as we shall see in Chapter 8, Niedt used similar techniques as a basis for keyboard improvisation, though it is possible that he was influenced by Speer. But I have been unable to find examples from other composers of a common bass line linking separate suites across different collections.[12] Sadly, the limited harmonic possibilities of this recurring motif are matched by the limited imagination shown in the suites of all three Quodlibets; for twenty-first-century ears, they seem uninspiring and often little more than barely competent.

The last two printed collections under consideration in this chapter are the work of composers who had court experience before taking up posts as municipal organists. Despite the court influence, both collections are firmly rooted in town music and both suggest directions the tradition might have taken had it survived longer. The first is Johann Friedrich Meister's *Il giardino del piacere overo raccolta de diversi flori musicali* (Hamburg, 1695), printed in moveable type; the second is Johann Pachelbel's engraved *Musicalische Ergötzung bestehend in sechs verstimten Partien* (Nuremberg, n.d.). Both *Musicalische Ergötzung* and *Il giardino* are trio-suite collections, a format that, as we have seen, had been largely discarded in the printed collections of previous decades. Along with Reincken's *Hortus musicus* (see Chapter 7), these collections appear to indicate a revival of interest in the trio-suite perhaps instigated by the popular *à3* extracts from Lully's stage works printed in Amsterdam around this time.

The early part of Meister's career had been as a court musician but, by the time of *Il giardino*'s publication, he had been organist of the *Marienkirche* in Flensburg for twelve years. It has been suggested that Meister's instrumental music may have been written for performance at the nearby ducal court of Schloss Glücksburg; if this is correct, then the court must have been one of the few to resist the influence of Lully's music and the *frantzösischen Manier*.[13] Accordingly, Meister emphasised the Italian features of this work by giving it an Italian title and going as far as to identify each of the twelve suites by the whimsical title 'la Musica'; perhaps in emulation of Johann Kusser, who changed his name to the French equivalent, Jean Sigismond Cousser, Meister used 'Giovanni Frederico Maestro' – the Italian version of his own name – on the collection's title page. Table 5.1 details its contents.[14]

The contents of each 'Musica' are not only shown by the titles but also by the outer movements, always a Sonata and Gigue (the spelling of the latter varies between 'Gicque' and 'Gique'). The increasingly popular Menuet is also found at least once in all but two of the suites. Apart from this, Meister's scheme is more flexible. The opening Sonatas are multi-sectioned movements often containing fugues or canons and triple-time slow sections, while the technical requirements of movements such as the opening of the Sonata in 'La Musica Quinta' reflect Meister's time among technically accomplished musicians rather than the domestic *Collegia* described in Chapter 2.

Abstract music is not confined to the Sonatas. As well as the 'Fuga' in 'La Musica Sesta', there are a number of movements, mostly untitled, whose apparent purpose is to break up sequences of relatively simple dances with music that is often richly harmonised and chromatic. From the same fifth suite, Example 5.5 shows the start of the 'Arioso' that comes between the 'Corrente' and 'Menuet'.

100 *A time of decline: 1676–1700*

Table 5.1 Contents of J.F. Meister, *Il giardino del piacere overo raccolta de diversi fiori musicali, come Sonate, Fughe, Imitationi, Ciaccone, Passagaglie, Allemande, Correnti, &c.* (Hamburg, 1695)

Suite and key	Movements	Suite and key	Movements
La Musica Prima G major	Sonata Allemanda Sarabanda Corrente Menuet Gique	La Musica Settima F major	Sonata Allemanda Corrente Sarabanda Menuet Gique
La Musica Seconda D minor	Sonata Ciaconna untitled Menuet untitled Gique	La Musica Ottava B flat major	Sonata Menuet untitled Gique
La Musica Terza A major	Sonata Ballo Menuet Corrente Gavotta Gique	La Musica Nona G minor	Sonata Menuet untitled Gique
La Musica Quarta E minor	Sonata Sarabanda Variatio [I] Variatio [II] [delete space] Gique	La Musica Decima C minor	Sonata Passagaglia Allemanda Corrente Sarabanda Gique
La Musica Quinta C major	Sonata Corrente Arioso Menuet untitled Gique	La Musica Undecima D major	Sonata Menuet Fuga Menuet Gique
La Musica Sesta A minor	Sonata Menuet Fuga untitled Gique	La Musica Duodecima E flat major	Sonata Passagaglia Allemanda Corrente Sarabanda Menuet Gicque

The opening of the following example shows the E minor start of the movement within a suite in C major and this is typical of Meister's wide-ranging key schemes. While the opening and closing movements of suites are always in the same key, there is considerable variety in between. In the manner of Georg

Example 5.5 Meister, *Il giardino del piacere*, 'La Musica Quinta', 'Arioso'.

Table 5.2 Key relationships in Meister, *Il giardino del piacere*, 'La Musica Ottava'

Movement	Key
Sonata	B flat major
(Sonata) Fuga	B flat major
(Sonata) Adagio	G minor; ends in B flat major
(Sonata) [Adagio]	Chromatic modulation to C minor; ends in F major
Menuet	B flat major
Grave	G minor; ends in D minor
Gique	B flat major

Muffat's 1682 *Armonico tributo*, abstract movements often start in one key and finish in another. We can see this in Table 5.2, which shows the key relationships between movements and their sub-sections in the eighth suite.

It is hardly surprising that the dance movements themselves are Italian. The Gigues in particular are simple and propulsive; as with the *Correnti*, there is no suggestion of the German hybrid versions that often feature in town-music collections. The two sets of variations following the 'Sarabanda' of 'La Musica Quarta' are sets of *Doubles* in the traditional arpeggiated style.

In comparison with the moveable-type part-books of *Il giardino*, the engraved *Musicalische Ergötzung* makes a considerable visual impact, even if the layout is, at times, cramped.[15] The title page mentions Pachelbel's position as organist at the Nuremberg church of St Sebaldus; as the appointment was made in 1695, the publication must date from that year or later. Paul Whitehead has put forward a convincing case for 1699.[16]

There are three part-books in the only surviving exemplar: 'Violino Primo', 'Violino Secundo' and 'Cembalo'.[17] It is likely that a string bass part has been lost. While the use of *scordatura* tuning for both treble instruments recalling Wust's *EM 1* (see previous chapter) was perhaps regarded in dance music as rather old-fashioned at the time, the assertion that this hindered the sales of the collection is highly questionable.[18] There is no evidence to suggest that the dissemination of *Musicalische Ergötzung* was any better or any worse than other printed editions of instrumental music at the end of the century. Pachelbel does not employ these tunings for the virtuoso and dazzling effects achieved by Heinrich Biber; he merely requires a different sonority and a range of double-stopping techniques even if his use of the latter is relatively cautious – little more than chordal additions to final notes.[19] Like Kradenthaller's editions discussed in this and the previous chapter, the title page of *Musicalische Ergötzung* calls the collection 'music for recreation' and this may provide a reason for this caution.

The six suites of the collection are clearly identified and numbered as 'Partie' and there is none of Meister's experimenting with key. They fall into two basic patterns of movement sequences. All start with a Sonata; four close with a Sarabande and Gigue combination while the remaining two are shorter, and finish with a *Ciaconna*. In further contrast to *Il giardino*, the Sonatas themselves are not extended multi-section pieces but simple single-strain movements.

The choice of dance type clearly shows Pachelbel's court background; only two suites start the dance sequence with an Allemande and, without exception, the Courantes are French. The Viennese influence is apparent in the inclusion of a Trezza in 'Partie II' and 'Partie V'. Both *Ciaconna* are extended movements featuring a repeated bass-line formula. Like Meister, Pachelbel also provides *Double*-style variations for some of the movements although the 'Variatio' to the Ballet in 'Partie I' is the only set to be named as such. Here is further evidence of the quasi-improvisational approach that I discussed in Chapter 2; as we can see in Example 5.6, the second violin plays the original treble of the the dance movement while the first violin adds a layer of semiquaver figuration.

Finally we come to an example of a manuscript Sonata-suite by Dieterich Buxtehude.[20] It is surely an accident of preservation that only one consort suite by Buxtehude exists and, in a near-parallel with Weckmann in Hamburg, it is hard to believe that a composer with a substantial number of keyboard suites to his name should have composed so little in the consort genre. 'Sonata a 2 ex B. Con le Suite Violino è Violadagamba di Sig: Dieter: Buxtehude' (*BuxWV* 273) survives in manuscript *S-Uu* Instr. mus. i hskr.13:25, which comes from the 1680s or later.[21] While the copyist may have had Becker's *Sonaten und Suiten* in mind

A time of decline: 1676–1700 103

Example 5.6 J. Pachelbel, *Musicalische Ergötzung / bestehend in Sechs Verstimten Partien â 2. Violin nebst den Basso Continuo* (n.p., n.d.), 'Partie I', first strains of 'Ballet' and 'Variatio'.

Notes: the 'Cembalo' part of 'Variatio' is only indicated by repeat signs.

when it came to writing the title, there is no evidence to suggest that the work is from a now-lost printed edition.

Like the final suite in Becker's collection, Buxtehude's example is scored for violin, gamba and organ. The gamba has a fully independent part in the Sonata, but in the dance movements – Allemanda / Courant / Saraband / Gique – it mostly doubles or elaborates the bass *Organo* line. Buxtehude detached the Sonata from the dances when he included it as the fourth of his op. 1 sonatas, published in Lübeck in 1694 (*BuxWV* 255), but it does not follow from this that the dance movements were separately composed.[22] As we have seen, it was not unknown to reduce instrumentation from four or five parts in a Sonata to little more than the outer lines for ensuing dances. The part reduction further emphasises how, even away from the French tradition, composers such as Buxtehude had come to see dance music principally in terms of treble and bass.

Why were the suite movements excised from the printed version of the Sonata? Kerala Snyder considers that it was 'perhaps to bring this sonata into conformity with the others, perhaps to make it playable in church (although he does not mention this possibility in the title), or perhaps because he felt the predictable quality of the suite did not agree the prevailing aesthetic of the *Stylus phantasticus* that permeates the printed collection'.[23] While any of these reasons may be possible, Snyder's first suggestion seems the most feasible; Buxtehude wanted to include the piece in his printed collection and the dance movements were simply not required in a collection of Sonatas. As Snyder also remarks, there is no evidence that Buxtehude's Sonatas were ever intended for liturgical use. If a performance in church did take place, then it would probably have been at one of the *Abendmusiken* concerts that Buxtehude ran annually at the *Marienkirche* in Lübeck and there is no reason to think that the dance movements were not included. Example 5.7 shows the openings of the Allemande and Courante.

The Courante, along with the following Sarabande and Gigue, is a straightforward example of the Italian manner rather than the French or hybrid styles. Neither Sarabande nor Gigue is linked to the preceding dance pair. It is perhaps the simplicity of *BuxWV* 273 that led to Snyder's 'predictable' assessment of the suite section of this work.[24] This is surely too harsh. While the Courante here is basically a tertiary re-casting of the previous Allemande, Buxtehude does not present a slavish imitation. Unlike his keyboard suites, he varies the re-casting in order to make the Courante more idiomatic. This is particularly noticeable at the end of phrases where the Allemande original is extended in order to facilitate and enliven the cadences of the Courante. The dances may not be examples of Buxtehude's greatest music but, allied to a fine Sonata, the whole piece is worth more recognition that it currently receives.

So far in this book, I have drawn attention to the enduring strength of the town-music traditions in Leipzig and Hamburg, and it is time now to consider the music from these two major centres. It may be an accident of preservation, but more dance-music collections by Leipzig composers survive than from anywhere else in the German lands. It is clear that dance music was important for Leipzig musicians and that a strong tradition existed from the start of the seventeenth century in collections such as Schein's *Banchetto musicale*. One of the most important dance treatises of the early eighteenth century, *Rechtschaffener Tanzmeister*, was written by a Leipzig dancing master and we may see the strong link between the music of the dance and the Leipzig works of J.S. Bach as

A time of decline: 1676–1700 105

Example 5.1 D. Buxtehude (*BuxWV* 273), 'Sonata a 2 ex B. Con le Suite Violino è Violadagamba di Sig: Dieter: Buxtehude' (manuscript *S-Uu* Instr.mus.i hskr.13:25), first strain of 'Allamanda' and 'Courand'.

a further manifestation of this tradition. Chapter 6 divides the tradition into two parts: the string-based ensemble suite and the dance music played from towers and balconies.

In Hamburg, the tradition may not have been as productive in terms of output as Leipzig, but the town's composers still brought their own concepts of careful organisation and enhanced movement linking to bear upon the suite and printed collections. The Hamburg tradition will be dealt with in Chapter 7.

Notes

1. See S. Rose, 'Music, print and presentation in Saxony during the seventeenth century' *GH*, 23/1 (2005), pp. 1–19. See also H. Lenneberg, *On the publishing and dissemination of music 1500–1850* (Hillsdale, NY: Pendragon Press, 2005), pp. 60–61.
2. The British Library exemplar of the *Anderer Theil* 'Cembalo' part-book, *GB-Lbl* a.42.(2), does not have the equivalent *Erster Theil* part bound with it. This may be an indication that some *Anderer Theil* volumes were issued separately. But it is more likely that this exemplar was published as part of a two-volume set, the first of which became separated and lost.
3. See *CCS*, pp. 205–6.
4. See also *CCS*, pp. 220–22.
5. A. Layer, 'Scheiffelhut [Scheiffelhuet], Jakob [Jacob]' in D.L. Root (ed.), *Grove music online* (www.oxfordmusiconline.com) (accessed 27 October 2014).
6. Ibid.
7. L. Gerheuser, *Jacob Scheiffelhut und seine Instrumentalmusik* (Augsburg, 1931), p. 42. The rediscovery of part of the so-called 'Spitta collection' formerly in the Berlin *Hochschule für Musik* (who originally held the part-books) does not apparently include the missing first violin part. See C. Wolff, 'From Berlin to Łódź: the Spitta collection resurfaces' *Notes, Quarterly Journal of the Music Library Association*, 46/2 (1989), pp. 311–27. I have not been able to find any manuscript copies but it is possible to offer some reconstruction of the first violin line using the figured bass and the doublings by the keyboard in imitative passages.
8. Facsimiles of the title page and preface are given in the modern edition of the collection: J. Scheiffelhut (ed. K. Ruhland), *Leiblicher Frülings-Anfang* (Magdeburg: Edition Walhall, 2003). For comments regarding the basso viola, see Chapter 3, fn. 1.
9. It is unfortunate that the modern edition of these suites does not retain this barring but adds extra lines to conform to a modern interpretation of the triple-time signature. Scheiffelhut (ed. Ruhland), *Leiblicher Frülings-Anfang*.
10. It is unlikely that there is any great significance for performers in the use of both 'Lente' and 'Adagio'.
11. See S. Rose, *The musician in literature in the age of Bach* (Cambridge: Cambridge University Press, 2011), pp. 34–5.
12. Hammerschmidt links material across collections, but not in the way that Speer does. See Chapter 3.
13. A. Waczkat, 'Meister [Maistre, Maestro], Johann Friedrich' in D.L. Root (ed.) *Grove music online* (www.oxfordmusiconline.com) (accessed 27 October 2014).
14. Richard Hudson considers that one Allemande of the collection, identified by him as '32a', 'exhibits the motivic counterpoint that had developed in Italy'. But this is to ignore the long tradition of such Allemande writing that had developed in Germany. R. Hudson, *The Allemande, the Balletto and the Tanz*, 2 vols (Cambridge: Cambridge University Press, 1986), Vol. 1, p. 191.
15. For example, the Sonata of 'Partie IV' in the 'Violino Primo' part-book.
16. P. Whitehead, 'Austro-German printed sources of instrumental music, 1630 to 1700', PhD dissertation (University of Pennsylvania, 1996), pp. 662–3.
17. Facsimile edition: J. Pachelbel (ed. F. Dangel-Hofmann), *Musicalische Ergötzung* (Courlay: Éditions J.M. Fuzeau, 1992). For an overview of Pachelbel's career and output, see: M. Robertson, 'Johann Pachelbel 1653–1706' in *The Early Music Yearbook 2006* (Hebden Bridge: The National Early Music Association, 2006), pp. 5–10.
18. J. Pachelbel (ed. F. Zobeley), *Triosuiten für zwei Violinen und Basso continuo*, Hortus Musicus 54–56 (Kassel: Bärenreiter, 1960–66), Preface.
19. See also Robertson, 'Johann Pachelbel', p. 8.

20 I have used the spelling of the composer's name adopted by K.J. Snyder in *Dieterich Buxtehude: organist in Lübeck*, 2nd edition (Rochester, NY: University of Rochester Press, 2007).
21 Modern edition: D. Buxtehude (ed. E. Linfield), *The collected works*, vol. 14 (New York: Broude Trust, 1994), pp. 223–37.
22 There are minor differences between the manuscript and printed versions of the Sonata. It is likely that these were revisions made for the printed edition.
23 Snyder, *Dieterich Buxtehude*, pp. 349–50.
24 Ibid., p. 352.

6 Leipzig

If the 1660s marked the start of a trend towards clearer organisation of suite collections by town composers, the same thing happened a good deal earlier in Leipzig. In addition, and unlike suites written elsewhere, many Leipzig composers appear to offer the performer not just a choice of movement, but a choice of movement sequences. These concepts single out the Leipzig tradition as being independent of mainstream suite writing, and provide much of the focus for this chapter. Given the quantity of music under consideration, I have divided the chapter into two parts; the first deals with string-based ensembles, the second with wind-based ensembles. For the same reason, the music in both sections is dealt with by composer, and not chronologically.

String-based ensembles

Seventeenth-century Leipzig was 'the most significant trade centre for eastern Europe'.[1] Its position as a trade centre and university town meant that it 'had a magnified impact on the society and culture of early modern Germany'.[2] It was largely self-governing, but as one of the Imperial towns recognised in the Treaty of Westphalia, it was also partially subject to the Electoral court at Dresden. For example, the Elector could take it to war.[3] And it had suffered heavily during the Thirty Years War. Leipzig was under siege no fewer than five times, major battles were fought nearby and the inhabitants were subjected to periods of starvation.[4] Recovery was slow but the city's trading prowess brought it back to genuine prosperity by the 1680s. The frequent lists of civic dignitaries given at the start of many Leipzig suite collections suggest that the support and patronage given to Leipzig's musicians and composers was as good as anywhere else in the German lands, if not better.[5] And this is confirmed by the one-time Leipzig composer Johann Caspar Horn, who later in Dresden referred to the 'Welt berühmte' (world-famous) appreciation of music by the Leipzig municipal authorities.[6] Despite Rosenmüller's complaints in the preface to his 1654 *Studenten-Music* about the circulation of unauthorised manuscript copies of his music before it had reached print, it seems that most instrumental collections were issued as printed editions.

While suites for string trio were not unknown in Leipzig (see Rosenmüller's 1645 collection below), the standard string-based ensemble required four or five parts often with the *Fagott* or, in its later French form, the bassoon. The title page of Gottfried Taubert's Leipzig 1717 dance treatise, *Rechtschaffener Tanzmeister oder gründlicher Erklärung der Frantzösischen Tantz-Kunst*, shows just such an ensemble.[7] This is confirmed in the text of the treatise, where the bassoon, along with the *violone*, is described as having an association with the French dance ('als Violinen mit Violonen und Bassonen untermenget zum Frantzösischen Tantzen schicken').[8] It may be significant that no keyboard instrument or lute is shown; we should not assume that dance music was always played with a chordal accompaniment. Taubert also mentions trumpets, drums and oboes, but this is eighteenth- rather than seventeenth-century practice.

In additional to the domestic ensembles that were the target for Kuhnau's satire (see Chapter 1), Leipzig had an important tradition of university student performance. According to J.S. Bach, 'even my predecessors Messrs Schelle and Kuhnau had to avail themselves of assistance from the *studiosi* if they wanted to produce a full and well-sounding musical ensemble'.[9] The specific linking of the term 'Collegium musicum' with the Leipzig student body first appeared shortly after the middle of the seventeenth century.[10] Membership of the *Collegium* was clearly desirable, so it is not surprising that the *Nikolaikantor* Elias Nathusius noted in his 1657 application for the post of *Thomaskantor* that, in his time as a student, he regularly attended the 'Collegio Musico Practico'. And the civic official and lawyer Sigismund Finckelthaus did the same in a job application that had nothing to do with music. Former students could retain their membership, as long as they stayed in Leipzig, and the evidence pointing to a regular body of players is seemingly strong from the 1660s onwards.[11] Student participation in Leipzig secular events and evening entertainments is confirmed by Johann Rosenmüller in the preface to *Studenten-Music*.[12] And it is to the latter's music that I now turn.

'Der alhier wolbekante und berühmbte Musicus Rosenmüller' (the here well-known and famous musician Rosenmüller) was arguably the most influential Leipzig composer of dance suites in the seventeenth-century German lands.[13] Starting his study at the University of Leipzig in the summer of 1640, Rosenmüller gained a junior post of 'Collaborator' (teaching assistant) at the *Thomasschule* in the following year.[14] In 1645–46, he made his first trip to Italy and, by 1651, was organist of the Leipzig *Nikolaikirche*. By 1653, he was in line for the post of *Cantor* at the *Thomasschule*,[15] but this rapid career progress came to an abrupt end in 1655. According to a letter written by a minor court official in Dresden and dated 10 May 1655, Rosenmüller had been implicated, if not directly involved, in a scandal concerning sodomy among a group of pupils at the *Thomasschule*.[16] Before further enquiries could be made, Rosenmüller fled to Italy, where he became a trombonist at the church of San Marco in Venice. Around 1682, he returned to Germany and took up a court position in Wolfenbüttel.

Rosenmüller's first collection of dance music, *Paduanen, Alemanden, Couranten, Balletten, Sarabanden, Mit drey Stimmen / Und ihrem Basso pro Organo* was published in Leipzig in 1645, just before his first Italian trip, and scored for two treble parts (*Cantus* I and II, presumably violins), *Bassus* and *Bassus pro organo*.[17] The first twenty movements are not arranged by movement type, but divided into four suites, all with the same sequence of *Paduan / Alemanda / Courant / Ballet / Sarabanda*. In addition, the suites are arranged in ascending order of key, and Rosenmüller makes frequent use of variation techniques. Three of the suites seem to have a specific visual layout: apart from the opening Paduan, their movements are printed together on facing pages, and blank staves are inserted after the *Paduanen* to facilitate this layout. As we have seen, such careful organisation was all but unknown in the 1640s and, like Neubauer in Kassel, Rosenmüller could well have been influenced by Schein's *Banchetto musicale*. Given that Schein was *Thomaskantor* in Leipzig from 1616 until his death in 1630, this is hardly surprising. On the other hand, it is curious that, in the light of his subsequent heavy use of note blackening in the Courantes and Sarabandes of his later publications, Rosenmüller did not employ it here, even though there were plenty of opportunities to do so. Perhaps he was not aware of the technique's versatility at this stage in his career.

Rosenmüller's Italian trip appears to have exerted little influence on the structure of his next collection of dance music, *Studenten-Music* (Leipzig, 1654), but it would be surprising if it had done so. Italian dance-music collections at this time were mostly grouped by movement type and not as suites. For example, Biagio Marini's *Per ogni sorte di strumento musicale diversi generi di sonate, da chiesa, e da camera ... Libro terzo* (Venice, 1655) starts with four *Balletti* followed by four *Zarabandi* and four *Correnti*. *Studenten-Music* could hardly be more different.

If *Studenten-Music* does start with grouping by movement type – seven *à3 Paduanen* – it is hardly a reflection of Italian style; as we have seen, same-movement groupings were regularly used to open town-music collections. Thereafter, the collection moves to a five-part instrumentation comprising *Cantus primus, Cantus secundus, Altus, Tenor* and *Bassus continuus* for the ten suites that follow. The preface states that some parts 'oftermals in größter Eilfertigkeit aufgesetzet worden' (were often put together in great haste) but, despite this, there is the same sense of careful organisation that informs the 1645 collection. Both the opening *à3* sequence and following suites are arranged in ascending order of key; the start of each suite is clearly marked by the use of a Paduan that, with one exception, is followed by an Allemande. The *Paduanen* are all substantial movements of three strains and, in most cases, follow the diminution of note values and gradual intensification in rhythm that I discussed in Chapter 2. The five-part Allemandes in the collection, as Richard Hudson has pointed out, all 'utilize a dense and continuous texture'.[18]

The Courantes are a mixture of the Italian and German-hybrid styles, though with some important variety within the format. Example 6.1 shows the openings of '10. Courant. *Adagio*' and '11. Courant. *Alegro*'.

Leipzig 111

Example 6.1 Rosenmüller, *Studenten-Music / Darinnen zu befinden Allerhand Sachen Mit drey und fünff Violen* (Leipzig, 1654), openings of '10. Courant' and '11. Courant'.

While we should not interpret these *Adagio* and 'Alegro' markings in the modern sense – the *Adagio* is probably no more than an indication of slower than the norm – they do reflect the different characteristics of the two dances. '10. Courant', with its block chords indicated by *caesura* marks, is quite different from the livelier figuration in '11. Courant'. They are not the only dance types to be subject to this diverse treatment; Table 6.1 details the variety of Ballo movements in the collection.

As we can see, there are a number of *Balli* where the second strain has a different marking from the first. The use of two markings within the second strain of '14. Ballo' is reminiscent of Hammerschmidt's collections and it is likely that Rosenmüller knew of them. As with the former's music and the Courantes above, the markings should mostly be seen as changes of character and not as a wide divergence between fast and slow. On the other hand, the 'Adagio Adagio' of '53. Ballo' clearly indicates that a tempo much slower than the norm is required for the

Table 6.1 Ballo details in Rosenmüller, *Studenten-Music*

Movement title	First strain marking	Second strain marking
14. Ballo	Unmarked	*Adagio*, then 'Alegro'
19. Ballo	*Adagio*	'Alegro'
28. Ballo	Unmarked	Unmarked
33. Ballo	'Alegro'	Unmarked
38. Ballo	*Adagio*	'Alegro'
43. Ballo	Unmarked	Unmarked
48. Ballo	*Adagio*	'Alegro'
53. Ballo	*Adagio Adagio*	'Alegro'
58. Ballo	Unmarked	Unmarked

first strain. As the marking is the same in all the part-books, it is unlikely to be a printer's error.

Despite its clarity, the organisation of the collection does pose an important question. After the opening group of *Paduanen*, the first sequence of dance movements, all in the key of C major is as follows:

8. Paduan / 9. Alemanda / 10. Courant / 11. Courant / 12. Alemanda / 13. Courant / 14. Ballo / 15. Sarabanda

The first Allemande and Courante pair are linked; unusually, '12. Alemanda' is linked not to the following Courante, but to '15. Sarabanda'. But by linking the first and last, Rosenmüller is demonstrating that, beyond any shadow of doubt, movements 12–15 are intended as a unified sequence. The position of 8–11 in this scheme is less clear. Was the entire group intended to be played together or treated as two separate sequences? Or did Rosenmüller expect the performers to exercise some sort of choice in order to produce a sequence that is closer to the norm of Paduan / Allemande / Courante(s) / Ballo / Sarabande elsewhere in the collection? The same questions apply to movements 24–9, all in F major, where a Paduan is followed by a linked Allemande / Courante pair and an Allemande / Ballo pair before the final Sarabande. If the answers are not immediately apparent, important light is shed on them in Rosenmüller's next collection, the 1667 *Sonate da camera cioe Sinfonie, Alemande, Correnti, Balletti, Sarabande.*

If Schein's *Banchetto musicale* is arguably the finest suite collection from the first half of the century, Rosenmüller's *Sonate da camera* can make a similar claim for the second half. It was printed in Venice by Alessandro Vincenti and must have sold well, for a second edition was issued in 1670.[19] And while it was printed outside the German lands, there is no doubt that the collection is firmly within the Leizpig tradition. Had it been published inside the German lands, the title would have comprised a typically German list of movement types. However, there is one important Italian feature of this publication: along with nearly every other Italian printed collection of dance music, it carries a

Tavola (index). As a result of an arbitrary dismissal by Karl Nef in his 1904 edition of *Sonate da camera*, this *Tavola* is barely known even though it has very important things to tell us about the collection.[20] Table 6.2 details the contents of each suite as given in the part-books along with the *Tavola* variants in order.

Table 6.2 Contents, J. Rosenmüller, *Sonate da camera cioe Sinfonie, Alemande, Correnti, Balletti, Sarabande, Da Svonare Con Cingue Stromenti Da Arco, et altri* (Venice, 1667)

Suite	Part-book ordering	Tavola ordering
Prima	Sinfonia Prima / Alemanda / Correnta / Intrata à 5. obligati / Ballo / Sarabanda	Sinfonia Prima con la sua Alemanda, Correnta, Intrata, Ballo, e Sarabanda
Seconda	Sinfonia Seconda / Alemanda / Correnta / Ballo / Sarabanda	Sinfonia Seconda con la sua Alemanda, Corrrenta, Ballo, e Serabanda [sic]
Terza	Sinfonia Terza / Alemanda [I] / Correnta [I] / Ballo / Sarabanda / Intrata [à 5. Obligati] / Alemanda [II] / Correnta [II] / Correnta [III]	Sinfonia Terza con la sua Alemanda, Correnta, Intrata, Ballo, e Sarabanda
Quarta	Sinfonia Quarta / Alemanda / Correnta / Ballo / Sarabanda	Sinfonia Quarta con la sua Alemanda, Correnta, Ballo, e Sarabanda
Quinta	Sinfonia Quinta / Alemanda / Correnta / Intrata à 5. Obligati / Ballo / Sarabanda	Sinfonia Quinta con la sua Alemanda, Correnta, Intrata, Ballo, e Sarabanda
Sesta	Sinfonia Sesta / Alemanda / Correnta / Ballo / Sarabanda	Sinfonia Sesta con la sua Alemanda, Correnta, Ballo, e Sarabanda
Settima	Sinfonia Settima / Alemanda / Correnta / Ballo / Sarabanda	Sinfonia Settima con la sua Alemanda, Correnta, Ballo, e Sarabanda
Ottava	Sinfonia Ottava / Alemanda / Correnta / Ballo / Sarabanda	Sinfonia Ottava con la sua Alemanda, Correnta, Ballo, e Sarabanda
Nona	Sinfonia Nona / Alemanda / Correnta / Ballo / Sarabanda	Sinfonia Nona con la sua Alemanda, Correnta, Ballo, e Sarabanda
Decima	Sinfonia Decima / Alemanda / Correnta / Ballo / Sarabanda	Sinfonia Decima con la sua Alemanda, Correnta, Ballo, e Sarabanda
Undecima	Sinfonia Undecima / Alemanda / Correnta / Ballo / Sarabanda / Alemanda [II] / Correnta [II]	Sinfonia Undecima con la sua Alemanda, Correnta, Ballo, e Sarabanda

Note: the 'à5. Obligati' qualification to the Intrada of 'Sinfonia Terza' is missing from the violin part books, but present in those of the lower parts.

As we can see from the table, each suite is clearly identified by the numbering that appears in both *Tavola* and musical text. In addition to its movement-type identification, 'Sinfonia' is also used as a generic term for each complete sequence in the same way that 'Ballo' is used in Knoep's *Ander Theil Newer Paduanen*. Of most significance is the different movement order from the main musical text that the *Tavola* gives for the third and eleventh suites. As with *Studenten-Music*, this poses important questions; were the movements of these suites played in the written order of the text in the part-books, or does the *Tavola* offer some form of movement choice for the performer?

Given that Italian dance-music collections before the 1680s are often no more than sequences of like movements, it is likely that Rosenmüller, or his Venetian publisher was using the *Tavola* to draw attention to a specific concept of suite ordering little known in Italy at the time. For 'Sinfonia Terza' and 'Sinfonia Undecima' and *Studenten-Music*, the implication appears to be that there is a choice available to the performer of not just movements, but whole sequences. And while it is possible that the *Tavola* may be nothing more than a truncated list, this would be unusual, if not unique, among Italian dance-music publications.

It is likely that the first and second suites should be seen as exemplars for movement ordering for the whole collection. Thus, Rosenmüller's intentions in the third suite, which has been described as 'an improbable configuration', become clear.[21] Using the first two suites and the *Tavola* as a guide, the following choices of movement sequences are all possible:

1. Sinfonia Terza / Alemanda [I] / Correnta [I] / Ballo / Sarabanda
2. Sinfonia Terza / Alemanda [I] / Correnta [I] / Intrata / Ballo / Sarabanda
3. Sinfonia Terza / Alemanda [II] / Correnta [II] / Correnta [III] / Intrata / Ballo / Sarabanda

The *Tavola* also suggests that the contents of the collection could be performed as trios by simply leaving out the middle parts played by the violas ('A presente Opera Composta à cinque Stromenti, si potrà ancora Sonare à doi Violini soli è Basso'), and it is clear that some musicians took this instruction, either from Rosenmüller or his publisher, at face value. The so-called 'Rost manuscript' (*F-Pn* Rés.Vm^7 673) includes three Sonatas from the collection all arranged in this way. Where omission of the middle parts would do serious damage to the *Invention*, François Rost, the compiler of the manuscript, simply left out entire sections of music.[22] But Rosenmüller himself seems to be issuing a warning that not all the abstract movements are suitable for this treatment: all three Intradas carry the qualification 'à 5. obligati', presumably an indication that all five instrumental parts of are equal importance. And in each case, the viola parts do contribute significantly to the *Invention*. Clearly, they should not be dispensed with. It is curious that Rost did not include any of the dance music from the collection: these are effective in trio combinations and, as we can see in Example 6.2, the important material is confined to the two violins and bass. The viola parts are little more than fillers, suggesting that some of the dance music in the collection may well have started life as trios.

Example 6.2 Rosenmüller, *Sonate da camera*, 'Sinfonia Terza', 'Ballo'.

One of the most important features of this collection is the use of abstract movements, in this case the *Sinfonie*, to preface the main body of dance movements. It is not the earliest incidence of such use: a decade earlier, the court composer Johann-Jacob Löwe von Eisenach had used 'Synfonien' as a prefatory movement in his *Synfonien, Intraden, Gagliarden, Arien, Balletten, Couranten, Sarabanden. mit 3. Oder 5. Instrumenten* (Bremen, 1657–58), and it is possible that Rosenmüller's idea of using a prefatory abstract movement came from Löwe's collection.[23] More likely is the simple use of the *Sinfonie* as a more modern substitute for the increasingly old-fashioned Paduan that had been used previously in both *Studenten-Music* and *Paduanen, Alemanden, Couranten, Balletten, Sarabanden, Mit drey Stimmen*.

In the dances themselves, Rosenmüller makes frequent use of note-blackened off-beat rhythms for his hybrid-style Courantes and Sarabandes.[24] Example 6.3 shows the opening of the *Correnta* of 'Sinfonia Seconda'.

The Sarabandes also contain considerable amounts of note blackening and often exhibit a restless quality not always found in standard versions. Unlike *Studenten-Music*, each Ballo follows the standard double-strain format without variation of tempo; two are marked 'Presto' and this would seem to be appropriate for all the examples in the collection. Of the absolute movements, the three Intradas found in the first, third and fifth suites are more substantial than the single-strain versions often found elsewhere in the Leipzig tradition and, as we have seen, they contain musically important viola parts. All three are divided into three strains, but only the Intrada from the first suite has a section in triple time. But there can be little doubt that the finest movements in the collection are the opening Sinfonias that are, in effect, multi-sectioned Sonatas. They are detailed in Table 6.3.

As we can see, the duple-/triple-time combination of C; 3/2; C; 3/2 remains the same for each Sinfonia, but within this structure, Rosenmüller allows himself some variation. The common-time third section in each example never changes its *Allegro* designation, but the 3/2 sections on either side are sometimes *Allegro*,

116 *Leipzig*

Example 6.3 Rosenmüller, *Sonate da camera*, 'Sinfonia Seconda', 'Correnta'.

Table 6.3 Rosenmüller, *Sonate da camera*, details of 'Sinfonia' movements

Title	Key	Individual section details
Sinfonia Prima	F major	C: grave – 3/2: allegro – [C]: allegro – 3/2: allegro
Sinfonia Seconda	D major	C: allegro – 3/2: adagio – [C]: allegro – 3/2: adagio
Sinfonia Terza	C major	C: grave – 3/2: allegro – [C]: allegro – 3/2: allegro
Sinfonia Quarta	G minor	C: [unmarked] – 3/2: adagio – [C]: allegro – 3/2: [adagio]
Sinfonia Quinta	D minor	C: allegro – 3/2: allegro – [C]: allegro – 3/2: allegro
Sinfonia Sesta	A minor	C: allegro – 3/2: adagio – [C]: allegro – 3/2: adagio
Sinfonia Settima	G major	C: grave – 3/2: allegro – [C]: allegro – 3/2: allegro
Sinfonia Ottava	E minor	C: grave – 3/2: allegro – [C]: allegro – 3/2: allegro
Sinfonia Nona	B flat major	C: [unmarked] – 3/2: allegro – [C]: allegro – 3/2: allegro
Sinfonia Decima	A major	C: grave – 3/2: allegro – [C]: allegro – 3/2: allegro
Sinfonia Undecima	C minor	C: grave – 3/2: adagio – [C]: allegro – 3/2: adagio

and sometimes *Adagio*. Rosenmüller is fond of combining rich harmonies with rhetorical silences in the opening and subsequent linking sections. Again, the importance of the two viola parts is clear, and it is difficult to imagine this music performed without them.

Even though Rosenmüller went into exile before the publication of *Sonate da camera*, all three of his suite collections seem to have influenced other Leipzig composers. Werner Fabricius' *Deliciae Harmonicae, oder Musicalische Gemüths-Ergätzung* was published in 1657 in Leipzig, three years after *Studenten-Music*. Fabricius was organist at both the *Paulinerkirche* and *Nikolaikirche* in Leipzig and university music director.[25] He was unsuccessful in his application for the post of *Thomaskantor* in 1657.[26] We can be certain that he knew Rosenmüller or, at the very least, knew of his work. Example 6.4 gives the 'Continuus' and two treble parts of the identically numbered '38. Ballo' from both *Studenten-Music* and *Deliciae Harmonicae*.

The similarity is obvious, and the identical numbering is not coincidental; the arrangement of Fabricius' collection is nearly identical to Rosenmüller's. *Deliciae Harmonicae*'s suites are grouped into the same ascending order of key, finishing with a suite in C minor though, for reasons that are not clear, perhaps a printer's error, the expected penultimate suite in B flat is omitted and replaced by one in D major that may have been originally intended as the final suite.

Rosenmüller's influence can also be seen in the works of Johann Pezel (1639–94), a Leipzig town musician for much of his professional career. While the dedications in Pezel's surviving printed collections range from various tradesmen to Leipzig town council members, a background as a comparatively lowly town musician may have been an impediment when he failed in his quest to be appointed to the post of *Thomaskantor* in 1676.[27] Perhaps this setback prompted him to move away from Leipzig about five years later.

In addition to the eight extant printed editions of Pezel's instrumental music issued between 1669 and 1686, there may have been other collections that are now lost although it was not unknown for second volumes to be advertised but never actually published. His final dance-music publication may have been the *Musica Curiosa Lipsica* (Leipzig, 1686) listed in Gerber's *Tonwerke* catalogue, but this was probably a re-issue of his first collection of suites, *Musica vespertina Lipsica oder Leipzigische Abend-Music* (Leipzig, 1669, hereafter *MvL*).[28]

The 'Abend-Music' of *MvL*'s title suggests evening entertainment similar to Rosenmüller's *Studenten-Music* and we are told that the music can be played by anything from one to five parts ('mit 1. 2. 3. 4. oder 5. Stimmen zu spielen'). The collection is also said to be in 'Nach der neusten heut-tägigen Manier' (in the newest contemporary manner) but Pezel is not clear about what is meant by all this. And, despite the title page, there is no obvious music for solo instrument.[29] Presumably Pezel or his publisher was suggesting treble-line-only performance of the dances in the manner of a dancing master, although there is little to link this collection to functional dance.

MvL is made up of twelve readily identifiable suites, each one starting with a Sonata or a Sonatina. All but two of the suites have a second non-dance movement

Example 6.4 Comparisons between Rosenmüller, *Studenten-Music*, '38. Ballo' and W. Fabricius, *Deliciæ Harmonicæ, oder Musicalische Gemüths-Ergätzung* (Leipzig, 1657), '38. Ballo'.

Note: in each case, the *Altus*, *Tenor* and *Bassus* parts are not shown.

at the start, either an Intrada or a Prelude, a concept that may well have been copied by Becker in Hamburg (see the following chapter). While a gradual increase of sonority in the manner of collections from the previous decade would seem to be indicated by *MvL*'s title page, the instrumentation is more diverse than this, often changing during the course of a suite in the manner of Schein's *Banchetto musicale*. All the Sonatas and Sonatinas are in *à5* instrumentation of two violins, two violas and bass, but the following Preludes and dances are often in *à4* or *à3*.[30] The reduction is not made by leaving out instruments, but by doubling them. Example 6.5 shows the first strain of '16. Prælude'; in addition to the doubled violin and viola parts, we can also see the optional 'Fagotto' part that appears throughout the collection.

The final suite of the collection is an 'alternative'. Instead of a Sonata and an Allemande, Pezel starts off with a Capriccio that is followed by an extended Bransle sequence and a further set of closing dances. The seventeen movements of this suite are all in two-part instrumentation achieved again through doubling – the first violin part is merely reproduced in all the other part-books except the bass – which reflects Pezel's knowledge of single-line or treble and bass dissemination used in many Bransle sequences. So the suggestions that 'Pezel's imagination seems to have been restricted by the customs of the day and the limited audience for which he must have been writing' and that 'contact with a wide range of international styles and musicians must have been haphazard' are wide of the mark.[31] In fact, Leipzig's position as a major trade centre, the presence of law courts and the importance of its university suggest the opposite.[32] Charles Brewer has already pointed to the 'dissemination of Habsburg tradition to northern Europe' and we have already seen an example of it in Kradenthaller's *Anderer Theil* in southern Germany.[33] Peter Wollny has produced clear evidence to show the links between the day-to-day repertoire of the Leipzig student *Collegium musicum*

Example 6.5 J. Pezel, *Musica vespertina Lipsica oder Leipzigische Abend-Music* (Leipzig, 1669), '16. Prælude'.

and the Habsburg tradition in the manuscripts copied by Johann von Assig und Siegersdorff (the Assig collection now held in the Uppsala Universitetsbibliotek) while he was studying at the university between 1669 and 1672.[34] So it is highly likely that Pezel knew of a wide range of music from sources outside Leipzig. If he substitutes an Italian Ballo between '89. Amener' and '91. Gavotte' of the quasi-French Bransle sequence in the 'alternative' suite of *MvL*, it is surely a deliberate choice and not one arising from ignorance.

Pezel's next surviving suite collection is *Musicalische Gemüths-Ergetzung* (Leipzig, 1672) though only the 'Violino 1' part-book is extant. The title page tells us that the instrumentation is for the four-part 'Zwey Violinen, einer Viola, und Basso Continuo oder Violon' rather than the more usual five-part combination with two violas. Again, the influence of Rosenmüller is apparent. Example 6.6 compares '9. Sarabande' from *Musicalische Gemüths-Ergetzung* with the 'Sarabanda' from the first suite of *Sonate da camera*. Even if Rosenmüller's 'Sarabanda' is in F major and Pezel's apparently in D minor, the melodic similarity between the two is striking and surely no coincidence.

Table 6.4 lists the contents of *Musicalische Gemüths-Ergetzung*. Seven suites have sequences of dances containing duplication of movement types and, in all but suites 5, 6 and 8, it seems that Pezel is again following Rosenmüller in offering a choice not of individual movements, but entire sequences. To make it clearer for the performer, each alternative sequence starts with an Allemande. Thus, in the fourth suite of the collection, there are at least four possible sequences of dances to place between the Intrada and the final Sarabande–Gigue pairing:

1. 31. Intrade / 32. Allemande / 33. Courente / 34. Gauotte / 35. Sarabande / 46. Gigue
2. 31. Intrade / 36. Allemande / 37. Courente / 38. Ballet / 39. Sarabande / 46. Gigue
3. 31. Intrade / 40. Allemande / 41. Courente / 45. Sarabande / 46. Gigue
4. 31. Intrade / 42. Allemande / 43. Sarabande / 44. Allebreve / 45. Sarabande / 46. Gigue.

It may not be a coincidence that the first three of these possible combinations are similar in movement type and order to the following fifth and sixth suites. Perhaps Pezel, like Rosenmüller, was offering an exemplar. As with *MvL* and Rosenmüller's *Sonate da camera*, a second non-dance movement, this time an 'Allabreve', appears in the first four suites.

Delitiæ musicales (Frankfurt 1678, hereafter *Dm*) does survive complete and, with its quasi-Latin titles for some of the abstract movements, the collection of seven suites has every appearance of Pezel attempting to portray himself as a learned musician. Perhaps this was a response to being passed over as Cantor of the *Thomaskirche* two years earlier and linked to his efforts to find posts away from Leipzig. If the latter, Pezel certainly succeeded: as we have seen, it seems that he was given a post at Bautzen in 1681 on the strength of his publications.[35]

Leipzig 121

Example 6.6 Comparisons between J. Pezel, *Musicalische Gemüths-Ergetzung Bestehend Intraden, Allemanden, Balletten, Gavotten, Alle breven, Couranten, Sarabanden und Chiqven* (Leipzig, 1672), '9. Sarabande', and Rosenmüller, *Sonate da camera*, 'Sinfonia Prima', 'Sarabanda'.

Table 6.4 Pezel, *Musicalische Gemüths-Ergetzung*, contents

Suite	Content
1	1. Intrade / 2. Allemande / 3. Courente / 4. Allemande / 5. Courente / 6. Allebreue / 7. Courente / 8. Gauotte / 9. Sarabande / 10. Gigue
2	11. Intrade / 12. Allemande / 13. Sarabande / 14. Allemande / 15. Courente / 16. Allebreue / 17. Courente / 18. Ballet / 19. Sarabande / 20. Gigue
3	21. Intrade / 22. Allemande / 23. Sarabande / 24. Allemande / 25. Courente / 26. Allebreue / 27. Courente / 28. Gauotte / 29. Sarabande / 30. Gigue
4	31. Intrade / 32. Allemande / 33. Courente / 34. Gauotte / 35. Sarabande / 36. Allemande / 37. Courente / 38. Ballet / 39. Sarabande / 40. Allemande / 41. Courente / 42. Allemande / 43. Sarabande / 44. Allebreue / 45. Sarabande / 46. Gigue
5	47. Intrade / 48. Allemande / 49. Courente / 50. Gauotte / 51. Sarabande / 52. Gigue
6	53. Intrade / 54. Allemande / 55. Courente / 56. Gauotte / 57. Sarabande / 58. Gigue
7	59. Intrade / 60. Allemande / 61. Courente / 62. Allemande / 63. Courente / 64. Gauotte / 65. Sarabande / 66. Gigue
8	67. Intrade / 68. Allemande / 69. Courente / 70. Ballet / 71. Sarabande / 72. Gigue
9	73. Intrade / 74. Allemande / 75. Courente / 76. Gauotte / 77. Sarabande / 78. Allemande / 79. Sarabande / 80. Gigue
10	81. Intrade / 82. Allemande / 83. Courente / 84. Allemande / 85. Sarabande / 86. Allemande / 87. Courente / 88. Gauotte / 89. Sarabande / 90. Gigue

122 *Leipzig*

The collection's instrumentation is for *à5* strings and continuo with the addition of a 'Fagott' that may, as I have said earlier, be an indication of general Leipzig performance practice. Its contents are detailed in Table 6.5.

Dm has its weak moments; '41. Intermedium', for example, relies entirely on repetitions of an unremarkable rhythmic pattern that the often-predictable harmonic sequences do nothing to help. Similarly, the treble line of '34. Sursum Deorsum à4' follows the movement's title (up and down) far too literally. But taken as a whole, the standard is often impressive and the musical language of the dances in particular can be adventurous. Pezel includes *Adagio* Courantes in the manner of Rosenmüller and takes the opportunity in these movements to provide a harmonic language that is, for dance music, extraordinarily rich. As in parts of *MvL*, the dance movements use *à3* or *à4* instrumentation rather than the *à5* of the abstract movements. The *à4* reduction is enabled by the merging of the violin parts or, in *à3*, the merging of the viola parts as well.

At first, it seems that Pezel is again offering a choice of movement sequences in all but the third and fifth suites, but the 'Regeneratio' and 'Intermedium' movements that appear in the third, fourth and fifth clearly have an important function

Table 6.5 Contents of J. Pezel, *Delitiæ musicales, oder Lust-Music, Bestehend in Sonaten, Allemanden, Balleten, Gavotten, Courenten, Sarabanden, und Chiquen* (Frankfurt am Main, 1678)

Suite	Key	Movement numbers	Movement titles
1	C major	1–9	Sonata à5 / Allemande à3 / Courente à3 / Bal. à3 / Courente à3 / Bourre à3 / Sarabande à3 / Chique à3 / Conclusio à5
2	G minor	10–20	Sonata à5 / Bransle à4 / Gay à4 / Amener à4 / Courente à4 / Gavotte à4 / Courente à4 / Bal. à4 / Sarabande à4 / Chique à4 / Conclusio à5
3	D major	21–7	Sonata à5 / Allemande à4 / Courente à4 / Intermedium à5 / Sarabande à4 / Chique à5 / Conclusio à5
4	F major	28–36	Sonata à5 / Allemande à4 / Courente à4 / Regeneratio à5 / Allemande à4 / Courente à4 / Sursum Deorsum à4 / Chique à4 / Conclusio à5
5	C minor	37–47	Sonata à5 / Allemande à4 / Courente à4 / Sarabande à4 / Intermedium à5 / Allemande à4 / Courente à4 / Allegro à4 / Sarabande à4 / Chique à4 / Conclusio à5
6	A major	48–55	Paduana à5 / Galliarda à5 / Bal. à4 / Courente à4 / Gavotte à4 / Sarabande à4 / Chique à4 / Conclusio à5
7	C major	56–[63]	Sonata à5 / Allemande à4 / Courente à4 / Allemande à4 / Sarabande à4 / Gavotte à4 / Chique à3 / Conclusio à5

as a halfway point within their respective sequences. While the third suite is straightforward, the fourth and fifth suites point to a different, compound, construction emphasised by movement titles. In both, Pezel moves from the opening sonata to the *Regeneratio* or *Intermedium* middle point via one sequence of dances: a similar set leads back to the *Conclusio*. Three of the *Conclusio* movements are marked 'adagio' and all of them have a serious character reminiscent of the *Retirada* that composers at the Austrian imperial court used to end their suites.

Perhaps for the reasons discussed above, Pezel is attempting to demonstrate his originality and present a different concept of suite construction: unified and carefully structured with a deliberate repetition of dance types. The collection's 'alternative' suite is place second, and not at the end. It uses the four-movement Bransle sequence traditionally favoured by composers in the German lands but, as in *MvL*, Pezel idiosyncratically surrounds it with other dances.

Johann Caspar Horn also studied at Leipzig University and had quite a different professional background to Pezel. Medicine and philosophy ('Der Philosophie und Medicin weitberühmten *Doctori*, sowohl auch *Physico Ordinario* der löbl. Bergstadt Freyberg') is mentioned in the preface to the second volume of his *Parergon musicum*, and Walther's *Musikalisches Lexicon* calls him 'a doctor at Dresden'.[36] He does not seem to have been a professional *Stadtpfeiffer* but perhaps a member of a domestic *Collegium* if not the renowned student body. Horn spent most of his working life in Leipzig before the move to Dresden, and, while the musical quality of his work may not rival that of Rosenmüller's, the six-volume *Parergon musicum* is arguably the most influential collection of suites from the second half of the seventeenth century.

Published between 1663 and 1676, *Parergon musicum* was issued in paired volumes; the title pages call them 'Musicalisches Neben-Werck' (musical pastime).[37] The first and second volumes (Erfurt, 1663) are written in contrasting national styles, as are the third and fourth (Leipzig, 1672). The final two volumes (Leipzig, 1676) contrast instrumental sonorities; the *Fünfftem Theil* has suites for à5 strings and continuo while the *Sechsten Theil* concentrates on polychoral writing for mixed ensembles of wind and strings.

Parergon musicum Ersten Theil (hereafter, *PM 1*) is described as being in the Italian style ('nach der ietzigen Italiänischen Manier zu spielen') though, as I pointed out in Chapter 2, Horn's Courantes are mostly hybrids of both Italian and French styles. It was dedicated to the Leipzig Bürgermeister Wagner for his 'sonderbahrer Gewogenheit … gegen die Edle Music' (exceptionally favourable attitude to fine music). The printer and publisher was Johann Birckner, and if the accuracy of the text is sometimes questionable, *PM 1* is remarkable for the quality of its printing and presentation. Not only is the typeface a model of clarity, full-length bar lines are used throughout, a rarity for this time. Along with the companion second volume, *PM 1* was re-issued in 1670, this time by the Leipzig publisher Georg Heinrich Fromman in a print of poorer quality with inferior and often careless typesetting. It is likely that the 1663 edition was used as the source for the reprint rather than a manuscript *Stichvorlage* emanating from Horn; the layout is very similar and errors from the earlier print are carried over without correction. Fromman's typesetter also managed to introduce some further errors of his own.

PM 1 is arguably the most carefully organised consort-suite collection of the entire seventeenth century. Perhaps in this, his first publication, Horn's professional background made it important to demonstrate his intellectual and musical prowess. There are no sequences of independent dances or dance pairings. The sixty movements are divided into fifteen suites arranged in ascending order of first major then minor keys ('Aus unterschiedenen Thonen dur und moll') and all with the same doubled pairing of Allemande, Courante, Ballo and Sarabande (see Chapter 2). Each suite is printed on facing pages so that the performer sees the complete text without needing to make any turns. Presumably this layout was influenced by Rosenmüller's *Paduanen, Alemanden, Couranten, Balletten, Sarabanden*, though it is impossible to know whether Horn or his printer instigated it. The title page's 'zusammen getragen von [put together by] Johann-Caspar Horn' suggests the former.

Horn makes full use of a variety of variation techniques in all but two of the suites. In the fourth, the linking works on two levels; the Allemande becomes the Courante in a triple-time re-casting but there is also a common treble-line motif used in all four dances that rises from A to E. Horn is imaginative in the way he uses this rising treble; it is done through mostly consecutive notes in the first three dances, but elongated in the Sarabande so that each note of the rising progression is also the first note of each bar. To show this clearly, the rising sequence in the latter is marked with an 'x' in Example 6.7. There are also common bass lines to all the dances, but these come about as a result of the linking at other levels.

PM 1's preface does give us some interesting if contradictory information on performance practice. It is given here in its entirety:

An seinen Music-spielenden.

Günstiger Freund / etc. Diese Musicalische / zur Recreation studierenden Ubung / von mir aufgesetzte *Harmo*nien / können nicht besser gehöret werden / als wenn man die *Allemanden* nach einer langsamen Mensur, die *Couranten* hergegen etwas geschwinder / die *Ballo* aber so geschwind als es seyn kan / und denn die *Sarabanden* wieder langsam spielen wird. Worbey man sich eines reinen Strichs / nebenst einem netten Trillo / gebrauchen / und die Noten mit vielen *colori*ren und Gequerle nicht verdunckeln soll. Wird hierbey auch der *Violon* in siener Tieffe scharff gestrichen werden / kan die Anmuthigkeit desto vollkommener werden. Wo den dieses *Signum* φ stehet / da soll dieselbe *Clausul* nicht gantz / sondern nur von selbigem Orte an (und zwar *piano*) *repeti*ret werden. Im übrigen befehl ich mich deiner geneigten *Affection*, nebenst dienst freundlicher Bitte / du wollest dich mit deinem *Judico* nicht so bald übereiten / biß du zuvor dieses Musicalische *Parergon* in einer vollstimmigen Music eigentlich gehöret hast. Lebe wohl!

Leipzig   125

Example 6.7 Movement openings in J.C. Horn, *Parergon musicum, Oder Musicalisches Neben-Werck / Bestehend in allerhand anmuthigen Allemanden, Couranten, Ballo und Sarabanden ... Ersten Theil* (Erfurt, 1663, repr. Leipzig, 1670), '13. Allemande', '14. Courante', '15. Ballo', '16. Sarabande'.

(To the player [of this music].

Favoured friend! These musical [pieces], for recreation and study, are given with my own harmonisations. They are heard best when taken in the following way: *Allemandes* have a slow pulse; the *Courantes* are taken somewhat quicker, the *Balli* as quick as they can be, and again, the *Sarabandes* are played slowly. In these, [i.e. the latter] one applies a simple [bow] stroke in the company of a pleasant *trillo* and the notes should not be darkened with many colours [i.e. divisions] and restless ornaments. In addition, if the *Violon* were to be clearly articulated in its depth, the charm would become all the more perfect. Where the sign ɸ exists, the repeat of the strain is not played complete, but is made from the place of this sign and, in fact, played *piano*. In conclusion, I commend myself to your kind affection and, next to this, make the friendly request that you will withhold your judgement until you have heard this musical *Parergon* with a full-voiced ensemble. Farewell!)[38]

Horn's instructions for dance tempi are similar to those in many other printed editions. But, in his comments on the *petite reprise*, he appears to be at odds with French tradition when he clearly states that the normal repeat of the second strain is to be omitted when a *petite reprise* is present. The reference to ornamentation in the Sarabandes is ambiguous; Horn asks for a simple style of playing, but also encourages the use of 'a simple [bow] stroke next to a pleasant *trillo*'. The word 'trillo' itself does not necessarily imply a two-note trill. Johann Herbst's treatise on vocal ornamentation, *Musica moderna prattica* (Frankfurt, 1653), gives various examples of an accelerating same-note *trillo* as does de Brossard's *Dictionaire de Musique*. Brossard particularly equates this with Italian music and, given the proclaimed Italian manner of *PM 1*, Horn may well have intended just this type of ornament.[39] But it may be the case that the 'trillo' is not a trill at all; it may be nothing more than a bowed vibrato.[40] Again, this device was common in Italian music. We should also note Horn's statement that the pieces are given with his own harmonisations; it shows that he was familiar with the practice of court musicians providing their own harmonies to treble-line dance music.

Horn himself moved away from this concept of total organisation; perhaps he found sequences of nothing but the same four dances to be too restricting however imaginatively he dealt with the content. And his experiment with layout and organisation seems to have met with a mixed response by the copyists of two manuscripts that I shall now consider.

Despite occasional problems with spacing, the anonymous copyist of a manuscript conflation of the 'Violone' and 'Continuovo' parts from *PM 1* (*S-VX* Mus. Ms 5, headed 'Parergon Musicum oder Musicalisches Nebenwerck auff gesetzet von Johan [sic] Caspar Horn') follows the printed edition in setting out the movements of each suite on facing pages. The order and movement numbering of the original volumes have also been retained. No great harm is done by the conflation of the two bass parts; they are identical apart from the figures in the 'Continuovo'. Errors are few although the quasi-mensural C3/2 signatures of the Courantes and Sarabandes have been simplified to 3/2. Rather more seriously, the important note blackenings have been omitted; perhaps the copyist did not understand their significance.

Manuscript *D-Dl* Mus. 1/B/101 contains a carelessly written copy of the complete second violin part of *PM 1*. It is the work of a number of hands and the lack of care is demonstrated in the title 'ander [sic] Theil. C[aspar] H[orn]'.

While the movements are all given in the correct order, there is no attempt to reproduce the page layout of the printed editions. Fromman's 1670 reprint of *PM 1* is visually closer to Mus. 1/B/101 than the original 1663 edition and would seem to be the source for the copyists. In which case, it would appear that at least this part of the manuscript cannot have been copied any earlier than 1670. As well as extracts from *Parergon musicum*, it contains dance music by the Hamburg town composer Dieterich Becker (see the following chapter) along with vocal music by Hammerschmidt and Scheidt. The manuscript's title, 'VOX SECUNDA / Geistliche Colligirte Concerten von unterschiedenen Autoribus componiret' refers not only to the vocal items but to second-violin instrumental items.[41] This mixture is significant, for it accords with Kuhnau's description of a domestic *Collegium* and its mixture of singing and playing. Unfortunately, this is the only part-book to survive, making identification of some items difficult – the manuscript's index only lists the vocal items. It is possible that the instrumental items are all trios; the opening sequence is marked 'a 3'. And while the dance music from *PM 1* was originally *a5*, this manuscript may represent an example of five-part instrumentation being reduced to three by the removal of the two viola parts.

Horn's second volume of the series was *Parergon musicum Oder Musicalisches Neben-Werck ... Andern Theil* (Erfurt 1663, hereafter *PM 2*). The edition was badly reprinted by Fromman in Leipzig at the same time as the reprint of *PM 1*. In contrast to the *italiänischen Manier* of *PM 1*, the second volume is divided into 'fünff angenehmen Grossen-Balletten ... Nach der lustigen Frantzösischen Manier zu spielen' (five pleasant large Ballets to be played in the lively French manner). 'Lustigen' was often applied to French dances whether it was warranted by the material or not, but as I have pointed out earlier, it was above all a general performing indication and it seems that German town musicians would have understood the instruction.[42] According to *PM 2*'s preface, the music was written for the 'Pindus-Gesellschafft' (*sic*). *Pindisch* is synonymous with student and it seems that the *Gesellschaft* was originally a recreational group specifically for Silesian students at the university that later took members from other countries.[43] Members took on pastoral names and these may have played a part in the first Ballet, '1. Ballet. Pastorelle'.[44] *PM 2* comprises five sequences of apparently functional ballet music; the last of these, 'V. Ballet de Orphée', is by far the most substantial, with five acts. The latter must have also been a large-scale production; apparently nearly one hundred performers took part.

The practical purpose of this dance music is underlined by titles such as 'Les Ours dansants avec le Cupid' attached to '2. Amorosa' in the opening ballet, and it has been suggested that Horn modelled them on music taken from the dramatic stage works of Lully.[45] But this is doubtful. Lully had only just started on his career in 1663 and it is unlikely that his music was widely known in the German lands, especially in the towns. It is far more likely that Horn's model was the French *Ballet de Cour* from earlier in the century. Most *Ballets de Cour* were built around various *Entrées* for each character or group of characters. The *Entrées* were usually written in the same key and a *Grand Ballet* often acted as a conclusion that served to bring all the characters together.[46] Bransles and

Courantes are noticeably lacking; they were more associated with the ballroom.[47] A ballet typical of the genre is the 'Ballet de Louis 13, dansé à Gentilly, L'an 1635' preserved as one of the so-called Philidor manuscripts (*F-Pn* Rés. F 497). It has eighteen *Entrées*, mostly in G minor or major, and a 'Grand Ballet' at the end.[48] Horn's Ballets follow a similar format; the 'II. Ballet de Coloumbe' has the following movement titles:

    7. Intrade
    8. Spaniole (Coloumbe.)
    9. Bourree (Les Mariniers.)
   10. Retirade
   12. Mascarade (Les Mores. Jouants de tambourinets.)
   13. Grand-Ballet (des Mores.)
   14. Fortunate (Coloumbe avec des Mariniers.)
   15. Chiqve (Danse de eschange.)
   16. Gavotte Allegrò. (Les Matelots.)

It is curious that '13. Grand-Ballet' of this sequence does not come at the end. But we have no way of knowing if the *PM 2* music reflects the order in which it was danced.

Given the *Parergon musicum* title pages' reference to French and Italian styles, and the contrast between the instrumental-dance of *PM 1* and the functional dance of *PM 2*, we might expect that Horn would have taken the opportunity to reflect this in the style of the dances. There are times when he can be idiomatic: the '15. Chiqve' from 'II. Ballet de Coloumbe' does have the irregular phrasing of the French model. But in all of the Courantes, Horn fails to make any distinction between the French and Italian styles. Example 6.8 compares the openings of '22. Courante' from *PM 1*, ostensibly in the Italian style, and '19. Courante; L'Adolescence & les quatre saisons de l'Année' from *PM 2*, apparently in the French.

As we can see, the two are remarkably similar in rhythm and phrasing. And if '19. Courante' has little of the rhythmic complexity of the genuine French Courante given earlier in Chapter 2 (Example 2.2), its frequent use of note blackening to create off-beat accents provides a good example of the German hybrid style that surely provided Horn's model. In fact, there is a striking similarity between Horn's Courantes and those in *Erster Theil Darinnen begriffen X. Paduanen. X. Galliarden. X. Balleten, und X. Couranten* (Erfurt, 1652) by the Gotha court musician, Wolfgang Karl Briegel.[49] It is not known if Horn was familiar with Briegel's collection, but the similarity suggests that he was.

Horn also fails to make any difference between the scoring of *PM 1* and *PM 2*, suggesting either that he was ignorant of French instrumentation, or that he chose to ignore it. His five-part ensemble does not use the one-violin, three-viola and bass combination favoured by so many French composers and their German imitators. Instead, he uses the pairs of violins and violas preferred by the Italians. But Horn's possible ignorance could be explained by the single-line transmission

Leipzig 129

Example 6.8 Comparisons between Horn, *Parergon musicum ... Ersten Theil*, '22. Courante' and J.C. Horn, *Parergon musicum, Oder Musicalisches Neben-Werck / Bestehend in fünff angenehmen Grossen – Balletten ... Andern Theil* (Erfurt, 1663, repr. Leipzig, 1670), '19. Courante; L'Adolescence & les quatre saisons de l'Année'.

of French dance music in Germany; it is quite possible that he may have never seen a fully scored example of music from a *Ballet de Cour*.

Music from *PM 2* was also copied into manuscript Mus. 1/B/101. The copyists were selective; the entire first 'I. Pastorelle' Ballet is omitted, 'II. Ballet de Coloumbe' is lacking two movements, but 'III. Ballet de la Vanité' and 'IV. Ballet des Elements' are both complete. The longer fifth Ballet fares less well; the Bourée and 'Grand-Ballet' are missing from its first act, the opening Intrada and Aria 'Orphée jouant de sa Lyre' are omitted from Act II, and the opening Intrada is again missing from Acts III and IV. All of Act V is omitted. It is difficult to know why the copyist omitted so many movements.

The next pair of 'Neben-Werck' volumes were published alongside the Fromman re-issue of *PM 1* and *PM 2*. The 'Italian' volume, *Parergon musicum*

Oder Musicalisches Neben-Werck Bestehend in allerhand anmuthigen Intraden, Allemanden, Couranten, Ballo, Sarabanden, Chiquen, &c. Mit Fünff Stimmen ... Dritten Theil (Leipzig, 1672, hereafter *PM 3*), has not been preserved complete; only the first violin and 'Continuovo' printed part-books survive. But it is reasonable to assume that the instrumentation is the same as *PM 1* – pairs of violins and violas along with the bass. Many of the previous concepts from *PM 1* are carried over, though precise ordering by keys is absent; Horn is content to have four major keys followed by four minor keys. Once again, the title page has 'zusammen getragen von Johann-Caspar Horn'. There are eight suites in *PM 3*; seven have a revised movement sequence, adding an opening Intrada and closing *Chique* to the Allemande, Courante, Ballo and Sarabande. This certainly provides greater musical variety but makes the page-to-a-suite layout of the first volume impossible.

The Intradas are very short, most having two strains of little more than six bars; the longest in the entire collection only lasts for a total of seventeen bars. There appears to be no imitative writing, although it is difficult to be precise about the musical content with so much missing. This style of Intrada is also found in Pezel's *Musicalische Gemüths-Ergetzung*, published in the same year as *PM 3*. Even if Horn did not know Pezel's collection, he must have heard the outdoor Intradas played by the Leipzig *Stadtpfeifer* and it is highly likely that they served as his model. The dances of *PM 3* show a greater variety and freedom than those in *PM 1*. Once again, movement linking plays an important part. Example 6.9 shows how Horn expands the linking concept one stage further in the fourth suite: the last two bars of the Intrada form the basis of the opening of the following Allemande and Courante.

To make sure that the link is fully understood, Horn also links the bass line in all three movements, only slightly simplifying it in the Courante by removing one chord. '21. Courante' is also noticeable for the dynamics of its ending, where Horn marks it *forte*, then *piano*, then *pianissimo*. There are also echo effects uniting the closing bars of '22. Ballo', '23. Sarabande' and '24. Chique'.

The Gigues of the collection follow examples by other town composers; there is inversion of the subject at the start of the second strain and, as far as we can tell, they are probably imitative. Horn's final suite of *PM 3* is an interesting variant of the 'alternative' concept. As we have seen, this alternative was often the French-origin Bransle sequence but Horn presumably felt he could not do this in a collection in the *italiänischen Manier*. Despite this, he does use the French term 'suite' to start the final sequence; after that, the movements are Italian:

43. Suite / 44. Courant / 45. Lamente / 46. Sarabande / 47. Serenata / 48. Ballo / 49. Saltirelle / 50. Chique

Presumably, the use of the word 'suite' is an indication to the performer that these movements form a deliberate whole, and not an appendage of seemingly random movements. Again, Horn uses these unusual movements in unusual ways, and the entire sequence shows his obvious delight in the use of variation technique. '43. Suite' is linked to '44. Courant', and '48. Ballo' to '49. Saltirelle', but neither

Leipzig   131

Example 6.9 Movement linking in J.C. Horn, *Parergon musicum, Oder Musicalisches Neben-Werck / Bestehend in allerhand anmuthigen Intraden, Allemanden, Couranten, Ballo, Sarabanden, Chiquen, &c. Mit Fünff Stimmen ... Dritten Theil* (Leipzig, 1672), '19. Intrada', '20. Allemande', '21. Courante'.

pair uses material from the start of the movements in the usual manner. Instead, Horn links the second section of '43. Suite' to the start of the second strain of the following '44. Courant'; '48. Ballo' and '49. Saltirelle' are also linked through their second strains.

The fourth volume of *Parergon musicum* (hereafter *PM 4*) was, like *PM 2*, written for the 'Pindus-Gesellschafft'(*sic*), it contains three 'Grossen-Balletten'. While the title page does not mention the 'lustigen Frantzösischen Manier', we may assume that Horn considered it to be a further exercise in the French style. Like *PM 3*, it is incompletely preserved; only the first violin and 'Continuovo' part-books survive, and the former is lacking four movements. According to the title page, the instrumentation is for 'Vier and Fünff Stimmen' (four and five parts) that we must assume are all strings.

The Ballets in *PM 4* are similar in scale and content to those in *PM 2*; 'I. Ballet. Des Affects avec la Raison' has sixteen dances and 'II. Ballet. De l'Amour' has fifteen; both end with a concluding 'Grand-Ballo' and Sarabande. Titles such as '17. Cupido cum Amorettis' and '18. Venus cum Nymphis' show most movements to be the character *Entrées* of the *Ballet de Cour* and there is little difference between the single examples of the Courante, Ballo and Sarabande of *PM 4* and the so-called *italiänischen* versions elsewhere.

132 *Leipzig*

The fifth volume of the series (hereafter *PM 5*) contains arguably the best music of *Parergon musicum*. It was published in 1676 simultaneously with the *Sechsten Theil* and the two were again clearly intended as a musical pair. This time it is the instrumentation that forms the principal contrast: *PM 5* retains Horn's usual *à5* combination of two violins, two violas and bass strings with continuo, while *Sechsten Theil* uses large-scale polychoral writing. But there are passages within each *PM 5* suite, parts of the opening Sonatinas and some of the dance movements, where the violins play in unison, creating a four-part texture. These passages are clearly marked in the part-books with an asterisk, and the preface gives the following explanation:

> Bey diesem fünfften Theil ist zu erinnern / weil die Sonatinen eine Clausul mit sich führen / darinnen beyde Violinen in Unisono gehen (welches denn ebenfals bey den Couranten und Balletten geschiehet / und mit * gezeichnet stehet) So ist darauff acht zu haben / daß die Violinen sein gleich in einen Strich zusammen mögen gespielet warden.

> (Remember that, in this fifth volume, where the Sonatinas contain a section with both violins in unison (which likewise appears in the Couranten and Balletten and is marked *), the violins must take care to start each bow stroke at exactly the same time).

Figure 6.1 shows an example from the first violin part-book.

We have seen other Leipzig composers vary the instrumentation of movements within a suite. Horn's variation of instrumentation within a single Sonatina movement marks a significant departure from the norm. Table 6.6 details the collection and these variations of texture.

The collection is on a smaller scale than the previous volumes of *Paragon musicum*. The reason for this is not hard to find. As a part of the pairing concept, it was likely to have been a deliberate intention on the part of Horn or his printer

Figure 6.1 J.C. Horn, *Parergon musicum Oder Musicalisches Neben-Werck / Bestehend in allerhand ammuthigen / Sonatinen, Alleman- / den, Couranten, Ballet- / ten, Sarabanden und Chiqven, Mit Fünff Stimmen / ... Fünfftem Theil* (Leipzig, 1676), 'Violino 1' part-book, '4. Ballo', shelfmark H 930 [1]: Kraków, Biblioteka Jagiellońska. Reproduced by kind permission.

Table 6.6 Contents of Horn, *Parergon musicum* ... *Fünfften Theil*

Movements (à5 unless stated)	Key	Sonatina structure (excluding optional repeat)	Linking
1. Sonatina / 2. Allemande / 3. Courante [à4] / 4. Ballo [à4] / 5. Sarabande / 6. Chiqve	G minor	C [à5] 3/2 *adagio* [à5] C *allegrò* [first strain à4, second strain à5]	None
7. Sonatina / 8. Allemande / 9. Courante [à4] / 10. Ballo [à4] / 11. Sarabande / 12. Chiqve	B flat major	C [à5] 3/2 *adagio* [à5] C *allegrò* [first strain à4, second strain à5]	None
13. Sonatina / 14. Allemande / 15. Courante [à4] / 16. Ballo [à4] / 17. Sarabande / 18. Chiqve	G major	C [à5] 3/2 *adagio* [à5] C *allegrò* [first strain à4, second strain à5]	14 and 15 melodically and harmonically linked at start of first strain. 16 and 17 melodically linked at start of first strain.
19. Sonatina / 20. Allemande / 21. Courante [à4] / 22. Ballo [à4] / 23. Sarabande / 24. Chiqve	E minor	C *adagio* [à5] [C] *allegrò* [à5] 3/2 [à5] [3/2] *allegrò* [first strain à4, second strain à5]	First strain of 19 [3/2] *allegrò* melodically linked to all following dances in this suite.
25. Sonatina / 26. Allemande / 27. Courante [à4] / 28. Ballo [à4] / 29. Sarabande / 30. Chiqve	D major	C [à5] 3/2 [à5] [3/2] *allegrò* [first strain à4, second strain à5]	None

to give the fifth and sixth volumes the same number of movements. The expense of producing large numbers of part-books for the large-scale polychoral *Sechsten Theil* (see below) probably resulted in a limit of thirty movements and *PM 5* had to be the same, even if its content used fewer resources.

Even though *PM 5* contains less of the careful ordering that set *PM 1* and *PM 3* apart, Horn does not abandon all his earlier concepts. Example 6.10 shows how, in the fourth suite, the opening six notes of the fourth section of the Sonatina are used to link it with each of the following dances. The use of c♮ after the d♯ is deliberate – Horn uses the same interval in other parts of *Parergon musicum* – and allows the listener to recognise this link at every appearance even though, in the Courante, Ballo and Sarabande, the link has been imaginatively delayed. Once again, we notice Horn's delight in variation technique.

The Sonatinas are substantially longer than the Intradas of *PM 3* and follow the model of the Sinfonias found in Rosenmüller's 1667 *Sonate da camera*. In each of the *PM 5* examples, Horn gives the performer the option of repeating the opening section at the end. This was misunderstood by W.S. Newman: he asserts that Horn's Sonatinas 'can be repeated at the end of the suite, according to his foreword'.[50] This is incorrect and can only be based on a mistranslation or a misunderstanding of the word 'Clausul'. Horn's instruction, given in the preface, is clear and unambiguous:

Example 6.10 Movement linking in Horn, *Parergon musicum ... Fünfftem Theil*, fourth suite.

Nechst diesen so kan man auch bey den Sonatinen nach der letzten Clausul die erste repetiren / und damit schliessen.

(In the Sonatinas, it is permissible, after the last section, to repeat the first [section] and thus close.)

Finally in this part of the chapter, we come to two suites preserved only in manuscript. From its title, we can see that '8. Allemand, Courant, Ballet, Sarab: à 1.Violin. 2. Viol: di Bracc: è Violon. s. Cembalo. di S.K. Assieg. 1672' (*S-Uu* Instr. mus. i hs. 4:4) was copied by Johann von Assig und Siegersdorff. If the 'S.K.' refers to Sebastien Knüpfer, then the suite is by the Cantor at the *Thomaskirche* in Leipzig from 1657 until 1676. The music appears to be harmonically complete as it stands, albeit in a low tessitura, and the four instrumental parts carry the titles Viol. 1ma., Viola. 2., Viol. Tertia., Viol. quarta et Organ. But the Viol. 1ma. part appears to be a second, rather than first, treble part and, given the tessitura it is possible that the parts are incomplete, lacking a first violin part.[51]

There can be no doubts about the identity of the composer of a suite for two violins, three violas, bassoon and 'Violon con Continuo' preserved in the Sherard collection (*GB-Ob* MS Mus.Sch.c.93).[52] The composer is Georg Knüpfer, brother of Sebastian, and the manuscript is part of a collection assembled by the English amateur musician James Sherard that is now in the Oxford Bodleian library.[53] The suite contains a multi-sectioned Sonata followed by an Aria, Gigue and Sarabande. The Sonata is in G major and the dances in B minor, but the Sarabande has a five-bar common-time conclusion in G major, thus restoring the key of the opening. It is, of course, possible that the Sonata and suite were originally separate works; in which case, the Sarabande conclusion must have been added at the same time as the Sonata to give a tonal balance to the work. But as it stands in MS Mus.Sch.c.93, we must see it as a single entity. And while Knüpfer's arrangement of a series of dances in one key surrounded by abstract music in another stands outside the Leipzig tradition, circular key schemes are common, as we have seen, in the works of Viennese court composers whose music was clearly known in the town's musical fraternity.

The dances show a mixture of French and Italian styles. The 'Aria' contains the dotted rhythms and impetus of the Ballo used by many town musicians in the 1660s and 70s. The Gigue has the irregular phrase lengths of the French model although none of its imitation between parts. The Sarabande is closer to the Italian model and has little in common with the German hybrid version. In addition, Knüpfer's use of seven instrumental parts is not always assured, and his near-constant use of the full ensemble suggests a lack of experience. But this unusual work contains attractive music and deserves to be better known.

Wind-based ensembles

This part of the chapter deals with the so-called *Turmmusik* (tower music) played by the *Cornetti* and trombones of the Leipzig *Stadtpfeifer* from the town's towers and balconies. While other towns had tower musicians (see Chapter 2), the importance of the *Turmmusik* in Leipzig public life seems to have been greater than anywhere

136 Leipzig

else. Johann Pezel's *Hora Decima Musicorum Lipsiensium* (Leipzig, 1670) is a collection of wind Sonatas providing a clear link with the tower repertoire; it contains '40. Sonaten mit 5. Stimmen welche die Stadtpfeiffer besonders zum Abblasen warden gebrauchen können' (40 sonatas in five parts that the *Stadtpfeiffer* can use especially for their playing).[54] It is telling that, when re-issed in Dresden as *Supellex Sonatarum Selectarum, a quinq: instrumentis* (Dresden, 1674), the instrumentation listed on the collection's title page was changed to '2. Violinis, 1. Fagotto, vel Violono adjuncto Basso Continuo'.[55] While the original wind instrument names were included on the part-book covers along with the strings, suites for wind were clearly less popular as commercial ventures outside Leipzig.

Two more of Pezel's instrumental collections have clear associations with *Turmmusik*; the trio collection, *Bicinia Variorum Instrumentorum* (Leipzig, 1675, hereafter *Bicinia*), and *Fünff-stimmigte blasende Music* (Frankfurt am Main, 1685). While *Bicinia*'s part-books are headed 'Violino Primo', 'Violino Secundo' and 'Basso Continuo', its title page allows the options of '2. Violinis, Cornet, Flautinis, Clarinis, Clarino et Fagotto'. There are more specific indications within the music itself with parts for '2. Cornett', '2. Clarin' and 'Clarino & Fagotto'. It is possible that one treble part was taken by a wind player and another by a string player, but it seems more likely that the music was played by pairs of like instruments.

There is also an appendix for '2. Bombardinis vulge Schalmeyen et Fagotto' where the part-book identifiers are changed to 'Bombardino Primo', 'Bombardino Secundo' and 'Fagotto', while 'Flöthen' (recorders) and 'Schalmeyen' are listed as further alternatives. Walther's *Lexicon* defines 'Bombardino' as 'ein kleiner Alt-Pommer' (a small alto shawm); 'Schalmey' is the treble variety of the same instrument.[56] Given that alternatives in part-books usually refer to different families of instruments – for example, *cornetti* instead of violins – it is unclear why Pezel's alternative to the alto *bombardino* should be a treble instrument of the same family. With his intimate knowledge of such instruments, it is unlikely that this is a mistake on Pezel's part. If Walther's definition is correct, then we must assume an error or misunderstanding on the part of the printer. Unlike the main part of the collection, the Appendix has no continuo figuring in the bass part, a possible indication of outdoor origins. Although the collection was self-published by Pezel, the twelve tradesmen and merchants ('Weitberühmten Kauf-und Handels-Leuten in Leipzig') listed on the dedication page suggest that the edition received a high degree of patronage. It is reasonable to assume the dedicatees were keen to be associated with the public music of the towers.

There are seventy-five pieces in the main part of the collection and thirty-six in the Appendix. Some organisation of content is apparent, but not at the same level as Pezel's string-based collections. Movements are mostly grouped by key, and there are some Allemande-led sequences where the dances appear to belong together but linking techniques are conspicuously absent. Elsewhere, Pezel's intentions are not always clear and the collection seems to be looking back to an earlier time. This is certainly the case with the start of the main collection where the first twenty-four and final fifteen movements are all grouped together by type – all Sonatinas apart from the single '75. Sonata' at the very end. In addition to the dance types commonly employed by town musicians, Pezel uses the Viennese Trezza, and *Bicinia* contains five examples. As I pointed out in the first part of this chapter, music from the Viennese imperial court was known in Leipzig and this is another example of this influence. Example 6.11 compares '28. Treza' from *Bicinia* with an example from the third part of Johann Heinrich Schmelzer's *Balletto* 'Zu den geburts Tag Ihro Maÿ: der Khönigin in Spanien' (*A-Wn* Mus. Hs. 16583[II]). The similarities in rhythm and character are obvious; Pezel had a clear understanding of the dance's idiom.

Example 6.11 Comparison between J. Pezel, *Bicinia Variorum Instrumentorum ut à2. Violinis, Cornet, Flautinis, Clarinis, Clarino et Fagotto* (Leipzig, 1675), '28. Treza', and J.H. Schmelzer, 'Zu den geburts Tag Ihro Maÿ: der Khönigin in Spanien' (*A-Wn* Mus. Hs. 16583[II]), 'Trezza 97[a]'.

138 *Leipzig*

Unusually for this repertoire, Pezel also includes two examples of a *Ciacona* in the main section, one in duple time ('54. Ciacona') and one in triple ('36. Ciacona'). In keeping with the title, Pezel uses the Italian version of the dance as his model – there are no repeated bass lines or *Couplet* variations. Instead, Pezel repeats the rhythm of the opening bar throughout the duple-time example and does the same with the first two bars in the triple-time example. Given the use of this form of the *Ciacona* in the Viennese repertoire, it is a further example of the latter's influence.

In the Appendix, Pezel again seems to be reverting to the concepts of an earlier time with movements often set in pairs or grouped together by type; the pairings are between duple- and then triple-time movements, mostly *Intraden* followed either by a Courante or Sarabande. Some movements appear to be grouped together in longer sequences but Pezel's decision, perhaps reflecting limitations of the instruments or players, to place every movement in the same key of C major frequently makes his intentions difficult to follow. As we can see in Example 6.12, the first strain of '14. Courente', the contents of the collection are often little more than routine.

In the light of the other collections by Pezel that we have discussed earlier, the lack of clear organisation in both parts of *Bicinia* is difficult to understand and certainly at odds with the prevailing trends in printed suite collections of the 1670s, including Pezel's own publications. And there are none of the sophisticated choices of sequence that we have seen in the Leipzig string-based collections. But we must remember that at least parts of the collection were made up of functional music for the *Turmmusik* ensembles and there may well have been a lively now-lost tradition of performers making their own selections of movements for performance, perhaps even at the very last moment.

Example 6.12 Pezel, *Bicinia*, 'Appendix', '14. Courente'.

Pezel's *Fünff-stimmigte blasende Music* (Frankfurt am Main, 1685; hereafter *5-sbM*) was issued a decade after *Bicinia* at a time when Pezel had already moved away from Leipzig. But even allowing for this, we may still see it as reflecting the Leipzig wind repertoire with its instrumentation of *Cornetti* and trombones. Elwyn Wienandt suggests that the collection is a result of 'his continuing need to produce the kind of music for the performance of which he was employed' and dismisses the title page as 'lacking any evidence of artistic preparation'.[57] Wienandt may be correct, but it is more likely that Pezel was merely re-using the music from his Leipzig years and he may well have started work on the publication before he left the service of his former employers. The rather functional nature of the title page is probably nothing more than an indication that patronage for this collection was not forthcoming. Lack of patronage would also explain why there are none of the customary dedicatees, and the whole collection gives every indication of being produced on a limited budget. Given Pezel's move away from Leipzig before the issue of *5-sbM*, lack of patronage from a relatively new civic community would hardly be surprising.

There are seventy-six movements; some are divided into sequences of dances grouped mostly by type or in pairs. This again gives the appearance of a rather old-fashioned collection for its time, and Wienandt condemns it as having 'no apparent order of design'.[58] But the organisation of *5-sbM* has far more in common with Pezel's string-based collections than it does with *Bicinia*. As we can see in Table 6.7, four clearly defined suites are placed at important points; one at the start after a sequence of *Intraden*, two running consecutively in the middle forming the central focus of the collection, and one at the end before the final sequence of dances and *Intraden*. Wienandt's condemnation is clearly wide of the mark.

Within the groups themselves, Pezel is careful to order the contents with great clarity. In the opening group of Intraden, imaginative use is made of the duple-/triple-time relationship, and the suites themselves are clearly signposted by the use of the Allemande as a marker and by movement linking.[59] All but the last suite use some form of variation technique, Example 6.13 shows the relationship in the first between the openings of the Allemande and Courante.

If more unusual pairs are also used for linking ('20. Aria' to '21. Sarabande' and '24. Bal.' to '25. Sarabande'), there is further ordering beyond this; the first suite has three movements, the two central suites have four and the last five. The ordering may not be as elegant as some of the collections detailed later in this book, but it still shows the care that Pezel took with this publication.

We can also see the off-beat accentuation indicated by note blackening that is so typical of Leipzig writing, another indication that Pezel either used earlier music for this collection or did nothing to change his style on moving to his new post.

Throughout the collection, the music is given without any key signatures. Sharps and flats are all provided as accidentals within the musical text. This may be a result of the printer lacking a suitable number of print characters, and there is a precedent for this in Wolf Ernst Rothe's *Erstmahlig musicalische Freuden-Gedicte* (Dresden, 1660).[60] But given the content of the Appendix to *Biciana*, where all

140 *Leipzig*

Table 6.7 Movement sequences in J. Pezel, *Fünff-stimmigte blasende Music, Bestehend Intraden, Allemanden, Balleten, Courenten, Sarabanden und Chiquen* (Frankfurt am Main, 1685)

Movement numbers	Sequence type	Details and comments
1–16	*Intraden*, all in C major	
17–19	Suite in E minor	Allemande / Courente / Sarabande. Allemande and Courante linked melodically and harmonically at the start of the first strain, melodically (only) at the start of the second strain.
20–26	Dances of various types	Mostly grouped in duple-/triple-time pairs.
27–30	Suite in G major	Allemande / Courente / Bal / Sarabande. Courante is a partial re-casting (melody line only) of Allemande and Sarabande is a partial re-casting of Sarabande.
31–4	Suite in C major	Allemande / Courente / Bal / Sarabande. Melodic links between opening of 31. Allemande, 32. Courente and 33. Bal.
35–59	Dances of various types	Mostly grouped in duple-/triple-time pairs but finishing with a sequence of eight *Intraden*, all in C major.
60–64	Suite in C major	Allemande / Courente / Bal / Sarabande / Gique.
65–8	Intrade / Aria / Intrade / Sarabande	All in C major.
69–76	*Intraden*, all in C major	

the pieces are in C major, it is also possible that it was a tradition to write sharps and flats only in front of the required notes rather in the manner of eighteenth- and nineteenth-century horn and trumpet parts.

As we have seen in his string-based collections, there are times when the standard of Pezel's writing is little more than routine, and like *Biciana,* there are too many examples of dull, if functional, dance music. But there are times when he does rise above dull functionality and produce movements that are technically and musically highly imaginative. Example 6.14 gives the first strain and part of the second of '26. Galliard' from *5-sbM*. Like Rosenmüller, Pezel sometimes uses slow tempi for usually quick dances resulting, as we can see here, in a particularly dramatic movement, notably at the start of the second strain with its plunge from C major into E major. Comparison between this and Example 6.12 above shows the considerable distance between Pezel's best work and his poorest.

It may be that this variation of quality was a result of Pezel's duty to provide music for a wide range of ensembles during his time in Leipzig. It is not fanciful to

Leipzig 141

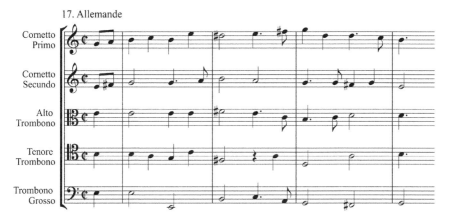

Example 6.13 Pezel, *Fünff-stimmigte blasende Music*, '17. Allemande' and '18. Courente'.

think that the music for *Biciana* was intended for one of the lesser groups of town musicians, while at least some of the pieces in *5-sbM* reflect the repertoire of the highest-grade *Stadtpfeifer*. If the best of *5-sbM* is typical of that heard from the town's balconies and towers, the standard must often have been high.

It is fitting that the final work in this chapter and sub-chapter dealing with the Leipzig tradition is perhaps the most monumental consort-suite collection to come from the seventeenth-century: the sixth and probably final volume of Horn's *Parergon musicum* (Frankfurt am Main, 1676: hereafter *PM 6*),[61] published, as we have seen, as a pair with *PM 5*. The comparison in *PM 6* is not between national styles as it was in the first four volumes but between sonorities, and it employs, in Horn's words, 'Einer vollstimmigen Musicalischen Compagnie' (a full-voiced musical gathering) for mixed wind and string ensembles of between five and twelve voices. For the wind instruments, *PM 6* calls for *cornetti*, trombones and *fagotti*, sometimes in pairs but, in the larger suites, in groups of three.

The different instrumental parts are shared around among the part-books; for example, both 'Viola ò Trombone' parts are printed on facing pages in the

142 *Leipzig*

Example 6.14 Pezel, *Fünff-stimmigte blasende Music*, '26. Galliard'.

'Fagotto' part-book. Even so, the production expenses must have been high, and this may explain the comparative brevity of the collection, standing at just thirty movements. But *PM 6* is also remarkable for the number of alternative instrumental options that Horn allows. When suitable players or instruments are not available, the preface suggests the following alternatives:

> Das Directorium kann zwar nach Gelegenheit der Personen und Instrumenten eingerichtet werden. Es ist aber zu erinnern / weil diese *Musicalia* benebenst den *Violen* zugleich auf blasende Instrumente gesetzet sind / daß 1. an statt der *Cornettinen* auch gar füglich Trombetten, (iedoch nur die ersten 6. Stücke), in gleichen Schalmeyen / oder auch *Flautinen* können gebraucht werden; Doch ist solcher gestalt der *Violen* – Chor desto

vollstimmiger anzuorden. Was 2. die Mittelstimmen anbelanget / kann man solche nach Belieben und Gelegenheit bestellen / oder auslassen; bis auf die letzten 3. Stücke / worrinen die Mittel-Partien sich alleine hören lassen / und also notwendig so viel möglich / besetzet seyn müssen. Ebenfalls 3. so kann auch der Violon ausgelassen werden / wenn der *Fagott* (oder an statt dessen eine *Trombone*) bestellet ist. Wenn aber der Fagott gar nicht darbey seyn kan / so soll auch der *Violon* nicht *à part*, sondern aus dem *Basso Continuo* mitgespielet werden. Schließlichen: I.e. mehr *Partien*, i.e. besser *Gratie*. Hiermit lebe wohl!

(The director may choose the players and instruments according to the circumstances. Therefore, in order to facilitate these alternatives in the music, the string parts have been set for the wind as well. Therefore:

1. Instead of the *Cornettinen*, *Trombetten* are also quite acceptable (however only in the first 6 pieces), in the same way, *Schalmeyen* or also *Flautinen* may be used; also, the string choir can be further augmented by such means.

2. One can arrange or omit the middle parts according to taste or circumstances. However, in the last three pieces, the inner voices must be heard distinctly and it is essential that as many instruments as possible are included.

3. Likewise, the *Violon* can be left out, as long as the *Fagott* (or a further Trombone) is available. However, when the *Fagott* is not present, the *Violon* should not play from its own part, but from the *Basso Continuo*.[62]
Finally, the more parts, the better. With this, Goodbye.)

There are further alternatives of instrumentation offered within the part-books: violas for trombones and *flautini* for *cornetti*. As we have seen, the preface allows the substitution of trumpets for *cornetti*, but this would need some adjustment for the second part to be playable on a natural instrument. The context makes it clear that when Horn says 'the more parts, the better', he is not referring to the reinforcement of instrumental parts, but to having as many inner parts available as possible.

Even with substitutions and allowed reduction of ensemble size, it is hard to know when such music might have been performed. As we saw in the main part of this chapter, *PM 2* was able to draw on 100 performers, although we have no way of knowing how many of these were musicians and how many dancers. Certainly there seems to have been large-scale dramatic performances in Leipzig during the 1680s, and Markus Rathey has suggested that 'that neither large-scale performances with processions nor quasi-theatrical performances with different characters were entirely unusual'.[63] But these were apparently for special occasions such as the Elector Johann Georg III's visit to Leipzig during the Michaelmas Fair of 1683 and there is no mention of such performances of the pieces in *PM 6* in Horn's preface.[64]

The alternation of wind and string choirs is common to all the larger-scale suites in this volume, and shows how skilfully Horn manages the polychoral writing. And while music emanating from the Austrian courts was known in Leipzig – though it is not clear if Horn knew of the polychoral works by J.H. Schmelzer, Biber and Vejvanovský – *PM 6* is remarkable within the context of town music in the German lands. The collection is arranged in order of increasing instrumentation, and details are given in Table 6.8.

Ordering by sonority in this looks back to some of the collections of the 1650s and earlier: for example, Hans Hake's 1654 *Ander Theil Newer Pavanen*.[65] Perhaps the contents of Horn's volume, albeit unpublished, were originally put together much earlier; but as we have seen in Pezel's two collections above, music associated with wind ensembles in Leipzig seems to have been conservative, if not old-fashioned, in content. It may not be a coincidence that the Galliard, certainly out of fashion in the 1670s and 80s features in both *5-sbM* and *PM 6*.

Table 6.8 Contents of J.C. Horn, *Parergon musicum Oder Musicalisches Neben-Werck / Bestehend in allerhand lustigen Intraden, Gagliarden, Couranten, Balletten, Sarabanden, Chiqven &c. ... Sechsten Theil* (Leipzig, 1676)

Movements	Instrumentation	Key
1. Intrada à5 / 2. Gagliarda [à5]	Cornettino I; Cornettino II; Violino I; Violino II; Fagotto; Basso Continuo.	C major
3. Intrada à 7 / 4. Intrada à7 / 5. Gagliarda à7 / 6. Sarabande fugue à7	Violino I & II; Cornettino I & II, Viola ò Trombone I & II, Fagotto, Basso Continuo.	C major
7. Intrade à10 / 8. Intrade à10 / 9. Courante / 10. Ballo / 11. Sarabande	Violino I & II; Viola I & II; Cornettino I & II, Trombone I, Trombone II, Fagotto, VioIono, Basso Continuo.	G major
12. Intrade à10 / 13. Courante / 14. Ballo / 15. Chiqve / 16. Sarabande	Violino I, Violino II, Viola I, Viola II, Cornettino I, Cornettino II, Trombone I, Trombone II, Fagotto, Violono, Basso Continuo.	G major
17. Intrade à11 / 18. Allemande / 19. Courante / 20. Gagliarda / 21. Ballo / 22. Chiqve / 23. Sarabande	Violino I & II, Viola I & II, Flautino ò Cornettino I, Flautino ò Cornettino II, Flautino ò Cornettino III, Trombone I & II, Fagotto, Violono, Basso Continuo.	C major
24. Intrade à12 / 25. Courante / 26. Ballo / 27. Sarabande	Violino I & II, Viola I, II & III, Flautino ò Cornettino I, Flautino ò Cornettino II, Flautino ò Cornettino III, Trombone I & II, Fagotto, Violono e Basso Continuo.	E minor
28. Intrade à12 / 29. Gagliarda / 30. Sarabande	Violino I & II, Viola I, II & III, Flautino ò Cornettino I, Flautino ò Cornettino II, Trombone I, II & III, Fagotto, Violono e Basso Continuo.	A minor

Leipzig   145

If some of the Intradas fail to move far enough from basic triadic material, it is clearly Horn's intention to emphasise the grandeur of the polychoral writing by adopting a straightforward approach. *PM 6* may not, in some respects, be as innovative as other Leipzig collections considered above, but its sheer opulence makes it worthy to stand as one of the most important of all seventeenth-century suite collections from the German lands. Example 6.15, '28. Intrada', fully illustrates this.

Example 6.15 Horn, *Parergon musicum ... Sechsten Theil*, '28. Intrada à 12'.

Notes

1 G. Webber, *North German church music in the age of Buxtehude* (Oxford: Clarendon Press, 1996), p. 74.
2 T. Kevorkian, *Baroque piety: religion, society, and music in Leipzig, 1650–1750* (Aldershot: Ashgate, 2007), p. 16.
3 Ibid.
4 Ibid., p. 19.
5 A reproduction of a list of civic patrons is given in Figure 1.1.
6 M. Maul, *'Dero berühmbter Chor': Die Leizpiger Thomasschule und ihre Kantoren (1212–1804)* (Leipzig: Lehmstedt Verlag, 2012), p. 131.
7 G. Taubert, *Tantzmeister zu Leipzig / Rechtschaffener Tanzmeister / oder gründlicher Erklärung der Frantzösischen Tantz-Kunst* (Leipzig, 1717); facsimile reprint ed. K. Petermann (Munich: Heimeran Verlag, 1976).
8 Ibid., p. 964.
9 A. Parrott, *The essential Bach choir* (Woodbridge: Boydell, 2000), p. 108.
10 The information here, and for the remainder of the paragraph, is taken from P. Wollny, 'Das Leipziger Collegium musicum im 17. Jahrhundert' in E. Fontana (ed.), *600 Jahre Musik an der Universität Leipzig* (Leipzig: Verlag Janos Stekovics, 2010), pp. 77–89 at p. 78.
11 Ibid., pp. 81–82.
12 'sondern meistentheils auff freundliches Begehren und Ansuchen denen Herren Studenten zu Dienst und Gefallen / wenn sie etwan vornehme Herren und Standspersonen mit einer Nacht-Music beehren wolle'.
13 Maul, *'Dero berühmbter Chor'*, p. 80.
14 P. Wollny, 'Rosenmüller, Johann' in L. Finscher (ed.), *Die Musik in Geschichte und Gegenwart*, 29 vols (Kassel: Bärenreiter, 2005), Personenteil 14, pp. 406–411 at p. 406.
15 'expectantz oder succession zur Cantorstelle in der Thomasschule'. Maul, *'Dero berühmbter Chor'*, p. 79.
16 Ibid., p. 80, where the entire letter is reproduced.
17 While the date of this collection places it outside the scope of this book, its importance warrants its inclusion.
18 R. Hudson, *The Allemande, the Balletto and the Tanz*, 2 vols (Cambridge: Cambridge University Press), p. 182.
19 In E.H. Meyer, *Die mehrstimmige Spielmusik des 17. Jahrhunderts in Nord- und Mitteleuropa*, Heidelberger Studien zur Musikwissenschaft 2 (Kassel: Bärenreiter, 1934), p. 239, the 1667 edition is listed as lost. But there is every reason to think that the exemplar *GB-Ob* Mus. Sch. c.158a-f is the first edition.
20 J. Rosenmüller, ed. K. Nef, *Sonate da camera*, DDT 1/18 (Leipzig, 1904), Preface, pp. ix–x. In addition, the important note blackenings have also been suppressed throughout. See Chapter 9.
21 P. Whitehead, 'Austro-German printed sources of instrumental music, 1630 to 1700', PhD dissertation (University of Pennsylvania, 1996), p. 186.
22 M.A. Eddy, 'The Rost Codex and its music', PhD dissertation (Stanford University, 1984), pp. 84–5.
23 *CCS*, pp. 101–102.
24 For a discussion of note blackening and further examples by Rosenmüller, see Chapter 9.
25 Fabricius' career in Leipzig is documented in M. Maul, 'Musikpflege in der Paulinerkirche im 17. Jahrhundert bis hin zur Einführung des "neuen Gottesdienstes" (1710)' in E. Fontana (ed.), *600 Jahre Musik an der Universität Leipzig* (Leipzig: Verlag Janos Stekovics, 2010), pp. 33–56, at pp. 35–6. See also C. Junge, '"Effigies XXI Clarissimorum Musicorum à Wernero Fabrico, Musico Lipsiensi":

Die Porträtsammlung berühmter Musiker des Werner Fabricius' in E. Fontana (ed.), *600 Jahre Musik an der Universität Leipzig* (Leipzig: Verlag Janos Stekovics, 2010), pp. 57–76.

26 See S. Rose (ed.), *Leipzig church music from the Sherard Collection: eight works by Sebastien Knüpfer, Johann Schelle, and Johann Kuhnau* (Middleton, WI: A-R Editions, 2014), p. xiv.
27 For a list of Pezel's dedicatees, see E.A. Wienandt, *Johann Pezel (1639–1694): a thematic catalogue of his instrumental works* (New York: Pendragon, 1983), p. xv.
28 C. Becker, *Die Tonwerke des XVI. und XVII. Jahrhunderts oder Systematisch-Chronologische Zusammenstellung* (Leipzig, 1855), p. 293.
29 If the part designations excluded the continuo, the '5. Stimmen' would then be incorrect.
30 Wienandt incorrectly calls this 'the five-part texture of the French orchestra'. His interpretation of Pezel's varying instrumentation also needs to be treated with some caution. Wienandt, *Johann Pezel*, Preface, pp. xxi and xxii.
31 Ibid., p. x.
32 For comments on Leipzig's courts and university, see Kevorkian, *Baroque piety*, p. 16.
33 C.E. Brewer, *The instrumental music of Schmelzer, Biber, Muffat and their contemporaries* (Farnham: Ashgate, 2011), p. 343.
34 Wollny, 'Das Leipziger Collegium musicum' pp. 84–5 and 89.
35 Pezel had applied for the post in 1680, but was not formally appointed until early the following year. See H. Biehle, *Musikgeschichte von Bautzen bis zum Anfang des 19. Jahrhunderts* (Leipzig: Kistner und Siegel, 1924), p. 35.
36 J. Walther, *Musicalisches Lexicon Oder Musicalische Bibliothec* (Leipzig, 1732); modern edition, ed. F. Ramm (Kassel: Bärenreiter, 2001), pp. 287–8.
37 It is possible that, in the use of 'Neben-Werck', Horn is indicating that he is not a professional musician and has composed these works in his spare time. I am grateful to Stephen Rose for making this suggestion to me (private communication).
38 It has not been possible to reproduce the symbol for Horn's *Signum* with any degree of accuracy.
39 S. de Brossard, *Dictionaire de Musique, contenant une explication des termes Grecs, Latins, Italiens, & François les plus usitez dans la Musique* (Paris, 1703); facsimile edition (Hilversum: Fritz Knuf, 1965), p. 192.
40 For a discussion of the bowed vibrato, see S. Carter, 'The string tremolo in the 17th century' *Early Music*, 19/1 (1991), pp. 43–60.
41 The manuscript is catalogued, though not with complete accuracy, in H. Kümmerling and W. Steude, *Die Musiksammelhandschriften des 16. und 17. Jahrhunderts in der Sächsischen Landesbibliothek zu Dresden* (Leipzig: VEB Deutscher Verlag für Musik, 1974), p. 13. The copying date of the manuscript is given here as 1675, but this appears to be based on an incorrect date for the *Parergon musicum* printed editions.
42 See also *CCS*, p. 25.
43 See C. Caemmerer, '„Des Hylas aus Latusia Lustiger Schauplatz von einer Pindischen Gesellschaft": der Bericht über eine Gruppe studentischer Liedermacher in Leipzig des 17. Jahrhunderts' in C. Caemmerer (ed.), *'Der Buchstab tödt – der Geist macht lebendig': Festschrift zum 60. Geburtstag von Hans-Gert Roloff von Freunden, Schülern und Kollegen*, 2 vols (Bern: Peter Lang, 1992), Vol. 2, pp. 775–98 at p. 793.
44 U. Seelbach, 'Die Altdorfer Ceres-Gesellschaft (1668–1669)' in K. Garber and H. Wismann (eds), *Europäische Sozietätsbewegung und demokratische Tradition* (Tübingen: Niemeyer, 1996), pp. 1361–80 at p. 1363.
45 M. Vaillancourt, 'Instrumental ensemble music at the court of Leopold I (1658–1705)', PhD dissertation (University of Illinois at Urbana-Champaign, 1991), p. 238; see also Whitehead, 'Austro-German printed sources', pp. 193–7.

46 For a full discussion of the *Ballet de cour*, see: D.J. Buch, *Dance music from the Ballets de cour, 1575–1651: historical commentary, source study, and transcriptions from the Philidor manuscripts* (Stuyvesant, NY: Pendragon Press, c. 1993).
47 See *CCS*, pp. 13 and 15.
48 The title is the one given in the manuscript's index. The ballet is reproduced online at http://gallica.bnf.fr.ark:/12148/bpt6k107418q (accessed 28 December 2015).
49 See *CCS*, pp. 98–9 and Ex. 5.2.
50 W.S. Newman, *The Sonata in the Baroque Era*, 3rd edition (New York: Norton, 1972), p. 230.
51 The parts in the Assig collection in *S-Uu* also suggest that Assig was a careless copyist, and the lack of a first-violin part could stem from a copying error.
52 The work is given in full in M. Robertson, 'The consort suite in the German-speaking lands, 1660–1705' PhD dissertation (University of Leeds, 2004).
53 The collection and its origins are fully documented in the introduction to Rose, *Leipzig Church Music*. See also M. Crum, 'Music from St Thomas's, Leipzig, in the Music School Collection at Oxford' in E. Herttrich and H. Schneider (eds), *Festschrift Rudolf Elvers zum 60. Geburtstag* (Tutzing: Hans Schneider, 1985), pp. 97–101, and the unpublished document M. Crum, 'James Sherard and the Oxford Music School Collection' (n.p., n.d.), held in *GB-Ob*.
54 The collection contains no specifically labelled dance music.
55 Wienandt, *Johann Pezel*, p. 21.
56 Walther, *Musicalisches Lexicon*, p. 95.
57 Wienandt, *Johann Pezel*, p. xvi.
58 Ibid., p. xxx.
59 Wienandt only finds three 'supportable' instances of movement linking but, again, his reasoning is hard to follow. Ibid.
60 *CCS*, pp. 102–104.
61 A further, but now-lost, volume of consort suites by Horn, *Allerhand anmuthige Sonatinen, Allemanden, Couranten, Balletten, Sarabanden und Giquen mit fünff Stimmen* was published in Leipzig in 1677. See C. Becker, *Die Tonwerke des XVI. und XVII. Jahrhunderts oder Systematisch-Chronologische Zusammenstellung* (Leipzig, 1855), entry: Horn, 1677. It is not known if this collection was meant to be a further part of *Parergon musicum*, but the fact that it was presumably a single volume and not one of a pair makes this unlikely.
62 By linking it with the trombone and *Fagott*, Horn appears to be suggesting here that the 'Violon' is an 8-foot instrument sounding at pitch rather than the octave below; he may well be thinking in terms of the six-string 'Bass-Violon' described by Speer. See Chapter 3, note 1.
63 M. Rathey, 'Rehearsal for the opera: remarks on a lost composition by Johann Kuhnau from 1683' *Early Music*, 42/3 (2014), pp. 409–420 at p. 416. Rathey does not mention *PM 6* in his article.
64 Ibid.
65 See Chapter 4.

7 Hamburg

'To be a citizen of Hamburg in the seventeenth century was probably, for Germans, the best guarantee of dying in one's bed.'[1] If Eda Sagarra's suggestion seems an exaggeration, we should not forget that Hamburg was one of the wealthiest cities in the German lands and was largely free from royal interference – 'in Hamburg, the burgher was master; no noble might reside within its territory'.[2] Governance was not restricted to a narrow group of long-established families; comparative newcomers were admitted to civic posts and were obliged to undergo legal training.[3] Indeed, 'one eighth of Hamburg's mayors from the time of the Reformation to the mid-nineteenth century were immigrants'.[4]

As we have seen in Chapter 1, a good deal of patronage could be expected from higher levels of town society, and this was surely reflected in Hamburg by an extremely high standard of music-making throughout the seventeen century. Performances of instrumental secular music took place in at least one of the large churches in the city with Matthias Weckmann, Johann Schop, Dieterich Becker, Johann Theile, Johann Adam Reincken and Christoph Bernhard among the many fine musicians active in Hamburg between 1648 and 1700. Thomas Celle and Heinrich Scheidermann also played important parts until their deaths from the plague that swept through the town in 1663. As director of the Hamburg *Ratsmusik*, Schop may have played an important role in these concerts, and the dedication to Becker's *Musicalische Frühlings-Früchte* pays tribute to the former's part in the 'Hamburgische Instrumental-Music'. Again according to Becker, public concerts in the Hamburg cathedral refectory were organised by Matthias Weckmann.[5]

If this chapter is limited to little more than the work of a handful of composers, it is a reflection of what appears to be a large amount of lost material. Advertised printed collections by both Becker and Theile have not survived and similar work by other composers is also likely to have been lost. Keyboard suites by Weckmann have survived, but no consort suites; it is difficult to believe that one of the leading figures of Hamburg's town music never explored the genre. In addition, a good deal of the suite output of Dieterich Becker, one of the most important Hamburg town musicians, was not printed but circulated in manuscript. And if the reliance on issuing suites in printed collections was not as strong in Hamburg as elsewhere, then we may see at least a partial reason for the loss of consort-suite repertoire. For the same reason, establishing a reliable chronology is often difficult, and the music in this chapter is therefore dealt with by composer and not primarily in chronological order.

The consort-suite tradition in Hamburg flourished from the 1660s until the early 1690s. While carefully organised collections were as common in Hamburg as elsewhere, the tradition embraced an enhanced use of variation techniques and placed great emphasis on the relationship between movements, including the prefatory Sonatas, of individual suites. In company with those in other large towns, Hamburg musicians were expected to play both string and wind instruments. According to Thomas Celle's 1642 'Verziechnüs derer Adjuvanten', the *cornetto* players were expected to play the violin and recorder and the trombone players were similarly expected to play violas and recorders.[6] But unlike the Leipzig tradition of the previous chapter, there does not seem to have been any tradition of publishing music written specifically for wind ensembles.

Establishing a background to the specifics of the Hamburg tradition is as problematic as establishing a reliable chronology. William Brade was an English musician holding the post of director of the Hamburg *Ratsmusik* in the early part of the century. Given that his *Newe ausserlesene Paduanen und Galliarden mit 6. Stimmen* (Hamburg, 1614) contains movement linking between duple- and triple-time dances, it is clear that basic variation techniques were known and used in Hamburg.[7] But nothing in this, or Brade's other collections, suggests the complexity of the tradition in the second half of the century. Likewise, there appears to be nothing in the so-called 'Anglo-German consort repertoire' of early seventeenth-century Hamburg that points to the adoption of enhanced variation techniques in suite writing.[8] Even in the 1633 *Erster Theil Newer Paduanen* by Johann Schop, also a director of the *Ratsmusik*, there is no anticipation of later trends.

The one composer whose work does seem to anticipate the tradition, albeit in the keyboard repertoire, is Johann Jacob Froberger. This is not to suggest that Froberger's influence was limited to Hamburg. In Leipzig, for example, the preface to Johann Kuhnau's *Biblischer Historien* (Leipzig, 1700) refers to the 'well-known' ('berühmten') Froberger, and the widespread circulation of the latter's keyboard works in Germany appears to have surpassed even that of Lully's dramatic stage music in the last two decades of the century. But it appears that Froberger had a number of friends and benefactors in and around Hamburg,[9] and the town's musicians certainly knew of Froberger's work. Peter Wollny has drawn attention to the 'Hamburg Froberger tradition', also tentatively suggesting that one of the town organists, Johann Kortkamp, was responsible for the copying of the important Berlin Sing-Akademie manuscript SA 4450 from the composer's autograph.[10] If this is correct, it is significant that SA 4450 includes the keyboard suites from Froberger's 'Libro Quarto'. Most important of all, a contest between Froberger and Weckmann had taken place in the winter of 1649–50 and the two men remained close friends. Not surprisingly, Weckmann, a fine keyboard player himself, seems to have possessed an unrivalled knowledge of Froberger's playing style and seems to have been responsible for a number of manuscripts containing the latter's music. According to Mattheson, this knowledge had been aided by Froberger providing one of his own pieces as an exemplar ('so daß Weckmann auch dadurch der frobergenischen Spiel-Art ziemlich kundig ward').[11]

Froberger's use of variation techniques was sporadic but, when he did use them, it was often with great imagination, and it is this feature of his work that particularly seems to have attracted the attention of Hamburg composers. Example 7.1 shows the openings of the third Partita (*FbWV* 609) from the autograph 'Libro Quarto' manuscript of 1656 that was copied by Kortkamp. The linking techniques are sophisticated: the opening motif of the Allemande appears in the Gigue, but only in the home key at the entry of the second voice. And while there is no direct melodic connection between these two dances and the following Courante, the latter shares a common harmonic progression with the Allemande that is also hinted at in the Gigue (marked 'x' in the example). The Sarabande is independent with no linking material. The construction methods of this suite could easily have come from the pen of a Hamburg composer.

When Dieterich Becker arrived in Hamburg, he may well have been familiar with Froberger's music and he would have certainly come into contact with it through Weckmann. If the Hamburg tradition reflects Froberger's influence

Example 7.1 J.J. Froberger, openings of 'Allemande', 'Gigue', 'Courante' in 'Libro Quarto: Toccate, Ricercari, Capricci, Allemande, Gigue, Courante, Sarabande' (*A-Wn* Mus. Hs. 18707), fols 100v–102v.

152 Hamburg

transferred to the consort suite, then Becker may well have been the one to make this transfer. It is to Becker's music that I now turn.

Born in Hamburg in 1623, Becker started his professional career as a court organist in Ahrensburg, moving on to be a violinist first at Stockholm and then at the court of Duke Christian Ludwig in Celle. Although he left for Hamburg in 1662, well before the Celle *Hofkapelle* was re-arranged along French lines by Princess Eléonore Desmier d'Olbreuse, it is likely Becker had already gained experience of writing in the French manner. According to the title page of his 1668 *Musicalische Frühlings-Früchte*, he held the position of 'Bestallten-Violisten' (official town violinist) in Hamburg and was still in this post when the 1674 *Sonaten und Suiten* were published. His work was widely circulated, especially in England. Roger North knew of consort music 'from Sweden by Becker composed from 2 to 6 parts which was too good to be neglected and lost, as it is at present', and the connection is confirmed by a number of English manuscripts containing Becker's work.[12] His known printed output is as follows although there may well have been more now-lost publications:

Musicalische / Frühlings-Früchte / Bestehend In drei-vier-und fünff-stimmiger Instrumental-Harmonia, Nebenst dem Basso Continuo. Gesetzet von Diedrich Beckern (Hamburg, 1668).[13]

Erster Theil zwey-stimmiger Sonaten und Suiten Nebest einem gedoppelten Basso Continuo gesetzet von Dieterich Beckern (Hamburg, 1674).

Ander Theil zweystimmiger Sonaten und Suiten nebest dem Basso Continuo. (Hamburg, 1679).

Musicalische Lendt-Vruchten Bestænd In dry, vier, vyf, Instrumentale-Hermoniale stemmen Beneffens den Bassus Continuus, door Theodorus Beckern (Antwerp, 1673).

The last of these is not a new publication, but a partial re-issue of *Musicalische Frühlings-Früchte* with most of the dance movements omitted. *Ander Theil zweystimmiger Sonaten und Suiten* is clearly a second volume of the 1674 publication. It is shown in Göhler's listings of seventeenth-century trade catalogues as '2 stim[miger] Sonaten ander Theil. Didr. B[ecker] Raths Violisten in folio. Hamb[urg] im Verl[egung] des Aut[oris]. 1679'.[14]

No doubt in connection with his appointment in Hamburg, *Musicalische Frülings-Früchte* was dedicated to Becker's new employers. Table 7.1 lists the contents of the collection; with the exception of the 'Canzon à4' and the two Bransle sequences at the end, it is organised by increasing order of sonority.

Musicalische Frühlings-Früchte (hereafter, *MF-F*) contains one of the earliest examples of a Sonata being used to preface a suite, although we have seen that the Paduan had fulfilled a similar function in a number of other collections during the previous decades. And Rosenmüller used 'Sinfonie' to start each of the suites in his *Sonate da camera* of a year earlier (see Chapter 6) while Löwe von Eisenach

Table 7.1 Contents of D. Becker, *Musicalische / Frühlings-Früchte / Bestehend In drei-vier-und fünff-stimmiger Instrumental-Harmonia, Nebenst dem Basso Continuo* (Hamburg, 1668)

Movement titles	Instrumentation	Key
1. Sonata à3	Violino I / Violino II / Violon / Basso Cont.	G major
2. Sonata à3	Violino I / Violino II / Violon ò Fagott / Basso Cont.	G major
3. Sonata à3	Violino I / Violino II / Viola da Gamba / Basso Cont.	A minor
4. Sonata à3	Violino I / Violino II / Viola da Gamba / Basso Cont.	A minor
5. Sonata à4 / 6. Allmand à4 / 7. Courant à4 / 8. Sarband à4 / 9. Giquæ à4	Violino I / Violino II / Viola / Violon / Basso Cont.	C minor
10. Sonata à4 / 11. Allmand à4 / 12. Courant à4 / 13. Sarband à4 / 14. Giquæ à4	Violino I / Violino II / Viola / Violon / Basso Cont.	E minor
15. Sonata à5	Violino I / Violino II / Viola / Viola da Braccio / Violon ó Fagotto / Basso Cont.	F major
16. Paduana à5	Violino I / Violino II / Viola / Viola da Braccio / Violon / Basso Cont.	G minor
17. Paduana à5	[Violino I] / [Violino II] / Viola / Viola da Braccio / Violon / [Basso Cont.]	A major
18. Sonata à5	Violino I / Violino II / Viola / Viola da Braccio / Violon ó Fagotto / Basso Cont.	B-flat major
19. Sonata à5	Violino I / Violino II / Violino III / Violino IV / Violon ó Fagotto / Basso Cont.	G minor
20. Ariæ à5 / 21. Ballet à5 / 22. Sarband à5	Violino I / Violino II / Viol[a] da G[amba] 1 / Viola da G[amba] 2 / Viola da G[amba] 3 /Basso Cont.	D major
23. Sonata à5 / 24. Allmand à5 / 25. Courant à5 / 26. Sarband à5 / 27. Giquæ à5	Violino I / Violino II / Viola / Viola da Braccio / Violon ó Fagotto / Basso Cont.	G major
28. Canzon à4. 2 Viol: 2. Cornettino è Basso.	Violin. I / Violino II / Cornetto I / Cornetto 2 / Violon ó Fagotto / Basso Cont.	C major
29. Brandle à4 / Gay / Amener / Gavott / Courant	Violino (I & II unis.) / Viola / Viola da Braccio / Violon / Bassus	C major
30. Brandle à4 / Gay / Amener / Gavott / Courant	Violino (I & II unis.) / Viola / Viola da Braccio / Violon / [Bassus]	B-flat major

Note: instrument names are given at the head of each movement in most of the collection; square brackets denote the places where they are missing.

did the same even earlier in 1657.[15] In the light of this, it is not Becker's use of the Sonata as a prefatory movement that is important; it is his deliberate integration of it into the total construction of the suite. Example 7.2 shows the start of each movement, including the Sonata, from the most impressive music in the collection, the second *à4* suite (movements 11–14) with its seeming imitation of Froberger's use of variation techniques.

The linking takes place at two levels; firstly the opening and closing movements (the Sonata and Gigue) share the same opening head-motif based on the descending interval b′–e′. The bass line for this shared motif is also the same.

Example 7.2 Becker, *Musicalische Frühlings-Früchte*, openings of '10. Sonata à4', '11. Allmand à4', '12. Courant à4', '13. Sarband à4', '14. Giquæ à4'.

Secondly, the head-motif is inverted to give an ascending interval b'–e", and this is used for the remaining dance movements – the Allemande, Courante and Sarabande. In the Allemande and Sarabande, Becker uses the bare interval; for the remainder, the gap between the notes is filled in. In the manner of Froberger's G minor keyboard suite quoted above, the most important feature of the linking between Courante and Sarabande is the common harmonic progression marked with an 'x' in the example. The opening and closing movements of the suite are further brought together by a similar use of counterpoint. Becker has therefore made it quite clear that the entire suite is a unity, and there can be no doubt on the part of the performer that the Sonata is an integral part of this scheme.

If the previous *à4* suite of the collection in C minor (movements 5–9) is less adventurous but still imaginative in its handling of variation techniques, the *à5* Allemande-led suite (movements 23–6) seems to show Becker experimenting with inversion of the head-motifs. As much of the thematic material in the suite is based on an ascending or descending scale, it is often difficult to know if there is an intentional link between movements, or if any similarity is coincidental. The material is not sufficiently distinctive; perhaps it comes from an earlier time in Becker's career. Curiously for a composer with such an interest in variation techniques, Becker does not use duple-/triple-time re-casting at any point in the collection.

If a model was needed for the organisation of the collection as a whole, Froberger had little to offer and, for this, it seems that Becker turned to Luder Knoep's *Ander Theil Newer Paduanen* published eight years earlier in nearby Bremen.[16] Becker's inclusion of *Paduanen* – hardly commonplace in the late 1660s – is telling. The multi-structured '20. Ariæ à5' is also reminiscent of Knoep; in both composers' examples, the music at the end of the first section returns to form a *coda* after the second section. Further parallels are to be found in the overall structures of the collections. Like Knoep, Becker uses two different suite formats in *MF-F*; the three Sonata-led suites are contrasted with a D major three-movement sequence ('20. Ariæ à5' – '22. Sarband à5'), which employs a different sequence of movement types (see Table 7.1 above). Unlike the three suites where variation techniques are an essential part of the structure, the D major sequence is restrained in its use of linking material and, above all, Becker uses a mixed ensemble of two violins, three gambas and continuo.[17] Even allowing for Druckenmüller's specified ensemble of three viols and continuo in his *Musicalisches Tafel-Confect* (published in the same year as *MF-F*), mixed violin and viol consorts are rare in the suite repertoire.[18] It is likely that Becker was responding both here and elsewhere to the tradition of viol playing that remained strong in Hamburg into the start of the eighteenth century.[19]

Knoep had concluded *Ander Theil Newer Paduanen* with a complete section devoted to functional dance music in the French manner. *MF-F* also concludes with French functional dance music – albeit not a complete section, but a pair of four-movement Bransle sequences, each with an additional Courante. Becker had clearly learned about instrumentation in the French manner from his time at Celle: the two violin parts double one another to give a reinforced upper line above the two viola parts and bass. And the material of each movement is equally idiomatic. However, Becker departed from standard French practice by introducing movement linking into the second of the two sequences. Here, he uses a short head-motif to link all the movements except the Courante.

Taken individually, the similarities between *MF-F* and Knoep's *Ander Theil* do not add up to very much; as we have seen, the use of French dance music to end a collection was not confined to the latter and there are many collections that provide contrasts of movement type. But the case for supposing that Becker used Knoep as the organisational model for his first publication is convincing when bringing the similarities between the two collections together as a whole. And taking into account the strong trading links and the comparatively short distance between Bremen and Hamburg, the supposition seems even more likely. *MF-F* exists in a modern edition, but despite this, the suites remain little known.[20] While not consistent in quality, they are still a worthwhile addition to the Hamburg tradition.

In 1673, the sonatas of the collection, along with the two *Paduanen* and the *Canzon* were published again in Antwerp under the title *Musicalische Lendt-Vruchten*. Bar lines are used instead of the more usual oblique slashes of Rebenlein's Hamburg edition but, in all other respects, the printing is inferior. Given the links between Sonatas and subsequent dance movements, it seems unlikely that Becker would have sanctioned such an edition and this, along with a lack of any preface or dedication, suggests that he had little or nothing to do with this publication.

Extracts from *MF-F* survive in manuscript sources. '5. Sonata à4', albeit in reduced *à3* instrumentation without the viola part, found its way into the so-called 'Rost' manuscript (*F-Pn* Rés. Vm7 673). Two further manuscripts confirm North's comment on the circulation of Becker's music in England. 'XLI. Sonata' was copied into *GB-DRc* MS Mus.D2, which was either in possession of, or written for, 'Sir John St. Barbe Bart neare Rumsey in Hampscheere',[21] and a near-complete version of *MF-F* is part of *US-NHub*, Osborn MS 515. The latter contains consort music by a number of English composers including Henry Purcell. Only surviving as a bass-line part-book, it appears to have been used in late seventeenth-century Canterbury.[22]

For his next publication, Becker turned to the trio format; *Erster Theil zwey-stimmiger Sonaten und Suiten* (hereafter *S&S 1*) was self-published in 1674. Becker's preface links the collection with *MF-F* and it is possible that at least parts of the collection may have been performed at the Hamburg public concerts. However, there are none of the opportunities for solo display that are found in the suites in manuscript *D-Hs* M B/2463 that are discussed below.

S&S 1 contains nine sonata-suites grouped in ascending order of key. The first eight are scored for two violins and bass but, in the final one of the collection, the second violin is replaced by a viola da gamba. Following the collection's title, the sequences of dance movements following each sonata are mostly given the collective title of 'suite' in the part-books; this is quite possibly the earliest use of the term in a printed edition by a German town composer.[23] Seven of the suites use the same sequence of movements:

Allmandt / Courant / Saraband (or Sarabanda) / Giguæ

Becker again includes a Bransle sequence in the collection, the shortened four-movement version followed by a pair of Courantes and a Sarabande. The sequence also has a prefatory Sonata. This combination of Bransle and abstract movement is unusual, but not unique. As we have seen in the previous chapter, Pezel's *Delitiæ musicales* and *Musica vespertina Lipsica* both contain similar examples.

Becker makes frequent use of movement linking between dances of *S&S 1*, but only one of the Sonatas is linked to its following suite. The opening of 'II. Allmandt' is given in Example 7.3.

The piece reflects the collection as a whole; it is well crafted but hardly demonstrates Becker's considerable musical imagination. The same is true of the choice of movement type. The seventh suite starts with an Aria instead of an Allemande, but the substitution is not the multi-sectioned Aria type found in the

Example 7.3 D. Becker, *Erster Theil zwey-stimmiger Sonaten und Suiten Nebest einem gedoppelten Basso Continuo* (Hamburg, 1674), 'II. Allmandt'.

1668 collection; it is a straightforward movement of two strains. Throughout the collection, Becker seems to be deliberately attempting to produce music of a simpler kind in contrast to *MF-F*. Perhaps he had the smaller, less ambitious domestic *Collegia* in mind of the type described by Kuhnau.

This did not stop parts of the collection finding its way to England. Manuscript *GB-Lgc* G mus 469–71 contains a section marked 'Sonata's, Almands, Courants & c: by Dieterich Beckron'. Subsequent pages are headed 'Beckrons Aires'. The manuscript only contains the first and second Sonatas and suites of the collection along with the third sonata. It is not possible to tell if this manuscript was copied directly from the printed edition or from another manuscript. As well as the extract from *MF-F* noted above, manuscript *GB-DRc* MS Mus.D2 also contains a shorter version of the sonata from the final suite in *S&S 1*.

If the shortened sonata suggests that the copyist of MS Mus.D2 may not have used the printed edition as his source, the scarcity of linking material between Sonatas and Suites in *S&S 1* suggests that at least some of the Sonatas originally had separate existences. This is further borne out by the existence of two suites from *S&S 1* without their sonatas in manuscript *S-Uu* Ihre 281–3. Only a small proportion of music in Ihre 281–3 is identifiable as the work of Becker, but it is possible that he is the author of the entire first section of the manuscript.[24] The first treble part-book carries the name 'Christian Kock', who registered with Lund University in 1696. He seems to have passed the manuscript on to Thomas Nilsson Ihre (1659–1720), a professor at both Uppsala and Lund universities. Ihre's collection is now at the Uppsala Universitetsbibliotek.[25] With this background, it does seem likely that at least some of the contents of the manuscript originated in Sweden. If this is the case, it is likely that the music by Becker came from his early career in Stockholm and before his move to Hamburg.

The two treble part-books are clearly for violins, as some of the suites contain *scordatura* tuning. The bass part-book is incomplete. All three are bound together with the equivalent voice in the Uppsala University Library exemplar of Wust's *EM 1* and share the same shelfmarks. As I have pointed out elsewhere, this has resulted in considerable confusion.[26]

Ihre 281–3 is arranged in three sections, each with its own sequence of movement numbers. The last of these sections contains music that is clearly from the court repertoire, and I have already dealt with it in *CCS*.[27] The contents of the first two sections are detailed in Table 7.2 along with duplications between parts of the manuscript and concordances with *S&S 1*.

The final three suites in the second section are not exact duplications of those in Section one; the two violin parts are both rewritten in *scordatura* tuning with extra chording. The variations following Sarabandes 28/46 and 31/49 are not present in the *S&S 1* concordance. They are technically more advanced than anything in the printed edition, and Becker may have considered them unsuitable in a collection apparently aimed at simplicity. But it is also possible that the variations are the work of another composer. As I have pointed out in Chapter 2, it was common

Table 7.2 Details of sections one and two of manuscript *S-Uu* Ihre 281–3

Movement titles (Section one)	Key	Concordances
1. Allemand / 2. Courand / 3. Saraband / 4. Gique	B-flat major	
5. Allem: / 6. Cour: / 7. Sarab:	B-flat major	
8. Allem: / 9. Cour: / 10. Sarab: / 11. Gigue	B-flat major	
12. Allem: / 13. Cour: / 14. Sarab. / 15. Gigue	C minor	
16. Allem: / 17. Cour / 18. Sarab: / 19. Gigue:	C minor	
20. Allem: / 21. Ballett: / 22. Sarab:	C minor	
23. Allem: / 24. Cour: / 25. Sarab: / Variation.[I] / Variat:[II]	D minor	
26. Allem: / 27. Cour / 28. Sarab: / Variation:[I] / Variat:[II]	D major	D. Becker, *S&S 1*
29. Allem: / 30. Gique: / 31. Sarab: Variation:[I] / Variat:[II]	D major	D. Becker, *S&S 1*

Movement titles (Section two)	Key	Concordances
1. Allamand / 2. Gique *a3* / 3. Aria *a3* / 4. Gique *a3* / 5. Capricio *a3* / 6. Gique *a3* / 7. Saraband *a3* / 8. Capricio *a3* / 9. Gique *a3* /10. Aria / 11. [untitled] / 12. Saraband *a3*	B-flat major	
13. Allemand / 14. Curant / 15. Saraband / 16. Gauott	D major	
17. [Allemand] / 18. Cour. / 19. Sarab: / 20. Aria	D major	
21. Allamand / 22. [Cour:] / 23. [Sarab:] / 24. Gique	D major	
25. [Allemand] / 26. [Cour:] / 27. [Sarab:] / 28. Gique	D major	
29. [Allemand] / 30. [Cour:] / 31. [Sarab:] / 32. [Gique]	D minor	D. Becker, *S&S 1* (one tone lower)
33. [Allemand] / 34. [Cour:] / 35. Sarab: / 36. [Gique]	D minor	
37. [Allemand] / 38. [Cour:] / 39. [Sarab] / 40. Gavott:	D major	
41. [Allemand] / 42. [Cour:] / 43. [Sarab: / Variation I/II]	D major	Movements 26–8 in Section one
44. [Allemand] / 45. [Gique] / 46. [Sarab: / Variation I/II]	D major	Movements 29–31 in Section one
47. [Allemand] / 48. [untitled] / 49. Sarab: [Variation I/II]	D minor	Movements 23–5 in Section one

practice for composers and performers to add their own *Doubles* in the keyboard and solo repertoires.

The first section of Ihre 281–3 has many of the appearances of a printed town-music suite collection; its contents are arranged in ascending order of key and each suite is clearly defined. Example 7.4 shows the openings of '16. Allem:' and '17. Cour' in Section 1.

160 *Hamburg*

Example 7.4 Manuscript *S-Uu* Ihre 281–3, Section 1, openings of '16. Allem:' and '17. Cour'.

Note: no corrections have been made. The readings are as given in the source.

The movement linking is rather more than the use of simple head-motifs; the avoidance of the Allemande's imitation at the start of the Courante highlights the differences in musical style between the two dance types. But while the movement linking is attractive, the part writing is not, especially with the parallel octaves between first treble and bass at the end of '17. Cour'.[28] And this is by no means an isolated example; a similar problem arises in the eighth suite in Section 1 of Ihre 281–3 (movements 26–8), a concordance with the dance movements in the final suite in *S&S 1*. As we have seen, the latter differs from the two-violin and bass format of the rest of the publication by the use of a viola da gamba for the middle part instead of a second violin. But in the manuscript, this process is reversed, with the gamba part being replaced by an entirely new one again for violin. The outer violin and bass lines remain largely the same. At first sight, the instrumentation for two violins and bass along with the parallel *scordatura* version in Section 2 (movements 41–3) of Ihre 281–3 appears convincing and might even reflect Becker's preference. But the attractiveness of the two-violin version is again negated by frequent faulty part writing that compromises all musical integrity. To give just one example, it is hard to believe that Becker would have sanctioned the blatant parallel octaves between the second violin and bass at the opening of '26. Allem[ande]'.

The obvious and persistent error in both first and second sections of Ihre 281–3 suggests that none of the three copyists involved with the manuscript possessed any more than the most basic musical knowledge. This is confirmed in movements 29–32 of the second section, a *scordatura* version of the penultimate suite from *S&S 1*. In the manuscript, the suite is written a tone higher than the printed edition's C minor, presumably to enhance the *scordatura* writing. But the bass part of the manuscript still carries the old two-flat key signature of the C minor version and the error is further compounded by a number of additional E♭s marked in at various points. It is not clear if the copyist was making the transposition himself from the printed edition or merely reproducing another faulty manuscript version. If the former, he either forgot, or was not aware of the need to change the key signature; if the latter, then he failed to correct the obvious error. Throughout both first and second parts of Ihre 281–3, there is enough significant error to render much of the content unplayable without far-reaching revision.

Unless fresh evidence comes to light, Ihre 281–3 will remain a mystery. It is possible that all of Section 1 and at least part of Section 2 is entirely by Becker, albeit in faulty transmission. But the quantity of error equally suggests that a good deal of the content was from the hand of an inexperienced musician, perhaps as a compositional exercise with Becker's music as an example.

Becker's otherwise-lost 1679 trio publication, *Ander Theil zweystimmiger Sonaten und Suiten nebest dem Basso Continuo*, may partially survive in manuscript transmission. A pencilled note in manuscript *D-Dl* Mus. 1/B/101 (see previous chapter) suggests that a sequence of movements headed 'a 3 Diderich Becker' is copied from the latter's 1668 *Musicalische Frülings-Früchte*.[29] This is incorrect, but it is possible that they are part of *Ander Theil*. We have seen how the copyists of this manuscript were highly selective in the movements taken from the printed originals, and it is likely that the 'Becker' movements in Mus. 1/B/101 may have suffered a similar fate. At the same time, it is also quite possible that some of the dances in this sequence are not by Becker at all.

In addition, the copying of this part of the manuscript, in possibly as many as four different hands, is not always careful. In a note above '17. Canzon', attention has been drawn to an error that resulted in the first violin part being entered at this point and not the second. The latter was similarly inserted into the now-lost first violin part. The reason for three blank staves before '25. Ballet' is not clear. It is equally unclear if this is the last dance of the 'Becker' sequence or an independent single movement. (With the exception of '25. Ballet', the incipits of the 'Becker' movements are given in Appendix 2.)

While the loss of everything except the second violin part brings a good deal of uncertainty, there are some examples of movement linking that seemingly point towards concepts of careful organisation. In a way that is typical of Becker, all three movements of the opening sequence are linked, as are '18. Ballet' and '19. Sarabande'. A possible 'alternative' suite is present in the form of the four-part Bransle sequence, movements 11–14. The Bransles appear to be idiomatically written – another feature that may suggest Becker's authorship. But there are also significant numbers of seemingly unrelated movements such as the D minor '7. Allemand' followed by '8. Giquæ' in B-flat major. There are also a number of possible movement pairings such as '9. Bauree' (sic) and '10. Sarab:' that may well have once been part of larger sequences.

Writing in 1934 before the Second World War, E.H. Meyer supposedly had knowledge of a copy in Hamburg of Becker's *Ander Theil*, and he lists the bass part containing forty dance movements followed by what appear to be a number of works based on chorales.[30] This exemplar has since been lost.

There is no mention of a Canzona, but the varied movement types listed by Meyer including a 'Gique Tambour', 'Ritournello' and 'Simphonie' have no parallels in the 1674 collection. The rambling sequence of

13. Sonata / 14. Allmand / 15. Gique / 16. Allmand / 17. Menuet / 18. Sonatino / 19. Gique

in his list also bears little relationship to Becker's careful organisation in his other publications.[31] In addition, it is unlikely that the chorale-based movements were part of a consort-suite collection. Meyer's attribution must be treated with great caution and the lack of any parallel with the 'Becker' sequence of Mus. 1/B/101 does not preclude this part of the latter from being a partial copy of the 1679 printed edition. It is to be hoped that further material will be discovered that sheds light on the matter.

Manuscript *D-Hs* M B/2463 has a number of titles and instrumental indications in English, and it seems reasonable to suppose that it was put together in England.[32] Arguably the most important manuscript of apparently unpublished works ascribed to Becker, it has been copied down as a score and not as individual part-books. Most of the remaining music appears to come from the eighteenth century and it is the work of a number of different hands.

Four sonata-suites and an independent sonata without dance music are all ascribed to 'D. Becker'. The independent sonata is similar to those that at the start of the four sonata-suites and may well have originally been linked to a sequence of dances. It is followed by a large number of blank staves presumably set aside by the copyist for their addition but never filled in. Stylistically and technically, these suites are works of considerable sophistication, and their imaginative use of variation technique is entirely consistent with the Hamburg tradition. There are clear similarities to the suites in *Musicalische Frühlings-Früchte* and there is no reason to doubt Becker's authorship. Given the likely mid-eighteenth-century copying date of the manuscript, it is fortunate that the copyist(s) appears to have resisted any temptation to modernise the score, and the notation is consistent with Becker's work elsewhere.

Dating is obviously a problem. All but one of the Courantes in these suites are in the French manner, and this could point to Becker's time at Celle. But it is far more likely that these suites were written at Hamburg. The instrumentation of two violins, two gambas and continuo for three of the suites is similar to the D major sequence of *MF-F* and clearly points to the continuing tradition of viol playing in Hamburg that I noted earlier. In addition, we shall see that the suites of M B/2463 offer greater technical sophistication than those in *MF-F*, and were presumably written later. Given the high quality of the music, arguably Becker's best work as a suite composer, it is curious that they never apparently found their way into print until modern times.

Three of the four suites follow the same order of Sonata, Prelude, Allemande, Courante, Sarabande and Gigue; the fourth inserts a 'Ballett' between the Courante and Sarabande. The sonatas are all extended multi-sectioned movements and three of the four have technically demanding solo sections for the main instruments including a remarkable *fagotto* solo from the opening suite – the only one to use the instrument.

These sonatas also show Becker making a particularly telling, and even dramatic, use of dissonance. Throughout these suites, even when his melodic lines seem to verge on the prosaic, Becker's love of dissonant harmonies often rescues the situation. Example 7.5 shows the harmonic progression that closes the sonata of the second suite, a passage of such boldness that the editors of the modern edition of the work felt compelled to change it.[33]

While they are not strict fugues, the 'Praeludi allabrevi' following each Sonata are all abstract single-strain movements using contrapuntal techniques. Becker is not alone in using a combination of two abstract movements at the start of a suite; there are parallels from the 1670s in Johann Wilhelm Furchheim's *Musicalische Taffel-Bedienung Mit 5. instrumenten* (Dresden, 1674) that contains suites starting with a Sonata followed by a Prelude, while the suites in the first volume of Clamor Heinrich Abel's *Erstlinge Musicalischer Blumen* (Frankfurt am Main, 1674) are prefaced by a Prelude and then a Sonatina. Becker, Abel and Furchheim were all, at various points in their careers, court musicians. Indeed, Abel arrived at the court of Celle in 1662, the year of Becker's departure from there in order to go to Hamburg. But there is nothing to suggest that the use of twin abstract movements at the start of a suite is in any way specifically linked to courtly music; and far from being examples of the latter, the collections by Abel and Furchheim were written in the municipal style and possibly associated with applications for posts as town musicians.

In the light of their likely Hamburg origin, it is hardly surprising that variation techniques play an important part in all of Becker's suites in M B/2463. As in *Musicalische Frülings-Früchte*, there are no examples of re-cast pairs of Allemandes and Courantes, but in every other area of the techniques, Becker explores new levels of intricacy and ingenuity. In the first suite, Becker sets out the brief, even

Example 7.5 D. Becker, 'Sonata â 4, 2 Violini & due Viola da gambæ, Nummer 2' (*D-Hs* M B/2463), Sonata, closing section.

minimal linking material in the opening bars of the Sonata; it utilises just two notes, G and A, but played at a specific pitch, and a bass line that rises or falls from C to F. The second and third suites use intervals between notes in a similar way. In all these manuscript suites, Becker shows considerable subtlety in the way that he handles variation techniques. As in *MF-F*, the linking often imitates Peuerl's in its brevity and simplicity, but unlike *MF-F,* there is never any doubt about the use of this material. Becker's intentions are set out with the greatest clarity, even when he is at his most ingenious.

This ingenuity is demonstrated in the linking material for the fourth suite that is characteristically based around the four notes A, E, F, E. Example 7.6 shows the Allemande, where Becker imaginatively divides the linking material between the two violin parts. (It is marked by an asterisk in the example.) Neither part, on its own, contains the entire thematic link, which only becomes apparent when both parts are played together. It is procedures such as this that typify the suites in this manuscript, and the Hamburg tradition as a whole.

Some of dances in M B/2463 are noticeable for their brevity; for example, the Ballo of the final suite is six bars long. But there is also variety. Courantes and Sarabandes are in the *lustigen frantzösischen Manier*, although the simplicity at the start of the first suite's Courante seems to be indicating the Italian style before Becker brings back the subtlety of the French style for the entire second strain. The *Ballett* of the final suite has little to do with Hammerschmidt's multi-sectioned versions; it is a Ballo of the 1660s and 70s under another name. But it is not the quality of individual dances that make this collection important; it is Becker's ability to bring them all together with the Sonatas and Preludes and make a highly cohesive whole. The suites in M B/2463 are among the best examples of their kind and it is curious that they appear largely unknown by present-day performers.

The quality of Johann Adam Reincken's *Hortus musicus* collection may not be as high as the best of Becker's work, but it was good enough for J.S. Bach to make

Example 7.6 D. Becker, 'Sonata â 4, 2 Violini & due Viola d[a gambæ], Nummer 4' (*D-Hs* M B/2463), 'Allemande'.

keyboard transcriptions of part of the content, albeit with considerable re-composition of the selected fugues. Reincken was an important figure in the Hamburg musical establishment from the mid-1660s until his death in 1722. He knew Buxtehude well, and was partially responsible for the establishment of the Hamburg opera in 1678. He is thought to be the principal figure in the foreground of Voorhout's 'Domestic music scene' painting.[34] The air of affluence portrayed in the painting appears to be accurate. *Hortus musicus*, seemingly Reincken's only printed collection of consort suites, was not printed in moveable type, but expensively engraved. Ulf Grapenthin has suggested that he wanted to show 'proof of his artistic prowess' and that 'he wanted to drive bad composers out of the sacred garden of music'.[35] This may be correct, but it is nothing more than a reiteration of the anxiety regarding unqualified musicians that inhabited the minds of so many town musicians in the German lands (see Chapter 1). The identity of the engraver is not known; perhaps Reincken undertook the task himself. The edition is undated, but the Frankfurt and Leipzig trade catalogues give the date of the publication as 1688 making it one of the earliest, if not the earliest, example of an engraved consort-suite collection.[36] There are four part-books: 'Violino Primo', 'Violino Secundo', 'Viola [da gamba]' and a figured 'Bassus Continuus'. For much of the time, the string bass plays a slightly elaborated version of the continuo; full independence only occurs in some sections of the sonatas and infrequently in the dance movements.

The six suites in *Hortus musicus* are arranged in ascending order of key: A minor, B-flat major, C major, D minor and E minor, with a final suite in A major. Each suite has the same sequence of movements: Sonata / Allemand / Courant / Sarband / Gique. The same degree of organisation is present within the music itself. Each Sonata is built around a fugue 'based on two themes that are written in double counterpoint'.[37] As each theme can be inverted harmonically, the subject or counter-subject is present throughout in various configurations. In the dance movements, the linking, often extending to the Sonatas, is extensive and multi-layered. In the third suite, a rising bass-line phrase links the openings of 'Sonata 11ma' to its following Allemande and Courante, while the openings of the Sonata and Allemande share the same repeated-note motif in the first violin part. Also in the first violin part, the opening of the *Allegro* section of the Sonata forms a third link with the Courante and Gigue. Only 'Saraband 14^{tia}' remains separate; Reincken follows Becker in keeping one movement free from linking.

The influence of Becker is clear, but, unlike him, Reincken makes extensive use of re-casting techniques: four of the six Courantes are linked with their preceding Allemandes in this way. While much of this uses the traditional relationship of half a bar of Allemande equalling a complete bar of Courante, Reincken is not afraid to offer a much freer association that allows, for example, the first bar of 'Allemand 22da' to be extended to no less than three bars in 'Courant 23^{tia}'.

As we have seen, Froberger and Becker use harmonic progressions to extend movement linking away from just the opening material. Reincken does this as well, but extends the link beyond a sequence of chords to several bars. In the first suite, the distinctive harmonic pattern from the eighth bar of the Sonata is reflected in the third bar of the following 'Allmand 2da' and its parallel in the linked 'Courant 3^{tia}'.[38] The passages are shown in Example 7.7.

166 *Hamburg*

Example 7.7 A. Reincken, *Hortus musicus recentibus aliquot Flosculis Sonaten, Allemanden, Couranten, Sarbanden et Giquen Cum 2 Violin. Viola, et Basso continuo* (n.p., n.d.), 'Sonata 1ma', 'Allmand 2da'.

For the dance types, Reincken keeps firmly to the simplicity of the Italian style. There is no suggestion of the more complex hybrid Courantes and Sarabandes. As with Becker's suites, the quality of the individual dances is not as important as their part of an overall scheme for each suite. As we have seen, both violin and gamba parts contain solo passages, but only in the Sonatas. These are similar to the opportunities for display given by Becker in his Sonatas that open the suites in M B/2463 and serve to highlight the close musical relationship between Reincken and Becker. But there is also one important difference: Becker was a violinist and obviously wrote idiomatically for strings. By comparison, Reincken's writing seems at times to suggest keyboard origins, though it is unlikely that the collection is an arrangement of keyboard music. The musical level of Reincken's work may not reach that of Becker's at his best, but the collection is an outstanding example of the Hamburg tradition.

It appears that *Hortus musicus* was the last printed collection of consort suites in the town-music tradition issued by a Hamburg composer.[39] However, there are surviving examples of individual suites. A sonata and suite for violin, viola da gamba and bass is found in the anonymous manuscript *S-Uu* Instr.mus. i hs.11:10. The dances following the opening sonata are 'Allemanda', 'Courant', 'Ballett', 'Sarabanda', 'Gigue'. RISM A/II lists the sonata separately from the suite, though this is not implied in the manuscript; the database also suggests that work is in the hand of Assieg (see Chapter 6), but this is also incorrect. The manuscript is the product of two different hands, and neither corresponds to manuscripts bearing Assieg's name. Apart from the closing Gigue, the dance movements and the opening Sonata are linked across their entire first phrase by material derived from the intervals a'-e"-a" or their inversion. Example 7.8 shows the violin-part openings of the linked movements. This is typical of the Hamburg tradition, as is the use of the gamba. And while it would be unwise to make any attribution of authorship on this basis alone, it must be a strong possibility that Instr.mus.i hs.11:10 is the work of a Hamburg composer or someone closely influenced by the tradition.

Johann Theile's 1683 *Sonaten, Prael, Allem, Cour, Arien & Chiquen* is now lost, but the manuscript suite *S-Uu* IMhs 009:001 may have been part of the collection.[40] While the instrumentation of the printed edition allows several options,[41] the basic combination of violin, two inner parts and bass agrees with the violin, two violas and bass of the manuscript suite. This French-influenced instrumentation points to Theile's background as a court musician; he was *Kapellmeister* at Gottorf from 1673 to 1675 and then at Wolfenbüttel from 1685 to 1691. But while he was never employed by a municipality, he stayed in Hamburg between these two positions at court. It is clear that he was well acquainted with the city's musical life and no doubt took an active part in it.

Example 7.8 Linking material in anonymous manuscript *S-Uu* Instr.mus. i hs.11:10, 'Sonata', 'Allemand', 'Courant', 'Ballett' and 'Sarabanda'.

168 *Hamburg*

The suite in 009:001 contains six movements: 'Sonata à4', 'Allemande', 'Courante', 'Ballo', 'Sarabande' and 'Chique'. All six movements follow the Hamburg tradition, the openings of the first five movements being melodically linked. Unfortunately, the violin part for the Gigue is lost, and while it is possible that the linking applied here is well, it does not automatically follow that this is the case. As we have seen, Becker and Reincken often preferred to keep one movement independent. As well as the melodic linking, the bass lines and harmonic structure at the openings of the Courante and Ballo are related, the latter in duple time being re-cast to become a triple-time Sarabande. Example 7.9 shows the first strains of the Courante, Ballo and Sarabande. Theile's delight in employing comprehensive and intricate linking on more than one level is obvious.

Example 7.9 Manuscript *S-Uu* IMhs 009:001; linking between 'Courante', 'Ballo' and 'Sarabande'.

Theile's treatise on counterpoint, 'Musicalisches Kunst-buch' contains two further consort suites that are firmly in the Hamburg tradition. The treatise was never published, but it survives in a number of manuscript copies, including one by J.G. Walther dated 1691.[42] It comprises a collection of studies in counterpoint – instrumental sonatas, fugues, canons and dance music along with settings of excerpts from the Latin mass. Given its wide range of contrapuntal device, it is not surprising that the work has invited comparison with J.S. Bach's *Musikalische Opfer* (*BWV* 1079).

Both of the treatise's suites use variation techniques, but it is the first one that is musically and technically the most interesting. There are six movements:

Præludium à4 – Allemande – Courante – Aria – Sarabande – Gigue

With the exception of the Aria – a two-strain, single-section movement – all the dances are melodically linked and, in addition to this, every single movement uses a contrapuntal device. In the Allemande and its linked Courante, for example, the bass line of the first strain is also the treble line of the second strain. Similarly, the treble line of the first strain, transposed, becomes the bass line of the second strain. There are similar arrangements in all the remaining dances and the Prelude.

Theile's work sums up the entire Hamburg tradition of suite writing: variation techniques, likely to have been influenced by Froberger, used with a freedom and complexity rarely encountered in other German municipalities. If, by the middle of the last decade of the century, this consort tradition had been swept away by the fashionable music of the German Lullists, it remained alive in the keyboard repertoire. As we shall see in the following chapter, the link between Hamburg composers and variation techniques carried on well into the eighteenth century in the keyboard suites of Handel and Johann Mattheson.

Notes

1. E. Sagarra, *A social history of Germany, 1648–1914*, 2nd edition (New Brunswick: Transaction, 2003), p. 58.
2. Ibid.
3. J. Gagliardo, *Germany under the old regime, 1600–1790* (London: Longman, 1991), p. 162.
4. Sagarra, *Social history*, p. 59.
5. D. Becker, *Erster Theil zwey-stimmiger Sonaten und Suiten* (Hamburg, 1674), Preface.
6. Celle was a Hamburg *Cantor* at the time. See A. Spohr, 'Wind instruments in the Anglo-German consort repertoire, ca. 1630–40: a survey of music by Johann Schop and Nicolaus Bleyer' *Historic Brass Society Journal* (2004), pp. 43–65 at p. 48.
7. The suggestion that 'Brade was not the sort of musician who would have been especially interested in reworking one piece closely to produce another' does not stand up to scrutiny. See W. Brade (ed. B. Thomas), *Pavans and Galliards for six instruments (1614)* (London: Pro musica edition, 1992), Preface.
8. P. Holman, *Dowland: Lachrimae (1604)* (Cambridge: Cambridge University Press, 1999), pp. 16–17.
9. Ibid. p. xix.

10 P. Wollny (ed.), *Johann Jacob Froberger, Toccaten, Suiten, Lamenti; die Handschrift SA 4450 der Sing-Akademie zu Berlin* (Kassel: Bärenreiter, 2004), Preface, pp. xviii–xix.
11 J. Mattheson, *Grundlage einer Ehren-pforte* (Hamburg, 1740); facsimile edition, ed. M. Schneider (Berlin: Kommissionsverlag von Leo Liepmannssohn, 1910), p. 396. See also: M. Weckmann (ed. S. Rampe), *Sämtliche Freie Orgel- und Clavierwerke* (Kassel: Bärenreiter, 1991), pp. xxi–xxii. Peter Wollny has suggested that this piece is 'Suite X' in the Berlin Sing-Akademie manuscript SA 4450; Wollny, *Froberger, die Handschrift SA 4450*, Preface, p. xix.
12 M. Chan and J.C. Kassler (eds), *Roger North's The musicall grammarian 1728* (Cambridge: Cambridge University Press, 1990), p. 263.
13 Facsimile edition, Huntingdon: King's Music, n.d.
14 *Göhler* 2/90.
15 See *CCS*, p. 101.
16 See Chapter 4.
17 It is unfortunately that the modern edition of *Musicalische Frühlings-Früchte*, printed alongside the suites of M B/2463, does not distinguish sufficiently between viola da braccio and viola da gamba. See D. Becker (ed. H. Bergmann and U. Grapenthin) *Musicalische Frülings-Früchte (1668) und hamburger Handschrift*, Das Erbe deutscher Musik 110, (Kassel: Nagels Verlag, 1995).
18 In neighbouring Lübeck, Buxtehude's church music uses gambas for the middle parts in a five-part ensemble, and it has been suggested that viols made a 'frequent appearance in the scoring of the new Lutheran church music ... Ensembles consisting of three viols with two violins superimposed were common'. See L. Robinson, 'Viol, Germany and the Low Countries from c. 1600' in D.L. Root (ed.), *Grove music online* (www.oxfordmusiconline.com) (accessed 15 March 2013).
19 See J.A. Sadie, 'Handel in pursuit of the viol' *Chelys*, 14 (1985), pp. 3–24 at p. 4.
20 Becker (ed. Bergmann and Grapenthin), *Musicalische Frülings-Früchte*.
21 B. Crosby (comp.), *A catalogue of Durham cathedral manuscripts* (Oxford: Oxford University Press, 1986), p. 52.
22 Osborn MS 515 and its copyists are discussed in P. Holman, *Life after death: the Viola da Gamba in Britain from Purcell to Dolmetsch* (Woodbridge: Boydell Press, 2010), pp. 70–71. See also RISM A/II, records 900007813–37.
23 Where this title is missing, it is presumably the result of a printer's error.
24 The previously unknown concordances between Ihre 281–3 and *S&S 1* were first put forward in M. Robertson, 'The consort suite in the German-speaking lands (1660–1705)', PhD dissertation (University of Leeds, 2004), p. 244.
25 See A. Grape, *Ihreska Handskriftssamlingen i Uppsala Universitets Bibliotek* (Uppsala: Almqvist & Wiksells, 1949), p. 587. I am grateful to Håkan Hallberg at the Uppsala University Library for drawing my attention to this catalogue and making parts of it available for me to see. See also J.J. Froberger (ed. S. Rampe), *Neue Ausgabe sämtlicher Werke*, Vol. 3 (Kassel: Bärenreiter, 2002), pp. lxx–xi.
26 *CCS*, p. 89.
27 Ibid., pp. 89–91.
28 From the number of instances found throughout the consort-suite repertoire, it seems that parallel fifths may not have been considered to be ungrammatical.
29 Also repeated tentatively in the Dresden *Landesbibliothek* catalogue; H. Kümmerling and W. Steude, *Die Musiksammelhandschriften des 16. und 17. Jahrhunderts in der Sächsischen Landesbibliothek zu Dresden* (Leipzig: VEB Deutscher Verlag für Musik, 1974), p. 13.
30 E.H. Meyer, *Die mehrstimmige Spielmusik des 17. Jahrhunderts in Nord- und Mitteleuropa*,(Heidelberger Studien zur Musikwissenschaft 2 (Kassel, 1934), p. 187.
31 Ibid.
32 The modern edition is Becker (ed. Bergmann and Grapenthin) *Musicalische Frülings-Früchte*. While M B/2463 is not mentioned, see R. Charteris, 'The music collection of

Hamburg 171

the Staats- und Universitätsbibliothek, Hamburg: a survey of its British holdings prior to the Second World War' *Royal Musical Association Research Chronicle* 30 (1997), pp. 1–138 for a description of how a number of English manuscript sources found their way to Hamburg during the nineteenth century,

33   Becker (ed. Bergmann and Grapenthin) *Musicalische Frülings-Früchte*, p. 182. In the second and third chords, the f in first violin part has been replaced by an e and the figuring changed accordingly. While there are significant copying mistakes in this manuscript, the treble line of the original reading is supported by the bass figuring, and there seems to be no justification for these particular changes. The fiercely dramatic impact of the whole sequence is considerably weakened. We should be aware that parts of the first suite have also suffered from unwanted editorial intervention in this edition.

34   The painting is now in the Hamburg Museum für Hamburgische Geschichte. It has been discussed in detail in C. Wolff, 'Das Hamburger Buxtehude-Bild: ein Beitrag zur musikalischen Ikonographie und zum Umkreis von Johann Adam Reincken' in A. Grassmann and W. Neugebauer (eds), *800 Jahre Musik in Lübeck* (Lübeck, 1982), pp. 64–77.

35   U. Grapenthin, 'Reincken … Johann Adam' in D.L. Root (ed.), Grove music online (www.oxfordmusiconline.com) (accessed 18 May 2015).

36   Göhler, 2/1223.

37   P.M. Walker, *Theories of fugue from the age of Josquin to the age of Bach* (Rochester, NY: University of Rochester Press, 2000), pp. 207 and 351.

38   In his keyboard arrangement, J.S. Bach strengthened the relationship between these two passages still further by adding the dotted rhythms of the bass of the Sonata to the bass of the Allemande.

39   The tradition carried on well into the eighteenth century in the keyboard repertoire. See Chapter 8.

40   Available online at: www2.musik.uu.se/duben/presentationSource.php?Select_Dnr=2208 (accessed 4 November 2015).

41   See Chapter 1, p. 9.

42   Modern edition: C. Dahlhaus (ed.), *Johann Theil Musikalisches Kunstbuch*, Denkmäler Norddeutscher Musik 1 (Kassel: Bärenreiter, 1965). Unlike this edition, I have retained the spelling 'musicalisches' given in Walther's manuscript.

8 Keyboard suites by town composers

As I pointed out at the start of this book, this chapter is not intended as a comprehensive survey of the keyboard suite. Instead, it examines the often-symbiotic relationship between town-music suites from the keyboard and consort repertoires. By its very nature, the keyboard suite was intended for a private, domestic audience, especially in winter when churches would have been unpleasant places for their organists. In keyboard tablature, it possessed a notation that was rarely used for consort suites, and Pieter Dirksen's description of Heinrich Scheidemann's keyboard-dance movements as cultivating 'a new style in which polyphony and virtuoso figuration of the earlier harpsichord manner are replaced by free voice-leading, simplicity and unpretentious melody' could easily apply to the majority of surviving keyboard suites from the second half of the seventeenth century.[1] However, it is the problem of survival that makes any overall judgement of the genre little more than tentative. The bulk of the surviving examples, particularly in manuscript, come from northern Germany, surely an accident of preservation. Composers are not always attributed and, where they are, these attributions are not always correct.[2]

Keyboard and consort-suite repertoires have movement types in common, most obviously the Allemande, Courante, Sarabande and Gigue; but especially with the Sarabande, the commonality often extends to little more than name and the use of triple time. In a theme that I will return to, it seems that, in writing for the keyboard Sarabande, town composers were often more concerned with providing a flowing *brisé* texture than with following the rhythmic characteristics of the dance found in the consort-suite versions.[3] The same concern for sonorous texture also inhabits keyboard Courantes and produces similar results; in many cases, the dance is frequently a good deal simpler than its consort counterpart. And while note blackening was sometimes used in the keyboard repertoire of the first half of the century to denote cross-beat accentuation, it was rarely, if ever, used in dance music of the second half. As a result, the hybrid versions of the consort Courante and Sarabande that rely so heavily on blackening are seemingly totally absent from keyboard suites.

On the other hand, the Gigue shared a common language in both repertoires. Its frequent use of imitation and propulsive rhythms were just as suitable for the

Keyboard suites by town composers 173

keyboard as they were for the consort and the harpsichord's clarity can be seen as a positive advantage in often-dense textures. Example 8.1 shows the second strain of the Gigue from the keyboard suite in G minor attributed to Buxtehude in the Ryge tablature manuscript (*BuxWV* 242, manuscript *DK-Kk* 6806.1399).[4] There is no imitation at the start of this dance, but Buxtehude imaginatively reserves it for use here at the start of the second strain. There is limited *brisé* figuration and the propulsive nature of the dance is clearly maintained despite the often-dense, chordal texture.

If the Gigue shares a common language between keyboard and consort, the dance that changes least in the transfer from one genre to the other is the Allemande. Example 8.2 gives two examples by the same composer, Johann Reincken; the consort version is from *Hortus musicus* (see the previous chapter) while the keyboard version is from his suite in C major in the so-called *Möllersche Handschrift* (*D-B* Mus. Ms. 40644).

As John Butt has pointed out, the '*Style brisé* is a particularly prominent element in Reincken's suites',[5] and it would be wrong to think that idiomatic writing is totally absent from keyboard Allemandes in the German lands; the *brisé* figuration in the second bar of the keyboard Allemande given below is not something that could ever become part of the consort genre. But there are also many points of similarity in Example 8.2, especially in the dialogue between the two upper parts.

In general, and throughout both genres, there are motif-like features that are frequently connected to Allemandes. Given that her example is compromised by the use of an editorial reconstruction of dubious material, Kerala Snyder has correctly pointed to the use of the same four-note descending motif from tonic to dominant at the opening of keyboard Allemandes by Reincken, Buxtehude and Froberger.[6] She puts this down to paying 'homage' to the keyboard suites of Froberger. This may

Example 8.1 D. Buxtehude (*BuxWV* 242), 'Gigue' (manuscript *DK-Kk* 6806.1399).

Example 8.2 Comparison between J.A. Reincken, *Hortus musicus recentibus aliquot Flosculis Sonaten, Allemanden, Couranten, Sarbanden et Giquen* (n.p., n.d.), 'Allemande 27^{tima}' and 'Suite ex C♮, Allemand' (manuscript *D-B* Mus. Ms. 40644).

be true, but the same opening is also present in a number of consort Allemandes that are less likely to be intended as an act of homage. As in the rising scale at the start of Reincken's 'Allemande 27^{tima}' shown above, this four-note motif is likely to be nothing more than a basic musical gesture associated with the Allemande in both its keyboard and consort versions. But if 'homage' is questionable in this particular case, there is no denying the extraordinary influence of Froberger on keyboard-suite composition. And as we shall see, he was a posthumous beneficiary of the new engraving techniques; printed editions of his music carried on well into the eighteenth century.

Despite the obvious quality of Froberger's music, this influence was not entirely positive. His apparently favoured combination of Allemande, Courante and Sarabande with a wandering Gigue seems to have dominated the manuscript tradition of keyboard-suite writing throughout the second half of the seventeenth century. In comparison, the consort genre presents a livelier tradition of movement choice. However, the influence was clearly felt by Reincken in Hamburg, which was, as we have seen, an important centre for the dissemination of Froberger's music, and the choice of Allemande, Courante, Sarabande and Gigue as unchanged dance types throughout *Hortus musicus* is surely a reflection of this. Not surprisingly, the same sequence is used exclusively in his keyboard suites where the propulsive and often-contrapuntal Gigues always remain at the end of the sequence. None of the extant keyboard suites contain any *Doubles*.

In keeping with the Hamburg tradition, Reincken's keyboard Allemandes and Courantes are frequently linked, either at their openings or as full re-castings. However, while the bass lines of the Sarabandes are often linked with the other movements in the suite, the treble lines are not. The reasons for this are not hard to find; as we have seen, Reincken frequently uses a flowing, sonorous *brisé* texture in his keyboard Sarabande writing, albeit at the expense of traditional rhythmic characteristics. Given the difficulty of producing a melodic line in such circumstances, linking becomes near impossible. For the same reason, Sarabandes are also the movements that have the least in common with their counterparts in his consort output. When Reincken abandons the over-reliance on *brisé* techniques, as he largely does in the Sarabande of the suite in C major, the results are extraordinarily fine.[7] It is the closest that any of his keyboard Sarabandes come to their consort counterparts.

We have seen in the previous chapter that only one consort suite by Buxtehude survives and, as Snyder has pointed out, the major sources for his keyboard suites have only come to light in more recent times.[8] Willi Apel dismissed them as 'disappointing when compared to his organ works',[9] and Snyder suggests that they 'lack the harmonic richness and dramatic intensity that characterizes so much of his other music'.[10] But both these comparisons ignore the often-deliberate simplicity of the dance-suite repertoire in its keyboard manifestation.

There are problems of attribution with Buxtehude's suites, but Snyder has identified a total of nineteen that appear to be genuine (*BuxWV* 226–44 and *BuxWV deest* [x 2]). Without exception, they have a strong affinity with the Froberger-influenced Hamburg suites of Reincken, and it has to be said that there is a stylistic anonymity about many of the dances. There are no abstract prefatory movements; like Reincken, Buxtehude apparently kept these for his consort-suite writing but, in the suite in E minor (*BuxWV* 237), he clearly emulates the Hamburg tradition of movement linking. The openings of all movements except the independent first Sarabande are given in Example 8.3.

Seemingly following the example of Becker, Buxtehude uses the interval E–B or its inversion to link the Allemande, Courante, second Sarabande and Gigue. The Courante starts each strain as a ternary re-casting of the Allemande

Example 8.3 D. Buxtehude, 'Suite in E minor' (*BuxWV* 237), linking between movements.

but diverges after the opening phrase, and we do see here some of the flexibility displayed in the consort suite *BuxVW* 273 (see Chapter 5). As with Reincken's suite in C major discussed earlier, the linking with the single-strain Sarabande is made possible by the avoidance of *brisé* writing and, particularly in the manner of Becker, the head-motif in the Gigue is split between two voices. It is noticeable that the independent first Sarabande (not shown in the example) also avoids *brisé* techniques; in this and its use of variation techniques, this suite could almost be an arrangement of a consort suite, although there is no evidence that this is the case. Of all Buxtehude's extant keyboard suites, it is the nearest to the consort genre.

Manuscript *D-Lr* Mus. ant. pract. 1198 is the work of two copyists, and it is possible that the first of these is Christian Flor (1626–97).[11] Flor was appointed organist of the town's *Lambertikirche* in 1654 and it seems that, while he retained this post for the rest of his career, he also became deputy organist and then organist of the neighbouring *Johanniskirche*. Mattheson speaks of him as 'the well-known Lüneburg organist'.[12] Dated 2 March 1687, the first part of the manuscript contains ten anonymous keyboard suites along with arrangements of twelve pieces extracted from Lully's dramatic stage music.[13] The material copied by the second hand also contains music arranged from Lully's work along with another four possible suite groupings. But the quality of these suites is very poor and does not appear to be related to the examples in the first part of the manuscript.[14]

The third of the suites from the first copyist's hand in MS 1198 also appears in the *Möllersche Handschrift*, where it has acquired a 'Fuga' as a new opening movement. Flor himself is named here as the composer. As a result, all ten suites in the first part of MS 1198 have been attributed to him.[15] But the *Möllersche Handschrift* is an unreliable guide to authorship and we should exercise a good deal of caution over making such generalised attributions.[16] And, as far as the 'Fuga' is concerned, the manuscript tradition in the German lands was a lively one, with copyists clearly uninhibited in carrying out additions and alterations. So it is uncertain if the suite in the *Möllersche Handschrift* is wholly or even partially Flor's work, and we cannot be sure that he is responsible for the remaining nine in MS 1198.

The first copyist of MS 1198, whatever his identity, was apparently uninterested in applying the concepts of careful organisation found in printed suite collections. Albeit with the absence of a suite in F major or minor, it would have been possible to place the ten suite groupings of MS 1198 in ascending order of key; but not only does the copyist fail to do this, he intersperses the suites with apparently unrelated dance movements in a way reminiscent of consort collections from more than twenty years earlier. Many of these dance movements are French-influenced, and it is surprising that the same national influence does not extend to the contents of the suites themselves. The choice of movement type in the latter is conservative and mostly limited to Allemandes, Courantes, Sarabandes and Gigues. The *Galanterien* so favoured by the German *Lullists* such as Cousser and Muffat are conspicuously absent, and the Courantes and Gigues are set in the hybrid versions favoured by German town composers.

Movement linking is used in the first, fourth, sixth, seventh and ninth suites, albeit without the rigour of Becker or Reincken. Example 8.4 gives the openings of the 'Allemanda' and 'Current' from the second suite of the collection. The Courante here is a triple-time re-casting of the Allemande, although it is hard to see this at the opening. Most town composers realised the importance of making the use of variation techniques clear to the listener. So it is curious that the Courante's re-casting of the Allemande is partially obscured in the treble until the second bar; its effectiveness is correspondingly reduced. An additional link between the Allemande and Sarabande of the same suite is clearer.

The second, third and eighth suites include *Doubles* or variations of select triple-time movements, and the first suite has a similar 'Variatio' attached to the opening 'Aria' along with the following 'Corrente' and 'Sarabande'. As we have seen, such variations were of the simplest kind; melody, bass and harmonies were all retained but broken up into *brisé* figurations and texture. David Schulenberg has rightly observed that 'anybody could have composed a variation [i.e. *Double*] at a later date' and drawn attention to 'orphan' movements that are 'free to wander from suite to suite at the whim of copyists'.[17] This tradition of adding variations or other dances to keyboard suites seems to have been particularly associated with the dissemination of Froberger's music. We can see it in manuscript *D-OB* MO

Example 8.4 Manuscript *D-Lr* Mus. ant. pract. 1198, 'Allemanda' and 'Current'.

1037, a collection of keyboard pieces and arrangements compiled in 1695 by the Ottobeuren organist Pater Honorat Reich. The collection includes a number of suites by Froberger.[18] 'Partia I^{ma}' of these is typical; it has three movements that survive elsewhere in Froberger's own hand followed by a Gavotte that appears in no other source and is almost certainly the work of another composer.[19] There is little or no parallel with this apparent freedom in the consort repertoire; as we have seen, it was commonplace for copyists working from printed collections to be selective in their movement choice, but adding extra dances to existing suites is seemingly rare.

If the relationship between copyist and composer in Mus. ant. pract. 1198 is unclear, it is apparently clearer in *D-Lr* Mus. ant. pract. KN 147, though not without problems. The manuscript contains keyboard music thought to be by Matthias Weckmann, but the attribution cannot be completely certain. Such doubts about this and other manuscripts of Weckmann's music have led to him being described as 'one of the most fascinating, but also most frustrating composers active during the mid-seventeenth century'.[20] The fascination comes from his links with so many important figures, the frustration because so much of his output has been subjected to questions of authenticity. However, Siegbert Rampe has suggested that the manuscript is 'largely written in Weckmann's own hand' and it is 'highly likely that Weckmann was indeed the author'.[21]

Included in KN 147 are five suites. If the Courantes and Gigues contain idiomatic examples of the French manner, Weckmann's obvious ease at writing in the style is hardly surprising; he had knowledge of French keyboard, lute and ensemble music that far surpassed most town musicians. Given the influence of Froberger on Weckmann's compositions (see the previous chapter), it is no surprise that these five suites contain the preferred sequence of Allemande, Courante and Sarabande with wandering Gigues and only one example of a *Double*. There is one introductory *Præludium* but there are no linked movements anywhere within these suites.

KN 147 appears to have been subjected to a number of physical alterations; it seems likely that, in its originally intended form, its content would have been organised by genre in a manner reflecting Froberger's own presentation manuscripts to the imperial court.[22] But even allowing for the changes to the manuscript, the content of the suites suggests that there was never any attempt to emulate the careful ordering of a printed edition. Table 8.1 details Weckmann's suites.[23]

Throughout the five suites, Weckmann shows himself to be an imaginative and resourceful composer of keyboard dance music; the standard of writing in these suites is very high, often matching Froberger's. We can see this in the Gigue from the B minor suite; Example 8.5 shows the start of the second strain and how Weckmann deals with F sharp major, one of the more distant keys in unequal temperament tuning.

Curiously, arrangements for keyboard of town-music consort suites are extremely rare; one example that has survived is the idiosyncratic arrangement of pieces from various volumes of Horn's *Parergon musicum* given in the so-called *Leutschauer Tabulaturbuch*.[24] Apparently dating from around 1676, the keyboard writing is crude. In a manner reminiscent of the treble- and bass-line transmission of French dance music, Horn's original outer lines are mostly maintained. Occasional harmony notes, not always agreeing with the printed sources, are then added, mostly for the left hand, and chords are given in the right hand for the concluding notes of a strain. More importantly, we can see the scant regard given to the careful ordering of *Parergon musicum* by the compiler of the tablature or the source from which he was working; for example, the Allemande from the third suite of the first volume and the *Saltirelle* from the final suite of the third volume both stand alone, while the first suite of Volume I is shorn of its Ballo.

Table 8.1 Manuscript *D-Lr* Mus. ant. pract. KN 147, suites by Matthias Weckmann

Suite key	Movements
D minor	Allemand / Courant / Sarabanda / Gigue
C minor	Allemanda / Gigue / Courant / Saraband / Le Double
B minor	Præludium / Allemanda / [Courante] / Saraband / Gigue
E minor	Allemand / Gigue / Saraband
A minor	Allemanda / Gigue / Courant / Saraband

Example 8.5 M. Weckmann, manuscript *D-Lr* Mus. ant. pract. KN 147, 'Gigue'.

180 *Keyboard suites by town composers*

Similarly, while making copies and transcriptions of individual French dances, town composers throughout the German lands were seemingly unwilling to write keyboard equivalents of the Lullian *Ouverture*-suite.[25] Even Weckmann, with his apparent ease of writing in the *frantzösischen Manier*, fails to follow the consort genre in its embracing of the new style derived from imitations of the stage works of Lully. And Weckmann was not alone in this. Table 8.2 compares the contents of one consort and two keyboard suites. The consort suite is by the *Lullist* Jean Sigismond Cousser, while the keyboard suites are by Johann Caspar Ferdinand Fischer, *Kapellmeister* at the Baden court at Schlackenwerth, and Johann Kuhnau, the Leipzig town composer.[26]

Table 8.2 Movements from select suites in J.S. Cousser, *La cicala della cetra D'Eunomio* (Stuttgart, 1700) and J.C.F. Fischer, *Les Pièces de Clavessin* (Schlackenwerth, 1696), J. Kuhnau, *Neüer Clavier Übung Andrer Theil* ([Leipzig], 1692)

Composer	Source	Movements
Cousser	*La cicala della cetra D'Eunomio* (Stuttgart, 1700).[a]	Ouverture II / Marche / Prelude / Entrèe /Air / Les Genies / Les Mesmes / Prelude / Air / Gavotte / Rondeau / Menuet / Les Vents / Les Matelots / Menuet [I] / Menuet [II]
Fischer	*Les Pièces de Clavessin* (Schlackenwerth, 1696).[b]	Præludium II / Ballet / Menuet / Rondeau / Canaries / Passepied
Kuhnau	*Neüer Clavier Übung Andrer Theil* ([Leipzig], 1692), pp. 51–60.[c]	Præludium / Allemande / Courante / Sarabande / Menuet

Notes: a. Modern edition: J.S. Cousser (ed. M. Robertson), *La cicala della cetra D'Eunomio; Suite Nr. 2* (Magdeburg: Edition Walhall, 2010); b. Modern edition: J.C.F. Fischer (ed. E. von Werra), *Sämtliche Werke für Klavier und Orgel* (Leipzig: Brietkopf und Härtel, 1901; repr. New York, 1965); c. Facsimile edition of 1696 reprint: J. Kuhnau, *Neuer Clavier Ubung* [sic] *Andrer Theil*, Monumenta Musicæ Revocata 20 (Florence: Studio Per Edizione Scelte, 1996)

Cousser's collection clearly has at least partial origins in the dramatic stage music performed in the 1690s by his touring company and it is typical of the consort suites written by the German *Lullists* at the end of the seventeenth century.[27] Fischer makes his keyboard imitation of this style clear on the title page of his *Les Pièces de Clavessin* (Schlackenwerth, 1696; re-issued in Augsburg in 1698 as *Musicalisches Blumen-Büschlein*) where the contents are described as 'unterschidlichen [various] Galanterien', precisely the type of quasi-theatrical dances employed by Cousser. In Fischer's later *Musicalischer Parnassus* (Augsburg, n.d.), the dramatic connotations are further heightened by the naming of each of the suites in the collection after the nine muses. As John Butt has pointed out, Fischer's approach in these collections 'immediately strikes a new tone'.[28] Kuhnau, on the other hand, keeps firmly to the town-music tradition. Only the concluding Menuet can be considered an example of *Galanterien*.

Keyboard suites by town composers 181

The conservatism of the keyboard genre can also be seen in one of the most important treatises relating to the dance suite of the late seventeenth century: Friederich Erhardt Niedt's *Musicalische Handleitung*.[29] It was published in three volumes in Hamburg between 1700 and 1717. Niedt died before the final part was printed, and the task of seeing it through to press was undertaken by Johann Mattheson, who also edited and annotated a reprint of the second part in 1721. Niedt himself never lived in Hamburg: he studied at the University of Jena during the early 1690s and took up a position in Copenhagen at the end of the same decade.[30] However, it is likely that he visited Hamburg in connection with the publication of the first and second parts of his treatise and presumably had contact with Mattheson. The second volume, the *Handleitung zur Variation* (Hamburg, 1706) deals with Niedt's version of variation techniques in suite writing, the purpose of the volume being clearly spelled out on the title page:

> how Preludes, Chaconnes, Allemandes, Courantes, Sarabandes, Minuets, Gigues, and the like may be easily constructed from a simple thorough-bass, as well as other necessary instructions.[31]

The references to thorough-bass and instruction indicate that the treatise was mainly intended for inexperienced keyboard players; as Robert Hill has observed, '[Niedt] wanted to show the pupil how improvisations or compositions can be structured, and how the activity of figured bass playing led the pupil to [musical] understanding, virtually without external help'.[32] This probably explains why Niedt pays comparatively little attention to more sophisticated techniques such as duple-/triple-time re-casting of complete movements.

Instead, he prefers to use the same bass line, albeit with slight modifications, for every movement of a suite. As we have seen in Chapter 5, he was not the first composer to use bass-line linking in this way; Speer had done it, albeit without much imagination, in his 'Quodlibets', written in the 1680s, and hinted at it in the first version of his theoretical treatise, *Grund-richtiger / Kurtz / leicht und nöthiger Unterricht der musicalischen Kunst* (Ulm, 1687). It is possible that Niedt had been influenced by his fellow theorist and, as a method of instruction and a probable reflection of his own teaching, it is undeniably practical and effective. Example 8.6 shows the first strains of a 'Couranten Bass', 'Sarabande Bass' and 'Menueten Bass'. In each case, a figured bass is provided in order to demonstrate the harmonies that are common to all three dances. The same example also shows Niedt's fully realised versions.

We can see from this that the Menuet is little more than a re-writing of the Sarabande. But while the Courante and Sarabande share the same bass line, the material in the upper parts is mostly quite different. And there is an important distinction to be made here. The treatise at this point is not showing how dance movements could be linked by the use of the same melodic or harmonic material. It is demonstrating the techniques of improvising over a common bass line, a modification of variation techniques rarely found in either consort- or keyboard-suite repertoire.

182 *Keyboard suites by town composers*

Example 8.6 F.E. Niedt, *Handleitung zur Variation* (Hamburg, 1706), 'X. Capitel'.

Niedt's purpose in writing this section of the treatise confirms the sentiments of the title page; it was to encourage the improvisational skills of his readership.

Handleitung zur Variation also includes descriptions of dance types, many of them French. However, it seems that Niedt's knowledge of the latter is often strangely deficient. His description of the 'Branle' makes no mention of a sequence of dances, even though he must have encountered them in consort-suite publications.[33] And as we have seen, Niedt's title page refers only to 'Præludia, Ciaconen, Allemanden, Couranten, Sarabanden, Menueten, Giquen'. The Preludes and Chaconnes are briefly dealt with, and it is telling that the instructions are principally focused on the standard Froberger-influenced dances along with the newly fashionable Menuet. It is against

Keyboard suites by town composers 183

this background that I now turn to a technological advance that had a profound influence on the keyboard repertoire.

In contrast to printed consort-suite collections, printed keyboard-suite collections by German town composers were unknown before the late 1670s. Even Reincken, who self-published an expensive engraved collection of consort suites, did not publish any keyboard equivalents. The reason for this is not hard to find; the moveable type process employed by German printers for nearly all of the seventeenth century did not easily lend itself to keyboard music.[34] There were two main problems for the printer: multi-beamed notes and the placing of two or more lines of music on a single stave. In most printed part-books of ensemble suites, each quaver and semiquaver were printed as separate entities (see, for example, Figure 6.1).

In the consort repertoire, the lack of joined-up note tails was obviously undesirable, and it is telling that manuscript copies of printed editions usually beamed together quavers and semiquavers in the normal way. But given that few consort dances required long sequences of notes shorter than a semiquaver, the separation was clearly regarded as no more than an inconvenience. In keyboard music, the problem was far more acute; groups of three- and even four-beamed notes might be an essential feature of the music and need to be joined in order to produce a coherent and legible text. But it was not until the final decade of the century that the technology of moveable-type setting had progressed far enough to allow notes to be beamed together. Figure 8.1, the Allemande from the first suite of Johann Krieger's *Sechs musicalische Partien ... auf einem Spinet oder Clavichordio zu spielen* (Nuremberg, 1697) shows the progress that had been made.

Figure 8.1 J. Krieger, *Sechs Musicalische Partien ... auf einem Spinet oder Clavichordio zu spielen* (Nuremberg, 1697), Partia I, 'Allemande', shelfmark 2 Mus.pr. 1293: Munich, Bayerische Staatsbibliothek. Reproduced by kind permission.

Despite this obviously careful work, Krieger still had some concerns; his preface states:

> Solten einige geringe Druckfehler noch verstecket geblieben / und den Augen des Correctoris in meiner Abwesenheit entwischet seyn; weilen solche nunmehr nicht können verändert warden / so wird ein iedweder hiemit ersucht / selbige zu excusiren / und nach Anleitung seines Judicii bester massen zu corrigiren.
>
> (A few minor print errors may still have remained hidden and escaped the eyes of the proofreaders in my absence. Unfortunately, such [things] cannot be changed at this point, so everyone is hereby requested to excuse the same and make corrections using the best extent of their judgement as a guide.)

While it is likely that entire movements in the collection were misplaced by the printer, this perceived lack of accuracy may also have been linked to the issue of note spacing and general layout when two or more lines of music were placed on a single stave.[35] Again, single blocks of moveable type provided serious obstacles. In the early years of the seventeenth century, the problem had been circumnavigated in polyphonic keyboard music by giving each part a separate stave, but such a layout was not possible in the *brisé* style that was applied to so much dance music in the keyboard repertoire. By the 1680s, it seems that at least some printers had overcome these obstacles and the 'Bassus continuus' part-book of Jacob Scheiffelhut's *Musikalischer Gemüths Ergötzungen Erstes Werck* (see Chapter 5), printed as well as published in 1684 by Jacob Koppmayer in Augsburg, contains *Bassetti* doublings of both violin parts on the same line of music. Koppmayer's printing staff were clearly craftsmen: the combination of the parts is clear and well set out.

If some printers took considerable care to produce a text of reasonable clarity, the results could be very different in the hands of the less skilled. Figure 8.2 shows an extract from Niedt's *Handleitung zur Variation*, printed by Benjamin Schiller. The layout of the musical text leaves a great deal to be desired.

As late as 1739, Mattheson was complaining in his *Der vollkommene Capellmeister* that two examples of keyboard music he wished to include had been truncated because the volume's moveable type could not cope with notes in close proximity to each other.[36]

Figure 8.2 Niedt, *Handleitung zur Variation*, 'X. Capitel', shelfmark a.31: London, The British Library Board. Reproduced by kind permission.

Keyboard suites by town composers 185

We may therefore imagine the delight with which composers and publishers of keyboard music greeted the arrival of copper-plate engraving techniques in Germany, albeit much later than other parts of Europe.[37] In Antwerp, music engraving had been practised since the end of the sixteenth century and, in England, from the start of the seventeenth. When German printers did eventually take up the technique, there was at least considerable knowledge of what was involved and many of the early efforts are surprisingly good. Figure 8.3 shows a page from *Diverse Ingegnosissime, Rarissime & non maj piu viste Curiose Partite ... Dal Eccellentissimo e Famosissimo Organista Giovanni Giacomo Froberger*, issued in 1693 by Ludwig Bourgeat in Mainz, and certainly the equal of anything issued in Amsterdam or London at that time. It is telling that no attempt was made to put the widely circulated keyboard music of Froberger into print until the onset of engraving.

This is not to say that the process was without its difficulties; print runs were small, perhaps no more than fifty copies, and the plates themselves degraded with use. It was also very expensive, with the total cost approaching twice as much as the moveable-type equivalent.[38] A great deal also depended on the skill and musical expertise of the engraver and, not surprisingly, some composers attempted to learn the skill for themselves. Not all of them met with success. In England, Roger North tried engraving on a copper plate, but the results 'miscarried a litle by the fury of the aqua fortis [i.e. acid], that made the caracter too course'.[39]

Figure 8.3   J.J. Froberger, *Diverse Ingegnosissime, Rarissime & non maj piu viste Curiose Partite ... Dal Eccellentissimo e Famosissimo Organista* ([Mainz], 1693), 'Capriccio 13', shelfmark c.51: London, The British Library Board. Reproduced by kind permission.

186 *Keyboard suites by town composers*

One composer who did manage the technical demands of engraving with success was Benedict Schultheiss, a town organist in Nuremberg for nearly all his professional career. Given that Nuremberg was a leading centre of German printing, we may assume that a good deal of professional expertise was available to assist him. As the title page of his *Muth- und Geist-ermuntrender Clavier-Lust / Erster Theil* (Nuremberg, 1679) points out, Schultheiss himself carried out the engraving in copper ('in Kupffer geetzt / und ans Liecht gegeben / durch Benendict Schultheis[s]') of this and a second volume that followed from the same publishers, Michael and Johann Friederich Endter, a year later. Both volumes were reprinted after the composer's death in 1693, but this time in Frankfurt.[40] It is likely that these volumes are the earliest published keyboard suites in Germany and a very early example of keyboard-music engraving, if not the first.

The first volume comprises four suites, all with the same movement sequence of *Præludium*, Allemande, Courante, Sarabande and Gigue. There is no 'alternative' suite of Bransles and the movement choice is conservative in comparison with the consort repertoire. Unusually, the contents are arranged by key in ascending fifths, starting in C major and ending in A minor. From a simple single-section start, the Preludes of each suite become progressively more complex. Margaret Seares has suggested that they appear to be 'one of the earliest if not the first appearance in Germany of the pattern of having an introductory movement to the suite'.[41] While it is not entirely clear if Seares is referring to the keyboard suite or the genre as a whole, we have seen that the practice of using an abstract movement to start a sequence of dance movements had been a part of the consort repertoire since the late 1650s. Schultheiss was merely following a trend set by town composers more than two decades earlier; it is an example of the transfer of tradition from consort to keyboard. And while the dance movements contain a good deal of *brisé* writing, their overall style clearly mirrors the consort repertoire of the late 1670s. There are also a number of occasions where Schultheiss loses no opportunity to include note values and divisions that would have been difficult, if not impossible, with moveable type. Example 8.8 shows the opening of '12. Allemande' with its sequences of semiquavers and triplet demi-semiquavers. While similar flourishes at the start of Allemandes are not unknown, it is difficult not to see this as a response to the new technology.

The second-volume *Anderer Theil* comprises six suites with the movement numbering following on in sequence from *Erster Theil*. The suites are again

Example 8.7 B. Schultheiss, *Muth- und Geist-ermuntrender Clavier-Lust / Erster Theil* (Nuremberg, 1679), '12. Allemande'.

arranged in ascending order of key, starting in E minor and rising consecutively by tones or semitones to C minor – the more usual ordering for printed suite collections. None of the suites has a Prelude and, apart from the final one, each suite has the same sequence of Allemande, Courante, Sarabande and Gigue. The replacement of the Allemande in the final suite with a 'Lamenta' is surely a reflection of the 'alternative' suite in the consort repertoire. Unlike the first volume, Schultheiss does use movement linking in the first, second and third suites, but it is only the latter that is linked throughout.

Again, it is possible to sense Schultheiss' delight in the possibilities afforded by engraving. Example 8.8 shows the opening of each strain of the duple-time '24. Gigue' from the first suite; it has an unusual and flamboyant demi-semiquaver flourish that would, like the Allemande in Example 8.7 above, be difficult to reproduce clearly in moveable type.

This is not the only Gigue of this type in the collection; '40. Gigue' in the fifth suite is also written in common time with similar sequences of quavers and semiquavers. As with the Gigues in the consort repertoire discussed in earlier chapters, it is again difficult to see how either of these could be successfully played in triple time, and there would seem to be little point in Schultheiss notating them in this way if he did not want them to be played as written. As in the first volume, the choice of dance type is highly conservative, and Schultheiss appears to be deliberately writing a collection with carefully organised contents. Even the preface to *Erster Theil* carries similar performance instructions to those found in many consort-suite collections: 'the Allemandes and Sarabandes somewhat slowly, but the Courantes and Gigues somewhat faster and lighter' ('die Allemanden und Sarrabanden etwas langsam / die Couranten aber und Giquen etwas geschwinder und frischer').

As we have already seen, the same conservative choice of movement type is found in Johann Kuhnau's two keyboard-suite collections. Most of the contents could, if written for consort, have found their way into town-music suite collections of two or more decades earlier. Kuhnau was J.S. Bach's predecessor as cantor at the Leipzig *Thomaskirche* and has been described as 'one of the foremost personalities of middle-German musical life around the turn of the 17th to 18th centuries'.[42] Educated in Dresden and Zittau, he received musical instruction from Vincent Albrici. He became organist of the *Thomaskirche* in 1684 and Cantor in 1701. The latter part of his career was overshadowed by poor relations with the city council and increasingly poor health.

Example 8.8 B. Schultheiss, *Muth- und Geist-ermuntrender Clavier-Lust / Anderer Theil* (Nuremberg, 1679), '24. Gigue'.

188   *Keyboard suites by town composers*

The first and second volumes of his *Neüer Clavier Übung* were published in 1689 and 1692 respectively; their distribution was apparently handled by the Leipzig book printer and dealer Johann Herbord Kloss.[43] They are in effect paired volumes in the manner of Johann Caspar Horn and it seems likely that the first volume of *Parergon musicum* was a strong influence on the layout and structural arrangement of Kuhnau's collections. Kuhnau's fourteen suites are divided equally between two volumes ('Sieben Partien aus dem Ut, Re, Mi, oder Tertia majore eines jedweden Toni' and 'Sieben Partien aus dem Ut, Re, Mi, oder Tertia minore eines jedweden Toni') while Horn's collection had been similarly arranged in ascending order of key – six in major modes and six in minor.

Both Kuhnau's volumes were self-published engravings and it is possible that Kuhnau, like Schultheiss, carried out the engraving himself. Even allowing for short print runs, both volumes appear to have been enormously successful; the first was reprinted in 1695, 1710 and 1718. The second was reprinted in 1695, 1696, 1703 and, posthumously, 1726. It is possible that at least some of these reprints contained both volumes bound together. In what may have been common practice, some plates were corrected or revised for a reprint; others were not.[44]

Erster Theil is ordered in a way that clearly reflects the consort-suite publications by Leipzig composers such as Horn and Rosenmüller. Six of the suites start with a *Præludium* and the remaining one with a Sonatina. The dance movements follow the order of Allemande, Courante, Sarabande and Gigue with the exception of the E major suite that replaces the Gigue with a Menuet, and the A major suite that replaces the Sarabande with an Aria. None of them have any *Double* variations. The final, imitative section of the first suite's *Præludium* is ingeniously linked with the following Allemande in a way that suggests Becker and Reincken. Apart from this, there is no apparently thematic or harmonic commonality between the abstract movements and their following dances; variation techniques are still present, albeit limited to movement linking of Allemandes and Courantes.

The dances in *Erster Theil* all have parallels with the consort-suite repertoire although Kuhnau choses the French rather than Italian style of Courante. The frequent use of ornament signs also points to the French repertoire and there is no reason to think that, working in a town with important trade fairs, Kuhnau was unfamiliar with keyboard music published in France. We can see both this use of ornamentation and a Courante in the French style in Example 8.9.

Of the six Gigues in the collection, one follows the simple and propulsive Italian manner (see Chapter 2), one is a common-time version of mostly dotted rhythms, but the remaining four are firmly in the hybrid form that relies on counterpoint and an inversion of the opening material at the start of the second strain. Example 8.10 shows the start of each strain of the Gigue from the second suite. The frequent ornamentation is again apparent.

If the second volume of *Neüer Clavier Übung* is more adventurous in its movement selection, it is still carefully organised along the lines of consort-suite collections of previous decades. The seven suites all have the sequence of Allemande, Courante and Sarabande at their centre, but Kuhnau frequently introduces *Double*

Keyboard suites by town composers 189

Example 8.9 J. Kuhnau, *Neüer Clavier Übung Erster Theil* (Leipzig, 1689), '25. Courante'.

Example 8.10 J. Kuhnau, *Neüer Clavier Übung Erster Theil*, '10. Gigue', opening of each strain.

variations along with a wider choice of closing movement. There are only two triple-time Gigues and one in common time. The third suite ends with a Bourée, the fourth with an Aria, the fifth with a *Double* of the preceding Sarabande and the sixth with a Menuet. Six of the seven suites start with a *Præludium* but, unusually, the fourth starts with a 'Ciacona'. And it is the fourth suite, standing at the midway point of the collection, which provides an example of the 'alternative' so popular in the printed editions of the consort repertoire.

Despite its Italian title, this 'Ciacona' is nearer to the French manner and the closest that Kuhnau came to writing in the courtly style of composers such as Johann Christoph Pez. The piece uses the traditional ♩♩♪ rhythm of the French Chaconne and there is also a descending *basse constraint*.[45] While it is in the minor key – most French composers considered that Chaconnes should be in the major – Kuhnau's intensification of the harmony in the upper parts along with a chromatic variant of the *basse constraint* at the mid-point of the piece is thoroughly idiomatic. The imposing character of the Chaconne often seems to have prompted court composers to provide the grandest and most complex music in any suite, and Kuhnau here seems similarly inspired. It is perhaps the finest movement in the entire *Neüer Clavier Übung*. The remainder of the suite comprises an Allemande, Courante, Sarabande and the final Aria. The latter, in A–B–A form and with an irregular five-bar opening phrase, uses ♪. ♪ rhythms throughout; and while it is reminiscent of a common-time Gigue, it is clear that Kuhnau wished to provide a suitably individual finale for his 'alternative' suite.

While Johann Krieger was a court musician for most of his career, putting him ostensibly outside the scope of this survey, his *Sechs musicalisches Partien* clearly demonstrate the continuing influence of the earlier consort tradition even more strongly than collections by town musicians such as Kuhnau. Given his employment background, we might expect a volume of suites influenced by Lully and his German imitators and similar to those in *Les Pièces de Clavessin* by J.C.F. Fischer. But as we can see on the title page, the six suites, each designated 'Partita', are made up of 'Allemanden, Courenten, Sarabanden, Doublen und Giquen, nebst eingemischten Bouréen, Minuetten und Gavotten'.

'Nebst eingemischten' (along with, mixed together) implies that the *Galanterien* are adjuncts to each *Partita*, and this is borne out by the preface: 'Where some space or room occurs, I myself filled it with various Menuetten / Buréen and Gavotten').[46] So the Froberger-inspired sequence of Allemande, Courante, Sarabande and Gigue that we have seen in Kuhnau's and Schultheiss' collections is again used here.

The same sequence also appears as the norm in *VI Suittes Divers Airs avec leurs Variations & Fugues*, presumably the pieces advertised as 'Ses Suiten meenigen Arien met variation en verscheide Fuguen voor't Clavier' in the *Amsterdamsche Courant* of May 1710 and printed at Roger's Amsterdam publishing house. The title page of the edition does not identify the composers, merely noting that the contents are 'de divers excellents maîtres'. The clarity and quality of the engraving are excellent. As Peter Dirksen has pointed out, there is some deliberate ordering of content; the six suites are followed by three sets of variations and three fugues.[47] Dirksen has also made a convincing case for Roger's use of a single now-lost 'manuscript X' source that may have come 'through Thuringian Bach circles or from Hamburg (via Mattheson?)'.[48]

The final suite of the collection is ascribed to Georg Böhm in the *Möllersche Handschrift*, and the Sarabande of the second suite also exists as part of Buxtehude's suite in D minor, *BuxWV* 234. Dirksen has suggested that, in addition to the final suite, Böhm was responsible for the third and fifth suites, Reincken the first, and Christian Ritter the fourth.[49] Dirksen's argument may be based too much on comparisons with the *Möllersche Handschrift*, which is sometimes unreliable over attribution, but there can be little doubt that this is a collection of keyboard music by German composers all of them, apart from Ritter, town musicians.

Apart from the music itself, the greatest interest of this collection is not in its origin; it is in the fact that, even at the end of the first decade of the eighteenth century, a commercially minded publisher was content to follow movement types common in the town-music suites of the seventeenth century. The influence of Lully, so successfully promoted by the Amsterdam publishing houses from the 1680s onwards, is largely absent from *VI Suittes*.[50] As a result, the first four suites of the collection follow the Allemande, Courante, Sarabande, Gigue sequence; *Double* variations are also used frequently. 'Suitte III' and 'Suitte V' have linked Allemandes and Courantes, while the latter, the only one to start with a Prelude, has an 'Air Adagio' and variation between the Courante and Sarabande. A Bourée and Menuet replace the Gigue. Böhm's final suite is arguably the best in the collection and the only one to reflect any French influence. It ends with an imposing Passacaille (given as 'Chaconne' in the *Möllersche* manuscript concordance) that Peter Williams has found 'faulty ... particularly confusing, being neither quite variations nor distinct episodes'. Williams also pointed out that 'there is no chaconne *ostinato*'.[51] But the lack of a repeated bass-line formula throughout the piece along with freedom of construction does not necessarily indicate faulty transmission. For instance, there are Chaconnes in Georg Muffat's *Florilegium Primum* (Augsburg, 1695) where the bass-line formula never reappears after the first strain.[52] Whether Chaconne or Passacaille, many examples of the movement type were often little more than a series of simple repetitions.[53] Böhm's repetitions may be haphazard, but there should be no doubting the integrity of the piece as given by Roger.[54]

I now return to Froberger. As we have seen, the continuing fascination with his suites seems to have exerted itself on keyboard composers well beyond the time when the consort counterpart had ceased to flourish. Despite this, their appearance in an engraved edition was surprisingly late. While the title page of Froberger's *Diverse Ingegnosissime, Rarissime & non maj piu viste / Curiose Partite ... Dal Eccellentissimo e Famosissimo Organista*, printed in 1693 by Ludwig Bourgeat in Mainz, mentions 'Alemande, Correnti, Sarabande e Gique', there are no suites or dance music in this or in any of Bourgeat's subsequent volumes of Froberger's keyboard music. The public had to wait until the early years of the following century when Roger, the newly established Amsterdam publisher, exercised rather more business acumen and issued a volume of ten suites, *10 Suittes de Clavessin Composées Par Monsr. Giacomo Froberger* (Amsterdam, n.d.).[55] As Siegbert Rampe has pointed out, 'Roger promised himself healthy profits by issuing this title so soon after founding his publishing house'[56]. Bourgeat's decision, for whatever reason, not to include any suites was clearly a commercial blunder; 'Dix suittes de Clavecin, composes par Forbergue' was still being advertised in Le Cene's 1737 *Catalogue des livres de musique* along with a more expensive edition 'beaucoup mieux grave & corrigé par E. Roger'.[57]

If Froberger's music was still being printed and circulated well into the eighteenth century, the town-music suite tradition was similarly long-lived in its revitalisation through the keyboard repertoire. As we have seen, Kuhnau's *Neüer Clavier Übung* volumes were reprinted in 1718 and 1726 while the dances listed on the title pages of Johann Mattheson's *Pieces de Clavecin en deux volumes* (London, 1714) are 'Allemandes, Courents, Sarabandes, Giques, et Aires'. Even when the 'Suite Dourzieme' of the second volume starts with an *Ouverture*, the following dances are not the French *Galanterien* favoured by Cousser and Muffat; instead, Mattheson uses:

Allemande / Courante / Sarabande / Double 1^{mier} / Double 2^d / Double 3me / Gigue / Menuet 1^{mier} / Menuet 2$^{d.}$

192 Keyboard suites by town composers

Mattheson linked three of his Allemandes and Courantes in this collection, and, perhaps demonstrating the influence of his time in Hamburg, Handel was still using variation techniques in his keyboard suites; even as late as the *Suites de Pieces pour le Clavecin Composées par G. F. Handel, Premier volume* (London, ?1720), the Allemande and Courante of the suite in E minor (*HWV* 429) are linked. And while the material of *Suites de Pieces pour le Clavecin. Composées par G.F. Handel. Second Volume* (London, n.d.) may well come from an earlier time than the publication date of the early 1730s, it is again telling that Handel continued to employ the variation techniques of the previous century in his linked Allemandes and Courantes.

Notes

1. P. Dirksen, *Heinrich Scheidermann's keyboard music: transmission, style and chronology* (Aldershot: Ashgate, 2006), p. 74.
2. For example, the so-called Ryge manuscript. See K.J. Snyder, *Dieterich Buxtehude: organist in Lübeck*, second edition (Rochester, NY: University of Rochester Press, 2007), pp. 277–8.
3. As its name suggests, *brisé* writing involved arpeggiation and breaking up chords into their component parts. The technique probably originated in French lute music.
4. Transcription from tablature based on 'Suite XV' in D. Buxtehude (ed. E. Bangert), *Klaverværker* (Copenhagen: Hansen, 1942, repr. Mineola: Dover, 2002). Available online at: http://img.kb.dk/ma/danklav/ryge_tabl-m.pdf (accessed 6 November 2015).
5. J. Butt, 'Germany and the Netherlands' in A. Silbiger (ed.), *Keyboard music before 1700*, second edition (New York: Routledge, 2004), pp. 147–234 at p. 195.
6. Snyder, *Buxtehude*, pp. 279–81. The Allemande given by Snyder as example '7–21c' is not the questionable reading in the *Möllersche Handschrift*, but the not-altogether satisfactory reconstruction by Klaus Beckmann in J.A. Reincken (ed. K. Beckmann), *Sämtliche Werke* (Wiesbaden: Breitkopf und Härtel, 1982), p. 24. The original text of the *Möllersche Handschrift* may be seen in R. Hill (ed.), *Keyboard music from the Andreas Bach book and the Möller manuscript* (Cambridge, MA: Harvard University Press, 1991), p. 152.
7. Reincken (ed. Beckmann), *Sämtliche Werke*, Suite 4.
8. Snyder, *Buxtehude*, p. 277.
9. W. Apel (trans. H. Tischler), *The history of keyboard music to 1700* (Bloomington: Indiana University Press, 1972), p. 623.
10. Snyder, *Buxtehude*, p. 280; she qualifies this with the observation that 'they cannot have been intended to please a large audience of ordinary citizens'.
11. Facsimile edition: B. Gustafson (ed.), *Lüneburg Ratsbücherei, Mus. ant. pract. 1198*, 17th Century Keyboard Music 22 (New York and London: Garland, 1987). The identification of Flor as copyist was put forward in C. Flor (ed. J. Jacobi), *Zehn suiten für Clavier* (Bremen: Edition Baroque, 2006), Preface.
12. J. Mattheson, *Grundlage einer Ehren-Pforte* (Hamburg, 1740); facsimile edition, ed. M. Schneider (Berlin: Kommissionsverlag von Leo Liepmannssohn, 1910), p. 66.
13. See Gustafson, *Lüneburg Ratsbücherei*, Contents.
14. Gustafson condemns the music copied by the second scribe as 'painfully incompetent'. Ibid., Introduction, p. viii.
15. Gustafson suggests that 'the suites are sufficiently consistent in style to suggest that they were the work of the same composer', Ibid., Introduction, p. viii. See also Flor (ed. Jacobi), *Zehn suiten*, Preface and RISM A/II, record 450101751.

Keyboard suites by town composers 193

16 See R. Hill, '*Echtheit angezweifelt*: style and authenticity in two suites attributed to Bach' *Early Music*, 13/2 (1985), pp. 248–55.
17 D. Schulenberg, 'Recent editions and recordings of Froberger and other seventeenth-century composers', *Journal of seventeenth-century music* 13/1 (2007) (http://sscm-jscm.org/jscm/v13/no1/schulenberg.html) (accessed 12 March 2014).
18 Facsimile ed. R. Hill (ed.), *Ottobeuren, Benediktiner-Abtei, Bibliothek und Musik-Archiv MO 1037*, 17th Century Keyboard Music 23 (New York: Garland, 1988).
19 Ibid., Preface,p. xv. For further commentary on MO 1037, see J. Froberger (ed. S. Rampe), *Neue Ausgabe sämtlicher Werke*, Vol. 3 (Kassel: Bärenreiter, 2002), Preface,p. lxxvii.
20 Butt, 'Germany and the Netherlands', p. 192.
21 M. Weckmann (ed. S. Rampe), *Sämtliche Freie Orgel- und Clavierwerke* (Kassel: Bärenreiter, 1991), Preface,p. xxv.
22 Ibid., p. xxv.
23 The movement titles are taken from Rampe's complete edition. Ibid.
24 The collection, emanating from the Slovak area of Europe, is sometimes known as *Pestrý zborník*. For a modern edition, see R. Schächer (ed.), *Leutschauer Tabulaturbuch 1676* (Stuttgart: Cornetto, 2001). See also L. Kačic, 'Die Suiten Johann Caspar Horns im Pestrý zborník, einem Tabulaturbuch aus dem 17. Jahrhundert' in G. Fleischhauer, W. Ruf, B. Siegmund and F. Zsoch (eds), *Die Entwicklung der Ouvertüren-suite im 17. und 18. Jahrhundert*, Michaelsteiner Konferenzberichte 49 (Michaelstein: Institut für Aufführungspraxis, 1996), pp. 169–78. RISM A/II also lists a tablature transcription of Hasse's *Delitiæ musicæ* (see Chapter 3) with the title 'Organist in S: Maria Kirck in Rostock / In Tabellatura Transportiret Durck Andream Törn Orga [...] / Anno 1696'. I have not been able to inspect this manuscript, but it may be a written-out chordal accompaniment for use with the original consort parts. See RISM A/II, ID no. 190007309.
25 It is possible that the keyboard suite in D major by Böhm in the *Möllersche Handschrift* is an arrangement of a consort original in the Lullian manner. The suite has been recorded in a reconstruction by Peter Holman on Hyperion records CDA66074.
26 Kuhnau has been described as a 'court musician', but this is incorrect. Apart from some early training, Kuhnau spent his entire career in the towns. See S. Zohn, 'Die vornehmste Hof-Tugend: German musicians' reflections on eighteenth-century court life' in S. Owens, B. Reul and J. Stockigt (eds), *Music at German courts, 1715–1760: changing artistic priorities* (Woodbridge: Boydell & Brewer, 2011), pp. 413–25 at p. 413.
27 See *CCS*, pp. 132–3.
28 Butt, 'Germany and the Netherlands', p. 205.
29 An online facsimile is available at http://petrucci.mus.auth.gr/imglnks/usimg/0/05/IMSLP296207-PMLP480263-Niedt_Handleitung_zur_Variation__1706__bsb10527644.pdf. Translated by P.L. Poulin and I.C. Taylor as *The musical guide* (Oxford: Clarendon Press, 1989).
30 A full biography is given in the Introduction to ibid.
31 Ibid., p. 56.
32 'Er wollte dem Schüler zeigen, wie er Improvisationen oder Kompositionen strukturieren kann und wie sich diese Tätigkeiten vom Generalbaßspiel auf fast selbstverständliche Weise ableiten lassen.' R.S. Hill, 'Stilanalyse und Überlieferungs-sproblematik' in A. Edler and F. Krummacher (eds), *Dietrich Buxtehude und die europäische Musik seiner Zeit: Bericht über das Lübecker Symposion 1987* (Kassel: Bärenreiter, 1990), pp. 204–214 at p. 206.
33 Mattheson's annotations in his 1721 edition of Niedt's *Handleitung zur Variation* show that he too was unaware of the *Bransle* tradition and dismisses 'these kind of dances ... because they have not been in style for a hundred years'. Poulin and Taylor (trans.), *Musical guide*, p. 135.

34 For an overview of the moveable-type process, see A. Devriès-Lesure, 'Technological Aspects' in R. Rasch (ed.), *Music publishing in Europe, 1600–1900* (Berlin: Berliner Wissenschafts-Verlag, 2005), pp. 63–88 at pp. 66–70.
35 The final Menuet and Bourée in A minor are arguably part of the penultimate suite in A major and not the final one in B-flat.
36 'denn weil es Clavier-Sachen sind, lassen sich die unter und in einander geflochtene Noten mit unsern Druck-Schrifften nicht füglich barstellen'. J. Mattheson, *Der vollkommene Capellmeister* (Hamburg, 1739; repr. Kassel: Bärenreiter, 1954), Erster Theil, Zehntes Capitel, §95.
37 It appears that engraving was known in England, Italy and the Netherlands in the early part of the seventeenth century. In France, it came into use about 1660. See H. Lenneberg, *On the publishing and dissemination of music: 1500–1850* (Hillsdale, NY: Pendragon Press, 2003), p. 51.
38 Devriès-Lesure, 'Technological aspects', p. 69. Clearly, Mattheson would have preferred *Der vollkommene Capellmeister* to be engraved, but it is likely that the costs were too high.
39 J. Wilson (ed.) *Roger North on music: being a selection from his essays written during the years c. 1695–1728* (London: Novello, 1959), p. 29.
40 See: B. Schultheiss (ed. R. Hudson), *Muth- und Geist-ermuntrender Clavier-Lust 1679–1680*, Corpus of Early Keyboard Music 21 (Neuhausen and Stuttgart: Hänssler-Verlag, 1993).
41 M. Seares, *Johann Mattheson's Pièces de clavecin and Das neu-eröffnete Orchestre* (Farnham: Ashgate, 2014), p. 37.
42 This, along with the following biographical details, are taken from: J. Kuhnau (ed. N. Müllermann), *Sämtliche Werke für Tasteninstrument* (Munich: Henle Verlag, 2014), p. ix.
43 Ibid., p. x.
44 Ibid., p. 201.
45 Pez's suites are discussed in *CCS*, pp. 193–9.
46 'Wo einig Spatium oder Raum vorgefallen hab ich selbigen mit etlichen Menuetten / Buréen und Gavotten erfüllet.'
47 P. Dirksen (ed.), *VI suittes, divers airs avec leurs variations et fugues pour le clavessin* (Utrecht: Koninklijke Vereniging voor Nederlandse Muziekgeschiedenis, 2004), Introduction, p. 17.
48 Ibid., p. 18.
49 Ibid., pp. 16–22. See also P. Dirksen, 'A Buxtehude discovery' (www.pieterdirksen.nl/Essays/Bux%20Discovery.htm) (accessed 6 November 2015).
50 The Amsterdam Lully editions are discussed in *CCS*, pp. 61–4. See also: C.B. Schmidt, 'The Amsterdam editions of Lully's music: a bibliographical scrutiny with commentary' in J. Heyer (ed.), *Lully studies* (Cambridge: Cambridge University Press, 2000), pp. 100–165.
51 P. Williams, 'A chaconne by Georg Böhm: a note on German composers and French styles' in *Early Music*, 17/1 (1989), pp. 43–54 at p. 43.
52 *CCS*, p. 186.
53 Ibid., p. 128.
54 As Dirksen has noted, '*VI Suites* provides a considerably better text of this suite than the Möller Manuscript'. Dirksen (ed.), *VI suittes*, Introduction, p. 19.
55 For a discussion of the printed editions of Froberger's suites, see Froberger (ed. Rampe), *Neue Ausgabe sämtlicher Werke*, pp. lix–lxxxvi.
56 Ibid., p. lx.
57 F. Lesure, *Bibliographie des éditions musicales publiées par Estienne Roger et Michel-Charles Le Cène* (Paris: Heugel, 1969), p. 67.

9 Note blackening and mensural notation

As Peter Holman has pointed out, 'the advice given by mid-18th-century writers such as Geminiani, Quantz and C.P.E. Bach cannot be assumed to apply to 17th-century music.'[1] There are still a number of issues relating specifically to seventeenth-century performing practice that were often dimly perceived by eighteenth-century writers and are, as a result, misunderstood or ignored by today's performers and editors. This chapter sets out to deal with arguably the most important of these issues, one that has been referred to many times during the course of this book – the use of mensural notation and note blackening.[2]

Throughout this book, we have seen instances of note blackening in the musical examples. In 1987, George Houle wrote that 'it is usually disastrous to disregard the original "time signatures" of seventeenth-century music, or to modify them according to a more modern idea of notation, as one loses the precise yet subtle meanings they are able to convey'.[3] And in 1989, the revised edition of Robert Donington's *The interpretation of early music* (London, 1963; repr. 1989) recommended that 'the notation [of blackened notes] should be left scrupulously as it appears in the original sources' even if it also suggests that the performers' parts should be modified when required.[4] Despite these warnings, the notation and its implications have been largely ignored or modified by modern editors despite cautions by twentieth-century scholars. A typical example of such modification occurs in Allen Scott's critical edition of Nikolaus Gengenbach's *Musica nova*, where mensural signs are transcribed into time signatures as follows: '¢ – C, ¢3 – 3/2, ¢3/2 – 3/4, ¢3/1 = 3/1, and 6/1 – 6/4'.[5] As we shall see, mensural notation, even in its often-misunderstood later seventeenth-century manifestations, is an essential part of triple-time dance notation. Sebastien Virdung in 1511 highlighted its importance stating that 'I cannot teach you [how to play an instrument] entirely satisfactorily without [teaching you] mensural notation'.[6] Albeit with considerable change, the system continued to be used in the dance music of both courts and towns for much of the seventeenth century. To ignore it is to run the risk of playing the music incorrectly.

Mensural notation was 'based on the idea of a chain of decreasing note-values', the maxima, longa, breve, semibreve and minim.[7] But the system was highly complicated and, as Rebecca Herissone has pointed out, 'theorists were fully aware of the muddled state of proportion and mensuration signs'.[8] Given this muddle, it is not surprising that musicians frequently came up with their own interpretations of the system.[9]

At the heart of the system was the *tactus*, not a precise unit of measurement, but a visual indication of basic pulse made by the lowering and raising of the hand. A division of the *tactus* into two (*tactus æqualis*) was indicated by simple down–up movements of equal length; a division into three (*tactus inæqualis*) still used two movements, but the first was twice as long as the second. Additional refinements to this basic scheme were known as 'prolations'. According to the third volume of Praetorius' *Syntagma musicum* (Wolfenbüttel, 1619), the mensural sign '¢' was used to denote the major prolation (*tempore perfecto majore*) and the division of the *tactus* into two semibreves. The sign 'C' gave the minor prolation ('[*tempore perfecto*] *minore*') and the division of the *tactus* into two minims. *Tactus inæqualis*, the division of the major prolation into three semibreves (*proportione tripla*), was denoted by 3/1; 3/2 was used to show the minor division of three minims (*proportione sesquialtera*).[10] Praetorius' musical examples of both *tripla* and *sesquialtera* prolations are shown in Figure 9.1.

In addition, Praetorius lists no fewer than thirteen other signs that could also be used to indicate the triple division.[11] But even though he complains about the number of musicians who 'do not observe their own precepts concerning these very matters and indiscriminately make use of one [signature] for another', Praetorius does not follow his own instructions.[12] In the illustration below, he uses '3' for the *tripla* instead of 3/1. While this may be an error by Praetorius, or his printer, it is telling that, in a likely 1619 second reprint of the treatise, the wrong note in the example (f″ at the end of the *tripla* line) was corrected, but the incorrect mensural sign remained unchanged.[13] So it seems that the '3' in the example was not considered to be a serious error, if an error at all. This is confirmed in Joachim Burmeister's *Musica poetica* (Rostock, 1606) that marks all the *tactus inæqualis* divisions with a simple '3'.

Figure 9.1 M. Praetorius, *Syntagmatis Musici, Michaelis Praetorii C., tomus tertius* (Wolfenbüttel, 1619), p. 53, shelfmark M.K.8.f.1: London, The British Library Board. Reproduced by kind permission.

Burmeister was certainly not alone in his apparent dislike of the varied mensural signs.[14] Seth Calvisius, the influential Leipzig-trained theorist, also condemned them in his *Exercitatio musica tertia* (Leipzig, 1611), calling them 'merely the clever devices of the musicians, who cause difficulty by this variety of beginnings'. It is telling that he goes on to suggest that 'only a single form [¢3] ought to have been proposed'.[15] His Leipzig pupil Nicolaus Gengenbach followed the same line in his 1626 treatise, *Musica nova, Newe Singekunst*, even though he states that 'in order to train boys better and to advance their efforts in music ... I procured for myself the third book of the *Syntagma musicum* by that incomparable man Michael Praetorius'.[16] But if the third volume of *Syntagma musicum* 'contains prescriptions that were a tremendous influence on later pedagogical writings', it is clear that the mensural system had all but broken down in Germany by the start of the seventeenth century.[17]

At the same time, it was widely perceived that the speed of the *tactus* could be varied, Daniel Speer, for example, making the distinction between a slow beat where the note values were quick ('geschwind'), a moderate beat ('ein mässiger Tact') for general use, and a fast beat for older motets.[18] Further problems arose from the now-widespread use of crotchet-based notation: with blackened minims identical in appearance to crotchets, the potential for confusion was high.[19] But as Gengenbach's treatise shows, it was the concept of the *tactus* itself, and not just its speed, that was changing.

Figure 9.2 shows Gengenbach's list of note values that his readers were likely to encounter.[20] Each note is given in terms of its relationship to the 'Schlag' (beat); the breve is '2. Schläge' while the *minima* is half. *Semifusæ* (semiquavers) are one-sixteenth. Gengenbach does relate the *Schlag* to the *tactus* (*Ein Schlag oder Tactus*).[21] But it is clear that for him, and no doubt many others, that the concept of a central, proportional *tactus* was no longer a consideration.

Despite this, the nomenclature associated with mensural notation was still being used in theoretical writings and treatises at the end of the seventeenth century. For example, Daniel Merck's *Compendium musicæ instrumentalis* (Augsburg, 1695) still talks of the *proportione tripla*, the *tripla major* and the *tripla minor* and, as we have seen above, Speer in 1687 was still assuming use of the *tactus* as a method of direction if not a theoretical standpoint. Gengenbach complained at the number of signs used for triple time, but he still discussed the *tripla* and *sesquialtera* proportions along with the use of the related ¢3/2 and C3/2 signs. Given that pairings of duple- and triple-time dances remained central to the German suite repertoire for much of the seventeenth century, the continued existence of these signs is hardly surprising even if they no longer carried the significance that they did in the early 1600s.

We have seen how the combination of Allemande and Courante became the principal vehicle for such dance pairings in the second half of the century, and there have been many examples in this book where, as part of variation technique, the two dances have been linked by the use of common material. And, as we have seen in Chapter 2, this was taken one stage further by the re-casting of duple-time Allemandes into triple-time Courantes (for instance, see Example 6.7 from

198 *Note blackening and mensural notation*

Figure 9.2 N. Genbenbach, *Musica nova, Newe Singekunst* (Leipzig, 1626), p. 54, shelfmark 498.1 Quod. (7): Wolfenbüttel, Herzog August Bibliothek. Reproduced by kind permission.

Johann Caspar Horn's *PM 1*). Typically one minim or half a bar of the Allemande equated to three minims or a whole bar of the Courante.[22] So should the two movements have a common pulse?

The first volume of Horn's *PM 1* uses the quasi-mensural C3/2 in all the Courantes except one, the exception probably being the result of a printing error.[23] At first sight, this use, by no means confined to Horn's music, could be seen as recognition of the rhythmic and melodic relationship between Courantes and their associated Allemandes along with a confirmation of pulse commonality.[24] But Horn's preface (given in its entirety in Chapter 6) tells us that 'die Allemanden nach einer langsamen Mensur, die Couranten hergegen etwas geschwinder' (the Allemandes have a slow pulse; the Courantes are taken somewhat quicker). This is ambiguous. In the re-casting of half a bar of the Allemande as a whole bar of the Courante, the pulse of the latter would still be *etwas geschwinder*. But if Horn really had intended something different – a common pulse between these two dances - it is surprising that his preface fails to mention it. Perhaps he was merely suggesting an approximate proportional relationship,[25] and we should therefore accept his instruction at its face value: the pulse of a whole bar of the Courante is 'somewhat faster' than half a bar of the Allemande without there being any direct relationship between the two.[26] The mensural sign has been retained, but the precise meaning lost or ignored.

C3/2 is used for nearly all the Courantes in all six volumes of *Parergon musicum*, whether they are related to the preceding Allemandes or not. But the general confusion over all this is tellingly illustrated in a manuscript copy of parts of *Parergon musicum* (*D-Dl,* Mus.1-B-101); here, all the C3/2 signs in the printed edition are replaced by ¢3/2. Despite this confusion, quasi-mensural signs remained in common use until almost the end of the century. In some cases, as we have seen, the C3 sign was further modified to become the hybrid C3/4.

Another demonstration of the same trend, and one that provides the central focus for this chapter, is the changing use of note blackening (*proportione hemiola*) during the seventeenth century.[27] At its simplest, note blackening was another way of indicating triple-time music, possibly with a proportional relationship to what had gone before. *Hemiola major* denoted three blackened breves or the equivalent; *hemiola minor,* three blackened minims or the equivalent. But it seems that there was little understanding of *proportione hemiola* by the start of the seventeenth century. Praetorius recommends the use of *hemiola major* where 'the frequent insertion of various signatures seems to produce a disturbance and to confuse' but warns that *hemiola minor* 'should be used only rarely'.[28] However, he gives few examples of recommended use and, perhaps as a result, many later treatises also mention blackening without seemingly understanding its true significance. Gengenbach is typical in suggesting that 'the black notes can be called *Tripla nigra, Sesquialt*[era] *nigra,* or else *Hemiolæ majors, Hemiolæ minores'* but failing to provide a clear description of their purpose.[29]

Despite Praetorius' warning against its frequent use, it was the *hemiola minor* that survived its *major* counterpart as the principal way of expressing note blackening in the seventeenth century. In the first half of the century, but far less so in the second, it was common for blackening to be used for entire movements. For example, Johann Schop's *Erster Theil Newer Paduanen* published in 1633 in Hamburg contains four Courantes, two of them entirely blackened.[30] Example 9.1 shows a 'Coranta à5' from William Brade's *Newe außerlesene Paduanen, Galliarden, Cantzonen, Allmand und Couranten* published in Hamburg in 1609. The notes with stems are not the crotchets of standard notation but blackened minims.

Again, we should consider the existence of a proportional pulse relationship between these entirely blackened Courantes and the movements that preceded them. If one did exist, then it follows that any preceding movement must be in duple and not triple time. But this is not always the case. For example, the Courante by Brade given on the following page is preceded by a Galliard, also in triple time. While it is possible that this is an error of movement ordering by the printer, similar instances exist in other collections. So it is reasonable to assume that, in a similar manner to Horn's *PM 1,* blackened movements are not precisely

200 *Note blackening and mensural notation*

Example 9.1 W. Brade, *Newe außerlesene Paduanen / Galliarden / Cantzonen / Allmand und Couranten* (Hamburg, 1609), 'Coranta à5'.

and proportionally related to other movements. In Italy, where the use of quasi-mensural notation seems to have developed in parallel with that of the German lands, the preface to Frescobaldi's *Ricercari et canzoni Franzese* (Rome, 1615), tells us that the tempo of the proportions can be changed depending on whether they are major or minor prolations. So the blackened minims of the minor prolation that Frescobaldi uses would presumably be faster than the norm. And while it is foolhardy to think that seventeenth-century musicians all held the same views, it is likely that entirely blackened movements are, in the same way, merely indications of performances that should be quicker than the norm.[31]

Note blackening also had another use, this time for specific circumstances within movements rather than a piece as a whole. Example 9.2 shows a passage from Georg Knüpfer's 'Sonata a 7. 2.Violin, 3.Viol, 1.Fag., 1.Violon con Continuo' (see Chapter 6). The note blackening here is showing an event-specific, as opposed to a movement-specific, context.[32]

Wolfgang Hase's treatise, *Gründliche Einführung in die edle Music oder Singe-Kunst* (Gosslar, 1657), gives an explanation of the three consecutive blackenings: 'When in *tripla*, three blackened breves that follow one another are worth two beats; and the middle note breaks the *tact*'. Hase's example uses breves, but it applies equally well to semibreves: each one of the latter equals two minims and the broken *tact* is where the bar line would normally be placed. Likewise, the second edition of Johann Crüger's *Synopsis musica* (Berlin, 1654) shows a similar example in breve notation, but emphasising the broken *tact* with a vertical line going through the second breve. This is nothing to do with a change of note value; as Crüger says, 'nulla perficitur' (nothing is perfected, i.e. shortened).[33] So it is clear that the purpose of the note blackening is to indicate the presence of syncopated cross-rhythms in triple time and the reversal of the normal hierarchy: that which is normally weak becomes strong; that which is normally strong becomes weak.

Note blackening and mensural notation 201

Example 9.2 G. Knüpfer, 'Sonata a 7. 2.Violin, 3.Viol, 1.Fag., 1.Violon con Continuo' (manuscript *GB-Ob* MS Mus.Sch.c.93), 'Sonata'.

A sequence of three blackened semibreves, along with the vertical line through the second, is labelled as 'Proportio hemiola' in 'Traicté de musique', a manuscript treatise by 'Martin vander Bist d'Anvers' dated 1622.[34] The labelling of the cross-rhythm as a 'hemiola' is a very early instance of the use of the term in this way. But along with Crüger's and Hase's comments, it does show the widespread use of this type of note blackening. As I have already suggested, there are many Italian parallels to the trends set out in this chapter and the blackened three-note formula is no exception. In France, note blackening was certainly used to warn the performer of the presence of cross-rhythms. Shirley Thompson has made a most persuasive case for Charpentier also using blackening as a demonstration of points of imitation and warning of changes of instrumentation.[35]

Knüpfer's example shown above is taken from a sonata movement. But it was in dance music that the blackened three-semibreve formula found its widest use, especially at cadences. As we have seen, it was an important feature of the hybrid Courantes and Sarabandes that frequently occurs in printed suite collections by German town composers. Example 9.3 is taken from the first strain of '15. Courante' from Horn's *PM 5*. If Horn or his printer do not seem to be bothered about the use of blackening for each of the three semibreves that make up the cadence, it was presumably considered enough of an indication for only the middle semibreve to be blackened at the point where it crosses the bar line. We may also assume that performers of the lines without blackening – in this case the treble – were, in any case, on the alert for cross-beat rhythms at such points.

202 *Note blackening and mensural notation*

Example 9.3 J.C. Horn, *Parergon musicum Oder Musicalisches Neben-Werck ... Fünfftem Theil* (Leipzig, 1676), '15. Courante'.

There was a further refinement of the cadential formula described above. As we have seen earlier in the example from Brade's *Newe außerlesene Paduanen*, blackened minims were often used in conjunction with blackened semibreves in completely blackened movements. As with semibreves, it is clear that there is no question of a change of note value. Indeed, Gengenbach states, 'If in *tripla* a black semibreve and a breve are written adjacent to one another, and in *sesquialtera* a black minim and semibreve are written adjacent to one another, one sings them as though they were white.'[36] But it is also clear that the purpose of blackened minims is to show with particular precision how the rhythms across the beat are meant to be applied. The blackened semibreves remain as the accented notes; the blackened minims show the correspondingly weak notes. We can see this in use in Example 9.4, the bass part of the triple-time section in 'XVI. Ballet à3' from Johann Rudolf Ahle's *Dreyfaches Zehn allerhand newer Sinfonien, Paduanen,*

Balleten, Alemanden, Mascharaden, Arien, Intraden, Couranten und Sarabanden (Erfurt, 1650). The two cadences marked (1) and (2) show a blackened minim followed by a blackened semibreve. The blackened minim, on the normally strong first beat of the triple-time bar, becomes weak; the blackened semibreve, on the normally weak second beat, becomes strong.

A further extension of this concept is shown in the following example. Example 9.5 is in open-keyboard score (along with an editorial two-stave reduction) and taken from Froberger's 'Ricercar 8' in his 'Libro di capricci, e ricercati ... Libro Terzo', apparently dating from around 1658.

It is clear that the note blackening is not intended as some form of proportion; neither is it connected with cadences. So what is its purpose? Froberger was influenced by French music, but there seems no obvious reason to highlight the musical text in any way and there are no points of imitation that need to be demonstrated to the performer. So it seems that the answer must be found elsewhere. Some composers, especially Leipzig town musicians, also used a parallel form of note blackening that is not linked with the cadences. Example 9.6, the start of the second strain of '52. Courant' from Rosenmüller's *Studenten-Music* (see Chapter 6), shows the three consecutive pairs of blackened minims and semibreves that equally do not correspond to cadential formulas.

Example 9.4 J.R. Ahle, *Dreyfaches Zehn allerhand newer Sinfonien, Paduanen, Balletten, Alemanden, Mascharaden, Arien, Intraden, Couranten und Sarabanden* (Erfurt, 1650), 'Bassus', 'XVI. Ballet à3'.

Example 9.5 J.J. Froberger, 'Libro di capricci, e ricercati ... Libro Terzo' (manuscript *A-Wn* Mus. Hs. 16560), 'Ricercar 8', excerpt.

204 *Note blackening and mensural notation*

Example 9.6 J. Rosenmüller, *Studenten-Music / Darinnen zu befinden Allerhand Sachen Mit drey und fünff Violen* (Leipzig, 1654), '52. Courant', start of second strain.

There is no reason to think that this is an error; similar blackening appears in the lower parts at this point and elsewhere in the collection. And the context makes it quite clear that, again, no change in note value is intended. But if we apply the same conditions that we have seen earlier, the blackened semibreve marks an off-beat accent and the normally weak second beat accordingly becomes strong. Likewise, the blackened minim is used to further emphasise the weakness of the first beat.

Leipzig composers were not the only town musicians to do this; as we have seen in Chapter 3, manuscript *GB-Lbl* Add. MS 31438 contains a sequence of movements that claim to come from the now-lost 1659 *Ander Theil, neuer Paduanen* by the Lübeck violinist and town musician Georg Züber (see Chapter 3). While I have shown this manuscript to be particularly unreliable in identifying its sources, it is likely that '5. Courant-Sarab: fort e pian.' has been copied from a printed edition, even if it is not Züber's. And by taking the trouble to include them, it is clear that the copyist realised the significance of the pairs of blackened notes (♩. ♪ | ♩. ♪.) at the start of the second strain. They are clearly an indication of second-beat accentuation. To return to my question posed by the keyboard music of Example 9.3 above, it is clear that the blackening serves the same purpose and warns the performer of off-beat accents creating duple-time patterns across the triple-time bar. If the harpsichord may not have the inflective qualities of a wind or string ensemble, the rhythmic distortions are still perfectly possible, especially in the hands of a skilled performer.

A single white or black minim followed by a single blackened semibreve provides yet another variant of the basic formula. We can see a particularly telling example of this in the first bar of the Sarabande from 'Sinfonia Sesta' in Rosenmüller's *Sonate da camera* (see Chapter 6) shown in Example 9.7

Here, the second beat of the opening bar is stressed, giving a profound change to the character of the dance and making it much closer to the slow Sarabande

Note blackening and mensural notation 205

Example 9.7 J. Rosenmüller, *Sonate da camera cioe Sinfonie, Alemande, Correnti, Balletti, Sarabande* (Venice, 1667), 'Sinfonia Sesta', 'Sarabanda'.

favoured in court circles of the seventeenth century and more widely during the eighteenth century. And four bars later, Rosenmüller further enhances the rhythm of the dance by using a series of three blackened semibreves to show three consecutive accents, the central one crossing the bar line in the manner of the cadential formula discussed earlier.

While Rosenmüller and, to a lesser extent, Horn considered this type of blackening to be an essential part of their musical language in triple-time dance movements, it was not confined to Leipzig; there are other examples, albeit less frequent, in the dances of German town musicians from elsewhere and, as we have seen, the German hybrid versions of the Courante and Sarabande frequently use such rhythmic distortions as part of their musical language.

Dotted blackened notes were used on occasion in the first half of the seventeenth century, but it seems that composers after that time largely avoided them. Example 9.7 above is an instance of blackening being limited to the lower parts; in the dotted notes of the first and second violin parts, it is absent. As we have seen, this was a common occurrence, and we must assume that those players with the blackening in their parts would use rehearsals to alert the other members of the ensemble to its presence.

In spite of the obvious importance of note blackening, composers, printers and copyists throughout the German lands were remarkably casual in its use. It is not unusual to find parallel bass parts, typically string bass and continuo, where the same passage contains one part with blackening and the other in conventional notation. In addition, poor-quality printing often made it difficult to distinguish between smudges and genuine blackening; there are also many surviving manuscript copies of printed editions where the copyist has ignored, or was not aware of, the blackening and written out the notes with their normal value.

If the present-day performer is not aware of the blackenings, the intended rhythmic distortions, an integral part of the music, will be lost. However, in many modern editions of seventeenth-century German music, note blackening seems to have been regarded as little more than a nuisance and is frequently omitted. In his 1904 edition of Rosenmüller's *Sonate da camera*, Karl Nef wrote: 'Ebenfalls aus der alten Zeit stammend ist die zur Anzeige von Synkopen noch vorkommende Notenschwärzung' (The use of blackened notes to mark syncopation also comes from earlier times).[37] But with the link between note blackening and syncopation being correctly identified, Nef then goes on to say, 'Neu daran jedoch ist, daß am Wert der Noten die Schwärzung nichts mehr ändert ... Solche Schwärzung tritt, wenn sie auch nicht ganz konsequent durchgeführt ist, doch in der Regel bei entsprechenden Stellen ein. In der Partitur wurde davon abgesehen, sie wiederzugeben' (However, it is a new development that the blackening no longer alters the note values ... The blackening is generally used in corresponding places but not with complete consistency. It is not used in the [present] score).[38] And so the performer is left without any idea of the full extent of the blackening, especially where it is not linked to cadences.

Nef seems to have started a trend that is still with us; editorial policies such as this one found in a modern edition of Andreas Hammerschmidt's 1635 *Erster Fleiß Allerhand newer Paduanen, Galliarden, Balleten* are common: 'In the original edition one finds "blackened-in notes" ... They indicate to the player special situations, e.g. hemiolas. There is no correlation for these blackened-in notes in today's notation and we do not show any indication of them as we believe that the modern notation with its bar lines is sufficient.'[39] But the facsimile illustration given as part of this edition clearly shows a sequence of note blackening in 'XIV. Sarabande 2 à5' that needs more than just the application of modern bar lines. Other editions resort to a system of brackets, but this still has unfortunate resonances with the editorial *hemiola* bracketing so popular with editors in the second half of the twentieth century and does not adequately show the difference between blackened note types.[40] At the very least, the inquisitive performer should be able to see the full extent of the blackening in its proper context.

The primary purpose of this chapter has been to draw attention to an aspect of seventeenth-century notation and the inadequate way in which we have hitherto dealt with this notation in many modern editions. I have deliberately refrained from making specific suggestions on how we should notate blackening – that is up to individual editors and the music software of their publishers. But as the musical examples in this book demonstrate, it is perfectly possible to notate blackening in a way that adequately represents the original notation. To repeat my quotation of Robert Donington from the start of this chapter, 'the notation [of blackened notes] should be left scrupulously as it appears in the original sources'. And modern editors should be scrupulous in following Donington's dictum.

Conclusion

In both this book and its companion *CCS*, I have assembled a body of evidence that clearly demonstrates the difference between two major traditions of consort-suite writing – one from the courts and one from the towns. Suites for keyboard belong to a further tradition, largely manuscript-based until the advent of music-engraving techniques in the German lands.

These traditions, albeit often symbiotic, were separate for much of the seventeenth century, and it is the failure of twentieth-century scholars in particular to define both separation and symbiosis that has led to the misunderstanding of the suite as a whole. A 'classical' order for the latter simply did not exist in the seventeenth century, and the concept of a rigid framework of dance types imposes a compositional structure unknown in the consort suites of both court and town composers. Only in the keyboard repertoire can any case be made for a framework of specific movements that imposed itself across the genre for a large part of the seventeenth century and this was seemingly the result of a desire to imitate Froberger. We can be certain that most town musicians had knowledge of both keyboard and consort repertoires, and it is telling that the two genres remained largely separate until the advent of engraved editions of the former. While the lack of keyboard arrangements of town-music consort suites is curious, this may be nothing more than an issue of preservation.

Throughout this book, I have constantly drawn attention to the concepts of careful organisation and ordering in printed editions. Such organisation came to be synonymous with publication. When they wished to publish collections of suites, court musicians recognised and emulated the edition formats of their town colleagues, even if this may have been partially at the behest of publishers wishing to retain a 'house' style. And we too should recognise these formats. In the twenty-first century, it is time to end the bonding together of the suite repertoire as if it were a single entity; it is equally time to end the concept of the 'classical' order and recognise in its place the concepts of careful organisation and ordering in so many printed editions. It is my great hope that this book will be part of the process.

To close, I echo the words of Johann Caspar Horn: 'Hiermit lebe wohl!'

Notes

1. P. Holman, 'Performing 17th-century music' *Early Music*, 41/2 (2013), pp. 335–7 at p. 335.
2. This chapter originated in 2012 as a conference paper and was then printed as M. Robertson, 'Edited out' *Early Music*, 42/2 (2014), pp. 207–218. For this book, it has here been extended and revised.
3. G. Houle, *Meter in music, 1600–1800: performance, perception, and notation* (Bloomington and Indianapolis: Indiana University Press, 1987), p. 34.
4. R. Donington, *The interpretation of early music* (London: Faber, 1963; repr. 1989), p. 658. Donington's discussion of 'coloration' was excellent for its time, but should now be treated with caution. I shall avoid the use of 'colouration' as a term for note blackening. *Coloriren* for German composers referred to the quick notes, typically semiquavers, used in divisions.
5. A. Scott (ed. and trans.), *Nikolaus Gengenbach's Musica Nova: Newe Singekunst; a commentary, critical edition and translation* (Ottawa, 1996), p. 38.
6. B. Bullard (trans. and ed.), *Musica getutscht: a treatise on musical instruments by Sebastian Virdung* (Cambridge: Cambridge University Press, 1993), p. 120.
7. A.M.B. Berger, *Mensuration and proportion signs: origins and evolution* (Oxford: Oxford University Press, 1993), p. 1.

208 *Note blackening and mensural notation*

8   R. Herissone, *Music theory in seventeenth-century England* (Oxford: Oxford University Press, 2000), p. 58.
9   For a comprehensive survey of the various interpretations of the *tactus* and its divisions, see Houle, *Meter in music*, pp. 1–34.
10 M. Praetorius (trans. and ed. J. Kite-Powell) *Syntagma musicum III* (Oxford: Oxford University Press, 2004), pp. 71–3.
11 Ibid., p. 72.
12 Ibid., p. 73.
13 Kite-Powell pays scant attention to the British Library source and wrongly dates it as 1618. Ibid., p. xxix.
14 J. Burmeister, *Musica poetica: definitionibus et divisionibus breviter delineata* (Rostock, 1606); facsimile edition, ed. M. Ruhnke (Kassel, 1955), p. 9.
15 S. Calvisius, *Exercitatio musica tertia* (Leipzig, 1611), p. 156: 'Interdum hasce absq; charactere denigrant, sed hæ funt argutiæ Melopœorum, qui hujusmodi diversitate incipientibus negotium facessunt, unicâ formâ tantùm scrib debebat, quam primam posui, & tripla proportio appellatur.'
16 A. Scott, *Nikolaus Gengenbach's Musica Nova: Newe Singekunst; commentary, critical edition and translation* (Ottawa, 1996), p. 45.
17 J. Butt, *Music education and the art of performance in the German Baroque* (Cambridge: Cambridge University Press, 1994, repr. 1996), p. 72.
18 The complete passage and translation is given in Houle, *Meter in music*, p. 17.
19 For a discussion of varying speeds of the *tactus*, see: B.V. Rivera, *German music theory in the early 17th century: the treatises of Johannes Lippius* (Ann Arbor: UMI Research Press, 1974; repr. 1980), pp. 46–9.
20 N. Gengenbach, *Musica nova, Newe Singekunst* (Leipzig, 1626), p. 54.
21 Ibid., p. 55.
22 There were exceptions to this; for example, Reincken makes a bar of Allemande correspond to a bar of Courante in parts of his *Hortus musicus*. See p. 201.
23 '6. Courante' from the first volume is given a ¢3/2 time signature. But there is little difference in overall rhythm notation between it and the other Courantes of the collection. If it is not a printing error, we must that Horn was not bothered about distinguishing between ¢3/2 and C3/2.
24 In the context of the direction of large-scale works such as *Messiah*, Peter Holman has suggested that 'we can also detect Handel stringing together sequences of movements with simple tempo relationships as Bach did'. The use of a common pulse to aid performance may well have also applied to large-scale seventeenth-century performances, but probably not to the simpler, smaller-scale performances of town *Collegia*. P. Holman, '*Before the baton*: a preliminary report' in *Early Music*, 41/1 (2013), pp. 55–63 at p. 61.
25 I am grateful to John Butt for suggesting this to me (private communication).
26 There were precedents for this outside Germany. In the preface to his *Ricercari et canzoni Franzese* (Rome, 1615), Frescobaldi suggests that the tempo of the proportions can be changed depending on whether they are major or minor prolations. As Horn was writing *PM 1* in the Italian manner (see Chapter 6), it is not fanciful to think that he had Frescobaldi's instructions in mind.
27 It should be noted that, in most cases, 'hemiola' in the seventeenth century had nothing to do with the modern use of the term indicating off-beat accentuation across the barline.
28 Praetorius (trans. and ed. Kite-Powell) *Syntagma musicum III*, p. 73.
29 Scott, *Nikolaus Gengenbach's Musica Nova*, p. 135.
30 The modern edition (ed. A. Spohr, Middletown, WI: A-R Editions, 2003) notes the presence of blackened notation in the critical report, but the main text is printed entirely in conventional notation.
31 Other scholars have reached a similar conclusion. Ibid., Preface p. xiv.

32 In the manuscript, note 1 of bar 2 in the 'Fagotto' is blackened, but this is almost certainly an error. The complete suite is reproduced in M. Robertson, 'The consort suite in the German-speaking lands, 1660–1705', PhD dissertation (University of Leeds, 2004).
33 J. Crüger, *Synopsis musica*, second edition (Berlin, 1654), p. 11.
34 Facsimile edition, Brussels: Éditions Culture et Civilisation, 1979.
35 S. Thompson, 'Colouration in the Mélanges: purpose and intent' in C. Cessac (ed.), *Les manuscrits autographes de Marc-Antoine Charpentier* (Wavre: Editions Mardaga, 2007), pp. 121–36.
36 Scott, *Nikolaus Gengenbach's Musica Nova*, p. 143.
37 J. Rosenmüller, ed. K. Nef, *Sonate da camera* (DDT 1/18, Leipzig 1904; repr., ed. H.J. Moser, Wiesbaden, 1957), Prefacep. x.
38 Nef's preface was repeated without change by Hans Joachim Moser, the editor of the 1957 re-issue of this edition.
39 A. Hammerschmidt (ed. L. and G. von Zadow), *Ester Fleiß: Suite I in C* (Heidelberg: Edition Güntersberg, 2000), pp. 4–5.
40 For example, see S. Rose (ed.), *Leipzig church music from the Sherard collection: eight works by Sebastien Knüpfer, Johann Schelle, and Johann Kuhnau* (Middleton, WI: A-R Editions, 2014), p. 271. From other volumes in the series, it seems that this is a policy decision by the publishers.

Appendix 1

Table A.1 Contents of A. Hammerschmidt, *Erster Fleiß Allerhand newer Paduanen, Galliarden, Balleten, Francoischen [sic] Arien, Courenten und Sarabanden, Mit 5. Stimmen auff Violen zu spielen / sampt dem General Baß* (Freiberg, 1636, repr. 1639 and 1650)

Movement title (I–XX)	Key, time signature	Movement title (XXI–XLI)	Key, time signature
I. Paduan à5. voc.	A minor – ¢	XXI. Courente à5	G major – ¢3
II. Paduan à5	G minor – ¢	XXII. Courente à5	G major – ¢3
III. Paduan à5	D minor – ¢	XXIII. Courente à5	A minor – ¢3
IV. Paduan à5	G major – ¢	XXIV. Courente à5	D minor – ¢3
V. Courente à5	E minor – ¢3	XXV. Courente à5	F major – ¢3
VI. Courente à5	D minor – ¢3	XXVI. Ballet 1. à5	D minor – ¢
VII. Ballet à5	D minor – ¢	XXVII. Sarabande 2. à5	D minor – ¢3
VIII. Ballet à5	G minor – ¢	XXVIII. Aria 1. à5	E minor – ¢
IX. Courente à5	G minor – ¢3	XXIX. Sarabande 2. à5	E minor – ¢3
X. Courente à5	A minor – ¢3	XXX. Ballet 1. à5	F major – ¢
XI. Mascharada 1. à5	C major – ¢	XXXI. Sarabande 2. à5	F major – ¢3
XII. Sarabande 2. à5	C major – ¢3	XXXII. Ballet 1. à5	C major – ¢
XIII. Aria 1. à5	A minor – ¢	XXXIII. Ballet 2. à5	C major – ¢
XIV. Sarabande 2. à5	A minor – ¢3	XXXIV. Galliard à5	G minor – ¢3
XV. Aria à5	D minor – ¢	XXXV. Galliard à5	D minor – ¢3
XVI. Ballet 1. à5	G major – ¢	XXXVI. Ballet à5	G minor - ¢
XVII. Sarabande 2. à5	G major – ¢3	XXXVII. Ballet à5	A minor – ¢
XVIII. Ballet à5	D major – ¢	XXXVIII. Ballet à5	G minor – ¢
XIX. Courente à5	D major – ¢3	XXXIX. Ballet à5	G minor – ¢
XX. Courente à5	B minor – ¢3	XL. Aria 1. à5	A minor – ¢
		XLI. Sarabande 2. à5	A minor – ¢3

Table A.2 Contents of G. Zuber, 'Erster Theil newer / Paduanen, Arien, Balletten, / Couranten, Sarabanden und / einer Sonat: / Mit 5 Stimmen nebenst dem / Baßo Continuo componirt / von / Georg Zubern: / beställter Violista und Musicus in / Lübeck' (manuscript *D-UDa* 38a/9)

Title in D-UDa 38a/9	Concordances in GB-Lbl Add. MS 31438	Key	Title in D-UDa 38a/9	Key
1. Paduan		D minor	25. Couranta	C major
2. Balletto	1. Balletto	D minor	26. Sarabanda	C major
3. Couranta	2. Courant	D minor	27. Paduan	F major
4. Sarabande	3. Sarab.	D minor	28. Couranta	F major
5. Paduan		D major	29. Balletto 1. Presto	F major
6. Aria	4. [untitled]	D major	[29. Balletto] 2.	F major
7. Couranta	5. Courant	D major	[29. Balletto] 3.	F major
8. Sarabande	6. Sarab.	D major	[29. Balletto] 4. Sarabanda	F major
9. Sarabande	7. Sarab.	D major	[29. Balletto] 5. Poco presto	F major
10. Paduan		G minor	[29. Balletto] 6.	F major
11. Balletto	8. Balletto	G minor	[29. Balletto] 7. Adagio	F major
12. Couranta	9. Courant	G minor	[29. Balletto] 8. Bataglia	F major
13. Sarabanda	10. Saraband	G minor	[29. Balletto] 9. Sarabanda	F major
14. Paduan		G major	30. Sonata: Flautino primo	G major
15. Aria	11. Aria	G major	31. Balletto 1. Poco presto	D major
16. Balletto	12. [untitled]	G major	[31. Balletto] 2.	D major
17. Couranta	13. Courant	G major	[31. Balletto] 3.	D major
18. Sarabanda	14. Sarab.	G major	[31. Balletto] 4.	D major
19. Paduan		A minor	[31. Balletto] 5.	D minor
20. Aria	15. Aria	A minor	[31. Balletto] 6.	D minor
21. Balletto	16. Ballet	A minor	[31. Balletto] 7.	D major
22. Couranta	17. Courant	A minor	[31. Balletto] 8. Bataglia	D major
23. Paduan		C major	[31. Balletto] 9. Adagio-Presto	D major
24. Aria		C major		

Note: After '22. Couranta', there are no further concordances in MS 31438.

Table A.3 Contents of A. Hammerschmidt, *Dritter Theil, Neuer Paduanen, Galliarden, Canzonen, Sonaten, Balleten, Intraden, Couranten und Sarabanden, Mit 3. 4 und 5 Stimmen* (Leipzig, 1650)

Movement title, printed edition	Movement title, D-UDa 38a/9	Key
I. Paduan à5	1. Paduan a5	E minor
II. Paduan à5	2. Paduan a5	G minor
III. Galliard à5		G minor
IV. Paduan à5	3. Paduan a5	D minor
V. Galliard à5		D minor

(*Continued*)

Appendix 1 213

Movement title, printed edition	Movement title, D-UDa *38a/9*	Key
VI. Paduan à5	4. Paduan a5	C minor
VII. Galliard à5		C minor
VIII. Paduan à5	5. Paduan [a5]	A minor
IX. Galliard à5		A minor
X. Canzon à3 cum Bass. Contin.	6. Canzon a3	D minor
XI. Canzon à3 cum Bass. Contin.	7. Canzon a3	G major
XII. Canzon à3 cum Bass. Contin.	8. Canzon a3	D minor
XIII. Canzon à3 cum Bass. Contin.	9. Canzon a3	C major
XIV. Canzon à3 cum Bass. Contin.	10. Canzon a3	E minor
XV. Canzon à4 cum Bass. Contin.	11. Canzon a4	A minor
XVI. Canzon à4	12. Canzon a5: cornetto o violino	C major
XVII. Sonata à5	13. Sonata a5: Trombona	G minor
XVIII. Sonata à5	14. Sonata a5: Trombona	A minor
XIX. Sonata à5	15. Sonata a5: Trombona	F major
XX. Quodlibet à5	16. Quotlibet a5	E minor
XXI. Ballet à5	17. Ballett a5	E minor
XXII. Sarabanda à5	18. Sarabanda	E minor
XXIII. Ballet à5	19. Ballett a5	A minor
XXIV. Couranta à5	20. Couranta a5	A minor
XXV. Ballet à5*	21. Ballett a5	G minor
XXVI. Sarabanda à5*	22. Sarabanda a5	G minor
XXVII. Ballet à5	23. Ballett a5	D minor
XXVIII. Couranta à5	24. Couranta [a5]	D minor
XXIX. Ballet à5	25. Ballett a5	C minor
XXX. Courant-Sarabanda à5	26. Couranta a5	C minor
XXXI. Ballet à5	27. Ballet[t] a5	D major
XXXII. Couranta à5	28. Couranta a5	D major
XXXIII. Ballet à5	29. Ballet[t] a5	G major – E minor
XXXIV. Courant-Sarabanda à5	30. Couranta Sarabanda a5	G major – E minor
XXXV. Ballet à5	31. Ballet[t] a5	F major
XXXVI. Couranta à5	32. Couranta a5	F major
XXXVII. Ballet à5	33. Ballet[t] a5	D major
XXXVIII. Sarabanda à5	34. Sarabanda a5	D major
XXXIX. Ballet à5	35. Ballet[t] a5	G minor
XL. Couranta à5	36. Couranta a5	G minor
XLI. Ballet à5	37. Ballet[t] a5	A minor
XLII. Sarabanda à5	38. Sarabant a5	A minor
[XLIII. Ballet à5]	39. Ballet[t] a5	G major – E minor
[XLIV. Couranta à5]	40. Couranta a5	G major – E minor
[XLV. Ballet à5]	41. Ballet[t] a5	D minor
[XLVI. Courant-Sarabanda à5]	42. Couranta Sarabanda a5	D minor
[XLVII. Ballet à5]	43. Ballet[t] a5	B-flat major
[XLVIII. Courant-Sarabanda à5]	44. Couranta Sarabanda a5	B-flat major
[XLIX. Ballet à5]	45. Ballet[t] a5	C major

(*Continued*)

214 *Appendix 1*

Movement title, printed edition	Movement title, D-UDa *38a/9*	Key
[L. Couranta à5]	46. Couranta a5	C major
LI. Ballet [à5]	47. Ballet[t] a5	A minor
[LII. Courant-Sarabanda à5]	48. Couranta Sarabanda a5	A minor
[LIII. Ballet à5]	49. Ballet[t] a5	A minor
[LIV. Sarabanda à5]	50. Sarabanda a5	A minor
[LV. Intrada à5]	51. Intrada a5	D minor
[LVI. Intrada à5]	52. Intrada a5	C major
[LVII. Intrada à5]	53. Intrada a5	G major
[LVIII. Intrada à5]	54. Intrada a5: Cornetto	C major
[LVIX. Intrada à5]	55. Intrada a5	C major – A minor
[LVX. Intrada à5]	56. Intrada a5	C major
[LVXI. Intrada à5]	57. Intrada a5: Cornetto	D minor
[LVXII. Intrada à5]	58. Intra[da a5]	C major
[LVXIII. Intrada à5]	59. Intrada a5: Cornetto	G major
[LVXIV. Intrada à5]	60. Intrada a5: Cornetto	A minor

Notes: An asterisk next to a movement title in the printed edition denotes a concordance with manuscript *GB-Lbl*, Add. MS 31438. Nos. XLIII–LVXIII. Intrada à5 are editorial additions derived from the manuscript source; they are absent from the incompletely preserved printed part-book.

Appendix 2

Example A.1 Incipits of 'Gregorig Zubern ander Theil', *GB-Lbl* Add. MS 31438.

(Continued)

216 *Appendix 2*

Example A.1 Incipits of 'Gregorig Zubern ander Theil', *GB-Lbl* Add. MS 31438.

Appendix 2 217

Example A.2 Incipits of 'a 3 Diderich Becker' in manuscript *D-Dl* Mus. 1/B/101.

(Continued)

218 *Appendix 2*

Example A.2 Incipits of 'a 3 Diderich Becker' in manuscript *D-Dl* Mus. 1/B/101.

Bibliography

Primary sources: Books, libretto and treatises (printed and manuscript)

Beer, J., *Musikalische Discurse durch die Principia der Philosophie deducirt* (Nuremberg, 1719).
—— (trans. J. Russell), *German winter nights* (Rochester, NY: Camden House, 1998).
Bist d'Anvers, Martin vander, *Traicté de musique* (n.p., 1622); facsimile edition (Brussels: editions Culture et Civilisation, 1979).
Brossard, S. de., *Dictionaire de Musique, contenant une explication des termes Grecs, Latins, Italiens, & François les plus usitez dans la Musique* (Paris, 1703); facsimile edition (Hilversum: Fritz Knuf, 1965).
Burmeister, J., *Musica poetica: definitionibus et divisionibus breviter delineata* (Rostock, 1606); facsimile edition, ed. M. Ruhnke (Kassel, 1955).
Calvisius, S., *Exercitatio musica tertia* (Leipzig, 1611).
Carr, W., *Remarks of severall Parts of Germanie, Denmark, Sweedland, Hamburg, Lubeck, and Hansiactique Townes* (Amsterdam, 1688).
Crüger, J., *Synopsis musica*, second edition (Berlin, 1654).
De Blainville (trans. G. Turnbull and W. Guthrie), *Travels through Holland, Germany, Switzerland and Other Parts of Europe ... by the late Monsieur de Blainville*, 3 vols (London, 1757).
Fuhrmann, M.H., *Musicalischer-Trichter: Dadurch Ein geschickter Informator seinen Informandis die Edle Singe-Kunst* (Brandenburg, 1706).
Gengenbach, N., *Musica nova, Newe Singekunst* (Leipzig, 1626). Modern edition, A. Scott (ed. and trans.), *Nikolaus Gengenbach's Musica Nova: Newe Singekunst; a commentary, critical edition and translation* (Ottawa, 1996).
Hase, W., *Gründliche Einfürung in die edle Music oder Singe-Kunst* (Gosslar, 1657).
Herbst, J., *Musica moderna prattica* (Frankfurt, 1653).
[Jordan de Colombier, C.,] *Voyages historiques de l'Europe tome VI ... Par Mr. De B.F. Nouvelle edition*, 2nd edition (Amsterdam, 1718).
Kuhnau, J., *Der musicalische Quack-Salber* (Dresden, 1700).
Mattheson, J., *Das neu-eröffnet Orchestre, oder Universelle und gründliche Anleitung* (Hamburg, 1713). Translated as M. Seares, *Johann Mattheson's Pièces de clavecin and Das neu-eröffnet Orchestre* (Farnham: Ashgate, 2014).
—— *Der vollkommene Capellmeister* (Hamburg, 1739; repr. Kassel: Bärenreiter, 1954).
—— *Grundlage einer Ehren-Pforte* (Hamburg, 1740); facsimile edition, ed. M. Schneider (Berlin: Kommissionsverlag von Leo Liepmannssohn, 1910).
Merck, D., *Compendium instrumentalis* (Augsburg, 1695).

220 Bibliography

Merian, M., (comp.), *Diarii Europœi* (Frankfurt am Main, 1667).
Niedt, F.E., *Handleitung zur Variation* (Hamburg, 1706). Available online at http://petrucci. mus.auth.gr/imglnks/usimg/0/05/IMSLP296207-PMLP480263-Niedt_Handleitung_ zur_Variation__1706__bsb10527644.pdf. Translated by P.L. Poulin and I.C. Taylor as part 2 of *The musical guide* (Oxford: Clarendon Press, 1989).
Praetorius, M., *Syntagmatis Musici, Michaelis Praetorii C[apellmeister], tomus tertius* (Wolfenbüttel, 1619); edited and translated by J. Kite-Powell as *Syntagma musicum III* (Oxford: Oxford University Press, 2004).
Priorato, Count G. (trans. J. Burbery), *The History of the Sacred and Royal Majesty of Christina Alessandra Queen of Swedland With the Reasons of her late Conversion to the Roman Catholique Religion* (London, 1658).
[Quinault, P.], *Le triomphe de l'amour: ballet dansé devant sa Majesté à S. Germain en Laie* ([Paris], c. 1680). Online facsimile at http://digital.library.unt.edu/ark:/67531/ metadc1689.
Rolle, C.C., *Neue Wahrnehmungen zur Aufnahme und weitern Ausbreitung der Musik* (Berlin, 1784).
Speer, D., *Grund-richtiger / Kurtz / leicht und nöthiger Unterricht der musicalischen Kunst* (Ulm, 1687).
Taubert, G., *Rechtschaffener Tanzmeister oder gründlicher Erklärung der Frantzösischen Tantz-Kunst* (Leipzig, 1717); facsimile reprint ed. K. Petermann (Munich: Heimeran Verlag, 1976). Translated by T. Russell as *The compleat dancing master: a translation of Gottfried Taubert's Rechtschaffener Tantzmeister*, 2 vols (New York: Peter Lang, 2012).
Walther, J., *Musicalisches Lexicon Oder Musicalische Bibliothec* (Leipzig, 1732); modern edition, ed. F. Ramm (Kassel: Bärenreiter, 2001).
Wood, A., 'The life of Mr Anthony a Wood … written by himself, and now first printed from a Copy, transcrib'd by the Publisher' in T. Caius, *Vinidiciæ antiquitatis academiæ Oxoniensis*, 2 vols (Oxford, 1730), pp. 438–603.
Wortley Montagu, Lady M., *Letters of the Right Honourable Lady M--y W---y M----e*, 4 vols (London, 1763–7).

Secondary sources: Books and articles, printed and online

Adams, P.G., *Travelers and travel liars, 1660–1800* (New York: Dover, 1962; repr. 1980).
Anderson, M., *War and society in Europe of the old regime 1618–1789* (London: Fontana, 1988, repr. Guernsey, 1998).
Apel, W. (trans. H. Tischler), *The history of keyboard music to 1700* (Bloomington: Indiana University Press, 1972).
Asch, R.G., 'Estates and Princes after 1648: the consequences of the Thirty Years War' *GH*, 6/2 (1988), pp. 113–32.
Becker, C., *Die Tonwerke des XVI. und XXVII. Jahrhunderts oder Systematisch-Chronologische Zusammenstellung* (Leipzig, 1855).
Berger, A.M.B., *Mensuration and proportion signs: origins and evolution* (Oxford: Oxford University Press, 1993).
Biehle, H., *Musikgeschichte von Bautzen* (Leipzig: Kistner und Siegel, 1924).
Brewer, C., *The instrumental music of Schmelzer, Biber, Muffat and their contemporaries* (Farnham: Ashgate, 2011).
Buch, D.J., 'The influence of the *ballet de cour* in the genesis of the French baroque suite' *Acta Musicologica* 57/1 (1985), pp. 94–109.
────── *Dance music from the Ballets de cour, 1575–1651: historical commentary, source study, and transcriptions from the Philidor manuscripts* (Stuyvesant, NY: Pendragon Press, c. 1993).

Bullard, B. (trans. and ed.), *Musica getutscht: a treatise on musical instruments by Sebastian Virdung* (Cambridge: Cambridge University Press, 1993).
Butt, J., *Music education and the art of performance in the German Baroque* (Cambridge: Cambridge University Press, 1994).
—— 'Germany and the Netherlands' in A. Silbiger (ed.), *Keyboard music before 1700*, second edition (New York: Routledge, 2004), pp. 147–234.
Caemmerer, C., '"Des Hylas aus Latusia Lustiger Schauplatz von einer Pindischen Gesellschaft": der Bericht über eine Gruppe studentischer Liedermacher in Leipzig des 17. Jahrhunderts' in C. Caemmerer (ed.), *'Der Buchstab tödt – der Geist macht lebendig': Festschrift zum 60. Geburtstag von Hans-Gert Roloff von Freunden, Schülern und Kollegen*, 2 vols (Bern: Peter Lang, 1992), Vol. 2, pp. 775–98.
Carter, S., 'The string tremolo in the 17th century' *Early Music*, 19/1 (1991), pp. 43–60.
Chan, M. and Kassler, J.C. (eds), *Roger North's The musicall grammarian 1728* (Cambridge: Cambridge University Press, 1990).
Charteris, R., 'The music collection of the Staats- und Universitätsbibliothek, Hamburg: a survey of its British holdings prior to the Second World War' *Royal Musical Association Research Chronicle* 30 (1997), pp. 1–138.
Collins, T.A., 'Of the differences between trumpeters and city tower musicians: the relationship of *Stadtpfeifer* and *Kammeradschaft* trumpeters' *Galpin Society Journal*, 53 (2000), pp. 51–9.
Corpis, D.J., 'Losing one's place' in L. Tatlock (ed.), *Enduring loss in early modern Germany: cross disciplinary perspectives* (Leiden: Brill, 2010), pp. 327–67.
Crosby, B. (comp.), *A catalogue of Durham cathedral manuscripts* (Oxford: Oxford University Press, 1986).
Crum, M., 'Music from St Thomas's, Leipzig, in the Music School Collection at Oxford' in E. Herttrich and H. Schneider (eds), *Festschrift Rudolf Elvers zum 60. Geburtstag* (Tutzing: Hans Schneider, 1985), pp. 97–101.
De Beer, E.S., *The diary of John Evelyn*, 6 vols (Oxford: Clarendon Press, 2000).
Defant, C., 'Becker, Dietrich' in L. Finscher (ed.), *Die Musik in Geschichte und Gegenwart*, 29 vols (Kassel: Bärenreiter, 1994–2005), Personenteil 2, pp. 618–19.
Devriès-Lesure, A., 'Technological aspects' in R. Rasch (ed.), *Music publishing in Europe, 1600–1900* (Berlin: Berliner Wissenschafts-Verlag, 2005), pp. 63–88.
Dirksen, P., *Heinrich Scheidermann's keyboard music: transmission, style and chronology* (Aldershot: Ashgate, 2006).
—— 'A Buxtehude discovery' (www.pieterdirksen.nl/Essays/Bux%20Discovery.htm).
Dodd, G. (rev. A. Ashbee), *Thematic index of music for viols* (Viola da Gamba Society of Great Britain, online edition, www.vdgs.org.uk).
Donington, R., *The interpretation of early music* (London: Faber, 1963; repr. 1989).
Eddy, M.A., 'The Rost Codex and its music', PhD dissertation (Stanford University, 1984).
Fuller, D., 'Suite' in S. Sadie (ed.), *The New Grove Dictionary of Music and Musicians*, Vol. 18 (London: Grove, 1980).
—— 'Suite' in D.L. Root (ed.), *Grove music online* (www.oxfordmusiconline.com).
Gagliardo, J., *Germany under the old regime, 1600–1790* (London: Longman, 1991).
Gerheuser, L., *Jacob Scheiffelhut und seine Instrumentalmusik* (Augsburg, 1931).
Grape, A., *Ihreska Handskriftssamlingen i Uppsala Universitets Bibliotek* (Uppsala: Almqvist & Wiksells, 1949).
Greve, W., *Braunschweiger Stadtmusikanten: Geschichte eines Berufstandes 1227–1828* (Braunschweig: Stadtarchiv und Stadtbibliothek, 1991).
Göhler, A. (comp.), *Verzeichnis der in den Frankfurter und Leipziger Messkatalogen der Jahre 1564 bis 1759 angezeigten Musikalien*, 3 vols (Leipzig, 1902).

Grapenthin, U., 'Becker [Bekker, Bäkker], Dietrich [Diederich, Diedrich, Dierich]' in D.L. Root (ed.), *Grove music online* (www.oxfordmusiconline.com).

―――― 'Reincken, ... Johann Adam' in D.L. Root (ed.), *Grove music online* (www.oxfordmusiconline.com).

Herissone, R., *Music theory in seventeenth-century England* (Oxford: Oxford University Press, 2000).

Herzig, A., *Der Zwang zum wahren Glauben: Rekatholisierung vom 16. bis zum 18. Jahrhundert* (Göttingen: Vandenhoeck & Ruprecht, 2000), p. 10.

Hill, R.S., '*Echtheit angezweifelt*: style and authenticity in two suites attributed to Bach' *Early Music*, 13/2 (1985), pp. 248–55.

―――― 'Stilanalyse und Überlieferungsproblematik' in A. Edler and F. Krummacher (eds), *Dietrich Buxtehude und die europäische Musik seiner Zeit: Bericht über das Lübecker Symposion 1987* (Kassel: Bärenreiter, 1990), pp. 204–214.

Holman, P., 'Thomas Baltzar (?1631–1663), the "Incomparable Lubicer on the Violin"' *Chelys*, 13 (1984), pp. 3–38.

―――― *Four and twenty fiddlers: the violin at the English court* (Oxford: Clarendon Press, 1993, repr. 1995).

―――― *Dowland: Lachrimae (1604)* (Cambridge: Cambridge University Press, 1999).

―――― 'From violin band to orchestra' in J. Wainwright and P. Holman (eds), *From Renaissance to Baroque: change in instruments and instrumental music in the seventeenth century* (Aldershot: Ashgate, 2005), pp. 241–57.

―――― *Life after death: the Viola da Gamba in Britain from Purcell to Dolmetsch* (Woodbridge: Boydell Press, 2010).

―――― '*Before the baton*: a preliminary report' *Early Music*, 41/1 (2013), pp. 55–63.

―――― 'Performing 17th-century music' *Early Music*, 41/2 (2013), pp. 335–7.

Houle, G., *Meter in music 1600–1800: performance, perception, and notation* (Bloomington and Indianapolis: Indiana University Press, 1987).

Howey, H., 'The lives of Hoftrompeter and Stadtpfeiffer as portrayed in three novels of Daniel Speer' *Historical Brass Society Journal*, 3 (1991), pp. 65–78.

Hudson, R., *The Folia, the Saraband, the Passacaglia, and the Chaconne: the historical evolution of four forms that originated in music for the five-course Spanish guitar*, 4 vols (Neuhausen and Stuttgart: Hänssler Verlag, 1982).

―――― *The Allemande, the Balletto and the Tanz*, 2 vols (Cambridge: Cambridge University Press, 1986).

Jaaks, J., 'Ducal courts and Hanseatic cities: political and historical perspectives' in K. Snyder (ed.), *The organ as a mirror of its time* (Oxford: Oxford University Press, 2002), pp. 31–59.

Junge, C., '"Effigies XXI Clarissimorum Musicorum à Wernero Fabrico, Musico Lipsiensi": Die Porträtsammlung berühmter Musiker des Werner Fabricius' in E. Fontana (ed.), *600 Jahre Musik an der Universität Leipzig* (Leipzig: Verlag Janos Stekovics, 2010), pp. 57–76.

Kačic, L., 'Die Suiten Johann Caspar Horns im Pestrý zborník, einem Tabulaturbuch aus dem 17. Jahrhundert' in G. Fleischhauer, W. Ruf, B. Siegmund and F. Zsoch (eds), *Die Entwicklung der Ouvertüren-suite im 17. und 18. Jahrhundert*, Michaelsteiner Konferenzberichte 49 (Michaelstein: Institut für Aufführungspraxis, 1996), pp. 169–78.

Karstädt, G., 'Zuber, Gregor' in L. Finscher (ed.), *Die Musik in Geschichte und Gegenwart*, 29 vols (Kassel: Bärenreiter, 1994–2005), Personenteil 17, pp. 1563–4.

Kevorkian, T., *Baroque piety: religion, society, and music in Leipzig, 1650–1750* (Aldershot: Ashgate, 2007).

―――― 'Town musicians in German baroque society and culture' *GH*, 30/3 (2012), pp. 350–71.
Kjellberg, E. and Whitehead, P., 'Beck, Johann Hector' in D.L. Root (ed.), *Grove music online* (www.oxfordmusiconline.com).
Kokole, M., *Isaac Posch 'diditus Eois Hesperiisque plagis – Praised in the Lands of Dawn and Sunset'* (Frankfurt am Main: Peter Lang, 2009).
Kuhnau, J. (trans. J.R. Russell), *The musical charlatan* (Columbia, SC: Camden House, 1997).
Kümmerling, H. and Steude, W., *Die Musiksammelhandschriften des 16. und 17. Jahrhunderts in der Sächsischen Landesbibliothek zu Dresden* (Leipzig: VEB Deutscher Verlag für Musik, 1974).
Layer, A., 'Scheiffelhut [Scheiffelhuet], Jakob [Jacob]' in D.L. Root (ed.), *Grove music online* (www.oxfordmusiconline.com).
Lenneberg, H., *On the publishing and dissemination of music 1500–1850* (Hillsdale, NY: Pendragon Press, 2005).
Lesure, F., *Bibliographie des éditions musicales publiées par Estienne Roger et Michel-Charles Le Cène* (Paris: Heugel, 1969).
Little, M. Ellis, 'Gigue (i)' in D.L. Root (ed.), *Grove music online* (www.oxfordmusiconline.com).
Little, M. Ellis and Marsh, C.G., *La danse noble: an inventory of dances and sources* (New York: Broude Bros., 1992).
Maul, M., 'Musikpflege in der Paulinerkirche im 17. Jahrhundert bis hin zur Einführung des "neuen Gottesdienstes" (1710)' in E. Fontana (ed.), *600 Jahre Musik an der Universität Leipzig* (Leipzig: Verlag Janos Stekovics, 2010), pp. 33–56.
―――― *'Dero berühmbter Chor': Die Leizpiger Thomasschule und ihre Kantoren (1212–1804)* (Leipzig: Lehmstedt Verlag, 2012).
McIntosh, T., *Urban decline in early modern Germany: Schwäbisch Hall and its region, 1650–1750* (Chapel Hill: University of North Carolina Press, 1997).
Medick, H., 'The Thirty Years' War as experience and memory: contemporary perceptions of a macro-historical event' in L. Tatlock (ed.), *Enduring loss in early modern Germany: cross disciplinary perspectives* (Leiden: Brill, 2010), pp. 25–49.
Meyer, E.H., *Die mehrstimmige Spielmusik des 17. Jahrhunderts in Nord- und Mitteleuropa*, Heidelberger Studien zur Musikwissenschaft 2 (Kassel: Bärenreiter, 1934).
Munck, T., 'Keeping up appearances: patronage of the arts, city prestige, and princely power in Northern Germany and Denmark, 1600–1670' *GH*, 6/3 (1988), pp. 213–32.
Nef, K., *Geschichte der Sinfonie und Suite* (Leipzig: Breitkopf und Härtel, 1921).
Nettl, P., *Die Wiener Tanzkomposition in der zweiten Hälfte des siebzehnten Jahrhunderts*, Studien zur Musikwissenschaft 8 (Vienna: Universal Edition, 1921).
Newman, W.S., *The sonata in the baroque era*, 3rd edition (New York: Norton, 1972).
Noack, F., *Sinfonie und Suite von Gabrieli bis Schumann* (Leipzig: Breitkopf und Härtel, 1932).
Norlind, T., 'Zur Geschichte der suite' in *Sammelbände der Internationalen Musikgesellschaft*, vol. 7 (Leipzig, 1905–1906).
Parrott, A., *The essential Bach choir* (Woodbridge: Boydell, 2000).
Patalas, A., *Catalogue of early music prints from the collections of the former Preußische Staatsbibliothek in Berlin, kept at the Jagiellonian library in Cracow* (Cracow: Musica Iagellonica, 1999).
Piersig, F. and Schröder, D., 'Knop [Knoep, Knopff], Lüder' in D.L. Root (ed.) *Grove music online* (www.oxfordmusiconline.com).

224 Bibliography

Rasch, R.A., 'Seventeenth-century Dutch editions of English instrumental music' *Music & Letters*, 53/3 (1972), pp. 270–73.

—— 'David Petersen [Pietersen]' in D.L. Root (ed.) *Grove music online* (www.oxfordmusiconline.com).

Rathey, M., 'Rehearsal for the opera: remarks on a lost composition by Johann Kuhnau from 1683' in *EM*, 42/3 (2014), pp. 409–420.

Rivera, B.V., *German music theory in the early 17th century: the treatises of Johannes Lippius* (Ann Arbor: UMI Research Press, 1974; repr. 1980).

Robertson, M., 'The consort suite in the German-speaking lands, 1660–1705', PhD dissertation (University of Leeds, 2004).

—— 'Johann Pachelbel 1653–1706' in *The Early Music Yearbook 2006* (Hebden Bridge: The National Early Music Association, 2006), pp. 5–10.

—— *The courtly consort suite in German-speaking Europe, 1650–1706* (Farnham: Ashgate, 2009).

—— 'Edited out' *EM*, 42/2 (2014), pp. 207–218.

Robinson, L., 'Viol. 7. Germany and the Low Countries from *c*1600' in D.L. Root (ed.), *Grove music online* (www.oxfordmusiconline.com).

Rose, S., 'Publication and the anxiety of judgement in German music life of the seventeenth century' *Music & Letters*, 85/1 (2004), pp. 22–40.

—— 'Music, print and presentation in Saxony during the seventeenth century' *GH*, 23/1 (2005), pp. 1–19.

—— 'The composer as self-publisher in seventeenth-century Germany' in E. Kjellberg (ed.), *The dissemination of music in seventeenth-century Europe: celebrating the Düben collection* (Bern: Peter Lang, 2010), pp. 239–60.

—— *The musician in literature in the age of Bach* (Cambridge: Cambridge University Press, 2011).

Sadie, J.A., 'Handel in pursuit of the viol' *Chelys*, 14 (1985), pp. 3–24.

Sagarra, E., *A social history of Germany, 1648–1914*, 2nd edition (New Brunswick: Transaction, 2003).

Scheibert, B., *Jean-Henry D'Anglebert and the seventeenth-century clavecin school* (Bloomington: Indiana University Press, 1986).

Schmidt, C.B., 'The Amsterdam editions of Lully's music: a bibliographical scrutiny with commentary' in J. Heyer (ed.), *Lully studies* (Cambridge: Cambridge University Press, 2000), pp. 100–165.

Schulenberg, D., 'Recent editions and recordings of Froberger and other seventeenth-century composers' *Journal of Seventeenth-Century Music* 13/1 (2007) (http://sscm-jscm.org/jscm/v13/no1/schulenberg.html).

Schwab, H.W., 'The social status of the town musician' in W. Salmen (ed.; trans. H. Kaufman and B. Reisner), *The social status of the professional musician from the middle ages to the 19th century* (New York: Pendragon, 1983), pp. 33–59.

Seares, M., *Johann Mattheson's Pièces de clavecin and Das neu-eröffnet Orchestre* (Farnham: Ashgate, 2014).

Seelbach, U., 'Die Altdorfer Ceres-Gesellschaft (1668–1669)' in K. Garber and H. Wismann (eds), *Europäische Sozietätsbewegung und demokratische Tradition* (Tübingen: Niemeyer, 1996), pp. 1361–80.

Sehnal, J. and Pešková, J., *Caroli de Liechtenstein Castelcorno episcopi Olumucensis operum artis musicae collectio Cremsirii reservata*, Artis Musicæ Antiquioris Catalogorum Vol. V/1 (Prague: Editio Supraphon, 1998).

Silbiger, A., 'Music and the crisis of seventeenth-century Europe' in V. Coelho (ed.), *Music and science in the age of Galileo* (Dordrecht: Kluwer, 1992), pp. 35–44.

────── 'The solo instrument' in T. Carter and J. Butt (eds), *The Cambridge history of seventeenth-century music* (Cambridge: Cambridge University Press, 2005), pp. 426–78.

Snyder, K.J., *Dieterich Buxtehude: organist in Lübeck*, 2nd edition (Rochester, NY: University of Rochester Press, 2007).

Spitta, P. (trans. C. Bell and J.A. Fuller Maitland), *Johann Sebastien Bach: his work and influence on the music of Germany, 1685–1750*, 3 vols (London: Novello, 1899).

Spitzer, J. and Zaslaw, N., *The birth of the orchestra: history of an institution, 1650–1815* (Oxford: Oxford University Press, 2004).

Spohr, A., 'Wind instruments in the Anglo-German consort repertoire, ca. 1630–40: a survey of music by Johann Schop and Nicolaus Bleyer' *Historic Brass Society Journal* (2004), pp. 43–65.

Thompson, S., 'Colouration in the Mélanges: purpose and intent' in C. Cessac (ed.), *Les manuscrits autographes de Marc-Antoine Charpentier* (Wavre: Editions Mardaga, 2007), pp. 121–36.

Vaillancourt, M.G., 'Instrumental ensemble music at the court of Leopold I (1658–1705)', PhD dissertation (University of Illinois at Urbana-Champaign, 1991).

Vierhaus, R. (trans. J.B. Knudsen), *Germany in the age of absolutism* (Cambridge: University Press, 1988, repr. 1991).

Voss S., *Die Musikaliensammlung im Pfarrachiv Udestedt* (Schneverdingen: Karl Dieter Wagner, 2006).

Waczkat, A., 'Meister [Maistre, Maestro], Johann Friedrich' in D.L. Root (ed.) *Grove music online* (www.oxfordmusiconline.com).

Walker, M., *German home towns: community, state, and general estate 1648–1871*, 2nd edition (Ithaca: Cornell University Press, 1998).

Walker, P.M., *Theories of fugue from the age of Josquin to the age of Bach* (Rochester, NY: University of Rochester Press, 2000).

Webber, G., *North German church music in the age of Buxtehude* (Oxford: Clarendon Press, 1996).

Whitehead, P., 'Austro-German printed sources of instrumental music, 1630 to 1700', PhD dissertation (University of Pennsylvania, 1996).

Wienandt, E.A., *Johann Pezel (1639–1694): a thematic catalogue of his instrumental works* (New York: Pendragon, 1983).

Williams, P., 'A chaconne by Georg Böhm: a note on German composers and French styles' *EM*, 17/1 (1989), pp. 43–54.

Wilson, D.K. (ed. and trans.), *Georg Muffat on performance practice* (Bloomington: Indiana University Press, 2001).

Wilson. J., (ed.) *Roger North on music: being a selection from his essays written during the years c. 1695–1728* (London: Novello, 1959).

Wolff, C., 'Das Hamburger Buxtehude-Bild: ein Beitrag zur musikalischen Ikonographie und zum Umkreis von Johann Adam Reincken' in A. Grassmann and W. Neugebauer (eds), *800 Jahre Musik in Lübeck* (Lübeck, 1982).

────── 'From Berlin to Łódź: the Spitta collection resurfaces' *Notes, quarterly journal of the Music Library Association*, 46/2 (1989), pp. 311–27.

Wollny, P., 'Rosenmüller, Johann' in L. Finscher (ed.), *Die Musik in Geschichte und Gegenwart*, 29 vols (Kassel: Bärenreiter, 2005), Personenteil 14, pp. 406–411.

226 Bibliography

——— 'Das Leipziger Collegium musicum im 17. Jahrhundert' in E. Fontana (ed.), *600 Jahre Musik an der Universität Leipzig* (Leipzig: Verlag Janos Stekovics, 2010), pp. 77–89.

Zohn, S., 'Die vornehmste Hof-Tugend: German musicians' reflections on eighteenth-century court life' in S. Owens, B. Reul and J. Stockigt (eds), *Music at German courts, 1715–1760: changing artistic priorities* (Woodbridge: Boydell & Brewer, 2011), pp. 413–25.

Music, primary sources and their modern editions

Where applicable, RISM references are included in square brackets

VI Suittes Divers Airs avec leurs Variations & Fugues (Amsterdam, ?1710; modern edition, ed. P. Dirksen, Utrecht: Koninklijke Vereniging voor Nederlandse Muziekgeschiedenis, 2004).

Ahle, J.R., *Dreyfaches Zehn allerhand newer Sinfonien, Paduanen, Balleten, Alemanden, Mascheraden, Arien, Intraden, Courenten und Sarabanden; Mit 3. 4. und 5. Stimmen* (Erfurt, 1650) [RISM A 484].

Bassani, G.B., *Balletti, Correnti, Gighe, e Sarabande à Violino, e Violone, overo Spinetta ... Opera prima* (Bologna, 1677; repr. 1684) [RISM B 1161; B 1162].

Beck, J.H. (ed.), *Continuatio exercitii musici Bestehend in außerlesenen Allemanden, Balletten, Gavotten, Giquen, Couranten und Sarabanden* (Frankfurt am Main, 1666) [RISM B 1522].

——— *Continuatio exercitii musici secunda, bestehend in außerlesenen Paduanen, Intraden, Allemanden, Balletten, Gavotten, Giqven, Couranten und Sarabanden* (Frankfurt am Main, 1670) [RISM B 1523].

Becker, D., *Musicalische / Frühlings-Früchte / Bestehend In drei-vier-und fünff-stimmiger Instrumental-Harmonia, Nebenst dem Basso Continuo* (Hamburg, 1668; repr. Antwerp, 1673 as *Musicalische Lendt-Vruchten Bestænd In dry, vier, vyf, Instrumentale-Hermoniale stemmen*) [RISM B 1525; B 1526]. Modern edition, ed. H. Bergmann and U. Grapenthin, Das Erbe deutscher Musik 110, (Kassel: Nagels Verlag, 1995).

——— *Erster Theil zwey-stimmiger Sonaten und Suiten Nebest einem gedoppelten Basso Continuo* (Hamburg, 1674) [RISM B 1527].

Brade, W., *Newe außerlesene Paduanen, Galliarden, Cantzonen, Allmand und Couranten* (Hamburg, 1609) [RISM B 4206].

——— *Newe ausserlesene Paduanen und Galliarden mit 6. Stimmen* (Hamburg, 1614) [RISM B 4207].

Cazzati, M., *Correnti, e balletti ... Opera XXX* (Bologna, 1662) [RISM C 1624].

Cousser [Kusser], J.S., *Composition de musique, suivant la méthode françoise* (Stuttgart, 1682) [RISM K 3079].

——— *Apollon enjoüé. Contenant six ouvertures de théâtre* (Stuttgart, 1700) [RISM K 3080].

——— *La cicala della cetra D'Eunomio* (Stuttgart, 1700) [RISM K 3081]. Suite 2, modern edition, ed. M. Robertson (Magdeburg: Edition Walhall, 2010).

Drese, A., *Erster Theil Etlicher Allemanden, Couranten, Sarabanden, Balletten, Intraden und andern Arien mit theils darbei befindlichen Doublen, oder Variationen* (Jena, 1672) [RISM not listed].

Druckenmüller, G.W., *Musicalisches Tafel-Confect; Bestehend in VII. Partyen / Balleten, Allemanden, Couranten, Sarabanden &c.* (Schwäbisch Hall, 1668) [RISM D 3587].

Fabricius, W., *Deliciae Harmonicae, oder Musicalische Gemüths-Ergätzung* (Leipzig, 1657) [RISM F 30].

Fischer, J.C.F., *Les Pièces de Clavessin* (Schlackenwerth, 1696; repr. Augsburg, 1698 as *Musicalisches Blumen-Büschlein*) [RISM FF 979a; F 980].

Frescobaldi, G., *Ricercari et canzoni Franzese* (Rome, 1615) [RISM F 1860].

Froberger, J.J., *Diverse Ingegnosissime, Rarissime & non maj piu viste Curiose Partite ... Dal Eccellentissimo e Famosissimo Organista* ([Mainz], 1693) [RISM F 2026].

—— *10 Suittes de Clavessin Composées Par Monsr. Giacomo Froberger* (Amsterdam, n.d.). [RISM F 2034].

Hake, H., *Ander Theil Newer Pavanen, Sonaten, Arien, Balletten, Brandlen, Covranten, und Sarabanden, Mit 2.3.4.5. und 8. Instrumenten mit dem Basso Continuo* (Stade, 1654) [RISM H 1895].

Hammerschmidt, A., *Erster Fleiß Allerhand newer Paduanen, Galliarden, Balleten, Mascharaden, Francoischen [sic] Arien, Courenten und Sarabanden* (Freiberg, 1636; repr. 1639 and 1650) [RISM H 1958; H 1959; H 1960]. Modern edition, ed. H. Mönkemeyer, Das Erbe deutsche Musik 49 (Kassel: Nagels, 1957); Suite I, ed. L. and G. von Zadow, (Heidelberg: Edition Güntersberg, 2000).

——, *Ander Theil newer Paduanen, Canzonen, Galliarden, Balleten, Mascharaden, Francoischen [sic] Arien, Courenten und Sarabanden* (Freiberg, 1639) [RISM H 1961]. Modern edition, ed. H. Mönkemeyer, Das Erbe deutsche Musik 49 (Kassel: Nagels, 1957).

—— *Dritter Theil neuer Paduanen, Galliarden, Canzonen, Sonaten, Balletten, Intraden, Couranten und Sarabanden, Mit 3. F und 5 Stimmen* (Leipzig, 1650) [RISM H 1962].

Handel, G.F., *Suites de Pieces Pour le Clavecin. Composées par G.F. Handel, Premier volume* (London, n.d.) [RISM H 1433].

—— *Suites de Pieces Pour le Clavecin. Composées par G.F. Handel. Second Volume* (London, n.d.) [RISM H 1438].

Hasse, N., *Delitiæ musicæ, Das ist Schöne / lustige und anmuthige Allemanden / Couranten und Sarabanden* (Rostock, 1656) [RISM H 2310]. Modern edition, ed. A. Bares (Albese con Cassano: Musedita, 2010).

Horn, J.C., *Parergon musicum, Oder Musicalisches Neben-Werck / Bestehend in allerhand anmuthigen Allemanden, Couranten, Ballo und Sarabanden ... Ersten Theil* (Erfurt, 1663, repr. Leipzig, 1670) [RISM H 7408; H 7409]. Modern edition of suites I–IV, ed. M. Robertson (Edinburgh: Thesaurus musicus, 2010).

—— *Parergon musicum Oder Musicalisches Neben-Werck / Bestehend in fünff angenehmen Grossen-Balletten ... Andern Theil* (Erfurt 1663, repr. Leipzig, 1670) [RISM H 7410, H 7411].

—— *Parergon musicum Oder Musicalisches Neben-Werck Bestehend in allerhand anmuthigen Intraden, Allemanden, Couranten, Ballo, Sarabanden, Chiqven, &c. Mit Fünff Stimmen ... Dritten Theil* (Leipzig, 1672) [RISM H 7412].

—— *Parergon musicum Oder Musicalisches Neben-Werck / Bestehend in Drey angenehmen Grossen – Balletten ... Vierdten Theil* (Leipzig, 1672) [RISM H 7413].

—— *Parergon musicum Oder Musicalisches Neben-Werck / Bestehend in allerhand ammuthigen Sonatinen, Alleman-den, Couranten, Ballet-ten, Sarabanden und Chiqven ... Fünfftem Theil* (Leipzig, 1676) [RISM H 7414].

—— *Parergon musicum Oder Musicalisches Neben-Werck / Bestehend in allerhand lustigen Intraden, Gagliarden, Couranten, Balletten, Sarabanden, Chiqven &c. ... Sechsten Theil* (Leipzig, 1676) [RISM H 7415].

Kelz, M., *Primitiæ musicales seu concentus novi harmonici* (Augsburg, 1658) [RISM K 369].

Knoep, L., *Erster Theil Newer Paduanen, Galliarden, Balletten, Mascaraden, Arien, Allemanden, Couranten und Sarabanden* (Bremen, 1652) [RISM K 994].

―――― *Ander Theil newer Paduanen, Galliarden, Arien, Allemanden, Balletten, Couranten, und Sarabanden, Mit 2. und 3. Stimmen nebenst dem Basso Continuo* (Bremen, 1660) [RISM K 995].

Kradenthaller, H., *Deliciarum musicalium Erster Theil à4. Viol. Von Sonatinen, Arien, Sarabanden und Giquen* (Nuremberg, 1675) [RISM K 1872].

―――― *Deliciarum musicalium Anderer Theil / Etlicher Sonatinen, Arien, Sarabanden und Giquen, &c* (Nuremberg, 1676) [RISM K 1873].

Krieger, J., *Sechs Musicalische Partien ... auf einem Spinet oder Clavichordio zu spielen* (Nuremberg, 1697) [RISM K 2451].

Kuhnau, J., *Neüer Clavier Übung Erster Theil* (Leipzig, 1689; repr. 1695, 1710, 1718) [RISM K 2982–85].

―――― *Neüer Clavier Übung Andrer Theil* (Leipzig, 1692; repr. 1695, 1696, 1703, 1726) [RISM K 2986–2990]. Facsimile edition, Monumenta Musicæ Revocata 20 (Florence: Studio Per Edizione Scelte, 1996).

―――― *Musicalische Vorstellung Einiger Biblischer Historien* (Leipzig, 1700) [RISM K 2997].

Kühnel. A., *Sonate ô Partite ad una o due viole da gamba* (n.p., 1698) [RISM K 2960].

Lully, J.-B., *Ballet du temple de la paix*, *LWV* 69 (Paris, 1685) [RISM L 3049]. Online facsimile at http://digital.library.unt.edu/ark:/67531/metadc69.

Mattheson, J., *Pieces de Clavecin en deux volumes* (London, 1714) [RISM M 1397].

Meister, J.H., *Il giardino del piacere overo raccolta de diversi flori musicali* (Hamburg, 1695).

Muffat, G., *Exquisitioris harmoniæ instrumentalis gravi-jucundæ selectus primus, duodecim rarioribus* [commonly known as *Ausserlesene Instrumental-musik*] (Passau, 1701) [RISM M 8132].

N.B.N., *Exercitium musicum Bestehend in auszerlesenen Sonaten, Galliarden, Allemanden, Balletten, Intraden, Arien, Chiquen, Couranten, Sarabanden, und Branlen* (Frankfurt am Main, 1660) [RISM B/I 16605].

Pachelbel, J., *Musicalische Ergötzung, bestehend in sechs verstimten Partien â 2. Violin nebst den Basso Continuo* (Nuremberg, n.d.) [RISM P 34]. Facsimile edition, ed. F. Dangel-Hofmann (Courlay: Éditions J.M. Fuzeau, 1992).

Peuerl, P., *Neue Padouan, Intrada, Däntz und Galliarda* (Nuremberg, 1611) [RISM P 1666].

Pezel, J., *Musica vespertina Lipsica oder Leipzigische Abend-Music* (Leipzig, 1669) [RISM P 1691].

―――― *Hora Decima Musicorum Lipsiensium* (Leipzig, 1670; repr. Dresden, 1674 as *Supellex Sonatarum Selectarum, a quinq: instrumentis*) [RISM P 1692; RISM P 1694].

―――― *Musicalische Gemüths-Ergetzung* (Leipzig, 1672) [RISM P 1693].

―――― *Bicinia Variorum Instrumentorum* (Leipzig, 1675) [RISM P 1695].

―――― *Delitiæ Musicales, Oder Lust-Music, Bestehend in Sonaten, Allemanden, Balleten, Gavotten, Courenten, Sarabanden, und Chiquen* (Frankfurt am Main, 1678) [RISM P 1696].

―――― *Fünff-stimmigte blasende Music* (Frankfurt am Main, 1685) [RISM P 1697].

Playford, J. (comp.), *Court-Ayres or Pavins, Almains, Corant's and Sarabands* (London, 1655) [RISM B/1 16555].

―――― *Courtly Masquing Ayres* (London, 1662) [RISM B/I 16628].

Praetorius, M., *Terpsichore, musarum aoniarum quinta* (Wolfenbüttel, 1612) [RISM B/I 161216].

Reincken, A., *Hortus musicus recentibus aliquot Flosculis Sonaten, Allemanden, Couranten, Sarbanden et Giquen* (n.p., n.d.) [RISM R 1072].

Rieck, J.E., *Neue Allemanden, Giques, Balletten, Couranten, Sarabanden, und Gavotten* (Strasbourg, 1658) [RISM R 1379].

Rosenmüller, J., *Paduanen, Alemanden, Couranten, Balletten, Sarabanden, Mit drey Stimmen / Und ihrem Basso pro Organo* (Leipzig, 1645) [RISM R 2563].

———— *Studenten-Music / Darinnen zu befinden Allerhand Sachen Mit drey und fünff Violen / oder auch andern Instrumenten zu spielen* (Leipzig, 1654) [RISM R 2564].

———— *Sonate da camera cioe Sinfonie, Alemande, Correnti, Balletti, Sarabande* (Venice, 1667) [RISM R 2565]. Modern edition, ed. K. Nef, DDT 1/18 (Leipzig, 1904; repr., ed. H.J. Moser, Wiesbaden, 1957).

Rothe, W.E., *Erstmahlig musicalische Freuden-Gedicte* (Dresden, 1660) [RISM R 2792].

Scheiffelhut, J., *Musicalischer Gemüths Ergötzungen Erstes Werck* (Augsburg, 1684) [RISM S 1369].

———— *Lieblicher Frühlings-Anfang, oder Musicalischer Seyten-Klang* (Augsburg, 1685) [RISM S 1370]. Modern edition, ed. K. Ruhland (Magdeburg: Edition Walhall, 2003).

———— *Musicalisches Klee-Blatt, Bestehend in lustigen Preludien, Entréen, Rondeau, Bourréen ... und andern Stucken* (Augsburg, 1707) [RISM S 1373].

Schein, J.H., *Banchetto musicale neuer anmutiger Padouanen, Gagliarden, Courenten und Allemanden* (Leipzig, 1617) [RISM S 1376]. Modern edition, ed. D. Krickeberg (Kassel: Bärenreiter, 1967).

Schop, J., *Erster Theil Newer Paduanen, Galliarden, Allmanden, Balletten, Couranten, unnd [sic] Canzonen* (Hamburg, 1633; repr. 1640) [RISM S 2102]. Modern edition, ed. A. Spohr (Middletown, WI: A-R Editions, 2003).

Schultheiss, B., *Muth- und Geist-ermuntrender Clavier-Lust / Erster (& Anderer) Theil* (Nuremberg, 1679) [RISM S 2302]. Modern edition, R. Hudson (ed.), Corpus of Early Keyboard Music 21 (Neuhausen and Stuttgart: Hänssler-Verlag, 1993).

Speer, D., *Recens Fabricatus Labor, Oder Neugebachene Taffel-Schnitz* (n.p., 1685) [RISM S 4070].

———— *Musicalischer Leuthe Spiegel / Das ist: Ein Extract auß dem Welt-berühmten Ertz-Schelmen Judas Tractat* (n.p., 1687) [RISM S 4071].

———— *Musicalisch-Türckischer Eulen-Spiegel / Das ist: Seltzame Possen von einem sehr gescheiden Türckisch-Käyserlichen Hof- und Feld-Narren* (n.p., 1688) [RISM S 4072].

Zuber, G., *Erster Theil newer Paduanen, [Gaillarden,] Arien, Balletten, Couranten, Sarabanden und iner Sonat. Mit 5. Stimmen nebenst dem Basso Continuo* (Lübeck, 1649).

Music: Secondary Sources

Brade, W. (ed. B. Thomas), *Pavans and Galliards for six instruments (1614)* (London: Pro musica edition, 1992).

Buxtehude, D. (ed. E. Bangert), *Klaverværker* (Copenhagen: Hansen, 1942, repr. Mineola: Dover, 2002). Available online at: http://img.kb.dk/ma/danklav/ryge_tabl-m.pdf.

Buxtehude, D. (ed. E. Linfield), *The collected works*, vol. 14 (New York: Broude Trust, 1994).

Dahlhaus, C. (ed.), *Johann Theil Musikalisches Kunstbuch*, Denkmäler Norddeutscher Musik 1 (Kassel: Bärenreiter, 1965).

Fischer, J.C.F. (ed. E. von Werra), *Sämtliche Werke für Klavier und Orgel* (Leipzig: Brietkopf und Härtel, 1901; repr. New York, 1965).

Flor, C. (ed. J. Jacobi), *Zehn suiten für Clavier* (Bremen: edition baroque, 2006).

Froberger, J.J. (ed. S. Rampe), *Neue Ausgabe sämtlicher Werke*, Vol. 3 (Kassel: Bärenreiter, 2002).

Gustafson, B. (ed.), *Lüneburg, Ratsbücherei, Mus. ant. pract. 1198*, 17th Century Keyboard Music 22 (New York and London: Garland, 1987).

Hill, R. (ed.), *Ottobeuren, Benediktiner-Abtei, Bibliothek und Musik-Archiv MO 1037*, 17th Century Keyboard Music 23 (New York: Garland, 1988).

—— (ed.), *Keyboard music from the Andreas Bach book and the Möller manuscript* (Cambridge, MA: Harvard University Press, 1991).

Kradenthaller, H. (ed. K. Ruhland), *Vier kurze Suiten* (Magdeburg: Edition Walhall, 2006).

Kuhnau, J. (ed. N. Müllermann), *Sämtliche Werke für Tasteninstrument* (Munich: Henle Verlag, 2014).

Pachelbel, J. (ed. F. Zobeley), *Triosuiten für zwei Violinen und Basso continuo*, Hortus Musicus 54–56 (Kassel: Bärenreiter, 1960–66).

—— (ed. R. Gwilt), *Partie a 4 in G major* (Hungerford: RG editions, 1998).

Reincken, J.A. (ed. K. Beckmann), *Sämtliche Werke* (Wiesbaden: Breitkopf und Härtel, 1982).

Rose, S. (ed.), *Leipzig church music from the Sherard Collection: eight works by Sebastien Knüpfer, Johann Schelle, and Johann Kuhnau* (Middleton, WI: A-R Editions, 2014).

Schächer, R. (ed.), *Leutschauer Tabulaturbuch 1676* (Stuttgart: Cornetto, 2001).

Weckmann, M. (ed. S. Rampe), *Sämtliche Freie Orgel- und Clavierwerke* (Kassel: Bärenreiter, 1991).

Wollny, P. (ed.), *Johann Jacob Froberger, Toccaten, Suiten, Lamenti; die Handschrift SA 4450 der Sing-Akademie zu Berlin* (Kassel: Bärenreiter, 2004).

Index

VI Suittes Divers Airs avec leurs Variations & Fugues 190

Abendmusiken 7, 12, 104
Ahle, Johann Rudolf 53–4, 63, 202; *Dreyfaches Zehn allerhand newer Sinfonien* 53–4
Ahrensburg 152
Albrici, Vincent 187
Allemande (Allmandt) xxv–vi, 14, 25, 30–1, 37, 50, 60, 63, 70–3, 78–9, 83–4, 94, 102, 104, 110, 112, 119, 120, 124–25, 130, 136, 139, 151, 155–56, 157, 160, 162–65, 169, 172–75, 177–79, 181–83, 186–88, 190–92, 197–99
Amener, *see* Bransle sequence
Apel, Willi xxvi, 175
Aria 32, 44–5, 48, 79, 85, 94, 129, 135, 157, 169, 177, 188–90
Arioso 99
Artus, *see* Leborge, Jean Artus
Assig und Siegersdorff, Johann von 120, 135
Augsburg 8, 60, 90, 92, 94, 180, 184

Bach, Johann Sebastian 104, 109, 164, 187; *Musikalische Opfer* (*BWV* 1079) 169
Ballet de Cour 14, 127, 129, 131
Ballo (Ballett, Balletto), *see also* suite 14, 32, 37, 45, 48, 50, 52, 71, 79–80, 85, 92–94, 111–12, 114–15, 120, 124, 130–31, 134–35, 162, 164, 168, 179
Baltzar, Thomas 5–6
Bassani, Giovanni, Battista 26; *Balletti, Correnti, Gighe, e Sarabande* 26
basse constraint 189
Bataglia 49, 80
Beck, Johann Hector 69, 71–3, 76, 78, 86
Becker, Dieterich xxiv, 8, 12, 55, 102–3, 119, 127, 149, 151–52, 154–58, 160–66, 168, 175–77, 188; *Ander Theil zweystimmiger Sonaten und Suiten* 152, 161; *Erster Theil zweystimmiger Sonaten und Suiten* xxiv, 12, 152, 156–58, 160; *Musicalische Frülings-Früchte* 8, 152, 154–56, 158, 162, 164; *Musicalische Lendt-Vruchten* 152, 156
Beer, Johann 4–6; *Musikalische Discurse* 4; *Teutsche Winter-Nächte* 5
Bernhard, Christoph 149
Biber, Heinrich 102, 144
Birckner, Johann 123
Bist d'Anvers, Martin vander 201; 'Traicté de musique' 201
Böhm, Georg 190–91
bombardino 136
Bourée 13, 32, 68, 129, 189–91
Bourgeat, Ludwig 185, 191
Brade, William 150, 199; *Newe ausserlesene Paduanen und Galliarden* 150, 199
Bransle (Branle) sequence xxiv, 13–14, 27, 37–8, 45, 58–9, 70, 83–5, 91, 119–120, 123, 127, 130, 152, 155, 157, 161, 186; Amener 37–8; Bransle Double 24, 38, 83; Bransle Gay 37–38; Bransle Simple 37–8, 84; Gavotte 37–8, 83, 120; Montirande 37–8, 58
Braunschweig 3, 8
Bremen 20, 54, 155–56
Brewer, Charles 2 (fn.2), 119
Briegel, Wolfgang Karl 128; *Erster Theil Darinnen begriffen X. Paduanen* 128
Brossard, Sebastien 14, 24, 126; *Dictionaire de Musique* 14, 126
Bruslard (Brülar) 38, 59
Buch, David J. xxv
Bürgermeister (burgher) 4, 6, 123, 149

Index

Burmeister, Joachim 196–97; *Musica poetica* 196
Butt, John 173, 180
Buxtehude Dieterich 7–8, 12, 102–4, 165, 173, 175–76, 190; Sonata a 2 ex B. Con le Suite' *BuxVW* 273, *see* manuscript *S-Uu* Instr.mus.i hskr.13:25; *VII. Suonate à due … Opera prima* 104

Calvisius, Seth 197; *Exercitatio musica tertia* 197
Canzona (*Canzon*) 46, 53–4, 152, 156, 162
Capriccio 119
Carr, William 2–3
Cazzati, Mauritio 22; *Correnti, e Balletti … Opera XXX* 22
Celle 152, 155, 162–63
Celle, Thomas 149–50
Chaconne, *see also Ciacona* 24, 181–82, 189, 191
Charpentier Marc-Antoine 201
Chique, *see* Gigue
Christina, Queen of Sweden 6, 12, 49
Ciaconna, see also Chaconne 102
classical order, *see* suite
Coleman, Charles 66–7, 73
Collegium musicum xxvi, 10–12, 45, 85, 99, 109, 119, 123, 127, 158
Cologne 2–4
Continuatio exercitii musici secunda, see Exercitium musicum III
Continuatio exercitii musici, see Exercitium musicum II
Corrente (*Corrente, Correnta, Corrento*), *see also* Courante xxvi, 22, 62, 69, 99–101, 110, 112, 114, 115, 117
Courante, *see also* Corrente xxv–vi, 13–14, 21–2, 24, 26, 32, 37, 48–50, 55–7, 60, 63, 70–72, 78–80, 92–4, 96–7, 102–4, 110–12, 115, 122–26, 128, 130–32, 134–35, 138–39, 151, 155–57, 160, 162–69, 172, 175, 177–78, 181–82, 186–88, 190–92, 197–99, 201, 205
Cousser (Kusser), Jean Sigismond 30, 99, 177, 180, 191; *Composition de musique* 30
Crüger, Johann 200–1; *Synopsis musica* 200

d'Olbreuse, Princess Eléonore Desmier 152
De Blainville 2–4
De Colombier, Claude Jordan 1–2
Diarii Europæi 12
Dirksen, Pieter 172, 190
Donington, Robert 195, 206

Double, see also Bransle Double 24, 46, 101–2, 159, 175, 177–78, 188–89, 190–91
Dowland, John 34
Dresden 5–6, 9–10, 108–9, 123, 136, 187
Drese, Adam 24, 81; *Erster Theil Etlicher Allemanden* 24
Druckenmüller, Georg Wolffgang 13–14, 36, 82, 84, 155; *Musicalisches Tafel-Confect* 13, 36, 82–3, 85, 155
Dumanoir, Guillaume 66, 70

Engels Speel-thresoor 67, 71, 73, 78
engraving techniques xxvi, 90, 174, 185–88, 190, 207
Entrée xxiv, 14, 127–28, 131
Erfurt 7–8, 54
Erlebach, Philipp Heinrich xxiv
Exercitium musicum I 32, 44, 65–7, 69–73, 78, 82, 86, 102, 158
Exercitium musicum II (Continuatio exercitii musici) 69, 71–3, 76, 78, 82, 86
Exercitium musicum III (Continuatio exercitii musici secunda) 69, 76, 78, 82, 84

Fabricius, Werner 10, 117; *Deliciæ Harmonicæ* 10, 117
Felsecker, Wolf Eberhard 85, 91
Ferdinand III, Holy Roman Emperor 6
Fischer, Johann Caspar Ferdinand 180, 190; *Les Pièces de Clavessin* 180, 190; *Musicalisches Blumen-Büschlein* 180; *Musicalischer Parnassus* 180
Flor, Christian 176–77
Frankfurt-am-Main 3, 63, 65, 71, 78, 165, 186
frantzösischen Manier 20–1, 49, 99, 127, 131, 164, 180
Freiberg 43, 52
Frescobaldi, Girolamo 200; *Ricercari et canzoni Franzese* 200
Froberger, Johann Jacob xxvi, 150–51, 154–55, 165, 169, 173–75, 177–79, 182, 185, 190–91, 203, 207; *10 Suittes de Clavessin* 191; *Diverse Ingegnosissime, Rarissime & non maj piu viste Curiose Partite* 185, 191; 'Libro di capricci, e ricercati … Libro Terzo', *see* manuscript *A-Wn* Mus. Hs. 16560; 'Libro Quarto', *see* manuscript *A-Wn* Mus. Hs. 18707
Fromman, Georg Heinrich 65, 123–24, 127, 129

Fuhrmann, Martin Heinrich 31–2, 38; *Musicalische-Trichter* 31
Fuller, David xxiv

Galanterien 38, 177, 180, 190–91
Galliard 29, 30, 45–7, 50, 52–3, 55, 70, 79, 144, 199
Gavotte (Gavott), *see also* Bransle sequence 38, 71, 97, 178, 190
Gengenbach, Nikolaus 195, 197, 199, 202; *Musica nova, Newer Singekunst* 195, 197
Gigue (*Chique, Giga, Gigè*) xxiv–vi, 21, 24–6, 71–3, 85, 91–5, 97, 99–102, 104, 120, 130, 135, 151, 154, 162, 165, 167–69, 172–73, 175–78, 181, 186–91
Gottorf 46, 167
Gradenthaller, *see* Kradenthaller
Grand Ballet, see also Grossen-Balletten 127–29
Graz 7
Grecke, Peter 6
Grossen-Balletten, see also Horn, *Parergon musicum II and IV* 14, 127, 131
Guth, Johann 78; *Exercitium musicum* 78

Hake, Hans 34, 55, 59, 63, 144; *Ander Theil Newer Pavanen* 34, 55, 59, 144
Hamburg 3–4, 6–9, 12, 20, 33, 35, 37, 55, 65, 68, 90, 102, 104–5, 119, 127, 149–52, 155–56, 158, 161–69, 175, 181, 190, 193, 199
Hammerschmidt, Andreas 8, 9, 22, 24, 32, 43–50, 52–4, 62–3, 72, 79, 85, 111, 127, 164, 206; *Ander Theil newer Paduanen,* 22, 45–6, 49, 52–3, 63; *Dritter Theil newer Paduanen* 8, 47–8, 52–4; *Erster Fleiß: Allerhand newer Paduanen* 24, 43–6, 48, 52–3, 206
Handel, Georg Fridric 37, 169, 192; *Suites de Pieces pour le Clavecin I* 192; *Suites de Pieces pour le Clavecin II* 192
Hase, Wolfgang 200–1; *Gründliche Einführung* 200
Hasse, Nicolaus 30, 35, 59–60; *Delitiæ musicæ* 30, 35, 59
Haupttänze xxv
hemiola major 199
hemiola minor 199
Herbst, Johann 126; *Musica moderna prattica* 126
Herissone, Rebecca 196
Hessen-Kassel, court of 19

Hintze manuscript, *see* manuscript *US-NH* Ma.21 H59
Hofkapelle 5–6, 46, 50, 90, 152
Holman, Peter xxiii, 195
Honoratioren (honourable families) 4
Horn, Johann Caspar 8–9, 14, 21–2, 29, 32, 35, 37, 65, 97, 108, 123–24, 126–28, 130–32, 134, 141–45, 179, 188, 198–99, 201, 205, 207; *Geistliche Harmonien* 8; *Parergon musicum I* 21, 35, 37, 123–24, 126–29, 130, 134, 188, 198–99; *Parergon musicum II* 21, 123, 127–29, 131, 143; *Parergon musicum III* 123, 130–31, 134; *Parergon musicum IV* 123, 131; *Parergon musicum V* 32, 123, 132, 134, 141, 201; *Parergon musicum VI* 9, 29, 35, 65, 123, 134, 141–45
Houle, George 195
Hudson, Richard 21, 32(fn.40), 99(fn.14), 110

Ihre, Thomas Nilsson 158
Inner Council 3–4
Intrada 35, 53–4, 70, 78, 84, 114–15, 119–20, 129–30, 134, 138–39, 145
italiänischen Manier 20–1, 27, 123, 127, 130
Iwe, Hans 8

Johann Georg III, Elector of Saxony 143

Kapellmeister 5–6, 20, 167, 180
Kelz, Matthias 10, 60, 62; *Primitiæ musicales* 10, 60, 62
Kindermann, Johann Erasmus 9; *Deliciæ studiosorum* 9
Kloss, Johann Herbord 188
Knoep (Knöp), Lüder 20, 32, 49, 54, 55, 78–80, 114, 155–56; *Ander Theil Newer Paduanen* 20, 32, 49, 78–9, 82, 114, 155; *Erster Theil Newer Paduanen* 54–5
Knüpfer, Georg 135, 200–1
Knüpfer, Sebastian 135
Koppmayer, Jacob 92, 94, 184
Kortkamp, Johann 150–51
Kradenthaller (Gradenthaller), Hieronymus 11–12, 85, 91–2, 102; *Deliciarum musicalium Anderer Theil* 91–2; *Deliciarum musicalium Erster Theil* 11, 85, 91
Krieger, Johann 183–84, 190; *Sechs musicalische Partien* 183, 190

Kromayer, Hieronymus 1
Kuhnau, Johann 10–12, 37, 109, 127, 150, 158, 180, 187–91; *Biblischer Historien* 150; *Der musicalische Quack-Salber* 10; *Frische Clavier-Früchte* 10; *Neüer Clavier Übung I* 188, 191; *Neüer Clavier Übung II* 188–91
Kühnel, August 19; *Sonate ô Partite* 19
Kunstgeiger, see Rollbrüder

Landstädte 3
Lawes, William 66, 78
Leborgne, Jean Artus 66, 68
Leipzig 7, 9–10, 12–14, 37, 52, 65, 90, 94, 104–5, 108–10, 115, 117, 119–20, 122–23, 127, 130, 132, 135–41, 143–45; *Nikolaikirche* 109, 117; *Paulinerkirche* 117; *Thomasschule* 109; *Thomaskirche* 120, 135, 187
Leopold I, Holy Roman Emperor xxiv, 91
Leutschauer Tabulaturbuch (Pestrý zborník) 179 (fn.24)
Liechtenstein-Castelcorno, Bishop Karl xxv
Locke, Matthew 71, 73, 76
Löwe von Eisenach, Johann-Jacob 115, 152; *Synfonien, Intraden, Gagliarden* 115
Lübeck 5–7, 12, 46, 76, 104, 204
Ludwig, Duke Christian 152
Lully, Jean-Baptiste xxiii, 20, 24, 90, 99, 127, 150, 176, 180, 190; *Ballet du temple de la paix, LWV 69* 24; *Le triomphe de l'amour* (LWV 59) xxiv

manuscripts
A-Wn Mus. Hs. 16560 203
A-Wn Mus. Hs. 16583 91, 137
A-Wn Mus. Hs. 18707 150–51
D-B Mus. Ms. 40644 173, 177, 190–91
D-Bsa SA 4450 150
D-Dl Mus. 1/B/101 126–27, 129, 161–62
D-EFu 13M. 8° 1222 46–7
D-Hs M B/2463 156, 162, 164, 166
DK-Kk 6806.1399 173
D-Kl 2° Ms. mus. 61a [I] 38
D-Kl 2° Ms. mus. 61d² 22
D-Kl 2° Ms. mus. 61k⁴ 49
D-Kl 4° Ms. mus. 27 (1–5) 50
D-Lr Mus. ant. pract. KN 147 178
D-Lr Mus. ant. pract. 1198 176–78
D-OB MO 1037 178
D-UDa 38a/9 8, 46–7, 52–3, 76
D-UDa 38b/8 46–7, 52, 76

F-Pn Rés F 496 30
F-Pn Rés F 497 128
F-Pn Rés.Vm⁷ 673 114, 156
GB-DRc MS Mus.D2 156, 158
GB-Lbl Add. MS 31438 47, 53, 55, 63, 71, 204
GB-Lgc G mus 469–71 158
GB-Ob MS Mus.Sch.c.93 135, 200
S-Uu Ihre 281–3 158–61
S-Uu IMhs 009:001 167
S-Uu IMhs 409 66
S-Uu Instr. mus. i hs. 4:4 135
S-Uu Instr.mus. i hs.11:10 167
S-Uu Instr. mus. i hskr.13:25 102
S-VX Mus. Ms. 4b 66
S-VX Mus. Ms 5 126
US-NH Ma.21 H59 68
US-NHub, Osborn MS 515, 156
Marini, Biagio 110; *Per ogni sorte di strumento musicale* 110
Mascharada 32
Mattheson, Johann 20, 37, 46, 151, 169, 176, 181, 184, 190–92; *Das neu-eröffnet Orchestre* 20; *Der vollkommene Capellmeister* 184; *Grundlage einer Ehren-Pforte* 46; *Pieces de Clavecin* 191
Meister (Maestro), Johann Friedrich 99, 102; *Il giardino del piacere* 99, 101–2
Mell, Davis 6, 73, 76
Menuet (Minuet) 13–14, 32, 99, 180–82, 188–91
Merck, Daniel 197; *Compendium musicæ instrumentalis* 197
Möllersche Handschrift, see manuscript *D-B* Mus. Ms. 40644
Montagu, Lady Mary Wortley 2
Montirande, *see* Bransle sequence
movement linking, *see* suite
Muffat, Georg 21, 100, 177, 191; *Armonico tributo* 101; *Auserlesene Instrumental-musik* 21; *Florilegium Primum* 191
Mühlhausen 54
Munich 7

N.B.N 67, 69
Nef, Karl xxiv–v, 113, 206
Niedt, Friederich Erhardt 11–12, 14–15, 22, 24, 28, 30, 32, 36–7, 98, 181–82, 184; *Musicalische Handleitung* (*Handleitung zur Variation*) 11, 22, 36, 181–82, 184

Neubauer, Johann 50–2, 54, 110; *Newe Pavanen, see also* manuscript *D-Kl* 4° Ms. mus. 27 (1–5) 50
Newman, William Stein 134
Nicolai, Johann Michael xxiii
Noack, Friederich 54
Norlind, Tobias xxiv-v
North, Roger 152, 156, 185
note blackening 21–2, 40, 48, 60, 69, 96, 110, 115, 126, 128, 139, 172, 195, 199–201, 203–6
Nuremberg 2, 102, 186

Pachelbel, Johann 25–6, 99, 102; *Musicalische Ergötzung* 25, 26, 99, 101–2
Paduan 27–9, 31, 43–5, 47–49, 51, 53–4, 55–7, 70, 79, 110, 112, 115, 152, 155–56
Passacaille 191
Passepied 14
Peace of Nijmegen 90
Petersen, David 46
petite reprise 126
Peuerl, Paul xxvi, 35, 37, 164; *Neue Padouan* 35
Pezel, Johann 4, 7, 9, 12, 22, 29, 117, 119–20, 122–23, 130, 136–40, 144; *Bicinia Variorum Instrumentorum* 136–9; *Delitiæ musicales* 120, 122; *Fünff-stimmigte blasende Music* 30, 136, 139–41; *Hora Decima Musicorum Lipsiensium* 136; *Musica Curiosa Lipsica* 117; *Musica Vespertina Lipsica* 12, 117, 119–20, 122–3, 157; *Musicalische Gemüths-Ergetzung* 4, 120, 130; *Supellex Sonatarum Selectarum* 136
Philidor manuscripts, *see* manuscripts *F-Pn* Rés F 496/7
Pindus Gesellschaft (Gesellschafft) 14, 122
Playford, John 66–7, 73, 76, 78; *Court-Ayres* 66–7, 73, 76; *Courtly Masquing Ayres* 73, 76
Praetorius, Michael 32, 66–7, 196–97, 199; *Syntagma musicum III* 196–97
Prelude (Præludium) 27, 53, 94–5, 97, 119, 162–64, 169, 178, 181–82, 186–89, 191
Priorato, Count G 2
prolation 196, 200
proportione hemiola, see note blackening
Purcell, Henry 156

Quodlibet, *see* Speer, Daniel

Rampe, Siegbert 178, 191
Rathey, Markus 143
Regensburg 85
Reich, Pater Honorat 178
Reichsstädte 3
Reincken, Johann Adam 35, 55, 95, 99, 149, 164–66, 168, 173–77, 183, 188, 190; *Hortus musicus* 35, 95, 99, 164–66, 173, 175
Rese, Joachim 1
Retirada 91, 123
Reusner, Esaias 19
Rieck, Johann Ernst 66–7; *Neue Allemanden* 66
Ritter, Christian 190
Roger, Amsterdam publishing house of 190–91
Rogers, Benjamin 73
Rollbrüder (Kunstgeiger) 7–8
Rose, Stephen 9
Rosenmüller, Johann 4, 9–10, 12, 22, 27, 49, 54, 108–12, 114–15, 117, 120, 122–24, 134, 140, 152, 188, 203–6; *Paduanen, Alemanden, Couranten* 110, 115, 124; *Sonate da camera* 9, 49, 112–13, 117, 120, 134, 152, 204, 206; *Studenten-Music* 10, 12, 27, 108–10, 114–15, 117, 203
Rost manuscript, see manuscript *F-Pn* Rés. Vm^7 673
Rothe, Wolf Ernst 139; *Erstmahlig musicalische Freuden-Gedicte* 139
Ryge tablature, see manuscript *DK-Kk* 6806.1399

Saltarella (*Saltirelle*) 91, 130–31, 179
Sarabande (Sarabanda, Saraband) xxv–vi, 20–4, 26, 37, 47–50, 54–7, 60, 62–3, 71–3, 78–80, 85, 91–4, 97, 101–2, 104, 110, 112, 114–15, 120, 124–26, 130–31, 134–35, 138, 151, 151–58, 162, 164, 166–69, 172, 175–78, 181–82, 186–89, 190–91, 201, 204–5
Scheidemann, Heinrich 172
Scheidt Samuel 127
Scheiffelhut, Jacob 90, 92–6, 184; *Lieblicher Frülings-Anfang* 92, 94, 96; *Musicalischer Gemüths Ergötzungen* 92, 94; *Musicalisches Klee-Blatt* 90, 92
Schein, Johann Hermann xxvi, 4, 35, 37, 50, 52, 104, 110, 112, 119; *Banchetto*

236 *Index*

musicale 35, 50, 52, 104, 110, 112, 119; *Diletti pastorali* 4; *Opella nova II* 4
Schelle Johann 109
Schlackenwerth 180
Schmelzer, Johann Heinrich 91–2, 137, 144; *Balletto* 'Zu den geburts Tag Ihro Maÿ: der Khönigin in Spanien', see manuscript *A-Wn* Mus. Hs. 16583
Schongau 60
Schop, Johann 4–6, 33–4, 149–50, 199; *Erster Theil newer Paduanen* 4, 33, 150, 199
Schulenberg, David 177
Schultheiss, Benedict 186–88, 190; *Muth- und Geist-ermuntrender Clavier-Lust I* 186–87; *Muth- und Geist-ermuntrender Clavier-Lust II* 186
Schutz, Heinrich 5
Schwäbisch Hall 1, 7, 83
scordatura 47, 57, 63, 65, 69–70, 102, 158, 160
Seares, Margaret 186
Sherard, James 135
Silbiger, Alexander xxv
Sinfonien 54, 63, 115
Snyder, Kerala 104, 173, 175
Sonata 99, 102–4, 114–15, 117, 119, 123, 135–36, 150, 152, 154–58, 162–69, 201
Sonatina 49, 66, 85, 91, 97, 117, 119, 132, 134–35, 137, 163, 188
Speer, Daniel 8, 36, 43, 96–8, 181, 197; *Grund-richtige/Kurtz/leicht* 43, 96, 181; *Musicalischer Leuthe Spiegel* 97; *Musicalisch-Türckischer Eulen-Spiegel* 97; *Recens Fabricatus Labor* 97; *Simplicianischer lustig-politischer Haspel-Hannß* 8
Spohr, Arne 4
Stade 55
Stadtpfeifer 7, 13, 130, 135, 141
Stockholm 49, 152, 158
Strasbourg xxiii
Style brisé 172–3, 175–77, 184, 186
Stylus phantasticus 104
suite; 37, 49, 54, 60, 71, 78, 85–6, 91, 119–120, 123, 130, 161, 186–87, 189, 190; 'alternative' *see also* Bransle sequence xxv, 32, 49, 54, 91, 110; Balletti xxiv-v, 32, 207; classical order of movements in 9–10, 19, 102, 119, 175; dissemination of 177; variation techniques (movement linking) in 35–7, 47, 51–2, 60, 63, 79, 95, 98, 110, 124, 130, 134, 139, 150–51, 154–55, 162–64, 169, 176–77, 181, 188, 192, 197

tactus 196–97
Taubert, Gottfried 12–14, 32, 109; *Rechtschaffener Tanzmeister* 12, 32, 104, 109
Tavola 113–14
Theile, Johann 9, 149, 167–69
'Musicalisches Kunst-buch' 169; *Sonaten, Prael, Allem, Cour, Arien & Chiquen* 9, 167
Thirty Years War xxiii–iv, 1, 3, 19, 33, 35, 37, 43, 49, 90, 108
Thompson, Shirley 201
tower musicians, *see Türmer*
Trezza 91, 102, 137
trillo 124, 126
Tunder, Franz 6
Türmer (tower musicians) 7, 135
Turmmusik 135–36, 138

Udestedt *Adjuvantenchor* 46, 52

variation techniques, *see* suite
Vejvanovský, Pavel Josef 144
Virdung, Sebastien 195
Voorhout, Johannes 165

Walther, Johann Gottfried 24, 27–8, 32, 46–7, 63, 123, 136, 169; *Musicalisches Lexicon* 32, 46, 123, 136
Wanderschaft 6
War of the Spanish Succession 2
Weckmann, Matthias 6, 12, 68–9, 102, 149–51, 178–80
weddings 7–8, 12–14, 32, 45
Whitehead, Paul xxv, 102
Wienandt, Elwyn 139
Williams, Peter 191
Wolfenbüttel 3, 109, 167
Wollny, Peter 119, 150
Wust, Balthasar Christoph 63, 65–73, 76, 78, 85–6, 102, 158

Zuber, Georg (Gregor) 5, 32, 46–50, 52–4, 55, 63, 71–2, 76, 204; 'Ander Theil, neuer Pad.' 63, 204; *Erster Theil newer Paduanen* 46, 55, 71